STEVE ALLEN
on the Bible, Religion, & Morality

Books by Steve Allen

BOP FABLES (1955)
FOURTEEN FOR TONIGHT (1955)
THE FUNNY MEN (1956)
WRY ON THE ROCKS (1956)
THE GIRLS ON THE TENTH FLOOR (1958)
THE QUESTION MAN (1959)
MARK IT AND STRIKE IT (1960)
NOT ALL OF YOUR LAUGHTER, NOT ALL OF YOUR TEARS (1962)
LETTER TO A CONSERVATIVE (1965)
THE GROUND IS OUR TABLE (1966)
BIGGER THAN A BREADBOX (1967)
A FLASH OF SWALLOWS (1969)
THE WAKE (1972)
PRINCESS SNIP-SNIP AND THE PUPPYKITTENS (1973)
CURSES! (1973)
WHAT TO SAY WHEN IT RAINS (1974)
SCHMOCK!-SCHMOCK! (1975)
MEETING OF MINDS, VOL. I (1978)
CHOPPED-UP CHINESE (1978)
RIPOFF: THE CORRUPTION THAT PLAGUES AMERICA (1979)
MEETING OF MINDS, VOL. II (1979)
EXPLAINING CHINA (1980)
FUNNY PEOPLE (1981)
THE TALK SHOW MURDERS (1982)
BELOVED SON: A STORY OF THE JESUS CULTS (1982)
MORE FUNNY PEOPLE (1982)
HOW TO MAKE A SPEECH (1986)
HOW TO BE FUNNY (1986)
MURDER ON THE GLITTER BOX (1989)
THE PASSIONATE NONSMOKERS' BILL OF RIGHTS (1989)
DUMBTH: AND 81 WAYS TO MAKE AMERICANS SMARTER (1989)
MEETING OF MINDS, VOL. III (1989)
MEETING OF MINDS, VOL. IV (1989)
THE PUBLIC HATING (1990)
MURDER IN MANHATTAN (1990)

STEVE ALLEN

on the Bible, Religion, & Morality

Foreword by
Martin Gardner

PROMETHEUS BOOKS
Buffalo, New York

94 93 92 91 90   5 4 3 2 1

Library of Congress Cataloging-in-Publication Data

Allen, Steve, 1921-
     Steve Allen on the Bible, religion, and morality / Steve Allen.
          p.   cm.
     Includes bibliographical references.
     ISBN 0-87975-638-1
     1. Bible—Criticism, interpretation, etc. I. Title.
BS511.2.A44   1990
220.6—dc20   90-39954
                                                    CIP

While no one person can grasp the truth adequately, we cannot all fail in the attempt. Each thinker makes some statement about nature, and as an individual contributes little or nothing to the inquiry. But the combination of all the conjectures results in something big . . . . It is only fair to be grateful not only to those whose views we can share, but also to those who have gone pretty far wrong in their guesses. They, too, have contributed something.

—Aristotle

I fiercely oppose those people who do not want Holy Writ translated into a vernacular to be read by nonspecialists; whether Christ's teaching were so involved as to be understood by very few theologians only, or the Christian religion could be protected only if it be ignored.

—Erasmus

Contents

CONTENTS

CONTENTS

Foreword

American actors and entertainers are seldom admired for the quality of their minds. Can you name one who delves deeply into philosophy, history, religion, and politics, and who is capable of writing an autobiography and 34 other books without a ghost? The only answer is Steve Allen. One marvels at the amount of research and courage it took to write this, his 35th volume.

Allen is a talented actor. Recall his superb portrayal of Benny Goodman in the motion picture about the band leader's career. On Broadway, he played the lead in *The Pink Elephant*.

Allen is also an accomplished pianist. Among his 40 record albums are two collector's items from the 1950s, *The Discovery of Buck Hammer* and *The Wild Piano of Mary Anne Jackson*, that testify both to his keyboard skill and his sly sense of humor. I wonder how many jazz buffs know that the piano solos on these records were played by Allen? "Hammer's death was a tragic loss to the world of jazz," wrote a New York *Herald Tribune* critic. The experts, Allen later observed, liked his playing much better when they thought he was black and dead rather than white and alive. All the melodies played by "Miss Jackson" were composed by Steve.

The *Guinness Book of Records* has called Allen America's most prolific songwriter. Among his more than 4,000 numbers are "Picnic" (the theme song of the film based on William Inge's play), "Gravy Waltz," "South Rampart Street Parade," and "This Could Be the Start of Something Big." He has also written the scores for numerous theatrical musicals, including the 1985 television production of *Alice in Wonderland*.

To the public, Allen is most admired as a brilliant ad-lib comedian and witty talk-show host, in which capacity he created and moderated the NBC *Tonight Show, Steve Allen's Comedy Hour,* and PBS's *Meeting of Minds,* which presented great thinkers of the past. In light of this hectic pace it is remarkable that Allen has found the time to write so many books. *Dumbth* (1989), his last book before this one, takes its startling title from

Allen's term for the fuzzy-mindedness of what H. L. Mencken liked to call our country's booboisie. Half the book consists of hilarious instances of dumbth, followed by 81 suggestions on how to overcome this widespread disability.

Allen's political views, generally those of an anti-Marxist liberal, have prodded him into clashes—albeit good-natured—with spokesmen on both the right and left. Two notable instances are his battle by correspondence with Dalton Trumbo, Hollywood's most famous Communist screenwriter (the letters were published in *Esquire,* October 1970), and his platform debate in 1963 with conservative William Buckley, Jr. I cannot resist quoting a limerick that Allen recited during the debate:

> There is a young man named Bill Buck-i-ly
> Who debates all the liberals quite pluckily,
> But when all's said and done,
> It must be just in fun,
> For few are persuaded—quite luckily.

Allen's books range over both serious and comic nonfiction, novels, short stories, plays, and even poetry, but the book you hold is the most impressive. It is no less than a detailed, scholarly (though Steve denies he is a scholar), skillfully reasoned analysis of Scripture. No other work by an American can be likened more favorably to Thomas Paine's classic, *The Age of Reason.* What press aside from Prometheus Books would have dared publish it?

It is astonishing how few present-day conservative Christians have even heard of Paine's explosive work. Theodore Roosevelt, as anxious as later presidents to woo conservative Christian voters, called Paine "a filthy little atheist," seemingly unaware that Paine was a great hero of the American Revolution, tall, neat, and a Deist. Paine not only believed in God but also in life after death.

How many conservatives, who talk constantly about restoring America's Christian heritage, have you heard mention that Washington, John Adams, Franklin, Jefferson, and most of the other founding fathers, as well as Lincoln, were not Christians? It was Washington who insisted that no reference to God appear in the Constitution. "The government of the United States," he declared, "is not in any sense founded on the Christian religion." Jefferson produced a life of Jesus (still in print) from which he removed all the miracles to let the heart of Jesus' teachings shine forth. Not one of the first seven presidents professed the Christian faith.

Like *The Age of Reason,* Allen's book is not written from the standpoint of an atheist. Again and again he reminds us that belief in God seems to him "less preposterous" than atheism. His central theme is simply this: The Old Testament's portrait of Yahweh is too loutish and brutal to be worthy of worship by any theist who accepts the ethics of altruism or who is familiar, even marginally, with modern science and biblical criticism.

In the two centuries since Paine wrote his book, an enormous amount of research on the Bible has been undertaken, much of it in recent decades by Catholic and Jewish scholars. Archaeologists, as well, are shedding light on what could and could not have happened during the Bronze Age, the era of the Pentateuch.

It is Allen's knowledge of this literature that gives his work a timeliness and persuasive power that Paine's book or the lectures of Robert Ingersoll necessarily lack.

William James, our most admired philosopher (he, too, was a theist), once said he could not imagine how an intelligent person could read the entire Bible and still believe it was throughout the inspired word of God. Millions of Catholics and Protestants who dutifully attend church, at least at Christmas and Easter, are almost as ignorant of the Bible as they are of the Koran or the Book of Mormon. Evangelicals and fundamentalists do study Scripture, but with minds so firmly clamped shut that they overlook or rationalize every error, absurdity, contradiction, and blasphemy with which the "Good Book" bristles.

In midlife, with considerable agony and effort, Allen constructed a philosophy of life that departs from his strict Irish-Catholic upbringing. Unshackled at last from certain of its ancient doctrines, he found himself free to apply his analytical intelligence to particular problems rooted in Scripture. The Old Testament God, he maintains, is as far removed from the loving Heavenly Father of Jesus as is Zeus or Shiva. To find analogies with Yahweh one has to turn to the jealous, cruel, bloodthirsty gods of ancient mythologies.

Is the God of St. Paul and the early Church much better? In some ways, yes. However, as Allen reminds us, he too is capable of inflicting unimaginable torment—not for a year, not for a century, but forever and ever—on those who are unable to perceive Jesus as God and as man's savior, and to believe that God raised him from the dead. At least Jesus reserved Hell for the rich and wicked. But Paul's God requires for salvation only a "rebirth" based on faith. The worst criminals, if they properly alter their beliefs an hour before they die, will go straight to Paradise, while persons of great goodness, if they cannot accept the Gospels, are destined for the flames. Has not that biblical "authority," Jimmy Swaggart, assured us that even Mother Theresa and most Catholic priests are on the road to damnation?

Allen puts it succinctly:

> The proposition that the entire human race—consisting of enormous hordes of humanity—would be placed seriously in danger of a fiery eternity characterized by unspeakable torments purely because a man disobeyed a deity by eating a piece of fruit offered him by his wife is inherently incredible.

Would any Christian believe such a tale if it were found in, say, an old Hindu document? Is it any less preposterous an explanation of human evil than the Greek myth about Pandora's box?

Repenting that he had ever created humanity, Yahweh—if we take Genesis as accurate history—once drowned every man, woman, and child, not to mention innocent land animals, except for Noah's family and the few animals saved by Noah. Dinosaurs, presumably, were too big to go on the Ark, but Noah would not have known about them and many other species.

Yahweh was a god who ordered Moses to slay entire tribes except for the virgin girls kept as slaves. He was a god who allegedly became so furious over the failure of Moses' nephews to mix incense properly for an animal sacrifice that, like Zeus, he struck them dead with lightning bolts. It was Yahweh who commanded Abraham to murder his son, Isaac. How many fundamentalists, I wonder, ever asked themselves how Abraham, a mere mortal, could have been certain he had heard God's voice and not the voice of Satan? Curiously, the Koran's overall portrait of Abraham is a much saner and thoroughly admirable patriarch.

Jesus urged us to love our enemies. Yahweh taught his chosen people to hate their enemies. Remember the lovely beginning of Psalm 137? "By the rivers of Babylon, there we sat down, yea we wept when we remembered Zion." The same psalm, Allen reminds us, ends: "Happy shall he be that taketh and dasheth thy [the enemy's] little ones against the stones."

Our political leaders are shameless in their efforts to curry conservative Christian support. Richard Nixon liked to recall how as a boy he was born-again at a revival meeting, but he lied to the American people and when he golfed with his "good friend" Billy Graham, he carefully suppressed the four-letter profanity we would hear on the Watergate tapes. Dwight Eisenhower never went to church until he entered the White House. John Kennedy lost his faith as a young man and was a notorious adulterer, but he never stopped going to Mass, because Catholics will vote for Protestants but never for ex-Catholics. Ronald Reagan, although no fundamentalist, nevertheless urged that creationism be taught in public schools and warned that Armageddon may be imminent! As president, however, he never went to church, a fact that never seemed to bother his fans.

George Bush is a lifelong Episcopalian, but these days an Episcopalian, like a Catholic or mainline Protestant, can be a liberal without the slightest interest in traditional doctrines. We know how Bush stands on taxes and broccoli. Does he believe Jesus was born to a virgin? If not, you can be sure he will never tell us. Who knows whether Dan Quayle, Mario Cuomo, or any other political leader who professes to be a Christian believes in the inerrancy of the Bible? A reporter today can ask a politician if he or she ever took drugs or committed adultery, but to ask whether he honors or ignores any fundamental Christian doctrine would be considered bad taste.

On May 12, 1990, Bush delivered the convocation address at Jerry Falwell's Liberty University, a college where students are taught that evolution is a theory inspired by Satan and that very soon the faithful will be "raptured"—caught up in the air to be with Jesus. Bush and his handlers know that Falwell is our country's top basher of homosexuals, with political and social views to the right of William F. Buckley and Pat Buchanan, but pleasing fundamentalists is more important to his advisers than pleasing some of the rest of us. Is it possible that one reason Bush picked Quayle for vice-president is that Quayle and his wife were once under the influence of Houston's fundamentalist preacher Robert Thieme, Jr., whose political views are even to the right of Falwell?

Falwell's Moral Majority was ominous enough, but far more menacing is the Reconstructionist movement that Allen touches on in his Introduction. Consider this passage from Leviticus: "If a man also lie with mankind, as he lieth with a woman, both of them have committed an abomination: they shall surely be put to death. . . ." (20:13).

Some Reconstructionist gurus maintain that this command still holds. In a future theocracy, which they would like to establish, any gay who practices his or her sexual orientation should be executed; the same goes for adulterers. Fortunately, Reconstructionists now number less than a thousand, but who can say whether their depraved doctrines will spread among the ignorant or fade like the adolescent dreams of Jim and Tammy Bakker? It was because of just such instances of spreading malignancy that Allen decided to publish his book now rather than posthumously.

Will the book have any effect on the rising fundamentalist tide? Allen is not optimistic:

> The fundamentalists, of course, are caught in a trap from which there
> is no escape, except that of abandoning at least the more absurd of
> their arguments. If we start with the unquestioned assumption that

there is a God and that he is, by definition, good, then it inescapably follows that the countless atrocities attributed to him in the Old Testament are not only lies, but insulting lies at that. Since this is something the fundamentalist cannot even consider, much less concede, they are, as I say, trapped in an intellectual prison from which there is not the slightest possibility of escape. Their greatest anger, alas, is reserved for those who would do them the great service of freeing them from their prison.

I have no doubt about the resentment this book will arouse. It will not surprise me to hear that some congregations plan to burn it, as they once burned Paine's *Age of Reason* and as in still earlier times their fanatical counterparts tortured and burned heretics and witches. But here and there, one dares to hope, people will have the courage to study all of this book's well-reasoned arguments with at least half an open mind. Perhaps it will send them to the Bible to find out for themselves whether every absurdity and horror Allen refers to is really there. It may even lead a few away from their narrow biblicism and back to God.

Martin Gardner
May 1990

Acknowledgments

I should like first to thank Cristina Gutierrez, of my office staff, for her tireless and quick-handed work transcribing the hundreds of tape-cassettes on which the various drafts of the present work have been dictated.

And secondly, Karen Hicks, who not only retyped all these materials and kept them appropriately filed for quick reference, but also made a number of helpful editorial suggestions.

Thirdly, I express my gratitude to the editor, Cynthia Brown Dwyer, whose knowledge of Scripture, archaeology, Islam, and ancient history proved valuable in scores of instances, and to Professor Joseph Barnhart for reading the lengthy text and making numerous helpful suggestions.

I am indebted, too, to Paul Kurtz, editor-in-chief of Prometheus Books, who suggested that I reduce the bulk of an originally enormous manuscript and print the individual commentaries in alphabetical sequence.

Dwyer and Kurtz also helped me perceive that the only way the original material could be introduced to the popular market was by dividing it into separate volumes. Should the point be of interest, they did not attempt to influence my judgment of the scriptural materials examined, except in places where there were questions of accuracy.

Needless to say, I was touched by Martin Gardner's willingness not only to offer encouragement but to provide a foreword to my report.

Lastly, I thank my wife Jayne Meadows and my secretary Pat Quinn for their devotion while I concentrated on my studies and writings.

Not one of those mentioned here, goodness knows, is responsible for any of the opinions expressed.

Introduction

Recently, while studying John Dart's *The Laughing Savior* (San Francisco: Harper and Row, 1976), it occurred to me that its opening paragraph suggested a perfect introductory statement for the book the reader holds in his hands. Dart explains that his work as religious writer (in this instance with the *Los Angeles Times*) led him "specifically to the dramatic, yet little known story of the Nag Hammadi gnostic library."

He is quite right that the story of the Nag Hammadi discoveries is a fascinating one that deserves to be better known. I think the same is true of another remarkable collection of ancient religious documents. I announce my intention, therefore, to relate the dramatic, yet still little-known story of nothing less than the Bible itself.

It might be objected that, inasmuch as the Bible is the best-known collection of books in history, it can hardly be described as little-known. But, having devoted many years of study to the matter, I am convinced that despite its popularity and influence, it is an imperfectly known work indeed, so far as the greater number of Christians and Jews is concerned.

The Scriptures have been referred to, quoted from, and applied to broad social issues and private problems for perhaps 2,500 years, but for all of that, the degree of common ignorance about them, even among the devout, is vast.

This assertion will hardly surprise Catholic readers, since members of that communion have for centuries been generally unfamiliar with most of the scriptural texts. It might be thought, by way of contrast, that Protestants are exempt from this observation. They are not. Many of them have done a good deal of *reading* of the Bible. But there is an enormous gulf between reading something and having an adequate understanding of it.

Part of the problem is that the majority of those who take time to give extended attention to the Bible bear a burden of preconceptions and prejudices. I imply no condemnation by this remark. The very fact that the great majority of serious Scripture readers, students, and even scholars are already firmly convinced Christians or Jews makes it almost impossible for them, except in rare instances, to bring to their study the sort of dispassionate analysis and open-minded critical understanding essential to true scholarship.

Another striking and inescapable factor is that there has been a steady weakening of confidence in specific religious positions as a result of the worldwide increase in human knowledge generally. It by no means follows that this process will suddenly end, at some future point, in the total absence of religious belief, but the phenomenon and its direction must nevertheless be recognized.

It is, of course, possible to argue that this general process is beneficial for religion, because it tends to purify it of superstitious and irrational elements, leaving a more reasonable, inspiring remainder. From the fundamentalist position, however, the astonishing increase in scientific knowledge over the past three hundred years has been viewed with alarm and hostility. This is not to say that religious conservatives close their minds totally to the accretion of scientific evidence, but such information as seems to have even a remote possibility of coming into conflict with long-cherished religious or philosophical assumptions is unlikely to be approached by such believers with any degree of open-mindedness. The conservative approach to new findings commonly reflects at once fear that yet one more defensive bastion will have to be abandoned and hope that the new fallback position will somehow still resemble the old faith.

I had been involved in my study for a very short time when it became clear that the degree of certain knowledge modern men and women can have about any ancient religious document is exceedingly modest. Among the reasons is that we make certain selections and interpretations from the massive volume of material available to us. We then classify our own selections as truth on the basis of our conditioning, or else take many matters on faith when knowledge fails us.

Let a dozen people walk into a room they have never seen before. The eyes of one are immediately drawn to wallpapers, of another to paintings, of another to musical instruments, of another to the view through a window, and so on. The room is the same for all, but each perceives it from different interests and each brings to the moment of observation a unique lifetime of experience. The old story of "The Blind Men and the Elephant" shows this clearly.

Obviously this is true a thousand times over about a massive collection of ancient writings, many passages of which are capable of more than one interpretation.

Another difficulty exists in our fundamental weakness in remembering, unaided, over periods of time, any statements that consist of more than a few words. If the reader doubts this, he may satisfy himself with a simple experiment. Let him compose a sentence consisting of, say, 30 words. He must write the sentence down, since—as he will shortly perceive—he will not be able to accurately remember it for long unless he does so, and even then will find that he has to refer frequently to his notes to see if his recollection is correct.

The second stage of the experiment involves nothing more than reading the sentence aloud to a second person, who must thereafter write the sentence down, as accurately as possible, and then read it privately to a third. The process is then repeated through eight more steps. The tenth person in the chain of communication, after writing his version on a piece of paper, reads it aloud. It will be a very unusual instance if the tenth version includes very many words from the original.

No one denies that there are *no* original texts of any part of the Scriptures, as there are, for example, Akkadian cuneiform inscriptions of the Mesopotamian Flood Story or the parchment manuscript of the Declaration of Independence.

All scholars have to work with are copies of copies, and these are chiefly translations from the original Hebrew or Greek. Occasionally, and most fortunately, a handwritten version of some portion of Scripture is discovered, but it is never claimed that such documents are originals. The original texts were generally written centuries before the copies whose discovery has excited archaeologists and biblical historians.

To sum up: Given the absence of first drafts, plus the notorious weakness of the human memory and powers of communication, it follows that the Bible could not possibly be a strikingly reliable record of any event or statement whatever, unless God intervened.

But the devout, alas, will not long find refuge in this alternative, for the Bible, far from being the sort of clear, bedrock exposition we should expect if God *were* its author, is in reality the cause of endless controversy, not only among poorly informed laymen, whom we would expect might become lost in its vast depths, but even among scholars, who spend a good part of their adult lives in an attempt to reason their way through the words and ideas the Scriptures present.

Although I set down these sobering observations for the reader's consideration, they do not represent the bias with which I originally approached my research. Rather, they gradually became clear over the course of years of painstaking reading, analysis, and consultation of sophisticated scholarship.

So confusing a documentary record is the Bible that scarcely any question one might raise about it can be answered to the satisfaction of all believers, much less the world's two billion or more nonbelievers in Judaism and Christianity. It is all but impossible to establish the makeup of the Bible, the Protestants asserting it consists of 66 books, the Eastern Orthodox of 43, and the Catholics of 73.

The reader who looks for order in the Bible is doomed to frustration and disappointment. To give but one illustration: Consider Judaism's traditional division of its Hebrew canon into three categories—Torah (Instruction or Law), Nevi'im (Prophets), and Ketuvim (Writings). The section called the Prophets concerns a good many people who were not prophets.

At my present age of 68, having the resources of leisure, a vast library, and a serious interest in the question as to whether the Bible is in fact what it has been represented to be for 2,000 years—i.e., the totally straightforward, literal word of God—I have undertaken a study of a fascinating question. I have been prepared to follow the evidence where it may lead and am equally disposed to acknowledge the scholarship and goodwill of authorities on each side of any question.

It is misleading, of course, to suggest that a fair-minded study of the Bible must incline one to decide between only two alternatives. As the multiplicity of Christian churches and sects makes clear, there are various points of view we might take about the integrity and divine inspiration of the Old and New Testaments. Nevertheless, there is one sense in which we may view two alternatives: either the Bible is—in whole or in part—divinely inspired or it is nothing of the sort. If the latter is true, then scripture is merely an imposing and valuable literary collection of ancient narrative, myth, legend, superstition, poetry, song, and religious codification. Ultimately, no reasonable person can stand with one leg in each camp.

Analysis is a time-consuming and exacting task. When the object of analysis is something so complex as an entire library, the difficulties are greatly increased. Again, there is not one but different versions of Scripture, each a large collection of separate books, some of which are excluded from other versions. One reason there is no one Bible is that a universally recognized authority would be required to identify it. No such authority is recognized by all branches of Judaism and Christianity.

In presenting my findings and views, I must beg the patience of scholars, to whom many of the questions raised here will already be familiar but which, in any event, have by no means been resolved to the satisfaction of everyone. No doubt a good many of the observations I make will have previously occurred to some specialists. The justification for their inclusion is that the present work is intended for the average reader who, by and large, will have done no critical thinking about or research on the Scriptures.

I want to put all possible cards on the table at the outset. A brief word is in order about the social biases and prejudices I have brought to this study. I am a product of the Catholic communion, having been a member until an automatic excommunication when I married a second time, in my early 30s. Having written at length elsewhere about the philosophical transition these experiences led to, I will not detain the reader with additional details. But I should point out that my leaving the Catholic church has not led to a fierce hatred of my former spiritual home, such as has been seen in so many emigres from the church over recent centuries.

Quite to the contrary, I have not only been accorded cordial, even affectionate, treatment by individual priests and nuns but have even from time to time lectured or entertained under formal Catholic auspices.

For about a dozen years my wife Jayne and I frequently attended the Bel Air Presbyterian Church in Los Angeles, where we were given a warm reception and developed deep respect for the many dedicated people we met there. Our first connection with this church came about because, having both been products of a Christian upbringing (Jayne's father was an Episcopalian minister and missionary to China), we agreed that our son Bill should have the benefits of the sort of moral training available in the Bel Air Presbyterian community, chosen because we lived nearby.

As a result of this background, I began with more of a sympathetic understanding of religious tradition than with any natural antipathy toward it.

I must also be honest enough, however, to state that from my mid-20s I began to have certain doubts about one aspect or another of the Catholic and/or Christian teachings and record. I do not refer here only to the obvious atrocities found in Christian history, of which there are more than enough to gratify the prejudice of the antireligious and to shame all decent Christians.

Nor did learning of the vulgar, sinful, corrupt, or warlike behavior of certain popes weaken my faith. The troubling questions arose from one source only: my intellect. To the extent that one has some respect for the rules of evidence, one cannot ignore those moments when a biblically based religious opinion comes into flat contradiction with either factual evidence or logical reasoning.

I suspect that, although there is little public acknowledgment of such private doubts and questions, the great majority of religious believers experience them at one time or another. One particular book, which I read in my late 30s, comes to mind as regards the kinds of religious disputes to which philosophical doubts have given rise. Titled *A History of the Warfare of Science with Theology in Christendom* (1896), it was written by Andrew White, the first president of Cornell University. It is by no means one of those unpleasant antireligious diatribes, nor is it the sort of more dignified but still heated attack upon organized religion for which certain freethinkers such as Thomas Paine or Ralph Ingersoll have been noted. It is, rather, a scholarly and fair-minded survey of a long list of specific instances in which science, intent only upon its own interests, came into conflict with religion, simultaneously intent upon its concerns.

It is almost as if two men of goodwill happened to bump into each other at a dark intersection while each was lost in his own speculation. The controversy, in other words, was by no means always sought; frequently there were conscious efforts to avoid it, but, of course, certain controversies, including those that are the most historically important, cannot be long avoided. In any event, as I read White's fascinating and soundly documented account, something quite remarkable, and at first disturbing, became clear. In every single instance where churchmen placed themselves squarely athwart the path of science, as regards a particularly knotty question, *the religious forces were eventually defeated for the very sound reason that they were wrong.*

It is hard to convey the profound importance this simple perception assumed in my mind. It led to the realization that while there is certainly a great deal of understandable controversy as to which religious views did or did not emanate personally and directly from God, the same confusion by no means prevails among the sciences. This is certainly not to say that all science is one solid body of opinion untroubled by argument. But scientific questions are not settled by debate, by democratic vote, by fiat of an infallible leader, or indeed by any means other than the inescapable verdict of factual evidence. And even then, strictly speaking, scientific views are said to have only a high degree of probability rather than absolute certainty, even though mountains of evidence and testing may support a given assertion.

By striking contrast, in the field of religion, where nobody tries to prove anything scientifically, a good many assumptions have been accepted as unquestionable.

Of all the embarrassing errors the church has made over the centuries, surely one of the most serious has been its frequent calumny of science.

For analytical convenience, we often treat as separate things which, in physical reality, are merged together. We tend, for example, to refer to *nature* and *science* as if they were two distinct things. Actually, the raw materials with which science works are the very phenomena that constitute nature. Though eventually we may distill scientific information and express it in abstract terms, it is encountered in a natural condition. Science deals not simply with mathematical symbols and laws but also with plants, with water, with all forms of animal life including the human, with sunsets, clouds, the daily birth and death of billions of living creatures, the flight of birds, the hunger of the shark, the jungle disguise of the tiger—with, in short, the only reality of which we can have any certain knowledge.

Those fundamentalist religious believers, therefore, who speak contemptuously of science as if they were merely expressing a political or social preference, reveal an astonishing insensitivity to the very world that they tell us God created. Granting, then, our prior assumption of a Creator, anyone who criticizes real science is in a direct sense criticizing God.

Parenthetically, most of the distinguished scientists of earlier centuries were not atheists, and a considerable portion were Christians. Newton was a believer, as were Galileo and Pascal. It is true that they often found themselves in philosophical conflict with the conservative orthodoxy of their day and that their religion was a very personal and unique thing. It is also true that they were, however intellectually gifted, products of their culture, one overwhelmingly dominated by Christian views.

It is not the purpose of this work to undertake something to which a library itself would be unequal, a survey of the totality of religious debate and dialogue over the past 2,000—or even 200—years. I limit the scope of the present investigation to the Bible alone, not unmindful that that in itself is a formidable undertaking and one which has troubled gifted scholars. Most scholars have devoted their entire adult lives to their investigations and know many languages, while I have conducted my studies as I was engaged in performing and in writing books, scripts, and songs.

But just as wars are too important to be left solely to generals, Bible study is far too important to be left to Christian apologists. There must be *something* to which a well-intentioned person of average intelligence can address himself or herself, and concerning which he or she can draw at least tentative conclusions.

A Word to Believers. During many years as a churchgoer I often heard or read Catholic or Protestant commentaries strongly critical of atheists or other persons who, it was said, "hated God." Only later did I come to realize that an atheist does *not* hate God; he simply is one who is unable to believe that a God exists. However, at that earlier time I embraced the implication that anyone who wrote critically of God would be intellectually depraved indeed. The strange thing is that it is not the atheists (many of them respected scientists, scholars, and philosophers) who have committed this offense. Rather, it is the mostly unknown authors of the Old Testament, who have, unwittingly or not, attributed to God hundreds of crimes as bad as, if not sometimes worse than, some of the enormities committed by humans.

In my first and second years of high school I attended two Catholic institutions, at both of which I was quite casually taught that while it was no longer necessary to believe that "six days" of creation in Genesis meant six 24-hour periods, one could nevertheless only go so far in interpreting the word *day* to mean *year* or *geological period.* Apparently many instructors were not themselves aware that the highest Catholic scholarship had already long conceded, as Jean Levie states in *The Bible, Word of God in Words of Men* (New York: Kennedy, 1961), that "this was a naive speculation which could not be upheld for long."

Even the esteemed Father Levie, however, and the many distinguished scholars whose work he represents, are unable to avoid all the traps into which the basic assumptions of their dogmatic theology inevitably led them.

> The repulses suffered in these fields had, like the unfortunate condemnation of Galileo, a fortunate result: Catholics began to understand that the Bible had not been written to anticipate the progress of science but to lead man to eternal salvation. And Leo XIII [1878–1903], in the Encyclical *Providentissimus,* laid down clearly that the Bible did not claim to give expression to a scientific explanation of the universe but to a judgment based on appearances as they are manifested to our human senses.

I recommend that the reader study this passage. One ought not to be misled by Father Levie's graceful and dignified language. What is important is that the passage contains an absolutely shattering concession: that the account of creation in Genesis *cannot* be squared with science— whatever the word *day* is taken to mean—and that furthermore it is a mistake and a waste of time to attempt to establish any such concordance.

Pope Leo's announcement should have been heralded on the first page of every important newspaper. How dare, one must ask, the best Christian scholarship make such concessions (the Pope himself going so far as to create a special encyclical) without the remarkable news having been transmitted to the hundreds of millions of the faithful? Why was I, during all my years of loyal residence in the Catholic world, never informed of this dramatic deviation from a theological view that had been sternly maintained for centuries?

The fact that such messages still have not been successfully transmitted is one reason why I trouble myself to publish the present volume. There is no reason the Catholic faithful should feel obliged to attend to my own views on matters biblical since I am without academic credentials. But

Catholics, as such, have no right to ignore the views of popes and major theologians on such questions.

To sum up: The ancient debate concerning the question as to whether the Bible can contain any scientific error is over and done with. It has been firmly settled that not only can the Bible contain error but it contains a good deal of it, if it is interpreted literally.

Rigid insistence on literalist interpretations of the Bible, incidentally, has probably done more to encourage religious apathy, agnosticism, and atheism than the writings of atheistic scholars, few of whom, in any event, have ever been read by the masses of Christians or Jews.

What about historical error? The same is true. Observes Levie,

> Religious respect for the Bible had habituated many minds readily enough to attribute a more definite, more certain historical value to the data provided by it than to the records of history or of archaeology. Traditional Biblical chronology, fixing creation in 4004 B.C., was still regarded by many as beyond doubt.

The scholars prepared to abandon literalist nonsense about the Bible are familiar with the archaeological records of peoples who flourished in various parts of the world many thousands of years prior to 4000 B.C., as well as the geological record, which, of course, pushes the time-line back millions of years.

Many distinguished Catholic scholars led the church out of the darkness from which it had originated and grown, but only at the cost of throwing overboard a great many opinions which had been firmly held for centuries.

Again, to the extent that my personal biases may be of the slightest interest, it would be perfectly all right with me if Jesus himself were to enter my study and say, "Look here. It's been good of you to trouble yourself to this extent but I propose to save you some time. There is indeed a God, as I shall prove in a moment by lifting your house seventeen feet above the ground and twirling it about three times. Oh, and by the way, I did indeed author every word of the Bible, including all its errors and absurdities. Don't ask me why."

At which I should answer, "So be it. And thank you, Lord, for saving me further trouble and doubt."

But in the absence of such an unlikely event, I have no personal *knowledge* that God authorized every verse of the Bible. We do, however, know that, if he exists, then it was he who implanted in my brain the capacity to reason, and I would be foolish indeed were I not to scrutinize any and all evidence that comes before me. If it is proper to do so about ordinary things so that one may not drink poison, walk into brick walls, buy shoddy merchandise, and so forth, it is equally as sensible to take care lest one be harmed by false intellectual or spiritual nourishment. I should have grave reservations about accepting the advice of anyone who would not say the same.

A Word to Nonbelievers. Many atheists, agnostics, freethinkers, Secular Humanists, and other critics of organized religion have made the mistake of assuming that since some aspects of Judeo-Christian belief seem preposterous to them, they must also seem so to most defenders. Therefore, it is reasoned that the latter are brazen hypocrites pretending to have faith in a philosophy that they do not in fact respect.

That Christianity and Judaism on the one hand and hypocrisy on the other are not mutually exclusive is, alas, all too well-established, but I believe that the majority of believers are sincerely convinced of the general reasonableness of their own versions of a faith.

I have known many priests, a category that old-style rationalists believed contained schemers, connivers, and hypocrites. Undoubtedly a few were—and still are—but the majority are nothing of the sort. Many that I have known have been dear men, hard-working, poorly rewarded for their labors, and certainly virtuous. The Protestant ministers I have known, including my own father-in-law, are the same. They have not taken an easy path in life; they carry the burdens of many on their shoulders; and I, for one, find them admirable. Many missionaries among them are often truly heroic in their selflessness. It would be hard to convince anyone who has seen missionaries in action in Latin American or African villages that these dedicated men and women are cynical manipulators.

To sum up: It is by no means necessary to presuppose hypocrisy on the part of ministers, priests, and rabbis. If they were deluded or conniving, they would be far less formidable opponents to those who differ with them. It is not their cynicism that provides their strength, it is their faith; the point is the same whether they are generally correct or very largely mistaken in their views.

Although most clergymen today, in my opinion, are superior, rather than inferior, to the average citizen so far as moral behavior is concerned, it does not, alas, follow that they will always debate charitably when their views are challenged. Each of us has an emotional investment in opinions considered important; certain kinds of emotions, springing from mysteriously deep wells, rise when one's spiritual assumptions are questioned.

The Assumption of God's Existence. Those rationalists and humanists who are also atheists may be displeased that in constructing the present study I have simply assumed the existence of God rather than subjecting it, too, to the same critical analysis devoted to other questions that float up out of the biblical text. As I have observed elsewhere, both the existence and nonexistence of God seem in some respects preposterous. I accept the probability that there is some kind of divine force, however, because that appears to me the least preposterous assumption of the two.

Scriptural Quotations in This Study. As Bible scholars will note, I have not restricted myself to one source for scriptural quotations. Roughly half of the present manuscript was written in various hotel rooms across the country; the Scriptures quoted in those portions are taken from the Gideon Bibles left on nightstands and bureaus. Other Bibles were from my own bookshelves or the libraries of friends, selected quite at random.

Only one sort of work has been consciously excluded: modern renditions such as the Good News Bible or the Living Bible. These, despite their obvious merits, present renderings of Scripture that will fall strangely on most ears. I have consulted only English translations.

Justification for the Present Study. It was my original intention to publish the result of my studies and speculations posthumously, but I have decided to permit the publication of at least the first volume of what may ultimately be a much longer report because an element of urgency has entered the public dialogue that was not present at the outset.

Because of the constitutional freedoms wisely established by our nation's founding fathers, Americans are at liberty to hold any religious beliefs at all, or none whatever. But there is a negative aspect to this, as there always is in the context of freedom. Along with beautiful, inspiring, uplifting, and morally instructive beliefs that flourish in such a climate, there will inevitably be a certain amount of destructive, superstitious nonsense preached.

Many of our nation's fundamentalist Christians, who, by and large, believe that the Bible is reliable as history and science, are no longer content with teaching their freely gathered congregations their theology and publishing their views, which they have every right to do. But just as my freedom to swing my arms about stops at the point of another's nose, so the freedom to preach unscientific superstition deserves to be limited when it attempts *to impose itself* on those who have not requested it and who may, in fact, hold contrary religious opinions, or none at all.

When, for example, America's fundamentalist believers in the inerrancy of the Bible insist on having historical and scientific errors taught in our nation's *public* schools, then they must be opposed by all legal means. That is a reason I have decided to delay publication of my views no longer.

When it becomes clear to even reasonably well-educated believers that the earth and all the rest of the vast physical universe cannot possibly be just a few thousand years old, as many fundamentalist Christians continue to insist, there is some danger that they will simply abandon their religious beliefs on the assumption that they have been sold a dangerously defective bill of goods. A careful reading of my argument will demonstrate that it is perfectly possible to continue to believe in God—and even one specific form of religious philosophy or another—while at the same time jettisoning beliefs about the *factual* nature of material intended as mythical illustration of philosophical or moral lessons.

One reason it is important to publish such a study at present is that the Christian conservative movement of the 1980s clearly requires commentary. For the preceding half-century progressive forces in the Protestant community were dominant in American life. This state of affairs had come about as the result of the long erosion of certain bedrock conservative beliefs, from dramatically increasing knowledge in the fields of archaeology, literary scholarship, astronomy, physics, geology, biology, and history. The conservative resurgence was the inevitable reaction, although the assorted excesses and mistakes of both Western liberalism and Marxism also played a role.

Before fundamentalist critics respond to this study, I want to make clear that by far the majority of my sources have been the studies of devout Christian and Jewish scholars. The best and most responsible religious scholars know that, despite the Bible's many treasures and enormous importance, it cannot be considered a perfect document, since too many imperfect human hands have been involved in its creation over many centuries.

Many clergymen are aware of the results of responsible critical analysis of the scriptural text. Even so, there have been few attempts to communicate the results of such brilliant analytical work to the ordinary faithful, those who do not read scholarly biblical journals. Therefore, not surprisingly, we now have a situation where the majority of Christians in the United States have a level of understanding of Scripture for which there might have been an excuse a century ago but for which there can be no defensible justification at present.

I have the clear impression, however, that a new day of biblical criticism has dawned, one likely to bring increased benefits to "both" sides. As noted earlier, there are many, not just two, interested camps, and within the individual groups there are various shades of opinion.

It is encouraging to note that Evangelicals, who a few generations ago were distinguished largely by their shallow and unlearned argumentation, have largely rectified that, and their scholars now present arguments that deserve to be responsibly engaged.

Unfortunately, there is one party to the debate in the U.S. that has, in a large, statistically measurable way, substantially abandoned the field. That is the enormous body of the Christian laity. There was never, needless to say, a time when the great majority were truly knowledgeable about Scripture, but whatever the high-water mark of popular biblical awareness was, the soundings at present reveal a much lower level. As noted earlier, Bibles continue to sell in great numbers, but for some people they seem to be used in the same way others employ Tarot cards or astrological charts. Even those who attend Bible classes are almost invariably told what —*not how*—to think about Scripture.

To position the present modest effort in a larger setting: I would hope to interest the average reader, whatever his or her background or biases, in a greater, more analytical study of Scripture, in *all* its parts. This last qualification is of crucial importance, for no one has ever denied that there are certain passages of Scripture that emanate sweetness, light, and comfort.

But, surely, even the most devout believers cannot responsibly argue that it is either reasonable or fair to place so much emphasis on the comfortable and lovely portions of the Bible and to ignore the far more numerous passages in which not comfort and encouragement but terror, moral revulsion, and puzzlement are perfectly reasonable reactions.

Despite what I have said, the question may again present itself: Given that books with a thousand and one points of view about the Hebrew and Christian Scriptures have been written during recent centuries, is there any particular reason, at present, why one more volume should be added to such an extensive library? Indeed there is.

To understand that reason, a few factors must be considered. First of all, if there is anything on which social critics and philosophers of all camps are firmly agreed it is that modern society is in an intolerable state of disarray. General conditions involving political corruption, sexual excess, criminality, funding of military terror, financial greed, and an overriding selfishness are nothing new. The Old Testament itself is full of dire descriptions of them. But, to limit our analysis only to the American scene of, say, the last 100 years, no one denies that there is serious cause for concern. The relevant debate, then, concerns the question as to which, among many proposed solutions, are reasonable and practical. Although many readers may be unfamiliar with such realities, the fact is that a growing number of Christians, and a few Jews, are presently recommending a general solution that, whatever its assorted merits, would *inevitably involve throwing overboard the American system as it has long been known.*

I am not exaggerating. One component of the American formula embodies the notion that the proper basis for the authority of government is the consent of the governed, which is to say the will of the majority.

However, certain rights of the minority are also guaranteed. No one has ever imagined that such a system is perfect. Despite democracy's flaws, the overwhelming majority of the population of democracies around the world (and no doubt repressed populations living under other systems) prefer this system.

Christian Reconstructionism. I believe it is the imposition of a dictatorship that increasing numbers on the Christian Right now wish to construct in the United States.

I refer specifically to a group of believers who call themselves Christian Reconstructionists. Some harmful organizations, throughout history, have disguised their basic agenda while in the process of appealing to a broad base of support. The Reconstructionists are quite frank about their social prescriptions. They believe that Christianity should be the official religion of the United States and that American laws should be specifically Christian.

As Bill Moyers put it, in a fascinating and strangely ignored program aired on public television December 23rd, 1987:

> The Reconstructionists would want to invent America all over again, with the Bible as its primary charter, and Washington, D.C., as a new kind of government where God's will is done on earth as it is in heaven . . . [they want] every institution of society for Jesus Christ. Their leaders include learned scholars, articulate speakers, and prolific writers. They represent a cross-section of faiths. They disagree on many things, but on this they agree: every area of American life, law, medicine, media, the arts, business, education, and finally the civil government must one day be brought under the rule of the righteous.

The patriarch of the movement is a man named Rousas John Rushdoony.

Because all of this has an aura of unreality, the question may occur: Do the new True Believers actually want the various levels of government—federal, state, and local—to become formally Christian?

If the question is posed in precisely these terms, spokesmen for the Christian Reconstructionist camp back off somewhat and say that they are only trying to educate the people in such ways that Americans themselves will demand the changes. However, the changes they want are, to even the most neutral of observers, indistinguishable from laws that a cruel and oppressive dictatorship might pass.

Since the new ultra-extreme fundamentalists are so displeased by democracy, what, specifically, do they recommend as its replacement? On this question, too, they are quite frank. A theocracy. Shades of Puritan England, Inquisition Spain, or Iran, 1979-1989!

Theocracy means: rule not by the people, not by elected representatives, but by God (and whoever has the power to enforce claims that he speaks for God). Those of us who assume that God exists would presumably object to such a system only in the absence of God from the earth in a physical form. God can take over the administration of the affairs of all the nations of earth anytime he wants to, so far as I am concerned, but this has never happened. In the governments throughout history that have considered themselves theocracies, we have witnessed rule by clergymen who simply asserted (and in many cases may have honestly believed) that they were God's specially chosen representatives.

Taking a leaf from the Reconstructionists, I have a startling proposal of my own as regards what would be a proper punishment for those found guilty of attempting to impose such beliefs. That is that they should be sentenced to a 12-year course in world history, with particular attention to the record of what transpired in Europe during the centuries when people's lives were ruled by popes or Protestant divines. Such study would increase the present small degree of knowledge about the slaughters of the Inquisition, the massacres of the Crusades, and the extirpation of massive numbers of women and men for the invented crime of witchcraft.

In fact, the long-standing system of civil and religious justice in which all of those suspected of crimes were arrested and subjected to the most hideous forms of torture imaginable was one factor that led the American Founding Fathers to feel so strongly about the wisdom of keeping church and state separated. Religion was perfectly welcome in American society, as it still is, but one church should never be permitted to dominate the civil state or its citizens.

Let us now consider specifics. As regards the question of homosexuality, it is clear that most Americans regard the sexual preference for a member of one's own gender as a problem. Some people have fascistic and heartless attitudes on the issue; others strive to be fair.

The Christian Reconstructionists are perfectly clear about a solution to the problem. That solution is nothing more complex than the prompt imposition of the death penalty.

To those unfamiliar with the recent drift of the public dialogue on this and related questions, what I have just said will sound like a libelous distortion. Would that it were. The Reconstructionist movement, which is chiefly Protestant although it has interested a few Catholics, absolutely insists that homosexuals ought to be killed. I do not mean that individual Reconstructionists consider themselves at liberty to arm themselves to the teeth and travel about their communities in vigilante bands, shooting or stabbing homosexuals on sight. That would, obviously enough, be a horrifying spectacle to witness. I refer to something worse.

The Reconstructionists insist that the slaughter of millions of their fellow citizens is to be conducted in strict accordance with the law. They argue, in other words, that homosexuality must simply be added to the list of capital crimes punishable by execution.

What other crimes would the new fascist movement like to see added to the list of capital offenses? Habitual juvenile delinquency, for one. Please do not take my word for this; consult the public statements and writings of leaders of the new movement. It should take only a few days of investigation to establish that yes, the group at present is working very hard to do nothing less than take over the administration of the local, state, and national affairs of the United States. It insists that swiftly imposed death is the proper punishment for the kind of lamentable and sometimes criminal behavior engaged in by millions of young men and women in our presently troubled society.

If, as is commonly believed, about 10 percent of Americans have homosexual leanings, it inescapably follows that if the Reconstructionists ever do take over control of our country, some 25 million Americans will shortly be executed. Statistics about juvenile delinquency may be variously interpreted, but let us say that in that category perhaps another 20 million young men and women would be killed, and this, bear constantly in mind, by those who consider themselves Christians. It is obviously impossible to get precise statistics concerning that percentage of the approximately 250 million American population who have committed the moral and sometimes legal offense of adultery. Most of us would be pleased if no one ever was unfaithful to a marriage partner, and the American home would clearly be a more secure institution if this were the case. But, as the scriptures constantly remind us, humans have apparently as much a gift for wrong-doing as for virtuous conduct. So let us arbitrarily say that 75 million Americans have offended the moral law in this way. Add that to the other arithmetic.

Hitler's Nazis became the objects of most of the world's contempt by killing six million Jews, equally as many, if not more, Balts and Slavs, and being responsible for waging war in which millions more civilians and soldiers died. The Reconstructionists do not seek to obscure the fact that they propose the slaughter of their fellow citizens in numbers that Hitler, Stalin, and Pol Pot may never have dreamed of.

I shall not go more fully here into all the programs proposed by the Reconstructionists, though I hope my readers will go to such trouble on their own initiative. But the question inevitably occurs: What has happened to drive so large and influential a group of citizens to proudly espouse a set of proposals for the governance of the United States, which to most observers will seem sadistically insane? The Reconstructionists draw their horrifying proposals for the ills of our society from only one source, *the Bible*.

It should immediately occur to us to wonder why only a very small percentage of Bible-believers build such a program when many millions of Christians, though respecting the Bible, do *not* advance to Twilight Zone social proposals. The difference between the two groups is that the Reconstructionists are ultrafundamentalists.

A Final Word. A number of people with whom I have discussed the present study have inquired as to whether the sometimes disturbing facts my research has unearthed have not weakened my faith in God. The answer is no. I confess, however, that my faith in man has not been additionally strengthened.

A Few Technical Matters

Feminist Concerns in Referring to God. I must beg the indulgence of staunchly feminist readers concerning references to the Almighty Creator of the universe as a *he*. This is merely a convenience. Since God is invariably defined as pure spirit, it logically follows that "he" is incorporeal and therefore cannot have any identity that could be remotely described by the masculine gender pronoun.

Alphabetical Form. I have chosen to present the topics in this volume in alphabetical form, from A to Z. It is offered as a collection of short essays containing my reflections on the Bible, religion, and morality. It is in no way intended as an exhaustive, scholarly study, but as statements of ideas and issues that have intrigued me and I hope will intrigue you as well.

A Note About Abbreviations. Wherever I have added italics for emphasis in a Bible verse or other quotation, the letters *IA* in parentheses will appear at the end of the passage.

Cross References. Capitalized words refer to topics that are treated in separate essays.

A

ABEL, the second son of ADAM AND EVE. "Now Abel was a keeper of sheep . . ." (Gen. 4:2), favored by Yahweh over his brother CAIN. The Bible gives no reason, thus leading us to assume, heretically, that God is capable of partiality and inherent unfairness. The Hebrews were first a nomadic people, tending flocks for an unknown period of many centuries along the fringes of the Fertile Crescent. The Abel story could imply that God preferred that they lead a nomadic life (at least until he promised them the land of CANAAN).

John L. McKenzie, S.J., has explained that the name *Abel* is derived from the Akkadian *aplu*, "son," which, he observes, "would indicate a Mesopotamian origin of the story . . . Abel is a pastoral culture hero, the first herdsman . . ." (See also GENESIS, *Chapter 4.*)

ABIMELECH, the king of Gerar, an ancient town in southern Judea, or Philistia. It once lay on the route between Gaza and Beersheba, and was a place where ABRAHAM reportedly sojourned (Gen. 20:1).

Abimelech has two curious encounters with Abraham in Genesis 20-21. He behaves impeccably throughout, even though Abraham offers him SARAH as a wife, calling her his sister. Ultimately, Abraham makes a peace covenant with him at Beersheba, and they exchange animals, but not before Abraham has revealed that Sarah is indeed his half-sister (a clear case of incest).

As often happens in the Old Testament, the Lord is the character who behaves outrageously. He "closed all the wombs of the house of Abimelech because of Sarah, Abraham's wife" (20:18), even though we are told that Abimelech never slept with her. God later "healed Abimelech, and his wife, and his maidservants; and they bore children" (20:17). The two stories of Abimelech are interwoven with those of Sarah's barrenness and eventual production of Isaac.

Why did God close Abimelech's wife's womb and then open it again, unless we are being told that Abimelech did not conceive any other children while he "took Sarah" (20:2)? It is as though the writer cannot make up his mind what did happen in those ancient, oral-tradition legends he is working with to create the book of Genesis. It is peculiar also that the author or compiler of Genesis made Abimelech a more honorable and persuasive character than Abraham. His stories, though minor, are beautifully told bits of vivid narrative. They do not, however, appear in illustrated Sunday School papers, for reasons that are obvious.

Poor Abimelech—he was so virtuous, generous, and careful not to offend Abraham or the Lord, and his life was complicated by the misbehavior of both. It would be enlightening to have a Philistine or Canaanite version of these events. Would they deal as kindly with Abraham as the author was forced to treat a man considered by later Israelites to be their deadly enemy? I cannot help wondering if the two Abimelech stories, which read like insertions, might not, in fact, have been Canaanite legends, which the compiler of Genesis inserted because they dealt with the Hebrews' first culture-hero, Abraham.

ABORTION. It is fascinating that the purest form of the respect-for-life philosophy that motivates at least some antiabortionists is consistent with the general thrust of Humanist thinking over the last couple of centuries, but it relates scarcely at all to much Christian behavior of the past 2,000 years.

Two basic questions are: (1) What is life? (2) When, in the human context, does it begin? While at first the answers appear obvious, the relevant realities are complex. For some time it has been possible to keep human tissues, separated from bodies, alive. They need only be placed in an aqueous environment and provided with such nutrients and methods of waste-disposal as their individual cells require. We can, then, point to a brain, a heart, a lung, or other portions of a once-conscious body and state, quite accurately, that it is alive.

Yet if someone were to destroy such an organ, would it be reasonable to accuse him of murder? There is no question that he was destroying living human tissue. But it is equally as clear that the individual organ was nevertheless not a human being. Why? Because it did not have a mind. If then, it is only the existence of brain-function and/or mind that establishes the existence of a human, it follows that the termination of a fetus that is just a few days old can hardly be equated with arbitrarily ending the life of a six-month-old child or of an adult.

On this point, incidentally, there is invaluable relevant information in

Exodus 21:22, which refers to two men who engage in physical combat and who, in thrashing about, bump into a pregnant woman who suffers a miscarriage as a result. In both rabbinical and early Christian commentary there is a clear distinction between punishments thought suitable for two outwardly similar crimes. If the fetus that dies is unformed, the common opinion was that the guilty individual need not receive the death penalty. But if the fetus is formed—which is to say in the late stage of development— then that is a much more serious matter and the death penalty is considered appropriate punishment. This makes clear that, quite aside from the question as to whether it is ever appropriate to refer to the medical disruption of a developing fetus as *murder,* it was not correct at one time to use such a term if the unborn individual was in a very early state of development.

For an excellent analysis of this question, see "Two Traditions: The Law of Exodus 21:22–23 Revisited" by Stanley Isser in the *Catholic Biblical Quarterly* (Jan. 1990).

As noted above, a growing segment of the Christian Right openly advocates that the proper solution to present-day social problems is to make the United States formally and legally a Christian nation with a government entirely under Christian domination and guided by the laws and principles of both the Old and New Testaments. This would require repeal of the First Amendment.

Needless to say, such Christians are members of the pro-death-penalty camp. If (1) they succeed in their ambitions, (2) abortion is outlawed because it is considered murder, and (3) all murderers must be executed by the state, then it logically follows that the many millions of American women who would beyond question continue to have illegal, secret abortions would have to be put to death if detected.

Concerning certain aspects of the abortion controversy, there is surprisingly little disagreement or debate. Statistically speaking, few people think it is permissible to end the life of a fetus in the last several weeks of its development. This is so simply because a baby in the eighth or ninth month is clearly a human being and is therefore entitled to all the rights that society is prepared to accord a newborn or any adult citizen. (An interesting sidelight on this point is that in Nationalist China, America's ally against the Communists, the practice of infanticide was widespread among poor families, particularly if the children were female. When the Communists assumed control of that country in 1949, they legislated against the practice.)

Fundamentalists have, of course, attempted to justify their stand against abortion by citing the Bible, just as an earlier generation of fundamentalists used scriptural texts to try to justify their opposition to new birth-control

3

devices or their acceptance of slavery. Among the passages used to oppose abortion are Ephesians 1:4, 2 Thessalonians 2:13, and Jeremiah 1:5. These and similar texts emphasize divine foreknowledge and election by stressing that God knew his prophets and apostles when they were in the womb.

Fundamentalists have pressed these texts further in the service of their metaphysical conjecture that the entity in the womb, from the moment of conception, is a person. What they failed to note was that their premises lead them into the heretical doctrine of reincarnation. According to the book of Jeremiah, the Lord said to his prophet, "*Before* I formed you in the womb I knew you." (IA)

According to Hebrews 7:9-10, Levi the priest was within the loins of his great-grandfather, Abraham. If one used Jerry Falwell's exegetical methods in interpreting Scripture, one might conclude that Levi existed as a 100 percent person in Abraham's loins. This suggests that Abraham would have been guilty of manslaughter or negligent homicide if by fortuitous nocturnal emission he had allowed the innocent Levi to escape from his loins. (See Joe E. Barnhart, *The Southern Baptist Holy War,* Austin, Texas Monthly Press, 1986, pp. 159-160.)

According to Luke 1:42, another antiabortion passage employed by fundamentalists, when pregnant "Elizabeth heard the greeting of Mary the babe leaped in her womb." Elizabeth herself is then quoted as saying "the babe leaped in my womb for joy" (1:44). But this does not prove anything, because a pregnant woman, feeling the fetus moving, can attribute any emotion she wants to the baby she is carrying. Most women simply speak of the baby's "kicking."

Barnhart also notes:

> For many years, a number of [fundamentalist] preachers like Jerry Falwell and W. A. Criswell raised no prophetic voice against the known brutalities of racism or unjust treatment of women. Now suddenly they have turned into bleeding hearts over almost microscopic zygotes. With little sustained concern for the civil-rights movement when it had to do with conspicuous persons of minority status, some of the antiabortion preachers have recently begun to deliver impassioned and eloquent speeches about the civil rights of the fertilized egg.

There is the general perception that the new organism, which in its early stages is a small blob of matter, can hardly be referred to as a human being, consisting, as it may, of only a few dozen cells. Nature itself daily aborts millions of such creatures and, in fact, not only at early stages. The majority of those who take a clear-cut, no-abortions-under-any-circumstances position naturally wish to make it impossible to terminate the life of even these forms.

Most opponents of abortion seem unaware of the fact that the European and American successes in legalizing the practice during the last half-century grew largely out of public concern about the thriving market in criminal abortions. Few of these were performed by licensed medical practitioners. Not surprisingly, the results were often horrendous, so far as the life and health of the unfortunate mothers were concerned. Informed citizens eventually said, in effect, "It makes no sense to continue to permit so much death and suffering. If abortions are going to take place, as they obviously will continue to do, then the procedure ought to be performed under controlled circumstances by qualified medical professionals." This is certainly not the only rationale for legalized abortion, but since it is part of the larger argument, it must be taken into account.

To the great number of those who have not yet taken a formal position concerning the difficult question of abortion but who have at least been exposed to arguments from both sides, it may seem that at one end of the field are those who think that abortion is, generally speaking, a positive and justified act, and those on the opposite side who believe that it is a simple act of murder.

If there is a single person on earth who views abortion as favorably as he views playing tennis or reading a good book, he would be in urgent need of psychiatric attention. Abortion, like many medical procedures, is a sad business.

As for my own position—with which I would not trouble the reader except that I have frequently been asked to state it for the record—I am opposed to abortion in the sense that I can envision an ideal state in which no such medical procedure would ever be necessary.

And it is not difficult, after all, to at least imagine, if not bring about, a utopian situation in which almost no further abortions would be desired or performed. Such a situation, of course, would involve far more widespread use of methods of birth control than is practiced at present. The debate as to whether there is an overpopulation problem has never, in the present century, been worth the attention of any serious or informed person because everyone sensible agrees that there is. Even the Catholic church acknowledges that there are too many people in certain places for the available food supplies to sustain.

Many sincere and intelligent Catholics are so disturbed that their church only acknowledges the population problem and resists serious efforts to alleviate it, that they simply ignore Catholic doctrine on birth control and make their own moral decisions. Nor do they have much difficulty in finding priestly confessors to tell them that they are entitled to let their conscience be their guide on such difficult questions.

Among the many prominent Catholic thinkers who are at odds with their church on the question of contraception is James T. Burtchaell, C.S.C. The details of his argument on the question may be found in *The Giving and the Taking of Life: Essays Ethical* (1989). Father Burtchaell is professor of biblical theology and ethics at the University of Notre Dame, and his collection of essays was published by the University of Notre Dame Press. Moreover, the book is referred to in respectful tones by the Jesuit magazine *America* (Oct. 14, 1989). None of this would happen if Burtchaell's was simply the voice of a lonely heretic. It is my assumption that, on this question, the majority of Catholic intellectuals are on the side of common sense and therefore in opposition to their church.

One of the reasons that millions of abortions will continue to take place, regardless of the views of American conservatives, is that, though great numbers of eggs are being fertilized, not all the potential children are *wanted by either or both of their parents*. In a large percentage of the cases, this is because the parents are not married. In some instances, they are married, but to other individuals. And in cases where a married mother and father are the parents-to-be, they too, by the millions, are deciding, for whatever good or poor reasons, that they do not want the particular birth that will result if nothing is done to interrupt the cellular development in the womb.

Life is difficult enough for even the more fortunate among us in the present day. For those new arrivals who are not welcomed by loving parents, the eventual results are almost invariably horrifying. This relates, in a very direct way, to the problem of child abuse in American society. In one city alone, New York, over a hundred children are killed by their own parents each year. Nor is such a death a sudden, swift release. It usually results from a long series of savage beatings, sometimes—the very soul shudders—accompanied by sexual abuse.

The future society that was serious about trying to diminish the need for abortion would incorporate a vigorous program of instruction on sex, starting at the appropriate early grade-level. There is a tendency to assume that because modern America is inundated by sexual themes on a morning, noon, and nightly basis, high school freshmen have absorbed so much information about the subject that they do not require further formal instruction. However, research has shown that the same old historic ignorance of sex prevails and is one of the factors contributing to the present unhappy picture.

Should instruction about sex restrict itself to a description of the plumbing, so to speak? Absolutely not. Should it incorporate moral and ethical considerations? Certainly. The only sort of moral component that is automatically ruled out in American public schools is that which represents a strictly sectarian religious viewpoint. In other words, the Catholic church, which still feels that masturbation and birth control are grave sins, clearly ought not to be permitted to impose that view on the American process of public education.

The sort of moral considerations that could quite properly be incorporated into a program of instruction are those indicated by common sense, social custom, and practicality. Young boys, to give a specific instance, must be taught that they have no right to force their sexual attentions on anyone else, that to persist in doing so is called rape, and that it is a grave crime, punishable by imprisonment, in our society. Furthermore, it should be explained to immature boys that rape is wrong not simply because it is illegal but also because it is a cruel violation of the Golden Rule.

Young men and women should also be taught that until they are absolutely certain they want children, they shouldn't even think of having them. The present situation would be an outrage if only one unwanted child was born, but we are talking about millions.

It must be stressed that for those teenagers, especially the older among them, who would, despite moral advice, continue to lose emotional control in certain instances, largely because of the dictates of nature itself, there would have to be a great deal of information provided concerning methods of birth control and, for the unmarried, birth prevention. This returns us to a key and dramatic factor in the ongoing public dialogue on the ancient problem of irresponsible sexual activity.

Nature itself has always provided one means by which intercourse may be avoided. That is masturbation. But the largely Christian participants in the antiabortion camp belong to churches which are very clear in their condemnation of the practice of self-stimulation. Many of them are also, though with less unity, opposed to all practical methods of birth control. As a result of these two views, those who would do away with abortion in fact contribute to an increase in unwanted pregnancies and therefore a demand, on the part of millions of young women, that those pregnancies be terminated. We see, therefore, that among those elements of society that worsen the problem are the forces that want to make abortion unavailable for everybody.

Another feature of the better society in which abortions would be unnecessary would be a humane and civilized adoption program in which every child that was either unwanted by its natural parents or which became suddenly orphaned would be taken into a new and loving home. But such visions are, of course, fantasy. We are unfortunately forced to address the problem in the context of present reality, which is deeply depressing. Millions of children are presently being born to parents who either have little or no interest in them or who, if they do feel some rudimentary form of love for their newborns, are themselves so socially handicapped that they are simply incapable of responsibly assuming the role of parents. There are few orphanages either and a tremendous shortage of foster-care homes.

Another crucial requirement in any society prepared to outlaw abortion would be a massive and well-funded program of health care for the poor, day-care centers for infants whose mothers must work, family-counseling services, and other such agencies. Unfortunately these are in painfully short supply at present, largely for the reason that the conservative elements of society refuse to underwrite such compassionate programs with their tax dollars. Moreover, when, despite their wishes, a certain amount of tax revenue is allocated to such benign programs, conservative spokesmen complain vociferously about these expenditures. They cannot have it both ways. If they are serious about bringing about a sharp revision of the long-standing legality of abortion, it follows that the number of births will rise by the millions. It would rise even more, of course, were it not for the inescapable fact that armies of women will continue to insist on abortions, and will get them, if new laws are passed, generally from the same type of back-alley practitioners who have provided such services for centuries.

There is evidence that at least a minority of antiabortionists realize this, and we find, in the field of Catholic social services, for example, admirable instances of willingness to lend additional support to orphanages, adoption agencies, and day-care centers. One hopes that if the wishes of the conservative minority prevail in law and abortions are, in fact, outlawed or sharply curtailed, then the victors will not simply turn their backs on the millions of unwanted infants. This will, of course, require antiabortionist forces to stop complaining about taxes and start making clear that they care about the poor in America in ways actually detectable to the poor.

ABRAHAM. Abram is the name by which the first biblical patriarch is called until the Lord renames him Abraham in Genesis 17:5 (when he is 99 years old), at which time the covenant is proclaimed. God tells the old man that he "shall be the father of a *multitude of nations*" (v. 4; IA). Since this formula—*nations,* in the plural—is used three times in Chapter 17, it is curious that *one group*—the Hebrews and their descendants—should claim exclusive descent as God's CHOSEN PEOPLE. At this point in the Bible, it seems clear that the writer believed that God had anointed Abraham to be the father of all peoples dwelling in that part of the Near

East, especially when we note the Lord's promises about ISHMAEL (Gen. 16:10; 17:20; 21:13, 18).

Since real place names are mentioned in the first Old Testament verses about Abram (Gen. 11:26), it is probable that the account of the patriarch's sojourning with his clan—from Ur (in Mesopotamia) to Haran (a town in southern Turkey), down into CANAAN, then on to the Negev Desert, to Egypt, and back again to Canaan—is a fictionalized version of the real wanderings of *several* nomadic tribes of Semitic speakers.

The reference to Ur of the Chaldees in Genesis 11:31 is one of the Bible's hundreds of mistakes. Explains Magnus Magnusson in *B.C., The Archaeology of the Bible Lands* (London: The Bodley Head, 1977):

> Ur of the Chaldees has always been one of the magic names in the Bible. Actually it is a misnomer; Ur was originally one of the ancient city states of Sumer, and did not become associated with the Chaldeans until the first millennium B.C., more than a thousand years *after* Abraham was thought to have been born there. So the name "Ur of the Chaldees" in Genesis is clearly an anachronistic reference. (IA)

Genesis 12:10 sounds plausible enough, given what we know archaeologically of the place and time: "And there was a famine in the land: and Abram went down into Egypt to sojourn there; for the famine was grievous in the land."

What follows immediately after is quite specific (hence, probably largely fiction) and also morally appalling to modern Jews, Christians, and Secular Humanists. Abram is revealed as a scheming liar. To avoid being killed by the Egyptians, he pretends that his "beautiful" wife Sarai is his sister, and she is taken into the Pharaoh's house, presumably as a concubine. Her "brother" Abram is rewarded with "sheep, and oxen, and he-asses, and menservants, and maidservants, and she-asses, and camels" (12:16). The Pharaoh, who is blameless in the matter, is nonetheless afflicted with plagues on the grounds that he had sexual relations with another man's wife. When he finds out the truth, he behaves far more honorably than Abram has.

> 18. And Pharaoh called Abram, and said, "What is this that thou hast done unto me? why didst thou not tell me that she was thy wife?
> 19. "Why saidst thou, She is my sister? so I might have taken her to me to wife: now therefore behold thy wife, take her, and go thy way."
> 20. And Pharaoh commanded his men concerning him: and they sent him away, and his wife, and all that he had.

If we assume that this Pharaoh/Sarai story was invented to explain how Abram became wealthy, why in heaven's name did the author of Genesis, a proud descendant of Abraham who is trying to tell why his ancestor found favor with God, present him as a devious scoundrel whose flocks and riches were obtained by acting as a pimp? These stories are never read from pulpits in the modern day. To its credit, the KORAN, written more than a thousand years later and claiming Abraham as an ancestor of the Arabs, does not contain such an account. Its references to Abraham are couched in respectful terms.

It is possible that *Abram* was a name arbitrarily given by later writers to a tribe or group of tribes from a particular area, from whom the later Hebrews thought they had descended. The "Abram people"—perhaps a more accurate way of putting it—may have become the wealthiest and most aggressive of the Near Eastern nomads of their day. One detail that argues for this explanation is that one of Abram's brothers was named Haran, and that is the name of the place (probably already established) where Terah, Abram's father, settled after he left Ur. The extreme longevity claimed for the patriarchs can be seen, then, as a later author's *estimate* of the time one particular *clan* prevailed at a certain place, since we know that humans do not live to be hundreds of years old.

A plausible account of the following chapters of Genesis is provided in the volume *The Israelites,* Charles Osborne, ed., in the Emergence of Man Series (New York: Time-Life Books, 1975):

> . . . *if there has been no hard physical proof that the individual patriarchs, Abraham, Isaac and Jacob, were actual human beings,* plenty of scholarly evidence does exist to support the conclusion that there is substantial historical truth in the patriarchal narrative. Discoveries of shrines and records—letters, legal codes and civil contracts—belonging to peoples who were contemporaries and neighbors reveal a great deal about the social structures, the manners and mores in Mesopotamia, Syria, Canaan and Egypt during the Second Millennium B.C.; and the story of the patriarchs as the Bible recounts it is filled with details that coincide with the archaeological data.
>
> It becomes increasingly possible to assume that the patriarchal roles parallel those of the ancient family chieftains. It is not at all clear, however, whether the Israelites they led were herders, moving their sizable flocks from pasture to pasture, and from time to time into the cities to sell their fleece and goat hair; or caravan traders who traveled the route between Mesopotamia and Egypt by way of the cities in Canaan.
>
> Archaeologists know that for a period of some 800 years, from

about 2000 B.C. to about 1200 B.C., several Semitic families, or tribes, pursued both activities. Though scholars differ over tribal identities and disagree about details of chronology, they nevertheless generally agree that the patriarchal age began no earlier than 1950 B.C. and ended no later than 1300 B.C. (p. 36) (IA)

Genesis 16 tells the famous story of Sarai, Abram's wife, who had borne him no children, and her maidservant, a younger Egyptian woman named Hagar. Sarai tells her husband that he should have sexual intercourse with her maid in order to produce an heir. "And Abram hearkened to the voice of Sarai" (16:2).

Indeed, human sexual nature being what it is, we may reasonably assume that he did so, and probably with all the alacrity possible to a man of 86. But Hagar, once she gives birth, becomes more secure and has less respect for her mistress. When Sarai complains to her husband about this, he tells her, in effect, to do whatever she wants with the woman. Having been thus authorized, Sarai treats Hagar so harshly that she runs away.

> 7. And the angel of the Lord found her by a fountain of water in the wilderness, by the fountain in the way to Shur.
> 8. And he said, "Hagar, Sarai's maid, whence camest thou? and whither wilt thou go?" And she said, "I flee from the face of my mistress Sarai."

The angel tells Hagar to go back home and submit to Sarai. Then, as if to make this instruction more palatable, the heavenly visitor makes one of those predictions for which the Scriptures are noted.

> 10. And the angel of the Lord said unto her, "I will multiply thy seed exceedingly, that it shall not be numbered for multitude."

Part of the true horror of the story of Hagar is that the source of loving protection, God Almighty, from whom Hagar might have expected just and merciful treatment, sided chiefly with Abram and Sarai.

I recommend, in this connection, Phyllis Trible's *Texts of Terror: Literary-Feminist Readings of Biblical Narratives* (Philadelphia: Fortress Press, 1984). Ms. Trible tells what she accurately describes as "sad stories . . . tales of terror, with women as victims." Her study refers to "the inferiority, subordination, and abuse of the female in ancient Israel and the early church." In the present day we hear many recommendations that the problems of our society could be solved if we would only "return to biblical morality." And follow the example of Abram and Sarai? Where is the edifying morality in these chapters of Genesis?

Chapters 17-23. The Lord then makes another convenant with Abram, changes the couple's names to Abraham and SARAH (these are merely variant spellings of the same names), and as we have seen, again promises Abraham that "I will make nations of thee, and kings shall come out of thee" (17:6). (This despite the fact that so far the Bible has mentioned only Hagar's son, Ishmael.) First, however, Abraham, Ishmael, and all male slaves had to be circumcised. We are not told how many died from such surgery performed in unhygienic goats'-hair tents. (See CIRCUMCISION.)

Well past menopause ("it had ceased to be with Sarah after the manner of women"), Sarah nevertheless conceives and bears ISAAC, but not before Abraham once again does the "she's my sister" routine (20:2), this time with King ABIMELECH. Abraham gives Sarah to the king. But the Lord warns Abimelech in a dream not to touch her, and then reasserts his partiality to Abraham: "he is a prophet." He may be a prophet, but he is also a panderer; Abimelech behaves more morally and plausibly, demanding to know:

> . . . "What hast thou done unto us? and what have I offended thee, that thou hast brought on me and on my kingdom a great sin? thou hast done deeds unto me that ought not to be done" (20:9).

I submit that there is not a minister or rabbi who would not be forced to side with Abimelech against Abraham, who is a coward despite all the evidence of God's favor he has been given. Now he reveals that Sarah is indeed his half-sister, and Abimelech, in gratitude for not having sinned, gives Abraham sheep, oxen, slaves, silver, and his pick of the land. This turn of events is incomprehensible to the modern reader and is almost a duplicate of Abraham's behavior earlier in Egypt.

All of this adultery or near-adultery with other partners suggests that the Hebrews may not have been sure of their legitimate descent from Abraham. After all, if Sarah was twice offered to another man and Abraham was over 100 years old, we can be forgiven for wondering who the father of Isaac really was. One could even construe one passage (21:1) as a hint that the Lord miraculously "fathered" Isaac, because the story of God's visiting Sarah loosely parallels the miraculous impregnation of Mary in the New Testament. For whatever the point may be worth, Abraham's sister-in-law Milcah was much more fertile than Sarah.

Chapter 23 tells us that Sarah died at the age of 127 and was buried in a cave in a field given to Abraham by the generous Hittites. (Scholars are not certain who these particular Hittites were, because the Hittites known to archaeologists lived far to the north, in present-day Turkey.) Abraham then took another wife, Keturah, who bore him six sons. He died at 177, was buried beside Sarah, and "gave all he had unto Isaac" (25:5), sending the sons of his concubines away to the east.

The chief information we get from all of this that may be accurate includes: (1) the Hebrews' plausible wanderings throughout the Near East and attempts to settle down in Palestine; (2) the *Hebrews' recognition that they were indebted to various settled peoples in Canaan and were related to tribes living east of the Jordan.* On the negative side, we find a sordid account of Abraham's relations with people who were generous to him, his unwavering egotistical belief that the Lord was promoting his welfare and his alone, and his stinginess toward all of his family except Sarah and Isaac.

For the bizarre story of Abraham and the near-sacrifice of Isaac, see ISAAC.

Altogether, the Old Testament inexplicably has presented Abraham as a hard-hearted man, a coward, a liar, a panderer, and an ingrate. How he came to be considered the revered ancestor of the Jews with these recorded traits is difficult to understand. If there *had* been such a patriarch and he had indeed behaved as Abraham is pictured, one would think that the Genesis author(s) would have invented some redeeming qualities. I challenge the reader to name any.

ACTS OF THE APOSTLES. We are brought face-to-face with one of the Bible's many mysteries when we examine the title of this 28-chapter book of the New Testament, for it is misleading. If you put to any person unfamiliar with the Scriptures the question as to what sort of text he might expect, given the title "Acts of the Apostles," he will, of course, respond, "Why, one that concerns the doings or experiences of the twelve Apostles." But this is not entirely accurate. Acts is generally a report of the experiences of only *two* of Jesus' original disciples, Peter and John, and of PAUL, who was not one of the original twelve although he considered himself an Apostle.

Another point almost never brought to the attention of the faithful is that there is no certain knowledge as to who wrote this book of the New Testament. There seems to be general scholarly agreement on stylistic grounds that whoever the author was also wrote the Gospel of LUKE. It is quite possible, of course, that Luke, a personal associate of Paul, did write these materials, but there doesn't seem to be any agreement about the matter. Most scholars date Acts at A.D. 80-85, or as late as 92.

The document was written as a general report, although, by a common ancient convention, it is presented as a letter to someone named Theophilus. Such "letters" were a common form of literary dedication. Scholars have not, however, been able to identify the gentleman, though he was probably a Gentile convert.

Chapter 1. Although the author describes the ascension of JESUS in clear-cut, unambiguous language, William Neil, in his *Harper's Bible Commentary* (New York: Harper and Row, 1962), suggests an allegorical interpretation.

> It is a pictorial way of saying that when our Lord had made it plain that the resurrection was a fact, and had convinced a sufficient number of his followers that this was so, the appearances ceased. The shroud and the angelic figures are a natural biblical accompaniment of divine mystery, conveying the message that Jesus is no longer confined to Galilee but is enthroned and exalted in heaven . . .

After relating the story of the physical ascension of Jesus into Heaven, the author describes, in precise terms, the manner of the death of Judas.

> 18. Now this man purchased a field with the reward of iniquity; and falling headlong, he burst asunder in the midst, and all his bowels gushed out.

A number of comments on this report are required. Either it is false, contradicting, as it does, the account of Matthew 27:5 that Judas hanged himself, or it is true. The Greek that is translated "falling headlong" probably means "he fell head first," with "from a height" understood. Such elliptical expressions are common in the New Testament.

It was certainly not necessary—if one thinks the matter through—that there be anything unusual about the physical death of Judas Iscariot. He has incurred, by his act of betrayal of Jesus, the contempt of hundreds of millions of Christians who would people the earth down through the centuries. Certainly the low repute in which Judas is held has nothing whatever to do with the fact that he either hanged himself or fell to his death.

Another extremely odd fact about the opening chapter of Acts is that, although Peter and his followers decided to name a new apostle to replace the dead Judas, they had trouble choosing between the two finalists, Joseph called Barsabbas, who was surnamed Justus, and one Matthias. In accordance with a widespread ancient custom for political appointments, a method of gambling, drawing lots, was used to make the choice between the two. What is odd about the matter is that after Matthias is chosen, there is not a single further word in any Christian writing about either of the two men, a strange literary fate for an actual apostle.

Chapter 2. This chapter is supposed to recount the events of the famous day of Pentecost. The residents of Jerusalem, it is asserted, their attention understandably attracted by the rushing, roaring sound of the wind, gathered round the house in which the visit of the Holy Spirit had just taken place. It is not made clear whether the apostles walked out of doors or how the visitors gained entrance, but, in any event, those who had been touched by the Holy Spirit now began to address the newcomers, who were astonished to be able to interpret what was said "each in his own language" (2:6).

> 12. And they were all amazed, and were in doubt, saying to one another, "What meaneth this?"
> 13. Others mocking said, "These men are full of new wine."
> 14. But Peter, standing up with the eleven, lifted up his voice, and said unto them, "Ye men of Judea, and all ye that dwell at Jerusalem, be this known unto you, and hearken to my words:
> 15. "For these are not drunken, as ye suppose, seeing it is but the third hour of the day.
> 16. "But this is that which was spoken by the prophet Joel;
> 17. "And it shall come to pass *in the last days,* saith God, I will pour out of my Spirit upon all flesh: and your sons and your daughters shall prophesy, and your young men shall see visions, and your old men shall dream dreams:
> 18. "And on my servants and on my handmaidens I will pour out in those days of my Spirit; and they shall prophesy:
> 19. "And I will shew wonders in heaven above, and signs in the earth beneath; blood, and fire, and vapour of smoke:
> 20. "The sun shall be turned into darkness, and the moon into blood, before that great and noble day of the Lord come:
> 21. "And it shall come to pass, that whosoever shall call on the name of the Lord shall be saved." (IA)

When we examine this chapter of Acts, we see that it is distressingly vague and so general that it is almost devoid of meaning. What does it mean, for example, for the Lord to say, "I will pour out my Spirit upon all flesh?" A dozen men are free to give a dozen mutually contradictory interpretations of the phrase. Nor is there anything more instructive in such statements as "your sons and daughters shall prophesy, your old men shall dream dreams and your young men shall see visions," for such things may happen in any place, at any time and are indeed alleged to have happened at many points during Old Testament times.

It will be instructive for the student to study the prophecy of Joel in full. If he does, he will conclude that *it has nothing whatever to do with a prediction about the coming of either Jesus of Nazareth or any other Messiah.* It is, in fact, but one more of those repetitive Old Testament prophecies of doom, characterized by an almost gloating tone of vengeance to come for those who fail to call on the name of the Lord.

Chapter 2 tells us that approximately 3,000 people were not only baptized but also promptly "sold their possessions and goods, and parted them to all men, as every man had need" (v. 45). The act of generosity described is beautiful and admirable; one can only lament that it is hardly ever encountered in the context of modern Christianity, nor has any such custom been known for many centuries.

Shortly thereafter, in preaching about Jesus, Peter asserts that MOSES referred to Christ when, as quoted in Deuteronomy 18:15, he said, "The Lord God will raise up a prophet like me from among you." But, alas, there is no way to determine whether Moses was referring to Jesus specifically or to the Messiah generally when he made the original statement. It is important, too, for the reader to remind himself that there is no way of knowing whether in fact Moses ever made the statement Peter attributes to him, since he did not write the books long credited to him.

Chapter 3. This chapter narrates the story of the miraculous healing of a lifelong cripple by Peter and John. The narrator tells us that those who had seen the recovered man gathered around the two apostles, to stare at them in wonder. Peter explains that the power to work such a healing was not his and John's but came from Jesus. Peter, in fact, takes the occasion to denounce his fellow Jews for having disowned and persecuted Jesus, although at one point he charitably says, "And now, brethren, I know that you acted in ignorance, just as your fathers did also" (v. 17).

Chapter 4 concerns the two apostles, who are thrown into jail overnight by the temple guard and the Sadducees. Annas, the high priest, and others question the two Christians; thereupon they utter a warning which continues to occasion discord in the churches—among Christians and other believers— to the present day. Peter says, in Verse 12, "And there is salvation in no one else, for *there is no other name under heaven that has been given among men, by which we must be saved.*" (IA)

Either this is indeed the case, or it is not. If it is a reliable prediction and threat, then it is a tragic shame that, after almost 2,000 years of effort, only a minority of the world's population has acknowledged Jesus Christ as a heavenly savior, since it has been alleged elsewhere that failure to do so will result in punishment in the eternal flames of HELL.

For whatever the point may be worth, many scholars point out that Luke, or whoever the author of Acts was, was not an eyewitness to the incidents he describes. (See also APOSTLES, THE.)

ADAM AND EVE, the first man and woman said to have been created by God. When it is first announced that God has created a man and then later a woman, in Genesis 2:7 and 22, they are not named. A fundamental error of the popular and even priestly interpretations of Genesis is in assuming that the word *Adam* was meant to be a proper name. Comments Father John L. McKenzie in *The Dictionary of the Bible* (New York: Macmillan, 1965): "the usual translation of the word as a proper name, Adam, is in error. He is called 'the man' until Genesis 4:1, where Adam is first given a proper name." (Actually, the name *Adam* is used in 2:19 and 3:21, if one consults a different translation of the Bible.)

For a very long time it was dangerous to question the strict interpretation of GENESIS, not to mention other portions of the Scriptures. The argument became particularly heated when the hypothesis of the physical evolution of all living species, including man, was developed. Catholic and Protestant authorities were united in the 19th century in stern condemnation of any accommodation with the evolutionists. As it gradually began to appear, however, that to a very considerable extent the evolutionists were right and the fundamentalists quite mistaken, the churches naturally had to modify their views, so as not to lose the loyalty of every intelligent person in Europe and the United States.

Today it is not unusual to find a statement such as the following, in *Old Testament Problems* by the Rev. Dr. L. Rumble, M.S.C.:

> As regards the formation of the first man, there is nothing in the Christian religion to prevent anyone from assuming the evolution of a body from some lower species of animal, until it arrives at a suitable degree of development for the reception from God of a specially created rational soul, with which it was combined to form the first truly human being.

This is a gracious, if quite necessary, concession on the part of the Catholic church, but many people were subjected to sometimes atrocious abuse for having suggested precisely as much in earlier centuries. It may be assumed that, inasmuch as the Jewish and Christian faiths have gradually made an accommodation of sorts with the Darwinian hypothesis, such development, however glacially slow, will continue, so that at some point in a perhaps

17

not too distant future most churches will have conceded the point totally, while still insisting on divine creation of the human soul. Unfortunately (or fortunately, depending on one's personal biases), the churches do not have sufficient space in which to make such a final maneuver. The reason they do not has to do with what is called ORIGINAL SIN.

Although a majority of Catholic scientists and scholars accept much of Darwinian theory, granting certain fundamental reservations required by dogma, the faithful in general are still taught an essentially fundamentalist interpretation of the first portions of Genesis. (See also CREATION, THE; DEATH; EDEN, GARDEN OF; FALL, THE.)

AGE OF ANCIENT CIVILIZATIONS. A great deal is known in detail about Middle Eastern culture before 2000 B.C. Archaeologists have found tombs, pottery, and settlement sites of earlier periods in different Middle Eastern countries, as well as in China, India, and Latin America. By 5000 B.C. not only had various cities in PALESTINE, Mesopotamia, Iran, Turkey and the Indus Valley reached high points in their development but about 6000 B.C., some populations of the Andean area in South America were beginning to establish permanent agricultural settlements and the rudiments of what is generally termed "civilization."

For details of early human settlement and development in that continent—all undreamed of by the authors of the Bible—read Frederic André Engel's *An Ancient World Preserved: Relics and Records of Prehistory in the Andes* (New York: Crown, 1976), particularly the chapter, "Ten Thousand Years of Andean History."

For the Archaic periods in North America, see Michael D. Coe's *Mexico* (London: Thames and Hudson, 1984), and John S. Henderson's *The World of the Ancient Maya* (Ithaca, N.Y.: Cornell University Press, 1981).

If God were only interested in his "creation" in the Middle East, as the Bible would have us believe, it must surprise fundamentalists of all faiths to learn that other peoples, whom we must assume were also created by God, were domesticating corn and cotton, building villages and rudimentary temples, and independently inventing pottery and weaving in places not even mentioned in the Bible. The Olmec civilization in Mexico, for example, was flourishing about the time David was allegedly ruling Israel. Obviously many cultures knew nothing of "the one, true religion," though they set great store by religions of their own, and some developed moral precepts higher than those found in much of the Old Testament.

The Archaeology of Mesopotamia by Seton Lloyd (London: Thames and Hudson, rev. ed., 1984) and *Persia: An Archaeological Guide* by Sylvia

A. Matheson (London: Faber and Faber, 1972) have fascinating accounts of what was going on in Southwestern Asia and the Iranian plateau back to 6000 B.C., among peoples not so far away yet perhaps little known to the earliest Israelite tribes.

The Sea Peoples: Warriors of the Ancient Mediterranean by N. K. Sandars (London: Thames and Hudson, rev. ed., 1985), covering the upheavals of 1250-1150 B.C., parallels in time the alleged Israelite wanderings and incursion into Palestine. Sandars notes:

> . . . by the time the Israelites felt themselves strong enough to attack the plains and the coastal cities, in the 10th century, it was the Philistines who were their chief antagonists. They possessed the land to which they have given their name: Palestine. The five cities of the Philistines—Gaza, Ashkalon, Ashdod, Ekron and Gath—are all in the coastal plain or the foothills of the Shephelah . . . ancient Ashdod has been dug and gives a most valuable stratigraphy. (p. 165)

Notable is the book's description of *the advanced stage of development of the Philistines,* especially their pottery. There is no clear evidence that the Israelites had then developed pottery, nor had they built permanent settlements, let alone cities like Gaza.

AGE OF THE EARTH AND THE UNIVERSE. The fundamentalist argument against the scientific assertion of the great age of our planet—to the effect that God created the earth only about 6,000 years ago, including fossils embedded in rocks—is unworthy of serious discussion. If we begin with the assumption that God can do anything he pleases, then of course he could have made the world 6,000 years ago, or last Tuesday, and planted *misleading evidence suggesting that it was billions of years older.*

One must speak very plainly in addressing the fact that neither Jewish nor Christian scholarship has any explanation as to how the author of GENESIS could speak with an air of such specificity about details of the creation of a universe so vast that even modern astronomers, with the best scientific instruments, cannot calculate with any accuracy the exact dimensions of it. Informed people have long concluded that, since the two conflicting creation accounts in Genesis cannot possibly be considered sound astronomy, geology, physics—or indeed sound science of any sort—the most reasonable conclusion is that they are myths.

But the fundamentalist Christian and Orthodox Jewish faiths, at the moment at least, cannot acknowledge such a conclusion, since the inevitable repercussions would—if people were in the habit of thinking such matters through—lead to a serious crisis of faith for many worshipers. Therefore, the very best that many religious scholars of the present age are able to suggest is that the account of Genesis, as Father Bruce Vawter puts it, *"is folk history, not circumstantial history, which means that historical and legendary elements frequently and inevitably appear side by side.* Note that I do not say Genesis teaches legend, but Genesis has used a partly legendary history to teach enduring truths." (IA)

I have shared this passage with a number of people, none of whom has the slightest reason for bias about such matters, and have yet to meet anyone who regards Vawter's reasoning as sound on this point. Nevertheless, Vawter—and to his great credit, reassuringly enough—states shortly thereafter in *A Path Through Genesis* (New York: Sheed and Ward, 1956): "Any interpretation of Scripture that contradicts a known fact of science we may be very sure is no true interpretation." Vawter should consider himself fortunate that he lives in the 20th century and not the 15th, since he might not have remained alive after preaching such a heresy, however reasonable.

It is, finally, discouraging—in the context of one's idealistic hopes concerning the essential ethicality of the human spirit—to study the record of the churches' arguments in the debate concerning the estimated age of the physical universe. Although many churchmen today freely speak of hundreds of thousands, millions, or in some cases billions of years as the temporal context of nature, they rarely acknowledge that they are indebted not to their predecessors in the faith, but to earlier generations of despised astronomers, geologists, and biologists for such calculations. Early churchmen long taught that the world dated back to about 4000 B.C. Any suggestions to the contrary were greeted with that hostility which the enemies of religion have, sad to say, been able to point to in accusing the churches of hypocrisy as regards their claims of preaching love and compassion.

One may respond with sympathy to the attempts of countless 19th-century Christian scholars to "reconcile" the astronomical, geological, and biological sciences on the one hand with the account in Genesis concerning the creation on the other. It is now recognized by every intelligent and informed person that the two cannot be reconciled. One is free to reject the scriptural version or the scientific evaluation; I am concerned merely to assert that one cannot respect both records for the reason that they are logically and factually incompatible. Nor should we be guilty of the error of assuming that the problem relates only to Genesis. It touches the New Testament as well, for both Romans and I Corinthians state that death came into the world with ADAM, whereas it is now clear that *death was a natural fact of life for countless ages before any of the higher animals including man, had evolved.* It is intellectual dishonesty to respond by saying, "Ah, but the Scriptures refer to the death of the soul."

If I may vouchsafe a modest observation on the speculations of philosophers and scientists concerning the age of the earth and the universe, I perceive an error in one of the basic assumptions on which such a debate rests. The assumption is clearly common, in much and perhaps all of the debate on this question, that if one somehow has correctly established the approximate age of such physical matter as exists at present, one has therefore established, with an equal degree of assurance, something or other about the time at which "the world was created," at which "time began," or at which "God made the world." Let us consider the legitimacy of this assumption.

It is part of one of the component building-blocks of such a case that matter in its presently recognizable form may be traced back to some point—let us arbitrarily say 20 billion years in the past—at which time a "Big Bang" occurred; as a result of such a massive explosion matter took on the physical properties by which we now apprehend it. But this leaves not only unanswered, but usually unrecognized, the question as to how such an explosion itself could take place in the absence of physical laws. Obviously one may posit the existence of a Supreme Mind, possessed of every conceivable power, as an explanation. If one simply assumes such a truth, then of course the argument is in a sense closed off.

But, alas for such simplicity of thought, a great many astrophysicists are not religious believers in any commonly acceptable definition of the term. While some have religious affiliations, a good many others are either agnostics or atheists. When, therefore, they address themselves to the drama of the massive explosion that took place 20 billion years ago, they must make the assumption that, *before* the Big Bang, matter existed in some earlier state and that, in fact, it has existed through all time. To an average mind—such as my own—there is something incomprehensible in such an assumption. But one must be impressed by the fact that there is something incomprehensible about *all* theories or assumptions concerning the still basically mysterious concepts of time and space. I have no wish to enter the discipline of metaphysics here, but I shall suggest that to establish that a particular massive explosion took place at some point in the distant past is by no means the same as automatically establishing that that is the point at which *everything* began.

Furthermore, if we believe that God made all things—as Christians, Jews, and Muslims are taught—then we must believe that he made radiocarbon. Whatever the reason for its creation, it has proved enormously useful to modern science because it enables us to determine the age of extremely ancient things. The substance serves as a sort of clock that was turned on and set to run at the moment some once-living object died.

The May 21, 1982, issue of *The Journal of Science* carried a story by Walter Alvarez, professor of geology at the University of California at Berkeley, and Ramachandran Ganapathy of the J. T. Baker Chemical Company detailing evidence, in samples taken from the Caribbean seafloor, that a large meteorite crashed into the earth approximately 34 million years ago and perhaps wiped out a number of species. The word *perhaps* was used because although the evidence points strongly to such a hypothesis, it is merely consistent with the evidence rather than conclusive. But there is no debate among geologists concerning the fact that a meteorite impact occurred some 34 million years ago.

The fundamentalists, however, have no alternative to believing that the physical universe is only a few thousand years old, because *that* is what the book of Genesis implies. It does not matter at all to the fundamentalists that the entire body of science says something quite different: that the universe is many billions of years old. The believers' reaction to such assertions is not a weakening of his or her faith; it is merely frustrated annoyance with science and its millions of representatives, no matter how well educated.

Those who are naive about this argument may assume that the debate can be quickly resolved by forcing the fundamentalists to consider relevant evidence. It might be supposed, for example, that simply placing in a fundamentalist's hands a three-million-year-old fossil of a fish would instantly disabuse him of his unsubstantiated notion that ours is a planet of recent vintage. But, no. The dynamics of the dialogue are far more complex. Nor would increasing the amount of material evidence improve the situation to any degree whatever. It would be pointless to talk of accumulating enough evidentiary material to fill, let us say, the Grand Canyon, or to pile up enough of it to shake the foundations of Europe itself. No, the entire incredible vastness of the universe itself *is* the very evidence of which we speak, but its existence has not the slightest effect on the closed minds of those who say that the world *must* be about 6,000 years old. (See also NOAH AND THE ARK.)

AMOS, a short book of the Old Testament, consisting of nine chapters that I feel add little to our understanding of virtue, compassion, and common sense. If the first two chapters are really the word of God, as the prophet Amos says, then we cannot avoid the conclusion that God is a pyromaniac. A number of peoples and cities are named, after which it is alleged that the Lord will set fire to their palaces. Included are Damascus, Gaza, Tyre, Edom, Ammon, Moab, Judah, and—surprise—Israel.

The rest of Amos is largely a lengthy recitation of threats. The Almighty, we are told, shall take endless vengeance, bring fire, sickness, military defeat, and other forms of destruction upon both his followers in Israel and Judah and their enemies.

Chapter 3. Although the Bible unfortunately abounds in ambiguous and puzzling passages, one of the most troublesome occurs when the prophet Amos tells the children of Israel that God has said: "You only have I known of all the families of the earth; *therefore* I will punish you for all your iniquities" (v. 2). The word *therefore* is italicized here to emphasize that whoever created the passage, whether God Almighty, Amos, or some other personage, seems to have intended to convey the idea that the Jews have suffered the countless tragedies that have been inflicted upon them *because* God ordained it.

It is important for the reader to pause to contemplate this passage, its meaning, and, to some extent at least, its implications. It does not require a remarkable exercise of the intelligence to perceive that if a wise and loving person—let us say a prophet, saint, or virtuous philosopher—were to regard some particular individual or social group with special favor, he would, to the extent that it was in his power, treat his chosen *better* than those toward whom he did not feel such affectionate regard.

But it is not incomprehensible that someone holding the common notion that crime deserves punishment might believe that Israel's criminal refusal to obey Yahweh was aggravated by all the favors Yahweh had shown Israel *alone,* and therefore Israel should be particularly punished.

It is not a meaningful response to this puzzling verse to restate the old observation that God's ways are not those of man since no one has ever supposed that they are. What it *is* perfectly reasonable to suppose is that, while God's ways are *not* those of man, they must be, by virtue of the very meaning of the word *God, superior* to the ways of man. It would be a very peculiar form of heresy indeed to announce that one had concluded, on the basis of careful study, that the primary way in which God's ways differed from those of humans was in their striking inferiority.

And yet, in this quotation of Amos, claiming to speak for the Almighty, it is unmistakable that both the motivation and behavior attributed to the Creator is not only inferior to that of wise and charitable saints and seers but is also inferior to that of some illiterate jungle tribes, whom, we may be sure, would not dream of expressing affection for a child by cruelly abusing him or her in a variety of ways.

In the present day, God help us, our society has become aware of one more social scandal, the problem of child abuse. Every year thousands of innocent infants are maimed, some killed, by their own parents. But

AMOS

who in their right mind would claim that such behavior is sanctioned by God's behavior toward his "children" in the book of Amos?

Whatever else Amos believed, he was clearly convinced that the unfortunate things that happen in the world, to both good and bad people, are at least partly the result, not of simple misfortune, but are the will of God. We see this in Verse 6, in which he says, "If there is a calamity in the city, will not the Lord have done it?"

Chapter 8. The author, said to be a shepherd, issues a perfectly sensible and morally sound condemnation of greedy merchants and others who take advantage of the poor. This may date from the 6th century B.C.

> 4. Hear this, O ye that swallow up the needy, even to make the poor of the land to fail,
> 5. Saying, When will the new moon be gone, that we may sell corn? and the Sabbath, that we may set forth wheat, making the ephah small, and the shekel great, and falsifying the balances by deceit?
> 6. That we may buy the poor for silver, and the needy for a pair of shoes; yea, and sell the refuse of the wheat?
> 7. The Lord hath sworn by the excellency of Jacob, Surely I will never forget any of their works.
> 8. Shall not the land tremble for this, and every one mourn that dwelleth therein? and it shall rise up wholly as a flood; and it shall be cast out and drowned, as by the flood of Egypt.

It would be interesting to know how many Bible-believing Christian and Jewish merchants and corporate executives have ever taken these passages to heart.

Chapter 9 continues the dire threats. The unfortunate shall be cut down by the sword. Those who might attempt to hide at the bottom of the sea, a small number one assumes, *at God's command* will be bitten by a serpent. These threats are addressed to the children of Israel.

In Verse 8, we are asked to believe that God will destroy the sinful kingdom of Israel "from off the face of the earth." But an exception is made. "I will not utterly destroy the house of Jacob, saith the Lord." Practically all modern Christian churchmen preach the love of God, his infinite capacity for forgiveness, his hope that sinners will repent and return to him. An idea of this sort finally appears in Verses 11–15, at the very end.

Though an often unpleasant book, Amos is not without merit. It contains a famous verse (5:24), which was used as a text by the Southern civil-rights movement. "But let justice roll down like waters, and righteousness like an ever-flowing stream."

Amos is probably one of those books of prophecy written sometime during the turbulent two centuries that encompassed the destruction of the Kingdoms of Israel and Judah (722 and 586 B.C.), so the writer may be trying to say that, though the children of Israel are *said* to be God's chosen, they sinned, and, consequently, the terrible things that occurred to them at the hands of the Assyrians and Babylonians represent God's punishments. That the Old Testament God appeared wrathful was perhaps inevitable. There were other peoples of the same era as the early Hebrews who were like them in conceiving of an angry God or of many gods as being responsible for all the evils that befell them. Jews today do not claim that God is like that.

No doubt some readers will feel that I have placed too much blame on Old Testament writers for their depiction of a savage God. But that is not my intent. The true objects of my criticism are those fundamentalists of the modern day who, by insisting that every word of the Bible is divinely authored or inspired, make such criticisms inevitable. Nonfundamentalist Christians feel that such a text as Amos has value partly because it gives us a point of comparison in demonstrating that the concept of God has evolved—and wonderfully improved—over the last few thousand years. This is a perfectly reasonable observation, but it is, of course, incompatible with the fundamentalist approach to Scripture.

On this point, some fundamentalists defend themselves by asserting that God really was once as punishing as the Old Testament depicts him but that he gradually changed into the far more loving deity of the New Testament. But this introduces a remarkable theological assertion, that God is not, after all, constant but, like all of his creatures, is capable of evolving. Whatever the merits of this claim, it is clearly heretical in the context of traditional Christian theology.

ANTI-SEMITISM. One social evil for which the New Testament is clearly in part responsible is anti-Semitism. Although relatively little has been published and widely distributed concerning Christian participation in anti-Semitic acts over the past 2,000 years—at least not until a stirred Christian conscience began doing so after the Holocaust—the record as it stands reveals perhaps the darkest blemish on the Western world, especially as it culminated in the Nazis' genocidal policy during World War II.

The fact that not all anti-Semitic literature is Christian and Bible-oriented is not entirely relevant. Over the centuries most anti-Semitic arguments have come from Christian sources. Catholic Professor Gordon Zahn's penetrating study, *German Catholics in Hitler's Germany* (New York: Sheed & Ward, 1962) is worth reading in this regard. It has been noted, in recent years, that an increasing number of Muslim writers and speakers of a fundamentalist bent or ones who are anti-Israel have taken up this theme, even though the KORAN specifies that adherents of Judaism, one of the "peoples of the Book," are to be tolerated and left alone to practice their religion, which is viewed by Muslims as an earlier revelation by God.

Professor Jack Sanders of the University of Oregon shows that Christian hostility toward the Jews began with the author of Luke-Acts. (See "The Salvation of the Jews in Luke-Acts," *Seminar Papers: Society of Biblical Literature,* Atlanta: Scholars Press, 1982.)

The chief notion that contributed to anti-Semitism is that the Jews were "Christ-killers." Being relatively disinterested in the specifics, I find it fascinating that so much argument has taken place among scholars over the centuries concerning the question as to whether the Romans or the Jews were primarily to blame for the death of Jesus. There is not the slightest doubt but that countless generations of Christians, of all denominations, have had it firmly impressed on them that the Jews were responsible for what they regarded as the most despicable crime in history, *even though the tragedy* (it is taught by the same authority) *was supposedly predestined by the Almighty* and was willingly submitted to by Jesus.

In the present century, of course, one has heard increasing expressions of guilt on the part of Catholic and Protestant spokesmen for anti-Semitism. This is understandable in light of the sordid and frequently atrocious persecutions of Jews by Christians over the centuries. But before taking up the question itself, one should grasp the larger point that, insofar as what allegedly happened 2,000 years ago can be said to have any reasonable connection with people in the present, one must ask the question: So what— after one has opted in favor of either Roman or Jewish primary blame for the death of Jesus? Given the fact that crucifixion was a Roman method of punishment and that there was clearly Roman participation in the act, would it have made sense also to harass and despise all descendants of the Romans, who—to the extent that they can be personally identified— are the Italians of the world?

The reason the question is a moral one among Christians today is that so-called Jewish "complicity" in the execution has been advanced as "justification" for the most despicable attacks, pogroms, and expulsions of populations.

Let us play the mental game, for a moment, of assuming that the Christians have been right about all this. But for them to be right, we must hold it a sound principle that an identifiable ethnic group of the present day must be held strictly accountable for offenses its predecessors committed thousands of years in the past. If one were to act consistently on this principle, few individuals would live long enough to mete out punishment to others. Not only would one be justified in hounding today's Jews but one would also be obliged to undertake a vigorous campaign against the Catholics because of the well-known atrocities of the Inquisition, the Crusades, the slaughter of the Huguenots, and the burning of witches; one would have to be an avenging angel against all present-day Protestants if one is sympathetic to the poor wretches brutalized, tortured, hanged, drawn-and-quartered, and burned at the stake by their Reformation and Puritan forefathers.

Come to think of it, the proper business of mankind would be nothing but constant wars of retribution, since it is observable that practically all ethnic groups, races, nationalities, tribes, religious sects, and political parties have been guilty of atrocities. I have deliberately drawn out the thread of logic here to demonstrate the utter absurdity of any Christian's notion that one is entitled to be beastly to *today's* Jews because an extremely small number of their distant ancestors were said to be, as the unlovely Christian phrase has it, "Christ-killers." Probably more Jews were his supporters than were those who urged his death. At any rate, Paul in I Corinthians said that those who killed Christ did not know who he was.

Having come from a lower-middle-class, Irish-Catholic family in Chicago and also having long familiarity with the Protestant culture, I know that many from such backgrounds are salt-of-the-earth. But they are, alas, exceptions to the rule that has greatly influenced both cultures. Even among relatively civilized Christians, there is still, I am saddened to report, a kind of anti-Jewish feeling, thought, and behavior. At times mindless and almost innocent, at other times vicious, it is not just a sort of unthinking add-on but is rather, God help us, central to their religious point of view.

There are a thousand and one reasons for this. Major among them is the 2,000-year tradition of active, formal Christian encouragement of anti-Jewish feeling that originated in the Jewish opposition to the earliest Christian groups from whom the New Testament derives. (See Acts 4:3; 5:17 f.; 6:10–15; 7:57–58; 8:1–2; 9:1–2, 23; 11:19; 12:1–3; 13:44–50, and in many places to the end.) These are referred to in many passages in Paul's letters.

However, after that is said, generous, intelligent people must let history be. God help the individuals and groups hatred of whom happens to be suggested by certain passages of Scripture. For then there have been almost no moral barriers to prevent the lashing out of the sickest possible sort of hatreds. Hitler, let us never forget, did not contaminate and corrupt a morally pure German people. The overwhelming majority were church-affiliated Christians in 1938. Rather, he was able to exploit to new depths of degradation a European anti-Semitic tradition of centuries.

Never should Christians of the modern day assume that the Nazis' behavior represented a slow falling away from early sweetness and light. The violence and viciousness were there all along; indeed, not even Hitler expressed *verbally* as much animosity as did the early fathers of the Christian church, although his state-sponsored genocide is one of the most barbaric the world has seen.

It is noteworthy that the extent to which American Christians today are less blameworthy in this regard than their recent and ancient ancestors has little to do with their religious beliefs. Such a tentative approach toward simple civic decency has come about because, as Americans, not as Christians, we have come to realize, as a nation of immigrants, that the U.S. Constitution forbids the acquisition of civic power by the churches and that we are all equal before the law.

It is these liberal, reformist currents, growing more out of a Humanist than Christian philosophy that have civilized America's Christians. Protestants and Catholics in our country were slowly, painfully, but, thank God, ultimately shamed into behaving more compassionately toward Jews and, for that matter, African-Americans and other minorities.

Many forces of social, economic, religious and political conservatism largely resisted such reformist currents, as some of their representatives still do.

On a personal note, although I early absorbed the idea of general Jewish "inferiority," it required nothing more than my attendance, in the third year of high school, at a school whose student body was largely Jewish, to disabuse me of any such idiotic notions. I saw at once that the new Jewish friends I made at that time were strikingly superior in intellectual achievement to the friends I'd known before. They were, for the most part, superior as citizens, too, actively interested in important issues, caring about the poor, sensitive to instances of injustice, whether personally touched by it or not.

There is nothing here of romanticizing the Jews. The worst judgment one can make of them, I suppose, is that they are, like the rest of us, human beings and hence prone to classic human weaknesses and failings.

All of the planet earth's tribes are justifiably proud of their individual representatives who have achieved fame and/or distinction. Members of religious bodies, too, point with pride to such members of their flocks as have enjoyed notable success. But somehow this sort of demographic bookkeeping seems rarely to get into print.

Although Jews number only about 3 percent of our population, they have been awarded 27 percent of the Nobel prizes won by American scientists. "Jews are overrepresented in medicine by 231% in proportion to the general population," report Dennis Prager and Joseph Telushkin in their *Why the Jews?* (New York: Touchstone–Simon and Schuster, 1983). "In psychiatry by 478%, in dentistry by 299% and in mathematics by 238%." Moreover, American Jews are twice as likely to go to college as Gentiles.

The family life of Jews has traditionally been remarkably stable, although this has changed somewhat in the last half of the 20th century. It hardly requires mentioning that Jews, as a class, are better educated than many of the Gentiles with whom they come into contact. And even though as a Christian I was raised in a culture which almost daily preached that charity is the greatest of virtues, I never saw the ideal properly and fully acted upon until I became aware of the inspiring generosity of American Jews.

It is probable that Jewish intellectual giftedness is based on nothing more complex than the centuries-old tradition, among Jews, of teaching not only the children of the well-to-do but all little ones to read. Those who know nothing of history and therefore who evaluate the matter on the basis of modern comparisons, will quite miss the point. Today, in the United States, there is the ideal that all children must be given instruction in reading, but, as we have learned, the ideal is far indeed from realization. For unknown thousands of years illiteracy was the norm in cultures all over the world. Only a tiny minority—priests, scholars, and the wealthy— were taught to read and write. The Jews, an exception to this deplorable state, were taught to read by 5 and, by age 13, to understand more sophisticated literature.

Some churches still do not seem totally at ease about Jews. There are, thank God, an ever-growing number of Christians who do reach out lovingly and with great understanding to their Jewish brothers and sisters. The churches conduct certain rare rituals as repentance for sin, but when does the worldwide campaign of atonement for 2,000 years of one of the most vicious sins imaginable get under way? I personally would attend such services if someone will tell me where they are to be held.

APOSTLES, THE, another name for JESUS' twelve disciples but generally extended to include certain other followers after his death. The lists given in the first three Gospels (Matt. 10, Mark 3, Luke 6) vary. The most popular list refers to the brothers Peter and Andrew; James and John, sons of Zebedee; Philip; Bartholomew, perhaps the Nathanael mentioned in John 1:43-51; Matthew; Thomas; James, the son of Alphaeus; Thaddaeus; Simon the Canaanite, also called the Zealot; and Judas Iscariot.

In *The New Testament and Early Christianity* (New York: Macmillan, 1984), Joseph B. Tyson of Southern Methodist University writes:

The leadership of the primitive community is far from clear. The city of Jerusalem seems to have been a focal point for [the leaders], although communities quickly arose in Damascus and Antioch. Our sources sometimes speak of leadership by the twelve disciples. It is frequently stated today that the idea of the twelve is a legendary conception of the times. The group is supposed to be representative of all Israel, which was originally made up of twelve tribes. That *there never was such a formal group* is shown by the fact that the Synoptic writers [i.e., the Gospels of Mark, Matthew, and Luke] differ widely in their lists of those who were in it. The term *apostles* points to a genuine, but loosely organized, group of leaders. It is impossible to determine how many apostles there were, but Peter, John bar Zebedee, and Paul certainly belonged to it (p. 278) (IA).

The Book of ACTS designates Barnabas as an apostle, and in Romans 16 Andronicus and Junias are called apostles, as is Apollos in First Corinthians 3. Sometimes, the word means something like "missionary" or "ambassador," that is, one sent forth. Paul seemed to be under severe pressure to justify his claim to apostleship; and, in turn, he labeled some of his rivals as "false apostles" (II Cor. 11:13). The word *disciple* is popularly thought to be interchangeable with *apostle,* but the lists of disciples, too, are riddled with problems and discrepancies. The author of the Epistle to the Hebrews (3:1) refers to Jesus himself as "the apostle," though he could hardly have been his own disciple.

The Apostle Paul and the author of LUKE-Acts do not use the term *apostle* in precisely the same way. For Paul, "an apostle is someone who has a *supernatural* experience of the risen Jesus and has been called to his service by such a vision" (G. A. Wells, *Did Jesus Exist?*, Buffalo, N.Y.: Prometheus Books, 1975, p. 126; IA). By contrast, the author of Acts repeatedly uses the term in a technical sense to refer to what he takes to have been an official body of twelve men who were witnesses to a physical ("flesh and bone") resurrection of Jesus and had been witnesses to his ministry from the day of his adult baptism.

Paul makes no reference to a physical resurrection and seemed not to have a concept of it. If Professor Wells' thesis is correct, Paul believed that an apostle had to have (1) encountered the risen Christ in a *supernatural* vision, (2) been called as a missionary or special ambassador, and (3) received special revelations directly from the risen Christ. In addition, (4) the working of miracles and of convincing manifestations of the Spirit were required. The controversy over Paul's own apostleship and over those he regarded as "false apostles" would *never* have arisen had the early churches already recognized the so-called twelve disciples as the apostles. It is especially the author of Acts, writing decades after Paul, who attempts to subordinate Paul's position and promote twelve other men as the "real" apostles.

The Book of Acts tries to bring Paul under the authority of Jerusalem, but in Galatians 1 and 2 Paul makes his claim abundantly clear:

> Paul an apostle—not from men nor through man, but through Jesus Christ and God the Father (1:1 RSV).
> For I did not receive it from man, nor was I taught it, but it came through a revelation of Jesus Christ . . . . I did not confer with flesh and blood, nor did I go up to Jerusalem to those who were apostles before me, but I went away to Arabia; and again I returned to Damascus (1:12, 16–17 RSV).

The favorite apostles seem to have been an inner circle of Peter, James, and John. In the Gospel accounts they alone were allowed to witness some of the important events in Jesus' life, such as the agony in the Garden of Gethsemane and the transfiguration. The Gospel of JOHN refers somewhat unclearly to the "beloved disciple." One tradition identifies him as John, son of Zebedee, but scholars cannot agree on his identity and some think he is an entirely fictional character.

For people of such importance in one of the world's major religions, surprisingly little is known about individual members of the group. Most are seldom mentioned in the Gospels and Acts. The exceptions are Peter, legendary founder of the Church at Rome; Thomas, who doubted Jesus' death until he was invited to touch the reportedly risen Christ's wounds; and the traitor Judas Iscariot.

What has confused many traditional Christians are the legends from the Dark and Middle Ages about the apostles, including the three named. All except Judas Iscariot are termed saints, and their relics are incorrectly supposed to lie in various places in Europe and the Near East. Andrew is the patron saint of Russia and Scotland. Bartholomew was said to have preached the gospel of Christ in India, Ethiopia, Iran, Turkey, Mesopotamia, and Armenia—a tall order in those days of slow camel caravans—and Indian Christians believe that Thomas founded a church in India, which still exists. On the basis of the claims for Bartholomew, both Abyssinians and Armenians claim to be the first mass Gentile converts to Christianity.

Since the writer of the Gospel of MATTHEW is thought by most biblical authorities to be anonymous, it is almost certain that the author was not Jesus' disciple; it is more likely that the unknown author simply used the apostle's name, thereby trying to claim authority for his work on Jesus' life, or else an early Church Father attached the name to the Gospel. This failure to be completely honest was common during the early Christian centuries, and there are various pseudepigraphical books bearing names of the apostles.

There is also no proof that the disciple John, son of Zebedee, was the author of either the Gospel of John or the Johannine letters, although Irenaeus, an early bishop, claimed that he was. Some Christians today assume that Irenaeus was correct and think that the same person also wrote the oddest book in the Bible, Revelation.

James, the son of Zebedee, could not have been the author of the Epistle of James in the New Testament, because that disciple was martyred before 44 A.D. Again, it is hardly likely that the illiterate Galilean Peter, as described in Acts, could have written either I or II Peter, as several recent commentaries have demonstrated.

Of the original twelve apostles, tradition holds that the following may have been martyred: Peter, James the son of Zebedee, Andrew, Philip, Bartholomew, and Thomas. Paul also was martyred. These stories of martyrdom are not accepted by all scholars, but they may have credibility, because we know that the Romans severely punished early Christians.

The Protestant clergyman Paul Hutchinson has observed that, with the exception of Peter, who seems fully human, the other eleven disciples "are shadowy figures." It is obvious that those who wrote the first "accounts" (some call them "fictions") of the life of Christ would concentrate chiefly on Jesus, whom they believed to be the son of God; it is nevertheless unfortunate that the Gospels provide so little information about eleven men who, if even the general outlines of the story of Jesus are true, would have been among the most privileged in all of history. This is one more instance, then, in which those who most fervently desire a clear historical record can find little accurate or directly relevant information.

The odd lack of detail about the apostles might have something to do with the fact that the Gospels were not even started until a good many decades after Jesus' presumed death. Some of the early contributors, since they were not eyewitnesses to the events they described, probably did not know the disciples and possessed little information about them.

The fundamentalist idolaters of the Bible appear not to have grasped the importance of what Hutchinson explained in "The Onward March of Christian Faith," written for *Life* magazine and published December 26, 1955. He says that the Christian religion first

> . . . develops as an institution (the Church), [then] as a teaching, a theology, a faith. The institution is named first because the theology came out of it, not the institution out of the theology. *The New Testa-*

ment—Gospels, Epistles, Apocrypha—is a product of the church. Little of it was written until there was a flourishing church all over the Roman world. It was not gathered in its finally agreed-on form until 692 A.D. (IA)

ATROCITIES, JUSTIFICATION FOR. In considering evidence of ancient savagery, the reader should not lightly dismiss the Old Testament's repeated demand for the vilest atrocities as something peculiar to Israelite military practice of some three or four thousand years ago; there have been more than enough instances in European and American history, over the centuries, when savageries that Christians perpetrated were supposedly justified by appeal to the authority of the Old Testament.

To cite but one such instance: when Oliver Cromwell's forces landed in Ireland in 1649, his 17,000 angry Puritans could hardly wait to slaughter the Irish; they actually marched forward into battle with a great deal of psalm singing and Bible reading, insisting that Irish soil had been assigned to them by their Protestant God. The native Irish were viewed as modern equivalents of the ancient Canaanites who, because of their "peculiar" forms of divine worship (that is, Catholic), deserved extermination by the sword.

Such Puritan preachers as Hugh Peters endorsed a war of extermination from the pulpit, invoking God's curse on any Puritans who might be reluctant to slay the Irish "while man, woman or child of Belial remains alive." Peters referred specifically to the conquest of Jericho to demonstrate that his hearers would be personally justified by God in killing "all that were, young men and old, children and maidens."

Cromwell himself had no doubts about the correctness of the incredible slaughter his men perpetrated. After his first military campaign at Drogheda, in which Irish men, women, and children were exterminated like insects, Cromwell stated, in a dispatch to the House of Commons:

> It has pleased God to bless our endeavor at Drogheda . . . the enemy were about 3,000 strong . . . I believe we put to the sword the whole number . . . I wish that all honest hearts may give the glory of this to God alone, to whom indeed the praise of this mercy belongs . . .

According to the *Encyclopedia Britannica,* sometime after 385, the Christian patriarch St. Theophilus of Alexandria, with the permission of the Christian Byzantine Emperor Theodosius I, began to persecute violently the non-Christians of the city. He destroyed the sacred temples of Mithra and Dionysius and the sanctuary of the Ptolemaic religion, about seven centuries older than Christianity. He also destroyed a large collection of classical literature, thought to have included manuscripts rescued by Cleopatra when the great Library of Alexandria was accidentally destroyed by fire. All in all, great treasures of literature, science, history, and philosophy from antiquity disappeared forever.

Scholars are, of course, aware of this cultural atrocity, but in the modern age, when sensitivities are dulled by the massive amount of crime and suffering brought to our attention daily, I suggest that the reader think for a moment about this fact, which all knowledgeable modern Christians readily and humbly concede was, in every sense, a Christian crime. The story of a Christian mob's murder of the neoplatonist philosopher Hypatia is also chilling. One scholar, incidentally, Hugh Lloyd-Jones, Professor Emeritus of Greek at Oxford, argues for the destruction of the library by Roman Emperor Aurelian in A.D. 273. Perhaps there were two such outrages. (See *The New York Review of Books,* 37 (10):27–30, June 14, 1990.)

To bring the ugly realities of Theophilus' act into even clearer focus, imagine that in the present day thousands of fanatics of one religion or another, not suffering a random fit but acting on orders from the highest authority, simultaneously attacked and destroyed the Library of Congress, the Smithsonian Institution, and a dozen or so other hallowed repositories of scholarship, and assume further that there were *no copies of the burned materials anywhere else on earth.*

That human ignorance has been only too slowly dissolved over the ages is partly attributable to such offenses.

Another massive crime, the perpetrators of which professed to be God-fearing, Bible-believing Christians, was the invasions of the North and South American continents. Blame for this atrocity is usually placed on mercantilism or early imperialism, and indeed the latter is the word for the world-wide process by which the nation-states of Europe, which assumed that they had every right to the territory of so-called primitive peoples, seized whatever portions of the earth's surface they wished, naturally by force of arms. While the motives for this were largely economic, the fact remains that the perpetrators were accompanied by priests and ministers with Bibles and prayer books, and they regarded the crucifix as their most sacred symbol.

To give but one sample of the results, we have only to look at the Andean portion of South America which, at the time of the Spanish conquest, was heavily populated, well-fed and organized, and highly civilized but whose culture was soon shattered by the military and cultural clash. The Andeans lost much of their civilization and art, and large populations were decimated by sword and disease and reduced to serfdom. To those who would like to know more of this tragic chapter of history, I recommend

AUTHORSHIP OF THE BIBLE

Frederic André Engel's remarkable study, *An Ancient World Preserved: Relics and Records of Prehistory in the Andes* (New York: Crown, 1976).

One of the most striking patterns in the Jewish Scriptures is that the most shameful atrocities often go unpunished, whereas the most inconsequential offenses are visited with a sudden violent or otherwise bizarre punishment. The wife of Lot, for example, turned to look back at Sodom and Gomorrah. The Bible would have us believe that for this offense she not only suffered execution on the spot but also that her mortal remains were turned to a pillar of salt. It is begging the question to say that she was punished for disobeying a divine command. It was a very stupid command, of that much we can be certain. We have no assurance whatsoever that it originated from God; its sheer inanity would argue that it did not.

It will no doubt occur to some that I am being disrespectful, but I do not see that anything so pointless as this story is deserving of respect, nor why I should apologize for having more respect for the creator of the universe than for the unknown author of what is clearly a mythical account.

The same interpretation may be placed on the punishment which resulted from another trivial thing, the alleged eating of a piece of fruit in the Garden of EDEN. Banishment is a severe penalty indeed, but at least it does not ravage reason. But it ravages not only reason but every decent moral impulse to suppose that a horrible punishment—resulting, be it remembered, from this one minor offense—should be visited not only upon ADAM AND EVE, but also upon their children, grandchildren, and the *entire human race*. Many scholars have said the story is shameful nonsense.

It would be erroneous to assume that, in pointing to the hundreds of instances of bloodthirstiness and savagery in the Old Testament, I am suggesting that the Israelites were in any sense unique in the degree of their xenophobia.

AUTHORSHIP OF THE BIBLE. There is no certain knowledge as to who wrote various portions of the Scriptures; but there is general agreement among scholars that, in addition to the figures nominally credited with the different books, there were many unknown authors and compilers who made contributions of various sorts. It is rather as if there are separate streams of influence which eventually flow together to make the Bible.

One of the Old Testament streams is called by specialists the E or *Elohist* version, which, it is believed, originated in the northern part of the Holy Land. The other, assumed to come from the south, is the J or *Yahwist* version. The blend of these two is, of course, referred to by the combined initials JE. Both of these are generally supposed to be limited to the first six or eight books at most; many scholars say five.

But no one assumes that the scriptural passages we have today represent the first drafts of the books in which they appear. There may have been certain other sources of information, now lost—presumably forever—which are referred to in the material we do have. For example, Numbers 21:14 mentions *The Book of the Wars of the Lord.* And in Joshua 10:13, we find a reference to *The Book of Jasher.* (However, just as we find fictional material in the book of Daniel, these references could also be fictions.) We must assume that, whatever the merits of these alleged "books," they could not have been inspired by God, since *if he had gone to the trouble to inspire them in the first place,* he would not have permitted their loss.

A third source of Old Testament material is called the P or *Priestly* version, which tends to be concerned with ritual, ceremonies, and genealogy. Scholars believe that the last touches of the PENTATEUCH were completed only about 300 years before Christ. William Neil, chief author of the helpful reference book *Harper's Bible Commentary,* says that it is the *composite* character of the first five books of the Old Testament that is responsible for the various contradictions and errors which are now commonly acknowledged. But Neil says an odd thing, when he observes that such discrepancies

> . . . at one time caused great distress to ordinary readers of the Bible since they could not understand how what they believe to be a miraculous, infallible book could possibly have two inconsistent versions of the same story.

If Neil imagines that such stumbling blocks were encountered merely "at one time," he is mistaken.

Ignorance of the Original Authors. While respecting them for such virtues or abilities as they might have had, we ought not to romanticize the original authors of the Bible. It is instructive to consider not only their general ignorance but the specifics of it. For example:

- They knew little about history.
- They knew almost nothing about geography.
- They knew nothing about geology.
- They knew nothing about chemistry.
- They knew nothing about anthropology.
- They knew nothing about archaeology.
- They knew nothing about physics.
- They knew little about biology, animal or human.

The writers of much of the Old Testament are called prophets. In the modern day the word *prophet* is associated with the act of prophesying, which is to say, predicting the future. Of this there is surprisingly little in the Old Testament, and what we do find has not always been borne out by events. The Old Testament prophets were primarily social critics. In all times and places there has been more than enough lying, deceit, financial dishonesty, sexual promiscuity, violence, cruelty, tyranny, selfishness, and other forms of wrongdoing. Even an otherwise neutral observer must respond with indignation to the staggering amount of injustice for which human beings are daily responsible. It is not required that the observer be personally saintly for him or her to become angry or dismayed at the spectacle of human misbehavior.

Although many fundamentalists seem unaware of the fact, the best Christian and Jewish scholarship readily concedes today that various authors contributed to Genesis. This concession has come about partly because to have continued to insist on the one-author theory—whether that one author is MOSES or someone else—would have forced the conclusion that this author, far from being inspired, was inordinately careless. Writes Jean Levie, S.J. (*The Bible: Word of God in Words of Men,* New York: P. J. Kennedy, 1962):

> There are two accounts of creation . . . These two accounts have been placed side-by-side in spite of their divergences. As against the well known order in the second, according to which man was created first (2:7), after man the plants (2:9; C.F. v. 4), then the animals (2:19), and finally woman (2:21). Moreover the second account is much more anthropomorphic than the first. There are two accounts of the flood (Chapters 6-7) combined into one. . . . They show considerable divergences.
>
> Some have maintained that two accounts of Joseph sold by his brothers can be identified . . . In one, Joseph is sold directly by his brethren to Ismaelite merchants at Judah's suggestion and taken by them into Egypt. In the other he is thrown into a well at the suggestion of Ruben, who counts on being able to free him afterwards. He is then taken out of the well by the Midianites who are passing that way . . . and taken by them into Egypt.

Levie concedes—as indeed he must—that such a method of writing history is "naive," but he cannot force himself to grant the obvious implication: that the Bible does not enjoy divinely inspired integrity. Rather, he must say that the method "has nothing in it that contradicts inspiration." This leads Levie to the absurdity that God has personally inspired an author (or two) to write two separate versions of a story, concerning which we can only say with absolute certainty: either only one of them is correct or they both are in error.

Moses' Authorship. As regards the once firmly held belief that Moses wrote the books that the churches for centuries insisted he wrote, I do not see how one can fail to be impressed by the fact that the more erudite a biblical scholar may be, the less likely he is to agree with this traditional view. In other words, those who know the most about the issue either strongly doubt that Moses wrote the Pentateuch or else assert firmly that he did not.

Joseph McCabe, who was for many years a Catholic priest and scholar—and who eventually left the church to devote the rest of his life to writing books critical of his former opinions—says, in *The Story of Religious Controversy* (Boston: The Stratford Company, 1929):

> Attempts to "reconcile Genesis and science" never come now from men who know science. The Hebrew text, which I know well, having had a course of Hebrew at Louvain University, is not one inch nearer to science than the English text. It is neither poetry—I have read it in Hebrew, Greek, Latin and English—nor accurate statement.
>
> There is first a dark chaos created by God. Why God created matter in a chaotic state and then, in six days, put it in order, is rather a puzzle to the believer. It would be just as easy for the "creative word" to make an orderly as a chaotic universe.
>
> Desperate apologists remind you how science (which they pretend not to believe) put a nebula at the beginning; and one might (if one did not know Hebrew) think of the chaos as a nebula. But a nebula is light, not dark; and it most assuredly has no water in it. . . . To the learned Babylonian, the first state of things was a watery waste, land and water mixed up together, and the gods had first to separate them. The Hebrew follows the Babylonian legend in all that it says.

For centuries many scholars—for the most part sincere Christians whose studies of the books attributed to Moses by firm religious tradition caused them to have certain doubts about his authorship—were excoriated, hounded, and attacked. Both Catholic and Protestant parties responded with heat to the slightest questioning of the solemn unity and authority of ancient Scriptures. But, in keeping with what is apparently a pattern in such controversies, it turns out that the critics were to a considerable extent correct and the defenders of the faith were mistaken. If only the long-dead questioners and doubters concerning the personal authorship by Moses of the Pentateuch, even those passages describing his own death, could be alive today to read the following passage from Father Bruce Vawter's *A Path Through Genesis:*

The scientific age had caught the champions of orthodoxy unprepared, and, with brilliant exceptions, *they had fled the field of debate and tried to ignore rather than interpret the real points that had been scored against traditional formulas* which they continued to repeat in a loud, clear voice. It is not surprising that they in turn were ignored by the scholarly world, which had to its own satisfaction *proved the Pentateuch to be a collection of Jewish legend and pious fiction composed at a late date,* edifying but hardly historical. (IA)

The churches have been faced with an acutely painful choice in regard to the Higher Criticism of the Bible. On the one hand, they were free to insist on the traditional, narrow, fundamentalist view, which is that literally every syllable of the Bible was inspired or dictated by God, a position that was successfully transmitted over long periods of Christian history. But to have opted for that alternative would inevitably have lost the church the allegiance of all but the most fanatical and uninformed. After all, even if the assumption is granted that an omniscient God exists, there has always been an incredibly wide variety of opinion as to what the Deity's views, acts, and wishes have been. But religious philosophers of all kinds have agreed that human intelligence was a direct and important gift of the Creator, and since the churches have generally been led by intelligent men, it was, we may assume, inevitable that the church—after first putting up a fierce show of resentment of those who had the temerity to question so much as a sentence of the Bible—would finally quietly commission scholars to study the Scriptures in the desperate hope that at least the basic building-blocks of the ancient faith would remain inviolate.

One problem that suggests itself to the mind of at least those scholars who might otherwise be favorably disposed to accept the Bible—in whatever language now rendered—as the literal word of God, is that there are frequent instances of what Father Vawter refers to as "grammatical blunders and a frequently tepid style, to name only the least faults." If we assume hypothetically for the moment that it is beyond question that God authored all of the sacred Scriptures, it would seem equally reasonable that a mind so vastly greater than any man's would also have produced a book that shone with a dazzling light of literary quality. But the observable, inescapable fact is that the Scriptures vary widely in literary quality. Some consist of beautiful, graphic poetry; others are poorly written indeed.

As regards the now well-established impossibility that Moses wrote all of the Pentateuch, note the following from the Scofield Bible introduction to the first five books.

Certain critics have denied that Moses wrote Genesis to Deuteronomy despite the fact that they were attributed to Moses by the Lord Jesus Christ. The arguments against Moses' authorship are chiefly based on the variation of the names of God (Elohim and Jehovah), the differences in style and vocabulary, and the presence of more than one account of the same event, e.g. the creation of man in Gen. 1:26 and 2:7.

These contentions have been adequately answered in that the variation in divine names is for the purpose of revealing certain aspects of God's character; the style is dependent on the subject matter; and the *so-called* parallel accounts, well known in ancient Near Eastern literature, are intended to add details to the first account. (IA)

It is, by all standards of responsible scholarship, absurd to say that the arguments of hundreds of brilliant scholars, many of them devout Jews and Christians, "have been adequately answered" by the pathetic counter-arguments offered by fundamentalists. It is absurd for these nonscholars to profess certainty that the author(s) of the Pentateuch used different names for God for the purpose of revealing certain aspects of God's character. This amounts to little more than attempted mind-reading across an expanse of millennia. The assertion that one knows what those who called God *Elohim* in one story and *Yahweh* in another had in mind would require intimate familiarity with a culture that left more documents or archaeological evidence than merely the earliest manuscripts we have of the Pentateuch. (It is important to understand also that archaeologists have found almost no *traces* of the early Israelites, although it is clear from ruins and other material evidence that other peoples lived there.)

It is presumptuous also to assert that the second accounts of the CREATION and FLOOD stories in Genesis are "intended" to provide details not given in the primary accounts, another instance of the classic "mind-reading" fallacy. We do not have manuscript or archaeological evidence of anyone's "intentions." Only *conjecture* can be applied to texts that may have been written *after* 600–500 B.C., a very long time after these events allegedly happened.

Another reason such argumentation is distressing is that it is addressed not to other scholars of Scripture but to unsophisticated Christian readers, few of whom would be knowledgeable enough to question the assurance that the second Creation and Flood accounts are given solely "to add details to the first account." That details are added should be clear to any reader above the age of seven who is shown both stories side by side. But unless one examines the stories carefully, one may miss the point that *the two stories contradict each other in certain details.* It is self-evident that when two accounts contradict each other, either totally or in specific details, either one story or both are false.

An error, encountered on the very first page of the Scofield edition, is the assertion that "the principle upon which the editorial committee undertook its task is that *the criterion of truth is the Scriptures.*" (IA)

Again, this is simply not the case. The Old Testament is important, but the importance of truth is paramount. How many millennia have passed between the time mankind evolved into homo sapiens and the writing of the first versions of whatever religious texts have subsequently been incorporated into the canon of the Bible? No one has a reliable way of knowing. But if the time difference between the two points were as small as ten minutes, it would still follow that mankind is not under the slightest obligation to use the Christian and Jewish Scriptures as a criterion of truth or as accurate history.

The same Scriptures have, as every intelligent person is by now aware, been shown to contain striking admixtures of error; it would be nonsensical to say that a published work which is to any significant degree either erroneous or otherwise untruthful can nevertheless serve as "*the* criterion" of truth.

For many centuries it has been the undeviating position of Jewish, Catholic, and Protestant faiths that every passage of Scripture was personally inspired by God Almighty. If only for purposes of clear thinking, it is important to distinguish between narrative inspiration and the hundreds of direct quotations attributed to God within the various books of the Bible. In the latter cases the logic of the churches' arguments leads one to conclude that at one point in time God would actually vouchsafe a personal spoken observation to a given prophet or follower of Jesus and that later, at a second point in time, he would inspire the same author to recollect what he had previously stated.

Some rationalist critics, observing the many errors in the Scriptures, have assumed that the authors of such tales must have been conscious prevaricators. While this may have been the case in some instances, we cannot accept the conclusion solely on the basis of available evidence. That people are indeed in the habit of lying we know, but most of the nonsense that one hears or reads is not the result of the intent to deceive. It comes, rather, from an even more common human failing, careless credulity. There is something in us that tends to believe almost anything we are told by a seemingly trustworthy person. Consider, for example, the stories that one hears, every few years, of children reared by wolves. Observes Tom Burnam in *The Dictionary of Misinformation* (Crowell):

> Stories of children reared by wolves are not only common, but they are only too often taken seriously, sometimes by persons as renowned as the famous Dr. Arnold Gesell. He apparently swallowed *in toto* the account by a Reverend J. A. L. Singh, of Midnapore, India, of the "Wolf-reared Waifs of Midnapore." Dr. Gesell repeated the story in the January 1941 issue of *Harper's* magazine. People have continued to believe in the tale ever since; it has been incorporated into textbooks, reported in newspapers and magazines, and is even the subject of Dr. Gesell's "Wolf-Child and Human-Child."
>
> Yet upon examination the whole story turns out to depend entirely on the unsupported—and quite unscientific—observations of the Rev. Mr. Singh.

One would think that a moment's reflection would suffice to demonstrate that no four-footed animal could possibly give the sort of care to a human infant that is required for its physical survival during the long months before it is able to sit up, stand, or walk about. No four-footed animal would be able to provide the infant with adequate food or water, with covering to protect it from the elements. Obviously such stories are inherently preposterous. Nevertheless, large numbers of people will continue to believe them, although they have examined no evidence whatsoever that supports them.

The highest authorities on the Bible have assured us that biblical authors often incorporated material drawn from a long oral tradition. If stories of the raising of human children by packs of wolves have become part of our more recent written sources, derived merely from oral tradition, then we may safely assume that in earlier times, when even reasonably well-informed men were far more superstitious, ignorant, and credulous than one trusts we are at present, equally preposterous stories could have eventually found their way into manuscripts by precisely the same means.

Does the Bible, then, *contain* God's word? Many, including myself, think it does.

As we shall see in this volume, it is impossible that every word of the Scriptures can be said to be divinely authored or inspired since some of it is nonsense, some is error, and some—after hundreds of years of scholarship—remains so obscure that we are unable to demonstrate what the original authors intended to convey. But those portions of the Scripture that speak wisdom and truth may indeed be said to speak the word of God. In that same sense, of course, *any true statement,* about any subject matter whatever, may be said to be God's word. (See also BIBLE, MYSTERY OF THE.)

B

BABEL, TOWER OF, a story found in Genesis 11:1-9. It follows the tale of the FLOOD, both of which appear to have their origins in the literature of Mesopotamia. They were probably part of the legends the Semitic-speaking tribes that migrated out of Mesopotamia took with them into the region of Palestine.

> 1. Now the whole earth had one language, and few words.

It is highly unlikely that the human inhabitants of the whole earth have ever spoken only one language. Whatever were the first rudimentary speech-forms of the earliest inhabitants of the African continent, we may be quite certain that they were not the same as those of the earliest inhabitants of, say, China or Java. Africa is probably where speech originated, although the writer(s) of Genesis did not know about the vast continent of Africa or the long development of speech and its proliferation in many forms in various lands. He may have been referring to a proto-Semitic language spoken widely in Mesopotamia in the early Bronze Age.

According to Genesis, after discovering how to fire bricks in the land of Shinar (modern Iraq),

> 4. Then they said, "Come, let us build ourselves a city and a tower with its top in the heavens, and let us make a name for ourselves, lest we be scattered abroad upon the face of the whole earth."

Although the legend is very primitive, it does give a rough suggestion of the coming of civilization to Mesopotamia that is described by archaeologists: the discovery of mud-bricks for construction of shelter and the rise of small city-states in what is now modern Iraq. Scholars almost unanimously agree that the Tower of Babel represents the remarkable ziggurats excavated throughout this region. Ziggurats were an early pyramid, which rose higher than anything man had yet been able to construct, and they were probably used for worship.

The famous Ziggurat of Ur was built under Ur-Nammu of the Third Dynasty of Sumer in approximately 2100 B.C. The Iraqi government has in recent years restored the lower portion of the ziggurat. It is a remarkable structure indeed, and since it originally had three even higher levels, it would have made a profound impression on anyone who saw it in ancient times.

The next verse describes a theological impossibility:

> 5. And the Lord came down to see the city and the tower, which the sons of men had built.

Then we get into the puzzling part of the story, for the Lord's jealousy is inexplicable, since he is supposed to have created man as an intelligent being in his own image. You would think he would have been proud of what men and women were accomplishing in Mesopotamia.

> 6. And the Lord said, "Behold, they are one people, and they have all one language; and this is only the beginning of what they will do; and nothing that they propose to do will now be impossible for them.

No sensible person over the age of ten, assuming his mind is not already clouded by the sort of religious commitment which simply disregards contrary evidence, could possibly believe that God—by very definition, the source and embodiment of all wisdom and intelligence—could have been guilty of such an inane assumption: that the speaking of a common language would enable humans to accomplish anything it might occur to them to attempt. Let the reader simply refer to the experience of his or her own family, workplace, social organization, community, city, state, or nation. While the sharing of one tongue is an aid to communication, it facilitates disagreement as well as agreement. Even in societies which are ruthlessly totalitarian, the combination of one language and one authority does not guarantee concurrence about anything.

> 7. "Go to, let us go down, and there confound their language, that they may not understand one another's speech."
> 8. So the Lord scattered them abroad from thence upon the face of all the earth: and they left off to build the city.

This nonsensical story, not even as believable as a well-loved fairy tale, actually alleges that the reason the Japanese speak as they do, the reason Swahili is what it is, the reason for the various Inuit tribal tongues, as well as the language forms of the Incas, the Aztecs, Australian aborigines, and numerous Native American tribes, is an alleged incident that took place at the Tower of Babel just a few thousand years ago. It explains nothing whatever about the origins and dissemination of the earth's thousands of languages. We can only conclude that a story of Almighty God deliberately creating hundreds of separate human languages as a form of punishment has no basis in fact.

> 9. Therefore is the name of it called Babel; because the Lord did confound the language of all the earth: . . .

It is typical of the religious literature of so-called primitive cultures not only that they attribute human emotions—even the most petty and spiteful—to their deities but also that they specify physical behavior which is intelligible only if human, and not at all if divine. The Old Testament, therefore, is full of instances in which God is said to travel from one point to another, to inspect and evaluate specific instances of human activity, in the way that a foreman or executive might report to a particular location to see how his workers are doing.

BELIEF. Despite the fact that PAUL, in referring to the three chief virtues—faith, hope, and charity—said that charity, or love, was clearly "the greatest of these" (1 Cor. 13:13), fundamentalists behave as though they believe nothing of the kind. They place simple belief or faith at the forefront, and are quite willing to attack those who think that on this particular question Paul was wiser than they.

And even if the debate is limited to the question of faith, our fundamentalist brethren take a weak position, for they appear to worship a *book* and spend an inordinate amount of their time defending *it* rather than addressing the love of the God they profess to adore. This particular problem is largely limited at the present to fundamentalist Protestants. Catholics, despite their profound respect for the Bible, refer to the fundamentalists' overemphasis on it as Bibliolatry.

A refreshing statement of the Catholic view on the question is that of William J. O'Malley, S.J., who teaches theology and English at Fordham Preparatory School in the Bronx, New York, and is an authority on Scripture. Writing in the February 4, 1989, issue of the admirable Jesuit journal *America,* O'Malley says in "Scripture from Scratch":

And yet how many people feel their faith shaken—or even shattered—when they discover that Gabriel really didn't need all those feathers to get from "way out there" to Nazareth? Or that a snake really didn't spend time nattering away to a naked lady in the park? *Obviously the author of Genesis didn't expect his audience to take him literally,* any more than Aesop, writing at about the same time, thought his audience believed foxes and donkeys talked. But when the evidently inadequate symbolism is threatened, the truth is thereby threatened. If the snake didn't talk, there goes Genesis! And original sin! And the whole damn shootin' match! (IA)

In his last few lines O'Malley is, of course, satirizing the fundamentalist position. Catholic scholars with the most impressive credentials perceived years ago that it is absurd to interpret every word of Scripture as literal fact. But even those portions which any disinterested person would at once recognize as mythical serve a profoundly important function. "Myth," says O'Malley,

... is a story or theory that intends to embody something true, but beyond literal, photographic description. *Genesis, for instance, is a myth.* It was written at least 300,000 years after the events it describes, not by an eyewitness . . . it attempts to embody something true (things obviously got here somehow . . .) (IA)

Likewise, the author goes on to explain, physical descriptions of God are myths in the sense that they are attempts to explain a reality that cannot be seen in terms of realities that can be seen. Like other scholars before him, O'Malley reminds us that the stories of the Prodigal Son and the Good Samaritan do not represent actual events either. Jesus contrived these parables to explain certain moral truths in ways easily understood.

The Effects of Christian Belief. At a National Catholic Conference for Inter-Racial Justice on the campus of Loyola University, Chicago, several years ago, the background paper supplied to participants urged consideration of the question as to how Christ's Mystical Body—the church—could have been involved in 300 years of prejudice, discrimination, and preferential treatment in the United States of America.

It is a good question, but only a fragment of the larger historical puzzle: How could the church have been involved in almost *2,000* years of prejudice, discrimination, and preferential treatment in all parts of what used to be called the civilized world? There have always been, thank God, individual churchmen and women who were not guilty of such un-Christian behavior, but it has never been seriously suggested that they constitute a majority.

It may be argued that the warlike tribes of Europe would have been considerably more barbaric had they not been converted to Christianity. Yet the fact remains that as Christians, and in their ethnic or national capacities, they have only occasionally demonstrated an inclination toward those qualities of mercy, compassion, meekness, humility, charity, rationality, and tolerance which are supposed to distinguish Christians from other people.

For evidence, consider the present tragic situation in Ireland, North and South, in which we see Christians resorting to the same savage violence that has plagued mankind throughout its history and is so common on our planet at the present moment.

That man has aggressive instincts we know. The question is: To what extent has Christianity sublimated his vicious impulses? To what extent does it do so on the streets of Londonderry today? To what extent has it done so throughout Catholic Latin America for the past 400 years? To what extent are the Christians of Catholic Sicily civilized by their religion? Members of the so-called Mafia "culture" imported into this country—whatever else they are—are Catholics. These are hard truths, but it is long past the time when they should have been faced.

The problem is not, needless to say, exclusively Catholic. The Protestant cultures face it as well. The members of the Ku Klux Klan and other right-wing hate groups in the United States have always *claimed* to be God-fearing Christians, have they not?

Then there is a particular episode in 20th-century history, which both Protestants and Catholics must look at carefully. Hitler was voted into power and subsequently supported by many supposedly God-fearing Christians—although I do not claim that any church or that *all* German Christians backed him. (See also ANTISEMITISM.)

The Catholic church in America, in the 1960s and 70s, came to a staggering realization which brought it to its knees in that hour of challenge—the recognition that it has so often failed to turn obedient Catholics into practicing Christians. John McDermott, writing in the November 1, 1966, edition of *Look* magazine, drew this shocking picture:

> Terrible evidence of the failure of the Church to teach racial justice came to light last summer, when Negro and white demonstrators from the Chicago Freedom Movement marched through all-white, predominantly Catholic neighborhoods to dramatize the need for an open and just housing market. Hundreds of policemen could not save the marchers, including Dr. Martin Luther King, Jr., from an avalanche of hate: hurled rocks, bottles and firecrackers. The score of nuns and priests who marched became a special target. "You're not a real priest! Where

did you get that outfit?" a heckler shrieked at one priest. "Hey, Father, are you sleeping with her?" a man screamed at a priest walking side by side with a Negro woman. *After one march, a Negro priest was dragged from his car and savagely beaten.*

Even the nuns were not exempt from obscenities and physical attacks. Bystanders cursed and spat at them. A rock felled Sister M. Angelica, OSF, a suburban nun who was spending her summer at an inner-city parochial school. *The crowd cheered wildly when she went down.* At the hospital, when her bleeding head was being sewed up, she said: "I feel no bitterness toward these people—but it hurts to think we haven't taught them better." (IA)

Whatever happened to love or charity, that Paul taught Christians to strive for?

A key word in the new approach to morality and faith is *relevance,* which relates to the ancient relationship between faith and good works. The conservatives have told us, consistently down through the centuries, that man should concern himself with the salvation of his own soul, then, if possible, with the salvation of the souls of others. To quote a statement by Father Gommer De Pauw, president of the Catholic Traditionalist Movement:

> Religions and their representatives, clergymen, are *not* supposed to concern themselves directly with social or any kind of temporal problems . . . we priests should leave the social and the other temporal problems to lay people, experts.

The underlying reason for this conservative view, I suspect, is that when you apply Christian principles to social questions, the poor actually get helped. For some reason, this practical effect has not interested most of the conservatives of history. Those who have attempted to do something concrete to better the social conditions of the poor and oppressed have, in almost all times and places, been attacked as either idealistic dreamers or dangerous revolutionaries. But that particular part of the historic debate has become a bore. It's over. The conservative position on this particular question is irrelevant. The hard fact is that unless the churches can now, in practical as well as spiritual ways, become relevant to the needs and concerns of the impoverished, the minorities, the politically persecuted, there are going to be even more defections from the ranks of the faithful by the poor, the young, the alienated, and the impatient.

Belief in Christ. At first, there is something appealing in the simplicity of the early and still persistent Christian belief: "Whoever shall believe in

Him shall have eternal life." But when we pause to reflect on this direct assertion, a number of questions automatically suggest themselves. Can it really be true—is it actually morally reasonable to believe—that all that is required for salvation is belief in JESUS Christ? The reality, alas, cannot possibly be that simple.

First of all, the doctrine has several component parts, each of which must be properly interpreted before we can even begin to discuss questions of agreement or disagreement. To believe in Jesus could, for example, be simply the belief that he existed, in precisely the same way that one may believe in the historical existence of George Washington.

We are then told that what is required is acceptance of Jesus "as Lord and Savior." If we concentrate on *Savior,* then we are involved in a circular statement that, if we believe that Jesus *is* our savior, he will in fact *be* our savior. What we are being saved from, presumably, is the fire of HELL. As regards the word *Lord,* the situation is less clear. Some Christians interpret it as meaning none other than God. Others interpret it as meaning the best, noblest human being of all time who was superior precisely because he was, in a unique sense, the personal son of God.

To return to the more troublesome question: Can it indeed be the case that all one has to do is believe? Before responding too glibly, we must grasp that, in accepting the assertion, we may be agreeing that it is not necessary to lead a moral life. This dogma stipulates that, whether or not moral behavior is important, simple belief in Jesus is the only thing required for entrance into HEAVEN.

His followers believed this because they also believed that the end of the world was very near and that he would shortly return to save believers and assure them of an everlasting life. The Gospels were not written with any idea that they would be read a hundred—much less 2,000—years in the future. They were not intended as a moral guide in a far-distant future, because the generation that followed Jesus believed that the world would end in their lifetime.

But since the world *has* continued, does this mean that the millions of moral monsters who have professed a belief in Christ are guaranteed the fate of better-behaved millions who, on this earth, would not have willingly shared their company? Does it mean that other millions of Jews, Muslims, Buddhists, Confucianists—and, for that matter, atheists and agnostics—will be consigned to the flames of Hell, despite their admirable personal lives, simply because they have held philosophical opinions that ruled out an acceptance of the divinity of Jesus? I think not. It is difficult to believe that even the pope accepts such an obviously absurd—because unjust—doctrine.

BELIEF

One of the most fascinating conclusions that emerges from even a casual survey of the field of religion is that many religious people are personally and quite consciously contemptuous of much religious belief and practice. That this hearty contempt is not more generally perceived is due to two factors: (1) in the modern age it is considered socially unseemly to indulge in that sort of fierce and fanatical religious contention common in our society until a century ago, and (2) religion itself is much less important to most people than it was in the days of our fathers and therefore does not lead to that loss of temper and ad hominem viciousness that characterized much religious debate of earlier times.

This civilizing process does not, of course, extend back merely a century. It has taken several centuries to move from the day when religious arguments were settled with the sword, the dungeon, the headsman's ax, the torture chamber, the hangman's noose, and the flames of the stake. But since the essential point—that most believers hold most religious practices in either heated or amused contempt—may at first seem strange to the reader, a brief explanation is indicated.

I do not assert that a typical believer has disrespect for the tenets of his own denomination, but it is clear enough that he considers much of all other religions as strikingly misguided. If there were only one true church, this would, of course, not be the case. But there are thousands of individual religious denominations and sects. In some primitive cultures, polytheistic beliefs are common. Those who believe in only one god are, understandably, horrified that in the 20th century there are some who still worship "false gods."

Among the now-diminished body of believers distinguished by their belief in one Deity, we find an incredible structure of subdivision. Christians, Jews, Muslims, Confucianists, Taoists, Buddhists, Parsees, and others, though they would concur that there is but one God, nevertheless may perceive that God in ways that are mutually exclusive.

A Deist, for example, believes in one God as surely as does a Baptist or a Catholic, but Baptists and Catholics believe in a God who rolls up his sleeves, so to speak, looks down at his world, and takes an active daily interest in everyone's business, intervening here, far more often mysteriously neglecting to intervene there, etc. The Deist views this particular perception as absurd. The Christian, of course, considers the Deist's idea of a nonintervening Deity as heretical.

It does not matter what individual fragment of belief or practice one examines for purposes of supporting the point—each believer has a sense of inhabiting a world in which he is surrounded by dunces, heretics, and unbelievers. But religions, per se, are neither good nor bad in themselves.

Only as regards specific content can value judgments be properly made: Is it good or bad to eat meat on Friday? Is it good or bad to burn heretics alive? Is it good or bad to permit, or enforce, the reading of the Bible in public schools? Is it good or bad to assert that God personally committed atrocities, as is clearly stated in the Old Testament? One can, it is clear, respond to such questions, but certainly not to such a broad question as the good or evil of any one religion or of religion itself.

BIBLE, MYSTERY OF THE. After almost 2,000 years of concentrated study by well-qualified scholars, not to mention the less dependable speculations of hundreds of millions of ordinary Christians and Jews, the Bible, unfortunately, remains a profoundly mysterious work. But this should not surprise the philosopher, since in time almost everyone begins to understand that mystery is not merely an annoying distraction but an essential element of life.

I believe in mystery, not in any dark-shadows-and-incense way, but as a matter of fact. The world is filled with mystery. Three of the most important philosophical questions—those concerning God, time, and space—remain questions, which is to say no answers to them have ever been proposed that convince all interested parties. Each has, or seems to have, aspects of either-or-ness. The difficulty arises from the fact that the three pairs of alternatives, the six individual answers, are essentially preposterous.

For example, if there is no God, then we are left with a profound puzzle as to how the intricate machinery of the universe came to exist. But if there is a God, a thousand and one troubling questions at once present themselves, since the vale of tears we live in is hardly consistent with the premise of an all-loving, all-knowing, all-wise creator with his eye on every sparrow. Carnivorous creatures survive by eating other animals alive.

As for time, either it began one morning, say, at 9:27—which is obviously ridiculous—or it never began, which appears equally ridiculous.

As for space, either one can go out to the end of it—which is absurd—or it has no end, which is equally absurd.

My own belief in God, then, is just that—a matter of belief, not of knowledge. My respect for the beloved figure of JESUS arises from the fact that he seems to have been one of the most virtuous inhabitants on earth. But even well-educated Christians are frustrated in their thirst for certainty about Jesus because of the undeniable ambiguity of the scriptural record. Such ambiguity is not apparent to children or fanatics, but every recognized Bible scholar is perfectly aware of it.

I have referred in other articles to errors in Scripture. The average believer has so little real understanding of the documents that make up the Bible that it comes as a shock to him to be informed that the Greek version alone, from which the King James rendition was largely translated, itself included more than 5,000 errors, every one of which was dutifully incorporated into the English Bible. Nor are most believers aware that there are more than 1,000 English words encountered in the King James version that have a different meaning now from that which they originally conveyed. This means that the number of errors—so far as simple interpretations are concerned—amounts to about 6,000! It is absurd to try to make this factual reality conform to the popular impression that the Bible, as one holds it in one's hands, is totally error-free because God personally not only rendered it originally in true form, but has, over the past few thousand years, personally seen to it that the Scriptures continue to be his personal word.

Despite its errors of fact, ambiguities, and contradictions, the Bible, in the context of Western civilization, is clearly the most important literary source. One should not, in reference to the whole of Scripture, use the word *book,* because, as even casual students are aware, what we have is a collection of numerous documents, written by an unknown number of mostly unidentifiable authors over a span of perhaps less than a thousand years. There are, of course, vast expanses of our planet and enormous populations in which and to whom the Bible is by no means as important as Muslim, Hindu, Buddhist, or Confucian works, but in the world as the mind-set of Western culture perceives it, the Bible is of profound importance indeed.

Even in so officially secular a society as that of the United States, where separation of church and state is a wise and abiding principle, the solemnity of public oaths is attested to by the ritual of placing one's hand on a Bible, obviously on the assumption that a promise made in such a form is taken more seriously than would otherwise be the case. How many witnesses have so sworn and then proceeded to lie shamefully, it is impossible to say.

Even to the millions in the West who are neither Jewish nor Christian, the Scriptures permeate popular thought, language, and custom. As Cyril Richardson, professor of church history at Union Theological Seminary, has aptly observed:

> No one can count himself educated unless he has read widely in the Bible. For this is the book of books, which has had a more far-reaching influence on our way of life than any other single factor. It can be read from many different points of view. Some may read it for

its literary quality, others for its historic interest, others again for its religious message. [But] no one, indeed, can read its stirring narratives, or moving poems, without being interested.

It is self-evident that Western culture, except for a small number of self-designated atheists or agnostics, has made a heavy psychological investment in the Bible. While every society has a moral code, many in the West feel that our morality depends on the Bible, that it has in fact, no other backing but the Bible. Those who hold such a view are therefore horrified at the slightest expression of intellectual doubt in the divine authority of Scripture. Frontal attacks generally produce responses running from mild resentment to outright malice. However unedifying such reactions might be (considered in the context of social civility), however violently some defenders of the Bible may behave, none of this need necessarily be added to the case against the Bible itself. For if one assumes that it is authentic because it was inspired by God, this would render the displeasure felt by its defenders and the vigor of their response to critics only the more understandable.

It is odd, of course, that during the last 2,000 years we Christians, who preach love and cheek-turning, have been far more violent in defending the Scriptures than have the Jews, to whom the OLD TESTAMENT is of greater importance than it is to Christians. It is, of course, difficult to say whether this marked difference in conduct is explained by some factor in Jewish social superiority or whether the explanation is in the fact that over the long span of Western history Christians have had it in their power to punish, whereas Jews have not. Christians, too, sometimes behave meekly and circumspectly—wherever they are a small minority.

As regards the Bible, it is impossible to know with complete certainty how the text we now have was achieved. Even if the various witnesses to the events it records were not long dead, the identity of most of them has never been determined. The original manuscripts no longer exist, and even the most sophisticated scholarship cannot, after the passage of so many centuries, know enough about the general conditions of the times in which the many separate parts of Scripture originated to properly analyze biblical writings. This is not to argue for giving up attempts to study the Bible. Fortunately, there are now small armies of scholars devoting their attention to scriptural study so that the drive toward fuller, more responsible knowledge progresses, albeit with continuing controversy.

The argument that there is something suspect about impartial Bible study is best answered by pointing to the admirably thorough work being done by great numbers of the devout within Christianity and Judaism.

Believers are usually not totally unaware that there are honest differences of opinion about the interpretation of Bible passages. Many Christians have at least a passing knowledge about certain portions of Scripture that are stumbling blocks to the faith of intelligent adults. But even those who are aware of these difficulties often imagine that about 99 percent of the Bible presents no such problems.

Such an opinion, however common, bears no relation to reality. The truth is the opposite; there are difficulties, including serious ones, on almost every page. There is not a book in the Bible that has not been the subject of controversy, even among believers, and all have been subjected to sometimes devastating critical analysis by those outside the Jewish and Christian folds. That mere humans were directly responsible for affixing words to clay tablet, papyri, or parchment has never been in question. The argument is between those who defend the Bible on whatever reasonable grounds there are and those who defend it in toto, with an unswerving faith that turns a blind eye to the enormous amount of evidence that questions much that is in the Bible.

This is not to say that the devout are told nothing about scholarly work on the Scriptures. But there is something shamefully dishonest in the way in which the rare fragments of information about this vitally important subject are sometimes transmitted. Pulpit preachers almost never explain that the scholars are theologians, loyal sons of one church or another, clergymen, professional historians or philosophers, and so forth. Rather, the implication is always that the critics are atheists, agnostics, haters of God, apostates, or irresponsible heretics. That practically all human institutions defend themselves in this unedifying fashion is recognized by every informed adult. But are the ethical standards of the churches no higher than those of the political or commercial components of our society? Is the Catholic church, any of many Protestant churches, one branch of Judaism or another no more obliged to speak honestly than are the CIA, the KGB, or an attorney for the Mafia?

At the university level, obviously, it is no longer possible to put blinders over the eyes of the faithful, although a good deal of church-sponsored scholarship on the Scriptures has, understandably enough, an apologetic rather than a disinterested viewpoint. Rome can hardly be expected to say to its university students, "Here are the facts and currently dominant academic theories about the Bible; make of them what you will." Fortunately, to those like myself who have not had formal instruction in this field and who therefore must pursue their own study, the world of Bible scholarship that gradually emerges is a vast, exciting, inviting territory, peopled partly by scholars of the most impressive credentials.

The Bible as Inspired? Among the few things that have become clear during my investigation is that *if* it could be established that the Bible, despite its merits, could not bear the imprint of personal, direct, divine inspiration, an important conclusion would inescapably follow: Those religious denominations that have always *insisted that their validity rested on the Bible* can be shown to have only *a modest amount of authority,* which is derived *solely* from custom, tradition, and habit. Such churches and synagogues would be, as Thomas Paine among many others believed, merely human inventions, not in any sense divine.

One could nevertheless point to the *social usefulness* of such institutions. One could argue that inasmuch as they teach ethics and morality they produce certain good effects upon society and that their ability to solemnize such important experiences as birth, marriage, and death is admirable; indeed an impressive defense of such positions could be mounted. *But the argument from social utility has no logical connection whatever with the argument from divine inspiration and authority,* a point well-recognized by all informed believers.

The naive may assume that responsible critical commentary on the Bible, of which the present volume is an exceedingly modest example, represents some new tendency. In fact, the Bible has been reasonably analyzed—in some of its parts at least—by highly intelligent and sometimes devout Christians and others for centuries.

A century ago an English bishop, J. G. Richardson, observed of the Old Testament that it was

> . . . no longer honest or even safe to deny that this noble literature, rich in all the elements of moral or spiritual grandeur . . . *was sometimes mistaken in its science, was sometimes inaccurate in its history, and sometimes only relative and accommodatory in its morality. It assumed theories of the physical world which science had abandoned and could never resume.*
>
> It contained passages of narrative which devout and temperate men pronounced discredited, both by external and internal evidence. It praised, or justified, or approved, or condoned, or tolerated, *conduct which the teaching of Christ and the conscience of Christians alike condemned.* (IA)

Literally thousands of similar testimonies—by devout and responsible Christians—could be introduced. But when will the churches at large begin to share with their theologically naive adherents the news of these gracious and fair-minded concessions?

A seldom-noted fact, to which Christians and others may attach different significance, is that whether the Bible is, in fact, what it is often represented to be—a direct message from God—it is the only major such document besides the KORAN so regarded. There are other alleged revelations, such as that of the Mormons, but these belong to relatively small sects. As for the Oriental holy books, they are by no means regarded as Chinese or Indian equivalents of the Bible.

It should occur to the reader to wonder why, specifically, the present article is titled the "*Mystery* of the Bible." The answer is that a careful analysis will reveal that the two Testaments are not the simple, open record they are represented to be by churches and synagogues. They are, in fact, profoundly puzzling works. For example: (1) No one knows exactly *when* the various books of the Bible were written. (2) No one knows *by whom* most of the Bible was written. (3) No one knows if many of the events and people described ever took place or existed—or whether scripture is, rather, somewhat analogous to the Arthurian cycle of legends and poems.

No preacher, priest, or rabbi can explain how, if—as they assert—the Scriptures are divine in origin, many of its stories and precepts are the same as those in older cultures. The latter were written down *long before* the books of the Old Testament were completed, and these texts have been unearthed and are available to scholars today. The Code of Hammurabi is, after all, available for examination on a stele of diorite in the Louvre. Moses' "commandments" on "tablets of stone" have never been found. Good archaeology has discovered hundreds of ancient civilizations, but no one has found a trace of "Abraham," "Moses," "Samuel," or "Saul."

Of all the phrases used to describe the Bible, the most inappropriate is "the Good Book," for the simple reason that this collection of books is not wholly good by any standard. Except for certain lyrical or inspirational passages, I do not regard it as particularly good literature. It is notoriously unreliable as history, and no knowledgeable person would possibly describe it as science. In the one area where it would be reasonable to expect it to be good—that of morality—it is most especially deficient and inconsistent, in that, in hundreds of instances, it condones acts which everyone knows to be illegal and/or immoral.

I argue that at the very center of both popular and, to a certain extent, scholarly approaches to the Bible there is a fundamentally irrational element. All other books are evaluated on their merits. In the case of the Bible, however, the churches have for centuries urged that we must first accept it as divinely inspired and then, to the extent that we might have a degree of rational curiosity about its components, our evaluative studies must consist of a defense of the original proposition. This, I repeat, is essentially irrational. If the Bible is indeed of divine origin, then its virtues ought to be so self-evident that an impartial and fair-minded analysis will serve only to confirm rather than undermine belief in them.

Many of the most complimentary assertions about the Bible grow, it seems to me, not so much out of the assorted merits of Scripture but out of the warm hearts and goodwill of individual believers. For example, F. Rossi Gasperis, S.J., of the Pontifical Biblical Institute of Jerusalem, has said that the Bible "aims at directing the people of God in the way of walking with the Lord." But an assertion of this sort is correct only if it is not taken at face value. The statement is true of only certain portions of Scripture. Clearly it cannot apply to those verses and passages which are a monstrous insult to the concept of an all-loving, all-knowing God.

This is by way of saying that Christians such as Father Gasperis are far more admirable personally than the unknown authors of the more un-edifying passages of Scripture, for those who earnestly seek to draw sweetness and light from the Bible are in reality often reflecting their own kindness and gentleness.

What would we think of the salesman or propagandist who mentioned only a product's virtues and never its failings?

Let the buyer beware has always been sound advice. But surely it cannot be seriously argued that the narrow-eyed methods typical of buying and selling are morally appropriate when the "product" is alleged to be the highest, most spiritual writing of which the human mind is capable.

A French philosopher with a good sense of humor once advised keeping a sharp eye on murderers. The man who would murder, he suggested, would almost certainly, in the long run, resort to theft. And anyone who would steal, would probably be readily disposed to lie. The cleverness of listing sins in reverse order of their seriousness painfully reminds us that, in defense of "the one true faith," mankind has, for several thousand years rushed headlong into murder, lying, thievery, persecution, tyranny, and serious sins of almost all kinds.

If these are the methods by which a faith is defended, then, if we assume that there is a God who is the very essence of virtue, can he be anything but saddened and repelled by the willing resort to such despicable means?

My Christian brothers and sisters, consider, I pray you, that you may be wasting precious time and energy, both of which are limited, in preaching to the poor and ignorant in backward parts of the world. Are not your dedication and courage far more needed in a massive, worldwide campaign to convert the millions with whom you daily rub shoulders, those who allegedly defend the God of love by the most hateful methods, defend the God of truth with the most disingenuous lies and circumventions, and defend the God of justice with the most outrageous injustice?

Problems with the Gospels. Since an all-powerful God, by definition, knows all things, it follows that he is aware of the weakness of that faculty in his human creatures called memory. Partly, perhaps, because it would serve no evolutionary purpose to remember literally everything we do, we in fact remember only an extremely minute fraction of the sensory impressions to which we are exposed, not to mention the endless river of interior thought that occurs to us during every waking and many sleeping moments as well. This, of course, is true even of those who enjoy a superior ability to recall the past. This fact, which apparently no one ever denies once he is made aware of it, gives us no trouble either in the abstract or as applied to our daily experience.

Oddly enough, this would seem to be inarguable except as regards one application: the ability of those who were followers of physical witnesses to Jesus' life to be certain that the testimony they heard was an accurate account of his sayings and doings. The recognition of the disturbing connection between this universal truth on the one hand and its relevance to the fair-minded search for the historical Jesus, of course, grows out of nothing more mysterious than the fact that, if the memory of those humans who actually saw and heard Jesus of Nazareth is no better than that of the human race generally, then it is unlikely that the NEW TESTAMENT record about him is totally accurate. There is one possibility which could have resolved this dilemma. That would have been the clear-cut, miraculous intervention of God into the three-year drama of Jesus' ministry so as to make certain that in this one instance in all of history the testimony of key witnesses would be consistent and perfect.

Unfortunately for our most fervent hopes, that possibility is automatically ruled out by reference to the available record. If the memories of all witnesses had been granted the temporary gift of perfection, we should find not the slightest hint of contradiction, ambiguity, or error in the Gospels, which Christians have been led to assume give an accurate picture of Jesus' ministry. Even the most devout Christians, if they are knowledgeable about the Bible, are all too painfully aware that contradictions exist, which could not be the case if God had decided that in this one instance all the important facts would be reported with absolute accuracy.

Bible Scholarship. While it is clear that a certain closed-mindedness—indeed in some cases apparent mindlessness—characterizes the argumentation of some of the defenders of the Bible's infallibility, it by no means follows that the great majority of its advocates in the Christian fold are individuals of modest intelligence, or that they lack scholarly credentials. Indeed, the most informed and morally responsible work of Christian and Jewish defenders of Scripture is characterized by a high-mindedness as well as a tireless, painstaking, and often remarkably insightful quality.

Fortunately for the possibility of the eventual triumph of truth and justice, there seems to be a correlation between the degree of true academic familiarity with the intricacies of Scripture on the one hand and willingness to make certain concessions to common sense on the other. Almost all the best critics, for example, have abandoned the simplistic position according to which practically everything in Scripture is interpreted precisely as it would be if we encountered it in a book that specialized in history, geology, or astronomy. But the armies of the faithful are, by and large, kept totally ignorant of such sophisticated research and analysis. There is an enormous gulf between the average Christian's perception of the Bible and that of the majority of serious scholars of Scripture.

There is, obviously enough, a small group of strict conservative fundamentalists who interpret almost every word of Scripture inerrantly, but I consider them in the same intellectual category as those who are honestly convinced that the earth is flat. It is important to note that there is a connection between these two schools of thought. That connection is encountered in GENESIS, since a totally unbiased examination of its early details makes clear that its authors, too, were flat-earthers who lived long before it was known that the earth was spherical and revolved around the sun. Apparently the Lord saw no reason to inspire them to grasp the true facts about the earth he had placed them on.

One reason it is absurd for fundamentalists to deny the existence of contradictions in the Scriptures is—to put the point as simply and clearly as possible—they exist. The issue is dealt with, with refreshing frankness, by William Neil in his helpful *Harper's Bible Commentary*. Of the book of Wisdom in the Catholic Bible, he says,

> . . . a further point of interest is that this book is, in a sense, a counterblast to the pessimism of Ecclesiastes. The author, in the guise of Solomon, replies to the other Solomon, who speaks in the words of the Preacher. It is not unusual to find one book of the Bible written to correct another. Job was written to protest Ezekiel's doctrine that a man receives his just desserts in this life. Ruth was intended to tilt at the prohibition of mixed marriages by Ezra and Nehemiah.

Wisdom's unknown author, in any event, is clearly condemning the general world-view of Ecclesiastes. Obviously this could not possibly be the case if every word of the Bible, every idea expressed represents the directly inspired word of God.

Ignorance of the Bible. The Christian churches have now had relatively unimpeded opportunity to preach the Gospel for some 2,000 years. For the last four centuries, the availability of printing presses and the greatly increased literacy that resulted have facilitated the large task. New editions of the Bible leap immediately to best-seller lists, the number purchased usually running in the millions. There are religious television and radio programs, Sunday School classes, university courses, adult study courses, books, pamphlets, tapes, lectures, sermons, ad infinitum. Incredibly enough, such a vast effort still finds the U.S. in a general state of biblical illiteracy.

In 1959, the Rev. Thomas Roy Pendell, a Protestant pastor of what he described as "quite a proper congregation in a boulevard church located in the college section of a rather large city," prepared a simple test about Jesus' life for the members of his flock. Reports Rev. Pendell:

> The results were staggering. Nearly one-fourth of the adult members of that Sunday's congregation could not identify Calvary as the place of Jesus' death. Over one-third did not know that Nazareth was the town where Jesus was brought up. Gethsemane rang no bell for 43%, and Pentecost had no significance for 75%. Only 58% could identify the Gospels.

There was complete confusion as to the number of converts baptized by Jesus, ranging from none (correct) to 300,000. Jesus was variously listed as living under Julius Caesar, King Saul, and King Solomon.

Concludes Pendell, "It seems plain that biblical ignorance is the rule among members of one particular congregation. If other Protestant congregations are like ours, Christian education still has a long way to go."

It does indeed. And Catholic church leaders have long conceded—and lamented—that Catholics know even less about the Bible than do Protestants.

In this connection, I recommend "American Catholic Intellectual Life" by Father George Hunt, editor-in-chief of *America* magazine, in that periodical's May 6, 1989, issue. In surveying American Catholic intellectual life, and referring to works distributed for a 60-year period by the Catholic book club, Father Hunt says:

> Up to 1970 or so, the most popular offerings were Catholic biographies (saints or other heroes, or converts for the most part) and Catholic fiction . . . only a handful of books on theology were offered and *none on biblical scholarship.* (IA)

This was, of course, in keeping with the long-standing general lack of interest among the Catholic laity in the Bible. It is encouraging to note that during the 1980s quite a different picture emerged. It remains to be seen whether the upsurge of Catholic Bible scholarship and lay interest will lead more to religious doubts or to renewed faith, but whatever the outcome, it is good that more and more Catholics are taking a serious interest in Scripture.

According to a 1980 Gallup Poll, 57 percent of Americans believe in unidentified flying objects, 10 percent believe in witches, 28 percent in astrology, 39 percent in devils, and 54 percent in angels. Those who believe in angels and devils are, of course, chiefly Christians, since teaching the literal reality of such creatures has been part of most Christian orthodoxy. However, astrology is anathema to Christianity, and UFOs are hardly compatible with the man-centered universe taught in Scripture.

See also the general articles AUTHORSHIP OF THE BIBLE; CHRISTIANITY; COMMANDMENTS, TEN; FALL, THE; GOD; ORIGINAL SIN; PENTATEUCH; RESURRECTION.

See specific figures such as ABRAHAM, JOSEPH, MOSES, and NOAH.

See the following books of the Bible: ACTS OF THE APOSTLES; AMOS; CORINTHIANS, FIRST; DANIEL; DEUTERONOMY; ESTHER; EXODUS; EZEKIEL; GENESIS; HEBREWS; HOSEA; ISAIAH; JEREMIAH; JOB; JOHN, GOSPEL OF ST.; JOSHUA; KINGS, FIRST; LUKE; MARK; MATTHEW; PSALMS; PROVERBS; RUTH.

C

CAIN, first-born son of ADAM AND EVE; "and Cain was a tiller of the ground" (Gen. 4:2).

> 3. In the course of time Cain brought to the Lord an offering of the fruit of the ground,
> 4. and Abel brought of the firstlings of his flock and of their fat portions. And the Lord had regard for Abel and his offering,
> 5. but for Cain and his offering he had no regard. So Cain was very angry, and his countenance fell.
> 6. The Lord said to Cain, "Why are you angry, and why has your countenance fallen?"
> 7. If you do well, will you not be accepted? And if you do not do well, sin is couching at the door; its desire is for you, but you must master it."

Of course, we all know the outcome. Cain was so jealous because the Lord favored ABEL that he slew him. Cain's diligence in cultivating "the fruit of the ground" apparently did not please the Lord, who wanted a bloody sacrifice. Like a bad parent, favoring one son over the other, he was indirectly responsible for the earth's supposed first murder. (For the rest of the story, see GENESIS, *Chapter 4*.)

God's apparent irrationality in favoring the nomadic sheep herder over the farmer is incomprehensible.

We know that agriculture is considered to be an "advance" over nomadism, leading to developments in civilization such as cities, a more dependable and varied food supply, writing, and a more complex governmental structure. So why did God favor Abel? The composer of this segment of Genesis is perhaps exalting the nomadic Israelites over their settled neighbors in the Fertile Crescent. Eventually they came to envy these neighbors, thus precipitating the alleged incursion into CANAAN, which they tried to justify by announcing that they were the CHOSEN PEOPLE. This belief, which certain scholars have seen as a myth, has caused the Jews no end of trouble down through the centuries.

I've always felt sorry for Cain. The poor fellow had toiled from dawn to dusk to raise food for his no doubt large family, following the Lord's injunction to Adam "to till the ground from which he was taken" (Gen. 3:23), but that wasn't good enough for the capricious Yahweh. Any child who has had a parent favor a sibling's Christmas gift and had his or her own go unnoticed will understand how Cain felt.

One of the serious difficulties with the Cain-and-Abel story, well known to scholars, is that if certain parts of Genesis are correct, then there would have been as few as four people on earth in the early days, those being, of course, Adam, Eve, Abel, and Cain. Even if, after the first couple's two sons were born, they might have had a few more children, it would nevertheless be the case that the population of earth during, say, the first 40 years would be such as could be accommodated on the average school bus. The problem starts when, in Chapter 4 of Genesis, after Cain kills his brother, the Lord sentences him to be a fugitive and wanderer. Cain and God have a conversation in which the possibility is discussed that Cain could be killed by strangers he might encounter on his life-long journey. Where did all the strangers suddenly come from? Who begat them?

All that this and other such classic problems establish, needless to say, is that the details of such narratives are purely legendary. In the present day, most Christians and Jews have no problem accommodating this obvious truth; the exception is the fundamentalists.

CANAAN. One of the strangest aspects of the story of ABRAHAM is that God would promise him the specific land of Canaan for his descendants (Gen. 15:18-21). To grasp this, it is necessary to remind ourselves that Egypt, where the Hebrews reportedly lived before the alleged invasion of Canaan, is a part of the continent of Africa. Even now, some 3,500 years later, Africa is a huge continent, containing fertile oases and, farther south, good farmlands. In the days of Abraham it was less populated than now. God, therefore, could have promised the ancient Israelites even more spacious territory, which, having fewer inhabitants, would not have made inevitable an almost endless series of expulsions, wars, and atrocities, which began again in that region in the 1930s and have continued to the present.

The land of Canaan—more or less the territory of Ottoman and British–Mandate Palestine and of present-day Israel—was inhabited by Philistines, Phoenicians, and Canaanites, who already led a settled existence in small cities about the time MOSES is said to have arrived. It was therefore inevitable that when, in the 13th century B.C. he supposedly led the Hebrews out of Egypt, a centuries-long process of war, pillage, and destruction would ensue. As to the question of why God, described in other contexts as all-loving and merciful, would deliberately *plan* for such an ongoing catastrophe, no satisfactory answer has ever been suggested. Indeed, by looking at the tragedy of the Middle East up to the present moment, we can perceive that the situation since 1948 bears a certain resemblance to that of the first century of the Israelite takeover of Canaan. (See also JOSHUA; PALESTINE.)

CAPITAL PUNISHMENT is a subject that often pits fundamentalists against Humanists and many enlightened Christians. Study of public attitudes toward the subject suggests that those who are quite certain they favor the death penalty, fall, generally speaking, into two classifications. The first group, an extremely small minority, consists of those who have taken the trouble to examine the pros and cons of the argument and who have, as a result, concluded that the electric chair, the firing squad, the gallows, and the gas chamber have some slight deterrent value and that therefore, however brutal, they ought to be retained for the protection of society.

The second classification, which I assume comprises over 95 percent of the pro-death-penalty forces, consists of those who know little or nothing of the particulars on the issue and who therefore almost certainly did not arrive at their positions by rational means. You can often identify the individuals in the second group by the heat and anger with which they present their arguments.

The death penalty, in democratic societies, will continue to be inflicted until the majority becomes civilized enough to appreciate its essential horror and depravity. The English writer George Orwell, describing a hanging he witnessed when he was working for the British government in Burma, told of the one moment when, for him, capital punishment ceased to be just a sociological abstraction and became, instead, a hideous reality.

> It was about forty yards to the gallows. I watched the bare, brown back of the prisoner marching in front of me. Once, in spite of the men who gripped him by each shoulder, he stepped lightly aside to avoid a puddle on the path. It's curious, but until that moment I had never realized what it means to destroy a healthy, conscious man. When I saw the prisoner step aside to avoid the puddle, I saw the mystery, the unspeakable wrongness of cutting a life short, when it is in full tide ("A Hanging," 1931).

An excellent book on the issue is *The Death Penalty in America* (Chicago: Aldine Publishers, 1968), a collection of various points of view, including arguments in its favor. Everyone opposed ought to be just as familiar with these arguments as he is with the arguments which please him more. The editor is Hugo Adam Bedau.

Much of the recent scientific and sociological research into the subject disposes once and for all of the argument that capital punishment must be retained because of its deterrent value. There is no concrete evidence that men are deterred from murder or other serious crimes simply because they fear being executed.

We have the death penalty now in most states, and yet murder and other serious crimes continue to increase. This wouldn't be the case if capital punishment were such a marvelous deterrent. The reason that common sense misleads us in this regard is that murder and other serious crimes are largely *irrational acts*. The people who murder tend to fall into three main categories. The first consists of the mental cases who are obviously not in a psychological position to be deterred, or to be approached on any reasonable grounds. They go right ahead and kill when they feel compelled by circumstances to do so.

Secondly, there are the more or less normal individuals who kill in a moment of blind emotion—passion, jealousy or rage, a fit of some kind. These people generally kill someone close to them—a husband, wife, brother, neighbor—sometimes over the most trivial cause, following a fight in a saloon over a baseball score or something of the sort, sometimes with drinking or drugs involved. If anything is clear it is that these people have killed impulsively and didn't give the slightest thought to the possibility that they might be punished.

The third category consists of professional criminals, essentially vicious people who go right on killing whether there's capital punishment or not. They do not expect to be caught, usually are not caught, and if they are, they generally hire an experienced lawyer, who can get them out of the chair or gas chamber.

Consider certain classic arguments in opposition to the death penalty.

1. Capital punishment is a vestige of barbarism, something from an earlier stage of civilization which we somehow haven't gotten around to getting rid of yet.

2. Innocent people have been put to death. We will never know how many.

3. Almost all of those who go to the chair, the gas chamber, or the gallows are the very poor and friendless, and the majority are members of minority groups, while wealthy people who have committed equally se-

rious crimes but can afford good lawyers are practically never executed.

4. The aim of the penal system should be the rehabilitation of prisoners, not their physical destruction. The practice of capital punishment is inconsistent with this ideal of reform and rehabilitation.

5. Capital punishment sometimes results in injustice to society, in that juries will occasionally let dangerous criminals go free because they are reluctant to bring in a verdict of guilty if there is a mandatory penalty of death associated with the crime.

6. Most prison executives—the people who have to do this dirty business—are opposed to capital punishment. It is not true that most policemen are opposed to it; they tend to favor it. And most prosecuting attorneys are in favor of it. This is to be expected. Prosecuting attorneys and policemen are generally decent people whom we send out to do battle with our criminal population. Generally the forces are uneven. And war, in every case, has among its destructive effects that of making us hate the enemy and assume he is some kind of subhuman creature who is almost totally evil.

7. The Judeo-Christian moral tradition teaches that killing is evil, except in self-defense. There are some who argue that killing is evil, period, and that we don't have the right to kill even in self-defense but theirs is a minority view. Be that as it may, society is already defended when a criminal is put behind bars and the most deviant ones are kept there.

8. When a society demands gas chambers and electric chairs, that society itself has become, to a certain extent, brutal; it becomes a killing society, and that affects everyone in it in one way or another.

9. The death penalty cannot undo the original crime. There is the ancient theory of "let the punishment fit the crime," or "an eye for an eye." In some instances this makes sense; if I steal $50 from you, the law ought to make me give your $50 back if I'm caught. But the death penalty cannot undo a murder. It only adds a killing by the state to a killing by the criminal.

As regards the eye-for-an-eye theory, bringing the Old Testament into the capital punishment debate is a waste of time. The Bible can be used to prove or disprove practically anything. There are two groups that seem to understand this well. First are the secularists who, since they do not have faith in the Bible, cannot see any reason to quote it as an authority. The other group consists of biblical experts, who are aware that some parts of the Scriptures are pro-capital-punishment and some are anti-capital-punishment. Those who oppose capital punishment frequently quote the commandment "Thou shalt not kill," but the Old Testament, unfortunately for consistency, lists dozens of offenses for which it not only condones but absolutely insists on death as a suitable penalty. For example, Exodus explains that if a man's ox kills another man, the owner as well as the ox is to be killed. If we took this and other passages in the PENTATEUCH seriously, half the people in the United States would have to be killed tomorrow. So much for the argument from religious authority.

The biblical concept of HELL has obviously failed as a deterrent. If Hell has not been effective an deterrent to murder, can mere hanging or gassing do the job?

Although the churches have sometimes failed to distinguish themselves in the march toward civilization, it is uncomfortable for their present adherents to concede as much. Even in the esteemed *Oxford Dictionary of the Christian Church*, an Anglican/Episcopalian source, the entry on capital punishment concludes: "Its abolishment in certain countries, however, and the great diminution since 1800 of the number of crimes punishable by death and others, may legitimately be ascribed to Christian enlightenment." To this comment, the reviewer Stanley Edgar Hyman, writing in *Commentary* magazine, wittily observes, "Perhaps the author means the enlightenment *of* Christians."

CHOSEN PEOPLE, THE, a term by which Orthodox Judaism, citing GENESIS, designates Jews, because of God's promises to ABRAHAM and the divine covenant made with him (Gen. 17:4-9). I am not here concerned with the question as to (1) whether Genesis is an accurate historical record (we must remember that it was written by Jews, possibly during or after the Babylonian Exile, and thus could be considered biased); (2) whether the Jews were indeed God's favorite people; or (3) whether he in fact loved them in any unique way—perhaps because they may have been among the first peoples to eschew idols and practice monotheistic worship. Let us assume that all of these suppositions are valid, but then proceed to reason further.

We are otherwise taught in Scripture that the Lord loves all of his creation, all of his children, which is to say he has no greater affection for the Germans, as such, than for the Poles; for Americans than for Japanese; for Mayan Indians than for Polynesians. How, then, can it be argued that he once loved—or still loves—the Jews most of all—and so much so that he has awarded them their own country in perpetuity, no matter what other historical events have occurred there or what other people have come to live there or what other religions have developed and flourished on its soil? Many people worship the same God Jews do, but they have never claimed he handed out real estate to them.

Do Christians believe God once declared Jews his chosen people? Do

Muslims believe it? Do Hindus or Buddhists or Native Americans? What percentage of today's Jews themselves are convinced of it? At least one branch of the faith, Reconstructionist Judaism, has officially repudiated the notion of the Jews as a chosen people. (See also CANAAN.)

CHRISTIANITY, a largely beautiful, warm, and touching philosophy, unfortunately much more honored in name than in observance. To the extent that we may depend on the testimony of the Christian Scriptures, JESUS and PAUL generally taught that the proper response to anger is love, that the wealthy ought to sell their belongings and share the proceeds with the poor, and that charity, or love, is the greatest of all virtues. Sadly, few Christians behave as if they had ever heard of such edifying moral advice.

Arguing from the Christian admonition that one can judge things by their fruits, it is sometimes suggested that the validity of the Christian message can be largely determined by the effect it has on the behavior of those who embrace it. But this is a very dangerous argument if its purpose is to demonstrate the superiority of Christianity, because it inescapably forces one to a consideration of the massive accumulation of evidence of despicable, atrocious, immoral, and destructive behavior on the part of some of those who have considered themselves Christians. Obviously there are many cases where people who have led destructive or criminal lives have been reformed by an acceptance of Christianity and have thereafter led saner, more edifying existences; but, as I say, such questions would have to be statistically surveyed on a very broad basis, and analyzed carefully, before one could draw conclusions.

Just as it is perhaps better for churchmen not to bring up the question as to what extent, if any, the acceptance of Christian belief changes the conduct of the individual acceptors, so it is also less embarrassing for the churches if they do not apply the same question to the conduct of Christian tribes and nations down through the last 2,000 years. For while it is true that there have been individual saints and even many nonsaints who have led exemplary lives, nevertheless many, many larger social entities have behaved throughout that history in a fashion that it is now a cliché to describe as unchristian.

The word *unchristian,* alas, falls far short of the reality it is intended to convey. *Anti*-Christian would be more apt since the various states of Europe have generally behaved in a sadistically criminal fashion. It is said that from the time of the formation of the Holy Roman Empire in the year 962 to the year 1862, a period of 900 years, Europe had 782 wars! And these formal military confrontations did not include the many slaughters by kings and armies, and even Crusaders, of their own citizens. Such glory as there is in the history of Europe may generally be credited to a small number of heroic and creative individuals. The Christian states themselves, for the most part, have disgraced Christianity, not ennobled it. The most, therefore, that defenders of the various forms of the Christian faiths might suggest is that if Christians in large numbers ever behaved in a Christlike manner, the world would be a safer place in which to live.

G. K. Chesterton once observed that Christianity had not really been tried and found wanting, but that it had been found exceedingly difficult and consequently was rarely tried. For such a statement to be accepted as reasonable, of course, one must interpret the word *Christianity* in a highly specialized and ideal sense, in which Christians would literally love their enemies, would really sacrifice to help the poor, would actually set aside self-interest of all kinds and devote their entire lives to the service of God's creatures as do, say, Mother Theresa, convert Mitch Snyder, advocate of the homeless, or Luis Espinal, S.J., the martyr-missionary to Bolivia, who was assassinated by the powerful bloodsuckers that forever attack those who dedicate their lives to the poor. Chesterton is right, if we employ the term *Christianity* in that sense. But precisely the same is true of HUMANISM, whether purely secular or qualified by the belief that a God created the universe.

There is a sense in which, though all religions can be shown to have failed—if only in terms of falling short of their hopes and claims—the failure of Christianity has been such that it does not even have a competitor in this particular race. For Christianity alone has made a certain claim: to be a religion of *love*. It is crucial to concentrate here on the fact that the love described is not merely the love of God, common to many religions. Nor is it simply the encouragement of love in its common and easy forms, such as love between parent and child, husband and wife, or between friends. No, the uniqueness of Christianity lies in its insistence that we love our *neighbor* as ourself, with the word *neighbor* interpreted as including all mankind, even enemies.

Since this constitutes the primary moral distinction between Christianity and all other religions, we are under the obligation to examine such relevant evidence as is available. Have Christians loved their enemies? The very question brings a bitter smile to the lips of both saints and anti-Christians. Jesus himself may have done so, forgetting for the moment the unresolved question of the historical reliability of the literary evidence for his teachings and acts. That the average Christian does nothing of the kind is so self-evident that the point is never even debated. If that does not represent failure, then the word has no meaning.

Martin Marty, an influential Christian thinker and leader, in an article titled "You're Going to Have to Be Institutionalized" (*The Critic*, Summer 1989), at one point decries the tendency of some to perceive Christianity largely as a philosophy. Marty says:

> The problems are evident. First of all, *Christianity is not very satisfying or original as a philosophy.* Find something in Jesus the philosopher (including "love your enemies") that you cannot find stated with at least as much eloquence and grounding in other ancients. (IA)

Marty's argument, largely, is that people ought to be Christians in the traditional sense by actually being affiliated with the institution of the church, observing its rituals and living by its precepts, rather than entertaining it at an intellectual and moral distance. However, he quite casually concedes the inadequacy of the total teachings of Jesus perceived in a philosophical context.

CIRCUMCISION. Customs of long-standing come to seem reasonable simply because they are rarely questioned or critically examined. This is certainly the case with circumcision, mentioned in Genesis 17. In any event, whether it is in fact a reasonable and hygienic custom or one as absurd as foot-binding among the Chinese or lower-lip extending among the members of the Ubangi tribe has not been easy to determine. It is clear that no one living has the slightest idea as to how—or for that matter why—the custom actually started, unless one is disposed to take Genesis literally.

The fact that it is commonly believed today that males who are circumcised are less likely to incur infections of the kidneys and urinary system can have had nothing to do with what primitive cultures thousands of years ago thought, since our knowledge about bacteria and viruses is relatively recent.

Since it is known that ancient societies not in contact with the early Hebrews also practiced circumcision, it is therefore not possible to say that it originated with the Israelites. Scholars are generally in agreement that the Egyptians practiced circumcision long before it was known to the ancient Jews. Primitive cultures that could not have acquired the practice from the early Israelites include ancient Mexican and South American tribes, as well as the Fijians and Samoans of Polynesia.

After I studied the history of eunuchs in China, the possibility occurred to me that circumcision may have been substituted for the barbaric custom of castration, which in some instances involves the removal of both male sexual organs so that the genitals of the affected male come to resemble those of a woman.

Those who arbitrarily assume that there is an essential amount of sense to practically all human customs are understandably taken aback to learn that their confidence in human rationality is not so well-founded. Among peculiar sexual customs, in some cultures, is that of circumcising women—sometimes at the age of puberty—by the surgical removal of the clitoris. This is still done in some African countries.

When we turn to Genesis 17, we find that circumcision is linked to the process of God's making a covenant with ABRAHAM.

> 10. This is my covenant, which ye shall keep, between me and you and thy seed after thee; every man child among you shall be circumcised.

When one considers how many important moral questions the Lord might have taken up on this most auspicious of occasions, his choice to require a minor physical operation seems incredible. Some details concerning this operation are elaborated:

> 11. And ye shall circumcise the flesh of your foreskin; and it shall be a token of the covenant betwixt me and you.
> 12. And he that is eight days old shall be circumcised among you, every man child in your generations, he that is born in the house, or bought with money of any stranger, which is not of thy seed.

Perhaps in our day, when most boy babies are circumcised shortly after birth, it will seem a matter of no great importance, one way or the other, that such a custom can be shown to be of great antiquity. But there is considerably more to it than that, as the account is rendered in Genesis, for it is not only one's own children who are to be circumcised, but any one "bought with money of any stranger, which is not of thy seed." This means that any slave living in a Hebrew master's house, no matter of what age, must be seized, held down, and forcibly attacked with a knife, without the benefit of anesthesia, the object being to mutilate the end of his penis. The violence associated with such an act has disturbed many people who do not practice circumcision.

What does the Lord propose for those Israelites who are not circumcised? The punishment, it turns out, is being treated as an outcast.

14. And the uncircumcised man child whose flesh of his foreskin is not circumcised, *that soul shall be cut off from his people; he hath broken my covenant.* (IA)

It might be thought that I am exaggerating in suggesting that not only week-old infants but also adults were to be cut in this way—and that in a day when there was no such thing as painkillers. But observe:

24. And Abraham was ninety years old and nine, when he was circumcised in the flesh of his foreskin.
27. And all the men of his house, born in the house, and bought with money of the stranger, were circumcised with him.

Max I. Dimont, whose fascinating study *Jews, God and History* (New York: New American Library, 1964) could be viewed as a beguiling work of pro-Jewish propaganda, says:

The rate of conversion [to Judaism] would have been even greater but for two factors: the rigorous dietary laws, and the necessity for circumcision. In Paul's time the early Christian sect dropped these two requirements, and the pagans flocked to the Christian religion, whose entrance specifications were less demanding than the Jewish.

COMMANDMENTS, TEN. It cannot be argued that an all-powerful deity would be unequal to the task of communicating ten or any number of commandments to his human creatures, by whatever means he might wish to employ. Once one accepts the existence of such a deity, it follows that the simple account of an act which is beyond human capability cannot be considered out of the question. On the other hand, it is entirely fair to expect that a divinely inspired account of such a wondrous circumstance would be *internally consistent,* and certainly not an insult to the intelligence.

I submit that any third-rate author could create a more attractive story of the transmission of an important message from a god to humankind than is offered in EXODUS, *Chapter 19.* (My own italics have been added, and I have omitted some verses.)

1. In the third month, when the children of Israel were gone forth out of the land of Egypt, the same day came they into the wilderness of Sinai. . . .
3. And Moses went up unto God, and the Lord called unto him out of the mountain, saying, "Thus shalt thou say to the house of

Jacob, and tell the children of Israel;

4. "Ye have seen what I did unto the Egyptians, and how I bare you on eagles' wings, and brought you unto myself.

5. "Now therefore, if ye will obey my voice indeed, and keep my covenant, then ye shall be a peculiar treasure unto me above all people: for all the earth is mine: . . .

9. And the Lord said unto Moses, "Lo, I come unto thee in a thick cloud, that the people may hear when I speak with thee, and believe thee forever." And Moses told the words of the people unto the Lord.

10. And the Lord said unto Moses, "Go unto the people, and sanctify them today and tomorrow, and let them wash their clothes,

11. "And be ready against the third day; for the third day the Lord will come down in the sight of all the people upon Mount Sinai.

12. "And thou shalt set bounds unto the people round about, saying, 'Take heed to yourselves, that ye go not up into the mount, or touch the border of it: *whosoever toucheth the mount shall be surely put to death:'*

13. *"There shall not an hand touch it, but he shall surely be stoned, or shot through; whether it be beast or man, it shall not live:* when the trumpet soundeth long, they shall come up to the mount." . . .

16. And it came to pass on the third day in the morning, that there were thunders and lightnings, and a thick cloud upon the mount, and the voice of the trumpet exceeding loud; so that all the people who were in the camp trembled.

17. And Moses brought forth the people out of the camp to meet with God; and they stood at the nether part of the mount.

18. And Mount Sinai was wrapped in smoke, because the Lord descended upon it in fire: and the smoke thereof ascended as the smoke of a furnace, and the whole mount quaked greatly. . . .

21. And the Lord said unto Moses, *"Go down, charge the people, lest they break through unto the Lord to gaze, and many of them perish.*

22. "And let the priests also, which come near to the Lord, sanctify themselves, lest the Lord break forth upon them.

23. And Moses said unto the Lord, "The people cannot come up to Mount Sinai: for thou chargedst us, saying, 'Set bounds about the mount, and sanctify it.' "

24. And the Lord said unto him, *"Away, get thee down, and thou shalt come up, thou, and Aaron with thee: but let not the priests and the people break through to come up unto the Lord, lest he break forth upon them."*

25. So Moses went down unto the people, and spake unto them.
(IA)

Nowhere in Exodus is there the slightest suggestion as to why a normal, highly religious curiosity, which would quite understandably move a believer in God to wish to approach the sight of an impending miracle, should cause the believer's death.

There is no question of an alternative interpretation here: "There shall not a hand touch it but he shall surely be stoned, or shot through; whether it be beast or man, it shall not live." Is there any intelligent person who will deny that this is a mixture of nonsense and savagery? If an innocent grazing animal wanders toward the mountain, is it flattering the Deity to attribute to him the wish that the poor, hungry creature should be struck dead?

The suspicion will occur to any reader of even inferior detective fiction that MOSES—already a murderer (Exod. 2:12)—was actually preparing some sort of religious fakery and that it was the fear of being caught in this deception that made him issue stern warnings that no one should approach the scene.

More Than Ten. Many good-hearted Christians and Jews who eventually become aware of disturbing discrepancies and errors in the Bible understandably choose to turn their backs on such problems, to leave them to scholars, and instead concentrate on such simple, bedrock verities as the Ten Commandments. It would be fortunate if such a course were reasonable. But such hopes are groundless, for when we study the chapters of Exodus—and also the book of DEUTERONOMY—we find that these passages of Scripture are as confusing as the others that have troubled us.

To begin with, I am ashamed of my former ignorance in having assumed—but then I was carefully taught—that there is indeed something unmistakably identifiable as *the* Ten Commandments in the Bible. As it happens, this is not the case.

The first surprise that awaits the new student of Scripture is that there is considerable difference between the common short version of the Commandments taught in synagogues, Sunday schools, and catechism classes and the more lengthy and complex messages actually presented in Exodus and Deuteronomy. I was taught, for example, in a series of Catholic schools, that the first commandment is: I am the Lord your God; you shall have no other gods before me. But the commandment attributed to God in Chapter 20 of Exodus reads as follows:

2. "I am the Lord your God, who brought you out of the land of Egypt, out of the house of bondage.
3. "You shall have no other gods before me."

Mark Twain, who seemingly approached every human commonplace with a fresh angle of vision, has this to say about the first commandment:

[God] did not say He wanted *all* of the adulations. He said nothing about not being willing to share them with his fellow gods. What He said was, "Thou Shalt Have No Other Gods *Before* Me." It is a quite different thing and puts him in a much better light—I confess it. There was an abundance of gods. The woods were full of them, as the saying is, and all He demanded was that He should be ranked as high as the others—not above any of them, but not below any of them. . . . He wanted to be held their equal.

But perhaps the most astonishing discovery for those who go to Exodus 20 for information is that there are not just ten commandments, but a great many more. Some are as follows:

> 24. "An altar of earth you shall make for me and sacrifice on it your burnt offerings and your peace offerings, your sheep and your oxen; in every place where I cause my name to be remembered I will come to you and bless you.
> 25. "And if you make me an altar of stone, you shall not build it of hewn stones; for if you wield your tool upon it you profane it.
> 26. "And you shall not go up by steps to my altar, that your nakedness be not exposed on it."

Perhaps the most noteworthy thing about the commandment given in Verse 24—concerning altars and the bloody slaughter of animals—is that no Jew has paid the slightest attention to it for centuries, nor did Christians ever observe it. Now if all these commandments were indeed authored by God Almighty, the omnipotent Ruler of the Universe, what right did the devout have to begin ignoring them one day?

Think through what is forbidden by the commandment of Verse 26. The author—who we may be sure was not God—actually gave attention to the possibility that if a robed priest ascended steps to a high altar, the faithful at the foot of those steps might be able, if a breeze passed, to see his buttocks or sex organs. This is either vulgarity or nonsense.

There is not the slightest evidence in the book of Exodus that the commandments given on Mt. Sinai were intended for the entire human race. What is clearly stated is that the commandments are intended for the people of Israel, for the allegedly divine speaker does not say "I am *the* Lord God" but "I am the Lord *thy* God, *which have brought thee out of the land of Egypt, out of the house of bondage.*" (IA) Christians adopted the Ten Commandments when early converts from Judaism declared their belief in Christ.

Source of the Commandments. Whatever the date on which the Ten

Commandments were first introduced—and whether this was done by God, by Moses, by Aaron, or by some forever-anonymous scribe or group of priests who lived centuries after the time of Moses—we may be certain that they did not come as a blinding flash of moral instruction in the sense that they suggested guides to behavior that had never before entered anyone's mind. Lying, the taking of others' property, of others' wives or husbands, of others' lives have been perceived as evil in all major cultures throughout recorded time and no doubt before. The parts of the Ten Commandments that might be considered unique concern the prohibition against statuary and painting and the forbidding of work on the Sabbath Day.

But if the commandments do not come from the creator of the universe, what is their source?

It has been the opinion of hundreds of scholars that a priestly group during the Babylonian Exile, presumably working from older sources both written and oral, created new materials out of the combination of their imaginations and good intentions, and thus drew up a moral and ritualistic code. Knowing that its strictures would become the object of debate if advanced under nothing more than their personal authority, they attributed the Code to Moses and/or God, perhaps believing in all sincerity that what they wrote down at that time did originate with God in the long-ago past "history" of their people. Some scholars believe that a clue to this is found in the apocryphal I Esdras 14:22: "I [Ezra] shall write all that hath been done in the world since the beginning and the things that were written by law."

Far from having received any or all of their commandments directly from God, the unknown authors of Exodus may have taken at least some from the Code of Hammurabi. This great Babylonian king, who ascended the throne shortly after 1800 B.C., lived several centuries before the time of Moses. Indeed, it has occurred to me—although I know of no scholarly exposition of such a theory—that the stone tablet that Moses brought down from Mt. Sinai may be a reference to the black diorite stone, eight feet in height and containing 3,654 lines of writing, on which Hammurabi's codification of Babylonian laws was not only inscribed, but happily, preserved. A Frenchman named DeMorgan located this priceless object in 1901. Today it stands in the Louvre in Paris.

A number of reputable scholars assume that the Israelites came from Mesopotamia. An extended period of residence in the Mesopotamian area would account for their familiarity with the laws of Hammurabi. Fred Gladstone Bratton, in *A History of the Bible* (Boston: Beacon Press, 1959), quotes a number of parallels.

Hammurabi

196,200—If a seignior has destroyed the eye of a member of the aristocracy, they shall destroy his eye. If a seignior has knocked out a tooth of a seignior of his own rank, they shall knock out his tooth.

199,201—If he has destroyed the eye of a seignior's slave or broken the bone of a seignior's slave, he shall pay one-half his value. If he has knocked out a commoner's tooth, he shall pay one-third mina of silver.

250,251—If an ox, when it was walking along the street, gored a seignior to death, that case is not subject to claim. If a seignior's ox was a gorer and his city council made it known to him that it was a gorer, but he did not pad its horns [or] tie up his ox, and that ox gored to death a member of the aristocracy, he shall give one-half mina of silver.

125—If a seignior deposited property of his for safe-keeping and at the place where he made the deposit his property had disappeared along with the property of the owner of the house, either through breaking in or through scaling [the wall], the owner of the house, who was so careless that he let whatever was given to him for safekeeping get lost, shall make [it] good and make restitution to the owner of the goods, while the owner of the house shall make a thorough search for his lost property and take [it] from its thief.

14—If a seignior has stolen the young son of a[nother] seignior, he shall be put to death.

Exodus

21:23-24—If any mischief follow, then thou shalt give life for life, eye for eye, tooth for tooth, hand for hand, foot for foot.

21:26-27—If a man smite the eye or tooth of his servant or his maid and destroy it, then shall he let him go for his eye's sake [or tooth's sake].

21:28, 29—If an ox gore a man or woman that they die, the owner of the ox shall be acquitted. But if the ox were wont to gore in time past, and it hath been testified to the owner, and he hath not kept him in, and he hath killed a man or woman, then shall the ox be stoned and the owner put to death.

22:7—If a man shall deliver unto his neighbor money or stuff to keep, and it be stolen out of the man's house, if the thief be found, he shall pay double.

21:16—And he that stealeth a man and selleth him, or if he be found in his hand, he shall surely be put to death.

As recently as 1952 the University of Pennsylvania's Noah Kramer revealed the discovery, in a Turkish museum, of a small tablet containing a portion of a legal code even older than that of Hammurabi, attributed to Ur-Nammu, an earlier king of Sumeria. Perhaps its most striking feature is that it is even more civilized and reasonable than that of Hammurabi.

Another odd aspect of this question, which I have never seen mentioned and which, in fact, occurred to me only after I realized that the commandments reportedly given to Moses by God on Mt. Sinai were so numerous and individually lengthy, has to do with the weight of the tablets of stone. It would require a very large slab of stone to accommodate such a voluminous text, so large in fact that Moses could hardly have carried them down Mt. Sinai.

The First Commandment. The phrase *no other gods* is one of the more remarkable in the Bible. For centuries Christians and Jews have firmly believed that there is—indeed that there can be—only one God. Consider what the response of the religious community would be if, say, in Cleveland today, a small sect erected a twelve-foot, green marble statue, called it Klodor, and began to worship it. The members would shortly be advised that, while they were free to attach any name whatever to the object they had constructed and were even protected by the Constitution of the United States in their peculiar behavior, they were nevertheless totally in error if they imagined that their statue was actually a God. They would be told that common sense itself requires the existence of one God and no more. But such sensible observations are never made concerning Moloch and the numerous other gods referred to in the Old Testament. Not only is their existence—as more than just statuary—never explicitly denied, but even the CHOSEN PEOPLE seem to have slipped sometimes and worshiped them.

The Second Commandment.

4. "You shall not make for yourself a graven image, or any likeness of anything that is in heaven above, or that is in the earth beneath, or that is in the water under the earth:
5. "You shall not bow down to them or serve them; for I the Lord your God am a jealous God, *visiting the iniquity of the fathers upon the children to the third and fourth generation of those who hate me:*
6. "but showing steadfast love to thousands of those who love me and keep my commandments." (IA)

Every Catholic church in the world is filled with "graven" images of all sorts. Indeed, one finds statuary, paintings, stained-glass windows and various other beautiful likenesses of God the Father, Jesus Christ, the Virgin Mary, the saints, and angels. During all the years I was a Catholic, and for that matter to the present day, I have not found it objectionable that one might be able to gaze upon a painting of a holy scene while inside a church. This is all very well, but there cannot be the slightest question that it is flatly forbidden by Verse 4.

Since I believe that the commandments were written by a human rather than a divine author, I am therefore perfectly at liberty to analyze and criticize them. Acting on that freedom, I conclude that it is utterly unedifying to be told that the Lord God, in what is supposed to be the moment of his most supremely important communication with the children of earth, is speaking in a bullying and threatening way, asserting that if a man does happen to bow down before a religious picture that he will not only punish that man but *also his children, his grandchildren and his great grandchildren!*

Furthermore, it is nonsense for the Deity to describe that man or woman, and their perhaps hundreds of innocent offspring, as "those who hate me." Humans who make such statements are usually identified as suffering from severe paranoia. Why a god is supposed to be admired for so speaking is unclear.

The almost infinite variety of interpretations of Exodus 20:4 is suggested by an incident in April 1964 in which Los Angeles Superior Judge Macklin Fleming entertained arguments in a case brought by a John Shubin, who had filed suit against the California Department of Motor Vehicles to have his driver's license issued without the usual photograph. Shubin, a member of the Russian Molokan Christian Holy Spiritual Jumpers sect, argued that the state regulation violated his freedom-of-religion guarantees under the First Amendment. One of the precepts of the Molokans is that the photographing of one's face is in violation of the second commandment.

The unprejudiced observer should be able to see that, far from being objects of ridicule, the Molokans are in fact, along with some Muslims, people who accept this commandment on its own terms. It cannot possibly be argued that a photograph is not a "likeness" of something "in the earth," and it is quite clear that the commandment prohibits the making of any likenesses. The only intelligent way out of the difficulty is to simply cast aside the alleged authority of the commandment or interpret it to mean a likeness of anything that suggests God. Which puts Michaelangelo, other religious artists, the popes who commissioned them, and the churches that display them in serious violation of the second commandment.

One of Voltaire's criticisms of the ancient Jews was that they were destitute of the arts. The observation, though an exaggeration, reflects reality but requires explanation. How could painting and sculpture have developed among a people who believed that Almighty God had personally forbidden the making of any graven image or physical likeness? The Italians and French, to name only two examples, produced numerous works of artistic merit, but they achieved this by ignoring this commandment or interpreting it to mean that a representation of God that was not worshiped was okay.

The Third Commandment. "You shall not take the name of the Lord your God in vain . . ." One of the many interesting things about this commandment is that there is no general agreement as to its meaning.

During the early years of my Catholic training, I was taught, in the clearest possible terms, that one thing only was forbidden by the commandment and that was using the name *God, Jesus* or *Jesus Christ* in a disrespectful way. It was said to be wrong, for example, to shout "Jesus Christ" if one hit one's thumb with a hammer, or to whistle and say "Jesus" if one saw a sleek new automobile or an attractive young woman. That the name of Christ is daily used in such a way by millions of people around the world is unfortunately clear. Others feel that what is forbidden by the commandment is any frivolous reference to either God or Christ. Perhaps the original interpretation applied to the name YAHWEH.

The Fourth Commandment. "Remember the Sabbath day, to keep it holy. Six days shalt thou labor . . ." (20:8-9). That the Jewish interpretation of the commandments may be different from the Christian is suggested by the following comment by Aaron Intrater and Leon Spotts, authors of *The Voice of Wisdom:*

> This Commandment usually is interpreted as ordering the observance of the Jewish Sabbath. At the same time, however, *the Fourth Commandment directs that we use the other six days of the week for active labor.* And so our ancestors did; work was an essential part of their lives. Even our rabbis of generations past supported themselves by active labor. Some of the great sages were blacksmiths, sandalmakers and carpenters. The gentle scholar, Rashi, whose commentaries on the Bible and the Talmud are still studied today, was a wine-presser. The Jewish sages insisted that work gives man dignity and develops his character. They saw idleness as leading to temptation and sin. (IA)

If there is any instruction which the Lord thought especially important it is that concerning the SABBATH day, so far as one can judge from the repeated references to the Sabbath in the Old Testament.

The Fifth Commandment. "Honor thy Father and thy Mother, that thy days may be long . . ." Since no rational person has ever suggested that fathers and mothers should be dishonored, this commandment has generally been puzzling. Perhaps it meant that the Israelites understood that if you did not *respect* your parents enough to learn from them, you would not *survive* in a precarious world. Also, unruly teens in those days could be put to death by town elders.

As for this commandment's validity today, thousands of parents criminally abuse their children. They should not be honored; they should be arrested.

The Sixth Commandment. "Thou shalt not kill." After God states some of the commandments, he points to specific and fearful consequences that await breakers of the law. As regards the sixth, however, he refers to no punishment. Although at first the sixth seems the most simple and clear-cut of all, there will apparently never be an end to debate as to its meaning. To most pacifists it means, quite simply, that we ought never to take human life. But some Indian sects go even further, saying that they are to kill nothing whatever, even animal and sub-microscopic forms of life. Most Christians, since like other tribes of the earth they have shown not the slightest reluctance to go to war, obviously have had to interpret this commandment in such a way as to free their hands in dealing with their enemies. The solution has been to argue that the commandment applies to only cases of murder, which is to say, unjust killing.

Concerning the well-recognized contradiction between the sixth commandment and the widespread killing of animals that occurs in western society, animal killers advance the argument that humans commit no moral offense by the act because it is obvious that they have a right to secure food to sustain themselves. The argument, needless to say, carries no weight with the millions of vegetarians, since it is obvious that men may live healthily their entire lives without ingesting animal protein. In fact, the vegetarian case has been considerably strengthened in recent years as it has become evident that diets high in animal fat are dangerous to health. But it is important to distinguish between the argument that we have the right to kill beasts for food and the completely separate question as to whether we have a right to kill them purely for our own amusement.

The proverbial impartial observer from another universe might have assumed that, after 2,000 years of unremitting Christian indoctrination, more Christians would want to be like St. Francis of Assisi than Rambo, but that is apparently not the case.

Another odd reality to be faced is that in the context of American and other societies, Christians are far more interested in hunting animals down and killing them than are Jews, Hindus, atheists, agnostics, Secular Humanists, Universalists, and Unitarians.

Since we have already seen many instances in which something in the scriptures does not make sense, we should not be surprised to find another example of poor reasoning and absurd morality in Exodus, Chapter 21:

20. And if a man smite his servant, or his maid, with a rod, and he die under his hand; he shall be surely punished.

21. Notwithstanding, if he continue a day or two, he shall not be punished: for he is his money.

The case itself would be laughed out of the most inefficient courtroom in the world since it clearly says that if two men brutally assault their slaves, male or female, and the victim dies immediately after being assauted in the one case but only three days later in the other, the second offender shall not be punished at all. Note that the crime is exactly the same, a brutal assault leading to the death of the victims. Is there any fundamentalist of the present day who would applaud such ridiculous injustice if he encountered it in his own community? Our modern fundamentalists are, in fact, generally quite insistent that judges are too lenient with criminals and that sentences, by right, ought to be much more severe than they are, but here we have a case of Holy Scripture saying it is perfectly all right for a murderer to walk off scot-free.

Another context, in which, in the opinion of many, it is difficult to know how to apply the commandment concerns individuals whose physical condition is so pitiable and hopeless that they themselves plead that their lives be ended. For a long time the churches were adamant in arguing that there were literally no circumstances in which there was any moral course other than keeping the sufferers alive. To their credit, however, the religions have in recent years modified this cold-hearted stance, though the larger issue has by no means been settled.

The large debate could no doubt be conducted in simpler terms if it were the case that those who insist that the Bible is most important in guiding their own conduct were rarely guilty of killing. Unfortunately there seems no such correlation, as anyone familiar with world history, including that of nominally Christian nations, will be all too well aware.

Millions of the most horrible murders and crimes are constantly being committed, as we know to our sorrow, but following the great majority of them there is at least the counterbalance of guilt which, if it does not restore the lives of those murdered, or recompense those who have been robbed, at least shows that the offenders have some vestige of human feeling. It is fascinating that the one exception to this feeling of remedial guilt is found in that theater of the human drama that prides itself on being most morally superior and that is, of course, religion.

Even the fanatic driven mad by political or patriotic considerations may, in the aftermath of his depredations, experience a degree of guilt, perhaps feeling that although he was justified in assaulting an enemy battlement or community he might nevertheless have "gone too far" in inflicting punishment on his opponents. But the religious fanatic never feels guilt at all and, in fact, compounds his crimes by being so proud of the havoc he has wrought that he sets his acts openly before God as instances not of shame but of great merit. It serves to dramatize futher this painful truth that even some of those who are considered saints—though they are never universally so regarded—have been guilty of it. Those, for example, most guilty of burning alive, in indescribable torment, sensitive human beings, for solely religious reasons, are not limited to the relatively few individuals who actually lighted the flames and brought them into contact with human flesh. Such men could at least relieve themselves of discomfort by observing, truthfully enough, that they were merely "doing their duty," in the sense that in the present day a man who throws the switch on the electric chair is simply following orders and himself has nothing to do with the decision and the sentence involved. Far more guilty were the church philosophers who supposedly justified such barbaric slaughters and the churchly judges who ordered them.

Limitations of space preclude saying more here about the matter, but it is a strange result of so important a divine commandment that it does not seem to have diminished the killing of fellow humans at all.

The Seventh Commandment. "Thou shalt not commit adultery." While I personally happen not to agree with him, there's no question that Martin Luther preached that a married man has a perfect right to commit adultery if his wife refuses him her sexual favors. He should ask her once, the great reformer advised, and then, to be on the safe side, ask again. If he is refused his sexual rights a second time then, Luther argued, he is guiltless if his natural appetites drive him elsewhere. Why have not the pre-AIDS proponents of the 20th-century sexual revolution quoted Luther in this context?

The Eighth Commandment. "Thou shalt not steal." Since there is little defense for stealing, except among professional thieves or those who are starving through no fault of their own, there is little necessity to comment at length on this divine law. Unfortunately, it is not always clear whether certain examples of acquisitive behavior constitute a form of theft. The free-enterprise economy provides numerous opportunities for dishonest, aggressive acts that, in bestowing success on the aggressor, work to the clear disadvantage of more scrupulously honest competitors, customers, and those who cannot afford the product or service.

The Ninth Commandment. "Thou shalt not bear false witness against thy neighbor." I have never known anyone who—whether the point was tacitly conceded or not—did not have a "situational" code of ethics and morals, so far as actual behavior is concerned. Many are, of course, perfectly aware that their actions in a given situation are dictated by considerations other than the bare, essential code they profess. But some—chiefly religious fundamentalists—are apparently unaware that in practice they too permit "mitigating circumstances" to affect both judgment and behavior.

Consider, for example, the case of those who profess strict adherence to this commandment. It is almost universally interpreted to condemn not only the bearing of false witness in the context of legal proceedings, which is apparently what the commandment specifically forbade, but also lying itself. Most people around the world are perfectly prepared to honor the general idea that truth is superior to falsehood and that it is better to tell a truth than to tell a lie. Some people are so morally superior in this regard that they very rarely lie, but even many morally well-behaved people constantly speak falsehoods in certain sorts of social situations. The secretaries of hundreds of decent, law-abiding conservative Christian businessmen are permitted to say to unwanted telephone callers, "I'm sorry but he's not in just now," "He's in a meeting," "He just stepped out for a moment," and various other falsehoods, since the telling of them is obviously preferable to such truths as "I'm sorry, but Mr. Thomas, as a matter of policy, never accepts calls from strangers," or "Mr. Thomas warned us that if you called he would under no circumstances talk to you," or "Mr. Thomas has been trying to avoid you for weeks and the time has come to tell you so."

Since the range of human behavior is very wide indeed I should not be surprised to learn that there are, scattered here and there, a few souls either so saintly and virtuous, or so priggish, that they will indeed tell such blunt truths rather than the polite lies that are the conventional social alternative. But I have no doubt that hundreds of those who criticize "situational ethics" nevertheless behave in as situational a way as possible when it is convenient for them to do so.

Consider a more dramatic case. A hijacker has taken over a plane, trapping hundreds of innocent hostages—men, women, and children. Where are the denouncers of situational ethics who will argue that the ethical thing to do is to speak absolute truth to the hijacker, despite the fact that doing so risks the lives of his captives? The police agencies, airline executives, and government officials of all nations naturally do not trouble themselves with such absurd debates. They have no compunction whatever, nor should they, about employing the weapon of falsehood when communicating with dangerous criminals toward the end of saving innocent lives.

The Tenth Commandment. "Thou shalt not covet . . ." Concerning this commandment E. C. Vanderlaan, writing in the *Progressive World* of September 1957, says:

It is not altogether fantastic to wonder just how to fit the implications of this Commandment into that uncritical adulation of business methods which, it is constantly being brought home to us, is the essence of loyal Americanism. How is a little business to become a big business if it does not covet another merchant's customers?

The value of this commandment is its injunction to control your cravings if you want to escape perpetual frustration.

Two Versions of the Commandments. The first significant difference between the two versions of the Ten Commandments—the one given in Exodus 20 and the other in Deuteronomy 5—comes when the two different authors undertake to explain why God forbids working on the Sabbath. In Exodus 20:11, we read:

> In six days the Lord made the heavens and the earth, the sea and all that is in them; but on the seventh day he rested. *That is why the Lord has blessed the Sabbath Day and made it holy.* (IA)

But in Deuteronomy 5:15 we read:

> For remember that you too were once slaves in Egypt, and the Lord your God brought you from there with a strong hand and outstretched arm. *This is why the Lord your God has commanded you to observe the Sabbath Day.* (IA)

It does not require the premises of an atheist to perceive that the two explanations are not the same, although each could be a half-truth.

As is the case of other instances of disharmony in the Old Testament, the concessions made by sophisticated scholars—however intellectually impressive—are socially scandalous in the context of the biblical views of most Christians. Comments John L. McKenzie, S.J., in his excellent *Dictionary of the Bible:*

> It is altogether probable that *neither of these recensions presents the Decalogue in its original form.* Most interpreters believe that all the Commandments were originally as brief as the Commandments on murder, adultery, theft and false witness. *The others have been expanded by the addition of homiletic motives for their observance.* (IA)

It bears repeating that, in light of the average believer's bias, this is an incredible concession, albeit one absolutely required by the tenets of rigorous scholarship. Since the Ten Commandments are widely accounted as the most important of all direct communications from the Divine, it is astonishing that the Old Testament is not a reliable source even for such essential material, a staggering perception that leads to the assumption that if the ancient documents cannot be trusted in regard to fundamental material, they are unlikely to be reliable about much else.

It must be unnerving to fundamentalists to be told by McKenzie, with whom a vast number of other scholars agree, that the story of the stone tablets being literally written upon by the finger of God and subsequently rewritten by Moses "is nothing more than a highly imaginative way of stating the Divine origin and authority of the Decalogue." But if, in fact, the story that Almighty God wrote with his own finger on stone tablets is false, then in what sense can it possibly be said that the Ten Commandments are of "divine origin and authority?"

This is not, of course, to argue that the moral laws proposed are of no value. Even if there were no God, common sense and the natural moral awareness that appears to reside in most human hearts would suggest that thievery, murder, and the bearing of false witness are crimes. They are regarded as such in all officially atheistic states, and rules forbidding them are an ingredient in the U.S.S.R. and other such countries' legal codes. Obviously, this is necessary if societies are not to disintegrate into social chaos.

There are some who gradually arrive at a perception of the confusion abounding in the Old Testament but who "resolve" the dilemma by arbitrarily separating the NEW TESTAMENT from the Old, assuming that the New can stand on its own despite the sagging of the Old. Theologians unite, however, in enlightening those who make such an error; *the New Testament cannot possibly stand if the Old is to any significant extent invalid.* Jesus himself refers to the Old Law, which he reportedly came not to destroy but to fulfill. If it were to be demonstrated that the Old Law is, despite certain virtues, not in the least divine, that one fact alone would make absolutely untenable the hypothesis that Jesus was either (1) Almighty God in human form, or (2) the supreme human son of God.

Those who raise analytical questions about the two versions of the Ten Commandments available in the Old Testament are sometimes challenged to "come up with something better." A proper response starts with the concession that, despite their obvious merits, the Commandments are not perfect. To say that something is not perfect is to agree that it can be improved upon.

Now that we have gotten past that barrier in reasoning, I have, in just a few minutes' time, dictated the following list of commandments, widespread adherence to which would certainly improve the world.

It will be seen, first, that there is an overlapping area of agreement between this particular collection of moral exhortations and the traditional set. The newer draft, of course, does not include the second commandment, which has never made a great deal of sense to the majority of the human race: the instruction to make no pictorial representations of any sort. It would have been perfectly reasonable if the commandment had read, "Thou shalt worship no graven images," although the degree of adoration that millions of Christians have, over the centuries, shown for material religious objects certainly confuses the issue. But it is fortunate that the commandment has been massively disregarded since, if it had been universally observed, we would have been deprived of many art treasures of the last 2,000 years. In that event, such figures as Leonardo da Vinci would be viewed not as heroic geniuses, but as diabolical heretics.

I do not delude myself that the following list exhausts the moral possibilities, nor that the ten specifics can be used, in a simple way, to apply to any and all relevant cases. The same thing, of course, is true of the original commandments, but the point should nevertheless be acknowledged.

1. Honor love as the greatest of virtues, for it brings both immediate and distant blessings, and turn your face against hatred for it produces much of the evil in the world.

2. Strive always to be honest, not only in deed but in word.

3. Be generous in all ways, for as you are grateful for the generosity of others bestowed upon yourself, so you must share your blessings with others, and not only in the material sense.

4. If there is an all-loving God, a person would be a heartless child who would not love such a Father. In the day of his coming, if it occurs, the loving heart will know how to respond. In the meantime, be compassionate to that concerning which there can be certain knowledge: the world and its inhabitants.

5. Educate your children and yourself till the day of your death, for knowledge brings power to improve the world, whereas ignorance leads to confusion and misery.

6. Value freedom by being philosophically tolerant, for, though all intellectual camps are certainly not of equal value or virtue, there is as yet no court of universal appeal. If you would have freedom to live by the light of your own conscience, you must grant the same to others, so long as they do not transgress reasonable legal codes.

7. Respect the property of others, as you wish the world to respect your own. You have the right only to what is freely given to you, what has fallen into your hands through the generosity of nature, or what you have worked to obtain in an honest manner.

8. The vows of mutual love, exchanged in marriage, are legally and

morally binding. Do not hasten into marriage, for by that act you renounce your freedom to engage in romantic or sexual conduct with others. This commandment, too, is largely an expression of the Golden Rule.

9. Because you would not want to be physically abused yourself, therefore do not abuse others.

10. You have heard it said that children must respect their parents. There is great wisdom in this instruction, but only insofar as parents respect their children.

COMMUNION. That faith is distinct from knowledge is clear enough. Indeed were everything in the world capable of being intelligibly apprehended, neither the word *faith* nor the concept would ever have entered our minds. One can have faith only in things which are not demonstrable since, by definition, if they are demonstrable then one simply knows about them, in which case there is no need to have faith that they are so. Consequently, faith applies to beliefs about matters which are inherently either mysterious or unprovable.

A good illustration would be the Catholic doctrine of transubstantiation, according to which the little starch wafer and the wine used in the communion service of the Mass *literally* become the body and blood of Jesus Christ. It is important—for non-Catholics and others not familiar with the belief—to understand that there is nothing whatever symbolic involved. In other words, it is by no means asserted that the carbohydrate and the alcoholic beverage *represent* the body and blood of Christ. What is specified is that they *become* such.

It is perfectly clear, of course, that there is no change whatever in the appearance of the wafer and the liquid. They continue to be indistinguishable from the form in which they existed the moment before the priest pronounced the magical, transforming words. To the overwhelming majority of the human population, who are not Catholic, the belief has always seemed absurd, as it clearly is by all standards of science and common sense. There's nothing in the least bit shocking in saying this; Catholic theologians not only concede the point but are quite prepared to make it themselves by way of distinguishing between simply sensory evidence on the one hand and what they perceive as the mysterious, hence unexplainable, element on the other.

The modern Catholic theologian freely acknowledges the fact that no such doctrine existed until it was asserted in the 12th century. Theologians naturally cannot accept that the magical transformation began in that century; they hold that the church merely formally recognized at that time what had always occurred from the moment of the Last Supper itself.

My purpose in referring to the connection between faith and mystery is to demonstrate the occasional imperviousness of the mind-set to either material evidence or logic.

CORINTHIANS, FIRST. Chapter 6. We are told that there are certain classes of people to whom the kingdom of God is closed:

> 9. Know ye not that the unrighteous shall not inherit the kingdom of God? Be not deceived: neither *fornicators,* nor *idolators,* nor *adulterers,* nor *effeminate,* nor *abusers of themselves* with mankind,
> 10. nor *thieves,* nor *covetous,* nor *drunkards,* nor *revilers,* nor *extortioners,* shall inherit the kingdom of God. (IA)

It is possible for those committing the various moral offenses listed to stop such practices and thereby, presumably, later to merit entrance into God's kingdom of HEAVEN. One of the categories listed, however, is separate in that it is not possible for an effeminate man to stop being effeminate. A homosexual, of course, can theoretically desist from homosexual acts, although such a thing rarely occurs, but if one is effeminate this is never the result of an act of will and in any event is a pattern of behavior that the individual cannot change. (This King James Bible uses the word *effeminate;* the Revised Standard Version employs *homosexual.*)

Chapter 7. In Verses 25-31, PAUL'S point, whether right or wrong, clearly contradicts the very first commandment referred to in Scripture, concerning the obligation to be fruitful and multiply (Gen. 1:28).

> 29. I mean, brethren, the appointed time has grown very short; from now on, let those who have wives live as though they had none.

A careless or quick reading of the entire passage might suggest that Paul is simply urging the single to remain in that state, while avoiding all sexual activity, but more strangely, he urges those who are already married to avoid sexual contact, thereby contradicting an earlier verse:

> 3. The husband should give to his wife her conjugal rights, and likewise the wife to her husband.

It would be interesting to see what the response would be if either the Holy Father in Rome or any of the influential television evangelists in our own country were to ask the married members of the faithful to pledge to avoid sexual contact.

That there are married couples who refrain from sex is clear enough. Sometimes this is explained simply by the unhappy fact that one partner no longer finds the other physically attractive. In other cases neither has any appetite for sex, at least with the marriage partner, and there is a category of cases in which illness precludes intercourse for at least one of the married pair. But we would be safe in saying that probably 99 percent of the best, most devout, married Christians pay not the slightest attention to the advice of Paul in Verse 29.

It is quite odd, incidentally, that on the one hand we encounter Christian apologists urging us to return, not to moral, sane and sensible family life—which is eminently wise advice—but to a specifically biblical mode of marriage behavior. But when we consult the Scriptures, Old and New, in search of guides to the moral conduct of marriage, we encounter a certain number of sobering surprises rather than the comforting ideal morality that our instructors carefully program us to expect. I know of no atheist or agnostic marriage counselor who either commands or advises married people to hate each other or their children, but that is precisely what JESUS is quoted in Luke 14:26 as requiring.

CREATION. If we accept the possibility that the natural world has *not* always existed, it is permissible to assume that there was "darkness" before the first moment of the creative process. Obviously this can be true in only one sense, for there can be neither darkness nor light if there are no organs of sight to perceive them. Nevertheless there is a sense in which one may refer to a precreation state of affairs as being one of darkness.

The same does not apply, however, as regards *chaos*. For it is absurd to speak of chaos in the absence of natural, physical, material objects. A defender of the ancient tradition may be unwise enough to fall back to the position that there may have been some sort of rough, unformed matter that existed before our planetary and stellar bodies were created. But if this *were* so—and there is not the slightest evidence for such an assertion—such matter can have existed only within the context of the philosophical understanding that it abided by physical laws. But if this is true, then it is necessary to conclude that there had already been some sort of creative act. All one can argue then, concerning the traditional details of "the creation" in GENESIS, is that the planetary and stellar bodies of our world emerged during some sort of secondary creative period. One may perhaps be complimented for developing such a philosophical construct, but it is certainly heretical in terms of any known Jewish or Christian theological formulation.

Although higher education in Christian countries now has no difficulty incorporating Darwinian essentials into its educational program, the long-standing debate between religious legend and science concerning the origin of animal life—including man—has by no means been disposed of to the satisfaction of all participants. As Hector Hawton observes in *Controversy: The Humanist/Christian Encounter* (London: Pemberton, 1971):

> The problem which orthodox theologians had to face is that Neanderthal man is a different species from *homo sapiens*. Yet the Neanderthal man made strong implements, used fire and buried his dead with a care that suggests rudimentary religious feeling. Did this clumsy, grotesque and even pathetic experiment in humanity come into existence before or after The Fall?

Father Georges Auzou (*The Formation of the Bible,* St. Louis: B. Herder Book Company, 1963) describes the separate components of belief about the physical world that are common to every ancient people of the Near East. It is important to grasp that every belief is false.

- They considered the earth as the center of the visible universe.
- It is placed above a mass of water, like a great island on mysterious pilings.
- From this unfathomable depth come springs, streams, rivers, and lakes.
- The earth is covered by a very firm, concave ceiling which rests, at its extremities, on high mountains and which supports the waters that fall from above through openings in the arch.
- The planets and the stars travel across the inner surface of the arch at night; they pass mysteriously beneath the earth during the day.
- Below ground level is the somber dwelling to which the dead descend.
- Above the sky, in the heavens, dwell the divinities.

Comments John L. McKenzie in his *Dictionary of the Bible,* "the order of enumeration [of the events of creation in Genesis] is obviously schematic and has no reference to the chronological development of the earth, of which the author had no knowledge."

As a host of devout scholars has clarified—at least to the satisfaction of one another even if their work has escaped the attention of many of the faithful—the two accounts given in Genesis are not only contradictory but were written by authors familiar with earlier Canaanite and Mesopotamian creation-myths. The Mesopotamian version, which is rendered in a document titled ENUMA ELISH, came first. A comparison of the Genesis account with the *Enuma Elish,* says McKenzie, "reveals that it [Genesis] is an explicit polemic against the Mesopotamian and Canaanite myth of creation." So much for the customary and sadly traditional nonsense about direct divine inspiration of all parts of the Old Testament.

Thomas Paine in *The Age of Reason* raises a fair question when he comments upon the manner of address of the opening portions of Genesis.

> As to the account of the Creation, with which the Book of Genesis opens, it has all the appearance of being a tradition which the Israelites had among them before they came into Egypt; and after their departure from that country they put it at the head of their history, without telling—as it is most probable—that they did not know how they came by it. The manner in which the account opens shows it to be traditionary. It begins abruptly; it is nobody that speaks; it is nobody that hears; it is addressed to nobody . . . it has every criterion of being a tradition; it has no voucher. Moses does not take it upon himself by introducing it with the formality that he uses on other occasions, such as that of saying, "The Lord spake unto Moses, saying . . ."

Paine became anathema among Christians and Jews for making such statements, though he remains a hero in American history. But the staggering fact is that many of his observations are now substantially accepted among devout scholars. The best Protestant, Jewish, and Catholic scholars now concede—though up until recently they refused to acknowledge it—that *the universe is billions of years old* and that the human experience on the planet earth may have started between three and four million years ago.

It is remarkable to contemplate the many once-unthinkable positions that the highest Christian and Jewish scholarship has now embraced. Concerning the scientific nonsense with which the first chapters of Genesis abound—as, for example, the view that the firmament is a solid platform in space containing reservoirs of water, the valves of which open to produce rain—Jean Levie, S.J., simply states that the original author wishes "to assert and to teach . . . God's creative activity and not these scientific concepts" (*The Bible: Word of God in Words of Men*).

It is, of course, reassuring to note that the churches—at least the best informed among them—have finally abandoned the pretense of many centuries that Genesis was perfectly sound scientifically. But, alas, they must not be permitted to suggest that they have happily resolved all aspects of the larger debate, for they now claim to know precisely what the author of Genesis "wishes to assert." Any man of average intelligence can see for himself what the author(s) wished to assert. Having studied the passages in question time and time again, I conclude that the original author(s) would be greatly surprised to hear what Levie and his like-minded colleagues of the 20th century now confidently claim the Genesis author(s) intended to establish. There can be no serious question, surely, that the original author(s) firmly believed the view of the natural universe just as they explained it.

Father Levie (ibid.) comments further:

> When the first inspired authors in Israel desired to describe for us the origin of man, and of their own people, *it could hardly be expected that they could be totally independent of the traditions and ideas of those powerful races who preceded them in history by many centuries and exerted a very considerable influence on the Near East.* All this necessarily raised Biblical problems in a light far different from that envisaged by scholars of the Middle Ages and of the Renaissance. (IA)

One point must be stated and restated: for centuries Christian scriptural tradition represented Genesis as a simple, factual description of creation. As to the reasonable question, "Precisely who is the describer?" the answer used to be equally straightforward: Moses. Of course, no one ever alleged that MOSES himself lived "in the beginning."

As Father N. J. LaGrange states in *The Historic Method,* it was long the traditional Christian assumption that Moses depended on the testimony of witnesses, who formed a relatively short genealogy going back to Adam, who—it was then believed—saw God in person, strolled with him through the garden, etc. The argument, LaGrange concedes, once seemed perfectly reasonable "but now unexpected witnesses have emerged from the shadows where they were thought to have been buried forever." By *witnesses* LaGrange means fossil remains which, as scholars have perceived, prove that the age of the earth is not the few thousand years which Jews and Christians had assumed covered the span of its history. This view, however opposed to reality, is still maintained by simple people in some Christian communities.

In mid-June of 1985 a condor chick that hatched in captivity after its egg had been taken from the wild to a California animal shelter, proved to be suffering from serious genetic defects. Authorities explained that because there were only 18 of the giant birds left in California, the sort of problems that invariably result from inbreeding of a small population group did not surprise them. The relevance of this information to the account given in Genesis is that if God created animals the same way that he is said to have created man, by starting with an original male-female pair, then the serious problems commonly associated with inbreeding would have troubled all animal species from their very beginnings.

The same difficulty, needless to say, would have affected the human animal. Christians and Jews now hold it to be illegal and immoral for brothers and sisters to marry and mate. Indeed, marriage even among cousins is strongly discouraged. Nevertheless, precisely such pairings would have been necessary not only in the time of Adam but also in that of NOAH, if we are to believe the Genesis account.

Although it is absurd for literalist fundamentalists to deny the existence of evolution, given that the reality of that process is readily observable, it is equally erroneous to suggest that if evolution has occurred, the mere fact of its existence disproves the possibility that there is a God. In reality, there is no necessary connection or lack of connection between evolution and God. The majority of well-educated Christians and members of other religions believe, in fact, that evolution has simply been God's practical method of creating and developing all aspects of nature that are alive, which is to say plants and animals. It is apparently only fundamentalists who are confused about this.

See also ADAM AND EVE; AGE OF THE EARTH AND THE UNIVERSE; EDEN, GARDEN OF.

CREATIONISM. See Fundamentalism.

CRUCIFIXION. If one approaches as rationally as possible the concept of the vicarious death-sacrifice of a presumably innocent individual as a means of counterbalancing the hundreds of millions of specific sins committed by all the rest of humanity, the first factor of the equation that impresses itself on the consciousness is its utter irrationality. Not all things which at first seem irrational, however, prove upon closer inspection to be so. It is perhaps possible that even if no such thing has ever occurred, nevertheless there is something therapeutic in the *belief* that such a thing has occurred or could.

Consider for a moment a model drama involving a small cast of characters, and therefore one more easily grasped by the intellect. Consider the story of an individual family—a father, a mother, and five sons. All members of the group are sinful, even criminal, except one, who is remarkably superior morally. Secondly, let us suppose that the authorities, having lost patience with the long-running depredations of this particular clan, have arrested them and sentenced all to death except the one guiltless of crime. Thirdly, assume that the spiritual son goes to the authorities and says, "I quite understand that the public sense of outrage at the many crimes committed by my family demands a formal blood-sacrifice. But I come to offer myself as food for this appetite, this lust for revenge. Spare, I pray you, my parents and my brothers. Perhaps from my example they will see the error of their ways and reform. In any event, the public weal can be as effectively benefited by the imprisonment of the members of my family as by their execution. I willingly give my life in the hope of preserving theirs and serving as an example to all men."

Quite aside from the question as to whether any civil authority would consider such a proposition reasonable, in purely dramatic and psychological terms, it is deeply touching. Any human death is tragic, and even in contexts where large numbers of deaths are to be expected, as in war, we are most particularly affected by stories of individuals who sacrifice their own lives—perhaps throwing themselves on a hand grenade—to save the lives of others. It is this element of the story of JESUS' sacrifice and atonement, combined with that degree of guilt which all humans feel—and should, because of their own moral transgressions—that explains the strong emotional appeal of this aspect of the Christian message.

Still, there is the unpleasant suggestion in the crucifixion story of regression to a belief in a God who required a human sacrifice, a notion long eradicated from most people's thinking. (But then Christians do not think Jesus quite the same as a young woman on an Aztec altar.)

CULTS, THE IRRATIONALITY OF. Could the so-called Jesus Movement of the last few decades have been predicted? It is difficult to say. It is instructive, in this context, to recall that, shortly before the emergence of the movement, leading Protestant theologians, having become uncomfortably accustomed to the dominance of secular currents in political and moral philosophy, had developed the God-is-dead theology. Since the gap between social realities on the one hand and the public perceptions of them on the other is invariably wide, we should not be surprised that the God-is-dead concept was misunderstood.

No theologian was ever so misguided as to interpret the phrase in literal terms. If there is a God, it follows, by definition, that such an entity could not possibly die. What the phrase meant—if I may run the risk of giving so important a phase of modern theological history only passing reference—was that something that had seemed to characterize earlier ages—namely, the belief in divine intervention into history and human affairs—was notably lacking during the 20th century.

To isolate only one instance among thousands that might be cited, the people of France made Joan of Arc a saint, as well as a national heroine, partly because they believed that God had intervened in her military campaigns in order to guarantee France and not England a victory. The French, of course, are not alone in holding what to many will seem an absurd as well as a nontheological view. How do they explain two subsequent defeats by Germany? Had God abandoned them?

Almost all cultures, civilized or primitive, throughout history have, in times of war, prayed for the victory of their own cause, however unjust, and moreover not only confidently expected divine aid but believed that it had actually occurred in all instances in which military victory was the outcome.

In any event, while the God-is-dead debate was still raging among theologians and interested scholars, not to mention the clergy, religious development on the street was taking quite another turn. Not only was there a sudden revival of interest in old-fashioned fundamentalist beliefs— the very sort of thing that had earlier been laughed to scorn by such popular American figures as Mark Twain, Clarence Darrow, H. L. Mencken, Thomas Edison, Robert Ingersoll, and other secularists—but religious and philosophical belief of an unashamedly nonrational nature suddenly burgeoned. At the outer fringes of religious fundamentalism, Pentacostals, Seventh-Day Adventists, Jehovah's Witnesses, speakers in strange tongues, and workers of mass revivalist frenzy were heard again in the land. Many Christians might have been indifferent had the phenomenon stopped at that point, but of course it did not. That it was enlarged much further became evident from the sharp revival of interest in astrology, witchcraft, demonism, numerology, belief in the magical power of pyramids, crystals, tarot cards, seances, and God knows what else.

Peter Berger has made an insightful comment, as he often does, on the relationship between reason and unreason within the Catholic context.

> The Catholic Church, out of anguished *aggiornamento,* decided to bring the faith closer to contemporary man by translating the mass from Latin into the vernacular. This act of accommodation was immediately followed by a period of convulsive disintegration unparalleled since the 16th century. One of the more piquant consequences of the effort to spare modern Catholics the spiritual difficulties of the Latin mass is that some of them are currently babbling away in *glossolalia* (in growing numbers, apparently) while others are chanting hymns to the Lord Krishna—in Sanskrit.

At a deeper level, Berger offers another clue to the resolution of the mystery which concerns us, or at least he describes a condition within which the strange religious revival is taking place. There is in the contemporary world, Berger has observed, "a very curious co-presence of modernizing and demodernizing processes." As a sociologist, Berger has centered his attention in recent years on what is called the Third World. From his studies he has drawn the unexpected conclusion that there are "resistances to development" in the very portions of our planet where the modern amenities—plumbing systems, clean-water systems, roads, automobiles, modern universities, etc.—would seem to be most needed. "What is most interesting is that these 'resistances' (which I prefer to call demodernization) increase rather than decrease as so-called development progresses." Having observed such a phenomenon in more primitive cultures, Berger then realized that it was occurring in the developed world as well. The cult movement is a prime instance.

The movement naturally assumes different proportions depending upon the view of the onlooker. Catholics and Protestants of the larger denominations regard the phenomenon, for the most part, as an unfortunate deviation from orthodoxy, however hazily that factor is perceived. Secular Humanists, on the other hand, assess the new movement as one more instance, among thousands in the record of history, of the natural tendency of religion to spawn highly irrational and sometimes socially irresponsible offshoots.

D

DANIEL. Any belief that a man named Daniel wrote the book sometimes attributed to him has long been abandoned by all serious scholars.

Among the last to proclaim Daniel the author of the whole book was E. J. Young in the 1950s. Says Father Athille Brunet (*Theology Digest,* Winter 1957) of another Daniel defender, Lindner:

> . . . even he vacillates. He speaks of the possibility of different authors for the stories . . . and the visions . . . of various editors and redactors . . . This was the last stand for the thesis. It never had been universally accepted, and since World War II it is evident that it is dead.

John L. McKenzie, S.J., points out that the "character Daniel as he is presented . . . is truly fictional." The best modern scholarship is agreed that most of the book was written around the year 165 B.C. Its unknown author or authors, however, dishonestly created the impression that it was written some 400 years earlier. For many centuries, during most of which time there was little serious biblical scholarship in the modern sense, even students of Scripture whose intelligence and knowledge of ancient history revealed to them strange discrepancies and discordances in Daniel, were nevertheless afraid to challenge the traditional view of the book.

As regards the book of Daniel, Isaac Asimov explains:

> Where Isaiah, Jeremiah, and Ezekiel make no anachronistic mistakes concerning the times supposed to be theirs, the Book of Daniel is replete with anachronisms as far as it deals with the period of the Exile. It treats, however, the Greek period with easy correctness, and while this might be explained by those dedicated to the literal acceptance of the Bible as a case of prophetic insight, it is odd that Daniel should be so correct in his view of what was to him the "future" and so hazy about his view of what was to him the "present." It is easier to believe that the writer was a man of Greek times, to whom the Exile was

an event that had taken place four centuries earlier and concerning the fine details of which he was a bit uncertain.

There is not even certainty that an actual Daniel ever lived, although he may have. The very fact that scholars are not clear on the point demonstrates that close to nothing about Daniel is firmly established. It may well be the case that by 165 B.C. a legendary character called Daniel had come to be part of an oral and perhaps some form of written tradition, but this no more establishes that he actually existed than do literary references to King Arthur or Robin Hood certify that such people really lived.

Another reason for skepticism is that a number of Daniel's separate stories are preposterous. One such is the tale of Shadrach, Meshach, and Abednego who, because they refused to pay homage to a 90-foot gold image erected at the order of King Nebuchadnezzar, were thrown into a fiery furnace. "The Song of the Three Children in the Fiery Furnace," given in the third chapter, is accepted in the Catholic canon but is rejected by Jews and some Protestants.

Father Jean Levie's comments (*The Bible: Word of God in Words of Men*) harmonize with those of Asimov.

> According to many critics, the book must have been written in the second century Before Christ, at the time of the Maccabees, whereas the supposed author, Daniel, lived in the Persian period. *The second century author recounts, in the form of prophecies, events which in fact took place from the sixth to the second centuries.* He relied on these to gain a more ready acceptance for his own prophecies concerning future events. (IA)

A possible defense for the author of Daniel is that there are nonbiblical examples, such as Homer's epics, in which the author casts the story as though he were speaking in the present of an earlier age. It is possible, of course, that the unknown author of Daniel intended nothing more than this.

The problem of Daniel might have been easier for Christians to deal with but for the fact that JESUS—at least according to Matthew 24:15— spoke of "the abomination of desolation announced by the prophet Daniel." Father Athille Brunet, S.J., in *Theology Digest,* Winter, 1957, says:

> Some insist that this testimony settles the matter. For them it would be impiety, almost heresy, to fail to see the apodictic proof that Daniel wrote at least chapters 7 to 12. *Otherwise Christ would be a fraud or in error.* (IA)

Since it is naturally out of the question for Father Brunet to accept the possibility of error in Jesus, he therefore is blocked by his most important assumptions from following out certain implications of his hypothesis. Still he writes with admirable frankness:

> A contemporary could not have accumulated so many improbabilities in such short narratives. The figure of Darius the Mede is composed from various sources; Balthasar was *not* the son of Nebuchadnezzar. We have *no* evidence that the latter was mad for seven years. Our book alludes to history, but it is *not* itself history. (IA)

I recommend Brunet's analysis of the book of Daniel. His treatment is scholarly and fair, although he is not at liberty to abandon the theory of divine inspiration.

The Rev. Jozef M. Milik, one of a team of eight international scholars who worked on translations of the DEAD SEA SCROLLS, announced in 1957 that one small Aramaic scroll, "The Prayer of Nabonidus," provided a clue to the apparent error about King Nebuchadnezzar. After giving accurate details of Babylonian history, the writer of "The Prayer" referred to King Nabonidus as the last ruler of the neo-Babylonian dynasty and then mentioned the King's sojourn of seven to eight years at the oasis of Tiema in Northern Arabia. Nabonidus, the writer of the prayer relates, was ill during those seven years but eventually enjoyed a recovery the author viewed as miraculous, thanks to the aid of one identified in the scroll only as "the Jewish astrologer." Father Milik and his associates believe the Jewish astrologer and the prophet Daniel are one and the same. They do not accept that Daniel himself was the author of the book attributed to him, but assume that the author or authors were familiar with the story of King Nabonidus.

Chapter 5. Although there is in the Old Testament no shortage of stories of fantastic and magical events, Chapter 5 of Daniel is nevertheless better known than some. It concerns a great feast held by Belshazzar, king of the Babylonians, with a thousand people in attendance. While the festivities and drinking among the king, his princes, wives, and concubines are taking place, suddenly the attention of the merrymakers is distracted by a remarkable event:

> 5. In the same hour came forth fingers of a man's hand, and wrote over against the candlestick upon the plaster of the wall of the King's palace: And the King saw the part of the hand that wrote.

Daniel is, in due course, sent for and proceeds to interpret the words *Mene, Mene, Tekel, Parsin.*

All we know of these words is that they do not appear in either the Hebrew or Babylonian languages. Had they been common words, there would have been considerably less mystery about their meaning. Says Daniel:

> 26. This is the interpretation of the thing: MENE: God hath numbered thy kingdom and finished it.
> 27. TEKEL: Thou art weighed in the balances and art found wanting.
> 28. PERES: Thy kingdom is divided, and given to the Medes and Persians.

Why the author refers in one instance to the word *Parsin* and a few verses later to a different word, *Peres,* is an inconsistency for which there is no explanation. *Pars-* is, however, a root meaning Persian.

Daniel is forthwith honored for his interpretation and that same night, we are told, Belshazzar is killed. Verse 31 states that Darius the Mede took control of his kingdom, being about 62 years old at the time. Actually, it was Cyrus the Great, a Persian Achaemenian king who conquered Babylon, in 538 B.C.

Chapter 7. The bizarre visions of Daniel are a strikingly poor method of conveying messages from God to man. To such observations the faithful sometimes reply that the ways of God are not those of man. Indeed they are not, but they should not be inferior to those of man. We are told that Daniel had confusing visions in his fevered dreams, but no living person has the slightest certainty as to the meaning of them. No Christian church has ever published an interpretation of Daniel's nightmares, which the faithful were nevertheless once expected to accept as a meaningful part of their religion.

Chapter 12. In this odd chapter we are told first that Michael, presumably the archangel, "stands guard over the sons of" the Jews. If this is indeed the case we would expect to have heard of many more instances in Scripture when Michael has protected the tribes of Israel. The evidence for such intercession is unfortunately scant.

Much of the chapter concerns the end of time. It is perfectly natural as an abstract intellectual exercise to be curious about the last days. Typically the authors of Daniel are annoyingly vague. We are told such things as "many will go back and forth, and knowledge will increase," but we are none the wiser. Daniel reports having seen a "man dressed in linen," who is apparently hovering above the waters of a river and of whom the prophet asks, "How long will it be until the end of these wonders?" Again, even the most devout believer must concede that the linen-clad gentleman's answer leaves a great deal to be desired. He is quoted as saying that "it would be for a time, two times, and half a time" (v. 7).

> 11. And from the time that the regular sacrifice is abolished, and the abomination of desolation is set up, there will be 1,290 days.
> 12. How blessed is he who keeps waiting and attains to the 1,335 days!

What is the "abomination of desolation"? It may refer to Antioch IV's offering of a pig on the Hebrew high altar. What do the two conflicting numbers mean? God only knows.

DAVID, youngest son of Jesse of Bethlehem, generally considered one of the two greatest Jewish kings. He is said to be the ancestor of JESUS, although there are widely acknowledged problems with Jesus' paternal genealogy. David was selected by the prophet Samuel to replace Saul as king of Israel, although he did not do so until after Saul's death. David's story begins in I Samuel, Chapter 16.

> 12. . . . Now he was ruddy, and had beautiful eyes, and was handsome. And the Lord said, "Arise, anoint him; for this is he."
> 13. Then Samuel took the horn of oil, and anointed him in the midst of his brothers; and the Spirit of the Lord came mightily upon David from that day forward. . . .

David became the favorite of King Saul on the grounds that his skillful performance on the harp soothed the troubled king.

> 23. And whenever *the evil spirit from God* was upon Saul, David took the lyre and played it with his hand; so Saul was refreshed, and was well, and the evil spirit departed from him. (IA)

This verse plainly says that God does evil. Does the reader believe it?

As every Jew and Christian knows, David's greatest exploit was the slaying of the Philistine giant, Goliath, said to be ten feet tall, who challenged Saul to send a champion to fight him to determine who would be enslaved by whom. Goliath's suggestion is clearly a great moral advance over the Israelite practice of slaying every man, woman, and child of the enemy.

David, his father's innocent young shepherd, performed the deed with a slingshot, having had plenty of experience, we are told, in fighting lions and bears. Of course, it was the Lord who favored David over the Philistine enemy and gave him courage and strength. Such divine intervention is always claimed by victorious champions, though a good many losers have also prayed to the same (or a similar) God for victory.

David and Saul eventually became estranged, due to Saul's great jealousy and mental disturbance, which appears to have been clinical depression. Saul's son Jonathan had become David's greatest friend, and David had won Saul's daughter Michel in marriage after he killed a great number of enemy Philistines.

Saul eventually attempted to kill David, but the young man escaped and formed a band of outlaws in the Judean hills; he was accepted by the priests of the house of Eli, and apparently lived somewhat like Robin Hood of English legend. Few Christians and Jews seem aware that at one point in his military career David fought *against* the Israelites, as is mentioned in the *Encyclopedia Britannica*'s summarization.

> Because he feared for his life, David, along with 600 of his men, fled to the Philistine city of Gath, where he became a supposed leader of one of their military contingents against the Israelites. . . . Some of the Philistine leaders distrusted David, who was sent back to his garrison town of Ziklag, which the Amalekites had overrun and in which they had taken many prisoners. Thus, David did not witness the defeat of the Israelites under Saul, who was mortally wounded by the Philistines and whose sons were killed. . . . [Saul] was caught between the old, conservative ways (led by Samuel) and the new, liberal views (championed by David).

Just from this account of the activities of David, who is so strongly identified with Israel and who yet allied himself against it at a crucial time in its history, when Saul was on the throne, it is possible to deduce that the fortunes of the Philistines and the Hebrews were entwined in ways that show that there was not always a sharp distinction or enmity between them.

Although the basic details of the story of Nabal, a rich man of Maon, are confusing and inherently unbelievable, it is instructive to look more closely at this story, in Chapter 25 of I Samuel. David, hearing of his impressive wealth, sent ten men to him with instructions to ask, or demand, that he give up an unspecified portion of his holdings for David's use. Nabal, however, asks a perfectly reasonable question.

10. And Nabal said, "Who is David? And who is the son of Jesse? There are many servants nowadays who are breaking away from their masters.

11. "Shall I then take my bread, and my water, and my meat that I have killed for my shearers, and give it to men who come from I do not know where?"

Leaving aside the question as to whether David had any right to demand—rather than purchase—Nabal's belongings, his response is sadly typical of Old Testament behavior. Far from saying, "Go again and explain to the man why my people are in need of provisions," he sends a military contingent to murder Nabal and steal his property. Abigail, Nabal's wife, rises to the occasion, hastily gathers supplies of bread, wine, sheep, corn, raisins, and figs, and has them sent toward the advancing avenger. This solution is not acceptable to the Lord, however. Abigail's intention to save the life of her husband is frustrated by a character who kills him anyway. Who is this murderous personage? None other than one whom the Old Testament authors persist in describing as one of the greatest mass murderers known to history, the Lord God himself.

38. And about ten days later the Lord smote Nabal; and he died.

Apparently, the Lord did this to avenge Nabal's "insult" to David. David wastes no time in taking the widow as his wife. The story does not reflect well on either David or the Lord, and no explanation is given for David's greed.

Once more we encounter a perverted morality in the Old Testament: the notion that "might makes right." This is a major flaw that has persisted in the outlook of many Jews and Christians, among others, to the present. Clearly, most people require—and somewhere obtain—moral instruction better than that available in much of the Bible.

DEAD SEA SCROLLS, the literature of an ancient Jewish sect, known as the Dead Sea Sect, which some people have thought might have influenced the origins of Christianity. The scrolls themselves are a fascinating and important collection of papyri found in the caves of Qumran, near the northwest corner of the Dead Sea, in the 1940s. Their importance lies in the fact that, with one exception, they constitute *the only premedieval manuscript texts of the Hebrew Bible.* Among the scrolls are fragments of about 180 different manuscripts of Old Testament books, dating from the 3rd century B.C. to the 2nd century A.D.

The scrolls include manuscripts of GENESIS, EXODUS, Leviticus, DEU-TERONOMY, JOSHUA, Samuel, ISAIAH, JEREMIAH, Lamentations, the Minor Prophets, PROVERBS, and DANIEL. For most of these, there is more that one copy. They were written in Hebrew and Aramaic.

For reasons that are not clear—and which may be suspicious—only a third to one-half of the material has been published, although Christian and Jewish scholars have been studying them for four decades.

According to the *Encyclopedia Britannica:*

> The scrolls formed the library of an ancient Jewish sect, which probably came into existence at the end of the second century BCE and was founded by a religious genius, called in the scrolls the Teacher of Righteousness. Scholars have tried to identify the sect with all possible groups of ancient Judaism, including the Zealots and early Christians, but it is now most often identified with the Essenes . . .

Just before and after the birth of JESUS, the world at the eastern end of the Mediterranean, called PALESTINE after the Roman conquest, saw the rise of numerous movements among the Jews. Some were messianic or apocalyptic, some were nationalistic. This trend was undoubtedly accelerated by the Jews' failure once again to ward off foreign domination. Some of these groups retreated to out-of-the-way places and behaved secretively. The success of the Dead Sea Sect in this regard is proved by the fact that their immense library of scrolls lay hidden and their very existence was generally unknown for 20 centuries.

In addition to manuscript copies of Old Testament books, the Dead Sea library contains books that are similar to some pseudepigrapha (that is, Jewish and Christian writings that, though revered, were *not* included in the Bible). It is possible that these long-known—although unfamiliar to the average churchgoer—pseudepigrapha are based on actual Dead Sea texts—or the traditions they preserve. Examples are the *Book of Jubilees,* the *Book of Enoch,* and the *Testaments of the Twelve Patriarchs.*

The Qumran library also held previously unknown *commentaries* on Old Testament prophets, notably Habakkuk and Nahum, and a remark-able and totally new, previously unsuspected text: *The War of the Sons of Light Against the Sons of Darkness.* Terming themselves the Sons of Light, the members of the sect describe the coming war, at the end of time, between themselves and, first, other Jews, and then Gentiles. The Sons of Darkness would be led by the Devil, here called Belial. This dualism, the struggle of good against evil, closely resembles the chief tenets of the ancient Persian religion, Zoroastrianism, which predated the Babylonian Captivity (587 B.C.) by about a century. The Jews could have encountered Zoroastrian ideas in Babylon after it was conquered by the Persians.

The English scholar, John M. Allegro, edited some of the most important of the scrolls and published his work early. In *The Dead Sea Scrolls and the Christian Myth* (Buffalo, N.Y.: Prometheus, 1984) it becomes apparent that the

> . . . difference between the Scrolls and the New Testament, in their understanding of the messianic office, underscores the fundamental struggle for supremacy that raged between the so-called heresies of early Christianity and their orthodox rival.
>
> We now know that the battle fought so ruthlessly by the Great Church [the early Catholic church], to suppress these heresies, was based on completely false assumptions about the historicity and purpose of the Gospels.

In the summer of 1989, the controversy over the nonpublication of many of the scrolls erupted into print. The *New York Times* reported, June 26, that historians and biblical scholars were accusing the small number of custodians of the Dead Sea Scrolls of obstructing research, and they demanded access to about 400 texts of unpublished material.

The editor of the *Biblical Archaeology Review,* Hershel Shanks, attacked both the Israeli Department of Antiquities, which obtained overall jurisdiction after the 1967 war, and the mostly Christian editors in charge of the scrolls for negotiating "a facade for further delay" that would extend past 1997. He spoke of a "conspiracy of silence and obstruction."

Dr. Robert Eisenman, professor of religious studies at California State University, Long Beach, said, "I don't think it's innocent, what's happening." The *Times* continued:

> He said some of the unpublished scrolls could be embarrassing if they contain information about the roots of Christianity at odds with Roman Catholic doctrine or about rabbinic Judaism that might be troubling to the Israeli government.

This was denied by Dr. Frank Moore Cross of the Harvard Divinity School. "There are too many of us of too many persuasions, Catholic and Protestant and Jewish, for there to be anything suppressed."

Later, the Associated Press reported, on July 1:

There also was early speculation linking Jesus to the Qumran community of ascetics called the Essenes, who produced the Dead Sea documents, but Strugnell [Dr. John Strugnell, editor-in-chief, and Harvard professor of Christian origins] said this has "virtually been dropped."

However, Jesus' movement and the Essenes were contemporary, he noted. "The two groups lived in the same century and there must have been some contact, but it is no closer than that," he said.

Concerning complaints about a still unpublished scroll letter from the Qumran community leader, the Teacher of Righteousness, to Jerusalem's high priest, Strugnell said it should be out by year's end. "That's a top priority," he said.

The high priest, whose leadership the Qumran community had rejected, was the same one that pushed for the elimination of Jesus.

A Jewish scholar later defended in the *Times* the publishing records of the Jewish editors and also defended the controversial John Allegro, who he said was hounded until his death by attempts to discredit him for his theories about early Christianity.

Interesting early books about the scrolls include: Millar Burrows' *The Dead Sea Scrolls* (1955) and *More Light on the Dead Sea Scrolls* (1958), both published by Viking, New York, and Edmund Wilson's *The Dead Sea Scrolls, 1947-1969* (New York: Oxford University Press, 1969). The scrolls themselves have been published in R. De Vaux and J. T. Milik, *Discoveries in the Judean Desert,* 7 vols. (New York: Oxford University Press, 1955-1982).

DEATH. There is a tendency to think that death—most specifically death imposed by others—is the greatest of evils. It is often assumed, for example, that the death penalty is the worst of punishments. But this cannot possibly be the case. This is proved by thousands of tragic instances in which people trapped in burning buildings and faced with the possibility of being painfully, though not necessarily fatally, burned leap to their deaths.

There are equally tragic cases of people so gravely and painfully injured that they have pleaded with bystanders to put them out of their misery by a bullet or sword. It is clear, then, that unendurable physical pain is far more abhorrent to most individuals than the inevitable cessation of their lives.

Absolutely nothing in the universe just happens, without cause. As for the process described by the word *decay,* it involves an essentially simple function of bacterial attack on living matter. Small organisms themselves survive by devouring, digesting, and eliminating even smaller fragments of plants and animals. This is simply nature's way and, for those who believe that the laws and function of nature were established by a conscious God, it is also God's way.

We would all be in an unfortunate predicament indeed if decay suddenly stopped, because then the millions of creatures, large and small, that die every minute on our planet would simply lie where they fell and in a very short time the surface of the earth would be littered with corpses, not to mention plant forms. This is all clear enough to be grasped by a five-year-old. It would never be a subject for controversy were it not for the first chapters of GENESIS in which it is implied that *decay was not part of God's original plan for the universe,* was not a natural process but only came about because of the sin of disobedience.

One cannot, of course, be disobedient in the abstract. Disobedience must take a specific form. In the Genesis story it takes the form of so simple an act as a woman eating a piece of fruit. Although we are nowhere told that ADAM AND EVE had ever, before the moment of their disobedience, used their mouths for ingesting liquid or food, a peculiar physical-medical question immediately presents itself: How did the wondrous digestive processes of their intestinal tracts function in the absence of decay?

To save the more incredulous readers discomfort, it must be stressed that every point I am going through in this particular exposition is utterly nonsensical. The problem does not exist—and never could have existed. It exists simply as a trivial puzzle produced by nothing more than the rigid insistence, by an exceedingly small minority of the earth's population now, that it is sinful to view such Old Testament accounts as Genesis merely as allegories, myths, or morality stories.

The traditional argument that neither pain nor death would have existed except as a direct result of Adam and Eve eating a bit of fruit against divine orders is precisely the sort of opinion anyone would instantly recognize as absurd if it were first encountered in the oral traditions of some Stone Age tribe.

Bertrand Russell observes:

> The world, we are told, was created by a God who is both good and omnipotent. Before He created the world He foresaw all the pain and misery that it would contain; He is therefore responsible for all of it. It is useless to argue that the pain in the world is due to sin. In the first place, this is not true; it is not sin that causes rivers to overflow their banks or volcanoes to erupt. But even if it were true, it would make no difference. If I were going to beget a child knowing that the child was going to be a homicidal maniac, I should be responsible for his crimes. If God knew in advance the sins of which man would

be guilty, He was clearly responsible for all the consequences of those sins when He decided to create man. *The usual Christian argument is that the suffering in the world is a purification for sin and is therefore a good thing. This argument is, of course, only a rationalization of sadism;* but in any case it is a very poor argument. I would invite any Christian to accompany me to the children's ward of a hospital, to watch the suffering that is there being endured, and then to persist in the assertion that those children are so morally abandoned as to deserve what they are suffering. In order to bring himself to say this, a man must destroy in himself all feelings of mercy and compassion. He must, in short, make himself as cruel as the God in whom he believes. No man who believes that all is for the best in this suffering world can keep his ethical values unimpaired, since he will always have to find excuses for pain and misery. (IA)

Let the reader ask himself and—more importantly—answer himself as regards the question: What would now be the physical condition of all living creatures if, for the past several million years, there had been no such thing as death? This means that if a boat foundered at sea and all of its passengers and crew were plunged into the waters, the individual bodies would nevertheless not die, even if none of them had the slightest knowledge of how to swim. And, should this tragedy occur in shark-infested waters, the individuals would nevertheless not die even though in hideous pain from being torn to shreds by sharks.

It also inescapably follows that in the tragically high number of burn cases the patients would never be released from their horrible suffering by the blessed anesthesia of death, no matter how piteously they longed for extinction. It also means that in the cases of persons who accidentally walk off cliffs or fall from other high places, the cases of those in airplanes dashed against mountainsides, indeed in any of the thousand and one daily physical tragedies, death would not occur.

It is not necessary to paint other fantasies to dramatize the total absurdity of the view of both the Epistle to the Romans and the book of Genesis concerning the origin of death. As not only every scientist but every child knows, death is the result of perfectly natural processes. Most people who have reached the age of 80 or 90 are quite prepared to accept it. Countless thousands, of all ages, consciously choose it over life every year because the conditions of their existence are too painful or otherwise intolerable. Tell the average infirm hundred-year-old man that he will go on living for all eternity and, if we assume that he accepts the news as true, one can imagine his dismay.

If it is argued that all humankind dies because of one human sinner—

which is absurd enough—it would also follow that animals die because some early animal—perhaps the serpent—sinned. This, too, is preposterous.

By the way, has any Christian fundamentalist mathematician ever computed the number of people who would now be trying to sustain themselves on planet earth if no human had ever died since the beginning of men and women's life here?

In some places the planet cannot sustain the numbers of humans who live on it at the moment. Famines occur. It might therefore be necessary to argue that such factors as lack of adequate food, though troublesome in the world we know, would somehow miraculously occasion no trouble at all in a world where humans could not possibly die simply because God had so decided. Perhaps we would all be very hungry, emaciated, and too weak to stand but nevertheless we would never die.

I am reminded of the old joke in which a resident of a small, backward community in Florida is explaining to a city fellow how alligators reproduce.

"The mother alligator," he says, "gives birth to dozens and dozens of little critters in a single year. But you know something? If she gets hungry, that mother alligator may actually eat most of her own offspring."

"How horrible," the visitor says.

"Horrible, hell," the old Floridian answers. "If she didn't, you'd be up to your armpits in alligators."

Again, I am not being facetious. The joke makes an important and clearly relevant point. If we lived on a planet where no plant life ever died, it would shortly become close to impossible to erect any sizable building except in desert or snowbound areas.

The same would apply to the uncountable billions of insects on our planet. It's appealing to envision a lion lying down with a lamb, but considerably less attractive to picture millions of black widow spiders, scorpions, and other such indestructible creatures lying down in your bed or mine. (See also LIFE.)

DEUTERONOMIST, THE. One element in the first part of the Old Testament is known by scholars as D. According to the *Encyclopedia Britannica:*

> The Deuteronomist, or D., has a distinctive hortatory style and vocabulary, calling for Israel's conformity with YHWH's covenant laws and stressing [his] election of Israel as his special people . . .

In addition to Deuteronomy, the D author or his "school" is probably also responsible for JOSHUA, JUDGES, I and II Samuel, and I and II KINGS.

(See also ELOHIST; PRIESTLY CODE, THE; and YAHWIST, designations given to three other strands or postulated authors of the Old Testament.)

DEUTERONOMY. Though *deuter* means *second,* this is the fifth book of the PENTATEUCH. It was probably written by a different author(s) from the ones who wrote GENESIS, EXODUS, Leviticus, and Numbers.

Some scholars have advanced the theory that it is the book of Deuteronomy that is referred to in II Kings, Chapter 22, which reports that during the process of repairing the Temple, a high priest named Hilkiah discovered "the book of the Law." (But do we know that such a priest or such a discovery ever took place?) We are not told why, if Deuteronomy was divinely inspired, as Christians insist, the Lord had permitted it to be lost for an extended period of time, nor do we know when the lost book was originally written or in what way it happened to be rediscovered. No matter how many Christians and Jews still believe that MOSES was the author of Deuteronomy, scholars assert that he was not.

To the reader who will be coming afresh to this sort of material, a word of warning. There is a strange, and in my view, essentially dishonest manner of writing about the countless errors that one finds throughout the Bible. For some reason, many critics simply will not use a word such as *falsehood* in describing such errata. A good example of this needlessly delicate language is the following comment by William Neil in the *Harper's Bible Commentary:*

> Allowance in this rather highly coloured description of Israel's "glorious" past must also be made for *the vivid imagination of the recorder.* As in the *pious exaggeration* of the size of Israel's "army" which we have already encountered in the book of *Numbers . . . ,* so also we may *take with some reservations the reference to wholesale extermination of hostile forces* here and elsewhere in the early books of the Bible. No doubt battles were fought and on both sides men were killed. On occasion, too, ruthless massacres were carried out, common in the ancient New East as sacrifices to a conquering deity . . . but we find most of these early enemies of Israel still plaguing them long after they are supposed to have been annihilated. (IA)

Chapter 2. A typical example of the sort of bloody massacre referred to by Neil is the following:

> 32. Then Sihon came out against us, he and all his people, to fight at Jahaz.

33. And the Lord our God delivered him before us; and we smote him, and his sons, and all his people.

34. And we took all his cities at that time, and utterly destroyed the men, and the women, and the little ones, of every city, we left none to remain:

The reader must choose between two uncomfortable alternatives. Either the people of God were sadistic terrorists or the authors of such reports were not telling the truth. But why they would want to brag about such mass murder is incomprehensible to us. Germans do not brag about the Holocaust.

Chapter 12. It is important to note that frequently in the Old Testament what appears to be the reason for a particular instruction is, in fact, not a reason at all and indeed may well be factually incorrect or impossible. An instance of such nonreason is found in the following:

23. Only be sure that thou eat not the blood: for the blood is the life; and thou mayest not eat the life with the flesh.

First of all, it is not physiologically accurate to equate blood with life. That blood sustains life is a matter of common knowledge; but air, water, and food are equally important to sustaining life, and yet may not be described correctly as life itself. But even if there were some sense in which it could be said that blood and life were the same thing, there would still be no physical reason why one could not absorb into one's own body the blood of an animal. We may observe, of course, that precisely this human ingestion and absorption of animal blood happens in hundreds of millions of cases around the planet every day, with no physical or moral ill effects whatsoever. The commandment serves, of course, as the explanation of why Orthodox Jews will eat only those meats which are considered *kosher,* meaning that the slaughtered animal has had most of its blood removed. It is important to perceive that it is only most, *and by no means all,* of the blood that has been removed by the kosherizing process.

Were even the most Orthodox Jews to adhere strictly to the commandment against ingesting blood, they would, of course, refuse the great medical benefit of transfusions, since taking human blood ought to be a much more serious matter than ingesting animal blood.

Chapter 20. One of the many odd things about the Bible is that Christians and Jews generally perceive its words, phrases, sentences, and chapters through a peculiar haze so that messages which would be readily understood if encountered in another book are, when read in a scriptural context, rarely brought sensibly into focus.

Consider, for example, the verses of Deuteronomy below. What they describe, in perfectly simple terms, is a massive atrocity. This fact must be grasped, as it would be if we heard it on the evening news. The slaughter of innocent civilians—according to all the world's moral theologians, Christians and Jews among them—is a matter of the most profound moral significance. Keep that one point in mind as you read.

16. But of the cities of these people, which the Lord thy God doth give thee for an inheritance, *thou shalt save alive nothing that breatheth:*

17. But thou shalt *utterly destroy them;* namely, the Hittites, and the Amorites, the Canaanites, and the Perizzites, the Hivites, and the Jebusites; as the Lord God hath *commanded thee* (that the Godites may have their land). (IA)

Chapter 21. Verses 18-21 are direct and forthright as to the proper method of dealing with the troublesome problem of juvenile delinquency. Since the Old Testament was written by a primitive people (I say *primitive* since there is no reason to assume that the ancient Hebrews were any more advanced than their neighbors), we are by now no longer surprised to observe yet another instance of sadistic barbarity.

18. If a man has a stubborn and rebellious son, . . .

19. Then shall his father and his mother lay hold on him, and bring him out unto the elders of his city, and unto the gate of his place;

20. Then they shall say unto the elders of his city, "This our son is stubborn and rebellious, he will not obey our voice; he is a glutton, and a drunkard.

21. *And all the men of his city shall stone him with stones, that he die.* So shalt thou put evil away from among you; and all Israel shall hear, and fear. (IA)

The next time the reader takes part in a public discussion at his or her church, school, or club about how to deal with rebellious teenagers, let him announce that the Bible insists that stoning is the answer and see what degree of concurrence he gets. Needless to say, no one—Jew or Gentile—any longer pays the slightest attention to such absurdities, although by what right Christians or Jews can dismiss some God-given commandments while insisting on others is by no means clear.

Chapter 23. This chapter leads off with one of the worst insults to God imaginable in that it attributes to him a truly stupid commandment. If a man suffers an injury to his testicles or, worse, has his penis cut off, he "shall not enter into the congregation of the Lord."

There are, of course, no statistics concerning what percentage of the male population of ancient Israel suffered castration, but it is no doubt safe to say that even in such bloodthirsty times very few men were abused in this specific way and lived. The idea that Almighty God would create a special commandment for such a minute portion of the population—either of a given tribe or the entire human race—hardly requires comment.

> 2. A bastard shall not enter into the congregation of the Lord;
> even to his tenth generation shall he not enter into the congregation
> of the Lord.

The preceding verse is, if not unique, at least moderately unusual in that it attributes an asinine statement to a God who is, by definition, incapable of any but the most sublime thoughts. There is a much wiser observation made in modern times, by a mere human: "There are no illegitimate children, only illegitimate parents." Since it is obvious that a child cannot possibly be responsible for the actions of the parents, it is moral nonsense to talk about punishing a child for such offenses.

In Verse 13 we are asked seriously to believe that God is reduced to instructing man as to the proper disposal of his own fecal wastes outside a military camp.

> 13. And thou shalt have a paddle upon thy weapon. And it shall
> be when thou wilt have a bowel movement outside the camp, thou
> shalt dig therewith and shalt turn back and cover that which cometh
> from thee.

The next verse is more nonsense; the reason for covering excrement is that God personally "walks" in the midst of the military camp.

Verse 20 teaches the shameful doctrine that it is perfectly all right to commit usury as long as the victim is a stranger but that one ought not to lend with interest to members of one's own faith. Sadly, this is one passage and practice that earned the Jews such a poor reputation in medieval Europe and that still haunts them today, though it is referred to chiefly by anti-Semites since everyone lends with interest at present.

Chapter 24. The first verse is clear-cut, forthright, and unmistakable as regards God's attitude toward divorce.

> 1. When a man hath taken a wife, and married her, and it come
> to pass that she find no favour in his eyes, because he hath found

some uncleanness in her: then let him write her a bill of divorcement, and give it in her hand, and send her out of his house.

Simple enough. No nonsense about alimony, child support, or the division of property. Perhaps, however, the always-to-be-unknown author of this passage was seized by a momentary pang of guilt about the poor woman for he next writes:

2. And when she is departed out of his house, she may go and be another man's wife.

But note the interesting plot twist of the next verses.

3. And if the latter husband hate her, and write her a bill of divorcement, and giveth it in her hand, and sendeth her out of his house; or if the latter husband die, which took her to be his wife,
4. Her former husband, which sent her away, may not take her again to be his wife, after that *she is defiled; for that is abomination before the Lord: and thou shalt not cause the land to sin, which the Lord thy God giveth thee for an inheritance.* (IA)

Chapter 25. This chapter is infamous for suggesting, in Verses 11 and 12, that God issued commandments that are in reality both disgusting and the height of stupidity. The situation is depicted as one in which two men are engaged in physical combat and the wife of one, in attempting to come to her husband's aid (certainly a praiseworthy act), grabs the other man by his penis and testicles. She shall be formally punished by having her hand sliced off with a sword, whether on the spot or by due legal process is not made clear. Could Jerry Falwell, Pat Robertson, Oral Roberts and Jimmy Swaggart convene, some Sunday morning, to enlighten their vast television audiences about the degree of wisdom in such an allegedly divine commandment?

I can assure the reader, on nothing more than my own modest authority, that (1) God never wrote, or caused to be written, anything so absurd, and that (2) any present-day theologian or clergyman who asserts that he did so is either a moral ignoramus or shockingly deluded and insensitive.

The farther one reads in Deuteronomy the more one is astonished by the presumption of the Judaic and Christian faiths. For more than 20 centuries adherents have insisted the book is divinely inspired. This chapter also specifies:

- That if two men contend against each other legally, the one judged to be most at fault shall be beaten precisely 40 times with a whip (vss. 1-3). Is this done today?
- That oxen ought not to have to wear muzzles while treading corn (v. 4). This was written to assert that the ox has the right to eat as a reward for its labor.
- That a man is *obliged* to have sexual relations with his brother's childless widow (v. 5).

Chapter 26. I am indebted to Paul Winchell, comedian and puppetmaster, for drawing to my attention the fact that in Verse 5 the Lord is quoted as stating that the Israelites are descended from the Arameans, who dwelt mainly in Syria. Winchell asks in his interesting book, *God 2000—Religion Without the Bible:* "Will that [news] bring peace to the Middle East?"

Chapter 28. This chapter is one of the most unusual and bizarre not only in the Bible but in all literature, in that it appears so sadistic. At first the people are told that if they observe *all* the Lord's commandments, including the nonsensical ones we have noted, things will go remarkably well for them. They will, in fact, be set "on high above all nations of the earth," and numerous specific blessings shall be enjoyed. Note the change of mood, however:

> 15. But it shall come to pass, if thou wilt not hearken unto the voice of the Lord, thy God . . . that all these curses shall come upon thee and overtake thee.

The following verses, up to number 68, list, with a sort of fiendish glee, various disgusting curses that will *surely* follow abandonment or neglect of the Lord's commandments.

Now, it might be argued, in defense of the Scriptures, that a curse is only a threat, however horrible, and therefore to be distinguished from the experiential reality of the events described. No scholar, however, would advance such an argument in the present context for the following reasons: (1) the threatener, the curser, is God himself, and (2) events which must automatically trigger the enactment of the curse have not only indeed transpired, which is obvious enough, but have taken place in countless millions of instances. What are some of God's curses?

> 16. Cursed shalt thou be in the city, and cursed thou shalt be in the field.
> 17. Cursed shall be thy basket and thy store.

18. Cursed shall be the fruit of thy body, and the fruit of thy
land, the increase of thy kine, and the flocks of thy sheep.

Verses 20, 21, and 22 not only threaten death, but death that will come
quickly. Why, after such a seemingly ultimate punishment, the Lord then
proceeds to threaten pestilence, consumption, fever, inflammation, fiery heat,
drought, blasting (whatever that is) and mildew only God could explain,
and he is not available for consultation on such questions.

It would appear that the author was getting such satisfaction out of
piling threat upon threat that he could not contain himself.

27. The Lord will smite thee with the boils of Egypt, and with
the ulcers, and with the scurvy, and with the itch, whereof thou canst
not be healed.
28. The Lord shall smite thee with madness and blindness, and
confusion of the mind; . . .

There is a particular fascination to Verse 36, which says that those
who do not hear the word of the Lord shall be given into the keeping
of another nation "*and there shalt thou serve other gods, wood and stone*"
(IA). What we have here is the remarkable spectacle of the God of the
Old Testament, who in countless instances denounces the worshiping of
rival deities as the gravest sort of sin, ordaining precisely that fate to any
sinful children of Israel.

Undoubtedly the most savage portion of this disgusting chapter—
perhaps the most barbaric in the entire Bible—is that which starts with
Verse 53.

53. And thou shalt eat the fruit of thine own body, the flesh of
thy sons and of thy daughters, which the Lord thy God hath given
thee, in the siege, and in the distress wherewith thine enemies shall
distress thee.

Now, in all civilized societies—and even in most that we ethnocentrics
do not consider as "civilized" as our own—cannibalism is regarded with
moral loathing. It is important to observe here that the Bible is not merely
talking about the act of cannibalism, horrible enough in itself. It is talking
about the fact that believers will absolutely, by the personal promise of
Almighty God, physically devour, obviously after personally killing, their
own sons and daughters. We are now entangled in such a web of savagery
and irrationality that the entire text has become an insult to even minimal

human intelligence.

Even if one wanted to be barbaric and declare that the Holocaust was God's punishment of the Jews for their abandonment of God's laws—thus implying that Hitler was God's instrument—we must note that the inhabitants of the concentration camps, although starving to death, never became cannibals. So far as is known, only in Uganda, when the tyrant Idi Amin ruled in the 1970s, has cannibalism occurred in an otherwise modern part of the world.

It may be objected that I have suggested that the Holocaust was God's punishment of the Jews. I believe nothing of the sort. What I am saying is that it seems peculiar that Orthodox Jews, who believe that every word of the PENTATEUCH is holy, can accept the notion that God punished them in biblical times and yet would find it intolerable were someone to suggest that he decided to do so beginning in 1934. I don't for a moment believe that anyone but Hitler and his henchmen persecuted the Jews, but then why would God have threatened to do so, so viciously, in ancient times?

Another disgusting moral low is reached with Verse 63, which says that God's personal attitude at the infliction of such calamitous sufferings shall not be sadness or regret but that he will *"rejoice . . . to destroy you."*

Is it really necessary to recall that among the many things we know are the following: (1) Humans are, in their more depraved state, capable of taking pleasure at the infliction of violent suffering, but (2) an ideal God is not. Is it any wonder that some religions have made the grave moral and tactical error of attempting conversions by the sword?

The last few chapters of Deuteronomy refer to the close of Moses' mission and his death in the land of Moab. Verse 10 of Chapter 34 states: "There arose not a prophet since in Israel like Moses." Considering the barbarous nonsense which it is claimed that Moses wrote, the house of Israel should be very grateful that prophets preaching such hatred, fear, and destruction were *not* seen again. (See also, COMMANDMENTS, TEN.)

DEVIL, THE. Whether the Devil exists or not, he provides a wonderfully effective service for one category of believers—those who, because of their unfortunate psychological makeup, appear to derive a good deal of satisfaction from feeling the emotions of hatred or guilt. Hatred misdirected can have destructive effects on the hater, as well as on the unfortunate object of his spite. If a man, let us say, hates his wife, his father, his employer, the very acidity of his venom can work against his own best interests. But there are certain tyrants and criminals whose conduct is so outrageous that they are quite properly objects of contempt.

In wartime, for example, entire populations—including those of Christian nations—are purposely stimulated to the most violent sort of hatred, as part of a formal, ongoing campaign. So haters feel perfectly justified when the despised target is indeed evil or perceived as such. What more suitable choice than the essential embodiment of evil, Satan? I'm sure the gentle of heart have moments of doubt as to whether any personage so vile could actually exist, but the naturally spiteful entertain no such questions.

Strangely enough, however, even naturally negative believers seem to feel chiefly fear of the Devil rather than hatred of him. This is decidedly odd, given that the same individuals experience no difficulty at all in hating communists, Jews, Catholics, blacks, Muslims, or other groups of whom they disapprove. If we were rational about our emotions (itself a laughable expectation), we would therefore hate the Devil most of all and various evil humans somewhat less.

Another service the Devil provides—whether he exists or not—concerns what I call the cop-out factor. In the late 1980s we saw public evidence of this when such popular fundamentalist clergymen as Jim Bakker and Jimmy Swaggart asserted, as regards their sexual misbehavior, that the Devil made them do it.

Even as a young Catholic, when I was obliged to believe in the Devil, I was never able to figure out why he needed to exist at all, for I had come to realize that humans were more than capable of seriously sinful behavior, so much so that they needed no encouragement from malign spirits.

Those who believe in the Devil also assume that he has been available, at all times, in all places, to tempt everyone who has ever lived. At the present moment, there are over five billion people on the planet earth. For all of them to be temptable by the evil one, it must follow that he can be present in over five billion different locations at once and carry on as many monologues or dialogues at the same time. Concerning which, one can say only that it is a remarkable assumption. That a God would have such power is simply a given, but there are supposed to be few if any godlike powers that are shared.

One of the most striking features of religious experience in the past quarter of a century has been the comeback of the Devil, or—as materialists might prefer—belief in the Devil. A number of popular books and motion pictures have presented as factual, stories which cannot be accommodated within the bounds of physical science.

Another remarkable factor of the controversy is that, although ours is a time in which nothing seems to be heard of miracles—except for certain cures of diseases, which may or may not be scientifically explainable— there are no reports concerning benign spiritual entities, but many of devils.

That portion of my brain out of which emanate humorous concepts perceives something bitter and ironic but nevertheless amusing about this. It is almost as if we are being told that though God is dead, the Devil seems more alive than ever.

One aspect found in modern reports of demonic possession seems to make no sense: the fact that those described as actually occupied and controlled by either the Devil or one of his evil servants are themselves decent and law-abiding. It would be understandable if those controlled by devils were themselves notoriously evil, depraved, or vicious individuals. Such moral monsters, one assumes, might even welcome an association with the very prince of evil. But what sense does it make that innocent children or other good people are said to be possessed?

There is also something inherently stupid in the exercise of actual or alleged demonic power in instances we have heard described. It would be perfectly understandable if, as a result of having been invaded by malign spirits, one went about the world doing evil—lying, stealing, raping, murdering. But such forms of behavior are never encountered in tales of possession. Instead, we are told that bodies hover in the air, spit up something that looks like pea soup as they speak with strange voices, or that they exhibit superhuman strength. If such reports are true, then we might derive considerable comfort in knowing that the Devil is stupid and not really so evil after all, since he apparently prefers to perform Halloween pranks rather than encourage evil deeds.

It is difficult to say which camp—the Christian or the skeptical materialist—is the more disturbed by reports of diabolical activity. That both are dismayed is clear enough: Christians because they accept the reports and are terrified by what seems to be the ascendancy of the powers of darkness, and rationalists because they either disbelieve the reports or else think it possible that at least a small percentage of them may concern phenomena responsibly observed and therefore especially perplexing.

Anthropologists working in the Andes tell us that, although the Quechua-speaking peoples believed in malignant spirits before the Spanish arrived, it was the Catholic clergy who introduced the idea of a totally evil being, Satan, and his devotees, witches, along with the Inquisition, one of the cruelest episodes in Christian history. (See also HELL.)

DISCIPLES, TWELVE. See Apostles, The.

E

EDEN, GARDEN OF, the legendary spot of perfection God is said, in Genesis 2:8, to have established as a home for the newly created ADAM AND EVE.

> 8. And the Lord God planted a garden in Eden, in the east; and there he put the man whom he had formed.
>
> 9. And out of the ground the Lord God made to grow every tree that is pleasant to the sight and good for food, the tree of life also in the midst of the garden, and the tree of the knowledge of good and evil.
>
> 10. A river flowed out of Eden to water the garden, and there it divided and became four rivers. . . .
>
> 14. And the name of the third river is Hiddekel, which flows east of Assyria.
>
> 15. The Lord God took the man and put him in the garden of Eden to till it and keep it.

There was trouble, however, in such a paradise.

> 16. And the Lord God commanded the man, saying, "You may freely eat of every tree of the garden;
>
> 17. but the tree of the knowledge of good and evil you shall not eat, for in the day that you eat of it you shall die."

Everyone, of course, knows what happened, and has heard of the elaborate theological edifice erected upon Adam and Eve's disobedience. See FALL, THE; ORIGINAL SIN.

It is obvious to intelligent readers that the Adam and Eve story falls into a common category called creation myth. All peoples have such myths, and some elements are similar. The idea of a Garden of Eden could represent a kind of pleasant memory, enshrined in legend, of a fertile area from which the Semitic tribes (some of whom became Israelites) emigrated long ages before they began to write down anything of their actual "history."

The first clues to the location of Eden are "in the east" in Verse 8 and "east of Assyria" in Verse 14; a third identifies the locale as being near the Euphrates River. Obviously the author or authors of GENESIS had no knowledge of the entire earth, so they spoke only of areas the Israelites had presumably traversed or heard of.

It has become common for people who study prehistory and myth, including some anthropologists, to believe that there may be a kernel of truth in important myths. This is an assumption also made about stories in the Old Testament—and not necessarily by people trying to prove their historical truth.

In a fascinating article in *The Smithsonian,* Dora Jane Hamblin tells about the work of archaeologist Juris Zarins, who has tried to pinpoint the location of the Garden and believes he has found it. He quite properly rejects many older theories that have named Atlantis, Mongolia, India, Ethiopia, and Turkey as its setting. It seems obvious, at least if the text of the Bible is reliable, that it lay in or near Mesopotamia.

> . . . Dr. Zarins, who has spent seven years working out his own hypothesis, believes that the Garden of Eden lies presently under the waters of the Persian Gulf, and he further believes that the story of Adam and Eve in—and especially *out*—of the Garden is a highly condensed and evocative account of perhaps the greatest revolution that ever shook mankind: the shift from hunting-gathering to agriculture.

Zarins worked from recent geological, hydrologic, and linguistic studies and from LANDSAT space images. The SUMERIANS had a myth of a beautiful land they called Dilmun, which was absorbed by the Akkadians and Babylonians. The Sumerians also had a word, *eden* or *edin,* which meant "fertile plain."

Dr. Zarins points to a crucial date, 30,000 B.C., at a time when the Ice Age caused the sea levels to fall by 400 feet so that what is now the Persian Gulf was dry land. It was watered by the Tigris and Euphrates Rivers and two now-extinct rivers in Saudi Arabia.

> It seems reasonable that technologically primitive but modern Man, in his endless search for food, would have located the considerable natural paradise that presented itself in the area where the Gulf now lies.

It was later, however, in about 6000 B.C., during a wet spell after a long arid time, that the period known as the Neolithic Wet Phase saw rains restore a belt of green in the Saudi Peninsula and southwestern Iran. Zarins offers as proof of intense human activity in this now-arid region animal bones and thousands of worked stone tools. It was in this area that hunters and gatherers encountered tribes that had already developed the art of agriculture and pottery making.

Since the Sumerian civilization that eventually developed from these early agriculturists preceded by more than several millennia the Israelite towns that were said by the Bible to have been built in Canaan, once again we find a common pattern: the Hebrew Scripture incorporates a borrowing from an older civilization. That in itself is perfectly acceptable, for borrowings and outside influences are the stuff of the history of civilization. But it plays havoc with the notion that there was a unique Creation by God at one moment in the history of the earth and that he always and continually has favored the specific people—the Jews—who much later wrote the story down in the form in which Western civilization has received it.

Had Christianity been the *direct* inheritor of the Sumerian-Akkadian-Babylonian tradition instead of indirectly through the medium and traditions of the Old Testament, there would never have grown up that peculiar preoccupation with ancient Jewish "history" to the exclusion of all else, as though it were the only civilized tradition in the ancient world. Nothing could be further from the truth.

A common misconception about the Garden story is that it was an apple that Eve and Adam ate. But an apple is nowhere mentioned in Genesis; it is only called a fruit. Isaac Asimov has explained that apples were not common in the Middle East and "may not even have grown in ancient Palestine." Other fruits, such as the apricot or the pomegranate, have been suggested, although of all the "fruitless" areas of scriptural research that have ever been launched, this is perhaps the most pointless.

The significant element of the Garden of Eden story, of course, has nothing to do with the proper identification of the fruit but with the fact that the eating of it, according to the narrator, suddenly made Adam and Eve able to distinguish good from evil, concerning which one can only marvel at the stupidity of any human being actually incapable of making such a distinction.

The tree of life and the duality of good and evil are concepts found in myths and earliest written records of many diverse peoples throughout the world.

EGYPT. The dramatically massive and world-famous pyramids of Cheops, Cephren, and Mycerinos were seven or eight centuries old by the time Abraham is supposed to have lived. Located in northern Egypt, they would certainly have come to the attention, even if only by report, of any people long subjugated and held in bondage by Egyptian rulers. The fact that the allegedly historical documents of the Old Testament make no reference to the pyramids during the ABRAHAM, JOSEPH, and MOSES periods suggests that the unknown authors of GENESIS and EXODUS had no first-hand knowledge of Egypt.

ELOHIST, THE. According to the documentary hypothesis of biblical authorship, the Elohist (E) is one of the three hypothetical strands found in GENESIS, EXODUS, and Numbers. This theory destroys the long-held tradition in Jewish and Christian teaching that MOSES authored these books, as well as Leviticus and DEUTERONOMY in the Pentateuch. The name derives from passages that use the Hebrew common noun for *god,* Elohim. The Elohist and the Yahwist (J) portions of these Old Testament books are thought to be the oldest sources of stories and legends in the Bible. The reader should understand however, that there is no existing tablet or manuscript or any concrete document that can be ascribed to "the Elohist." (See also DEUTERONOMIST, THE; PRIESTLY CODE, THE; YAHWIST, THE.)

ENUMA ELISH AND GILGAMESH. A number of scholars have commented on the resemblances between the celebrated Babylonian poem *Enuma Elish* ("when on high") and early portions of GENESIS. Since Genesis was written *after Enuma Elish,* it is difficult, if not impossible, any longer to maintain the simplistic traditional view that Genesis was directly inspired by God. To escape the logical difficulty, it is at least theoretically possible to argue that God simply inspired the unknown authors of Genesis to borrow certain components from a so-called pagan poem to a nonexistent rival god. However, it seems highly unlikely that an all-virtuous deity could have any possible connection with what would then have been an instance of plagiarism, let alone want to be modeled on a "pagan" god.

Concerning the obvious borrowing of the story of the deluge from another more ancient Babylonian document called *Gilgamesh* (the name of its leading character), even a scholarly professor of Sacred Scripture, Georges Auzou, is reduced to a reference to understanding "the way in which a tradition and a Babylonian document were 'reused' by the writers of Israel" (*The Formation of the Bible*). (See also FLOOD, THE.)

For understandable reasons Catholic theologians could hardly use a word like *plagiarism,* but the reader should understand nevertheless that, composers of ancient texts, and even Shakespeare, borrowed freely, although they did not write with any modern notion of plagiarism, with its pejorative meaning.

ESAU, the older twin son of ISAAC and Rebekah, brother of JACOB. He was born red and hairy, and became a skillful hunter, therefore the favorite of his father because the old fellow had a taste for wild meat. But as in the CAIN and ABEL story, the meddlesome Lord cannot permit *both* brothers to find favor with their parents. Esau commits the terrible "crimes" of (1) selling his birthright because he is hungry for bread and lentils, and (2) marrying two Hittite women, who "made life bitter for Isaac and Rebekah." (Gen. 34:35)

Rebekah is unhappy at Isaac's preference for Esau, and because of that, as well as the trouble with her daughters-in-law, she conspires with Jacob in one of the many shocking instances of injustice in the Bible. Esau begins to hate his brother and threatens to kill him. Does the Lord intervene on the side of the misused Esau? Of course not, but no explanation is given. Esau certainly got a raw deal.

Esau is also called Edom, so we are led to assume that he is the eponymous father of the Edomites, a neighboring tribe who lived east of the Jordan River when MOSES and the twelve Israelite tribes supposedly approached CANAAN. The Edomites were referred to as enemies of the Hebrews.

ESTHER. The book of Esther is, in the opinion of certain scholars, an unusual type of book to include in the Old Testament canon. Christians give it scant attention and, when it is addressed by Christian scholars, their comments seem invariably tinged with embarrassment. John Dart, religion editor of the *Los Angeles Times,* has referred to Esther as "the most embarrassing book of the Bible."

And it is, after the New Testament's Revelation, which one scholar said was written by a "cosmic terrorist." The following are some of the factors accounting for the unease with which Jewish and Christian scholars discuss the book:

- Esther contains no mention of the name of God.
- Specifically religious content is almost entirely absent.
- The book relates that the Jewish population of Persia, during the reign of Ahasuerus (identified as either Xerxes I, 486-465 B.C., or his grandson

125

Artaxerxes) was granted the royal privilege of slaughtering their enemies to the last man, woman, and child. It is not known whether Queen Esther is a real personage, although the description of the royal palace at Susa (Shushan) seems accurate, and the Muslims of Iran preserve a famous site at Hamadan said to be Queen Esther's Tomb.

• Modern Bible scholars were impressed, though hardly surprised, by the fact that when the DEAD SEA SCROLLS were discovered the book of Esther was the only Old Testament text not found. This is due to the fact either that Esther had not been written by the time the Scrolls were completed and hidden or that its inclusion in the Hebrew Scripture (and the celebration of the Jewish holiday of Purim) were both strongly opposed up to the third century A.D.

Another awkward fact is that there are no references to Esther in the New Testament. If Jesus had any awareness of this book, he seems never to have spoken from such knowledge. Martin Luther was so displeased by his study of Esther that he said he wished it did not exist.

No one has the slightest idea who wrote the book of Esther, although this in itself is not particularly weighty, considering that there is little knowledge concerning the specific authors of most of the Bible. Robert Gordis, emeritus professor at New York's Jewish Theological Seminary, has suggested that the author was Jewish but that, for unclear reasons, he wrote as if he were an official chronicler of the Persian royal court. It is for this reason, Gordis suggests, that the author "makes no reference to the God of Israel, to the practices and beliefs of Judaism, to the national history of the Jewish people, or to its ethnic concerns except, of course, for their resistance to the proposed genocide planned by Haman."

As regards the atrocious and troubling license granted the Jews to annihilate their enemies, Gordis sees this not as factual history but as an instance of irony. The reader should know that most Jewish and Christian scholars differ with Gordis. The most common view is that the book of Esther is neither history nor moral homily, but simply a "historical novel," something like *Gone With the Wind,* in which real and imaginary characters are mixed in the interest of nothing more than good storytelling.

It is hardly surprising that there is no factual knowledge as to when Esther was written. An important character of the story, Mordecai—a descendent of Jair, Shimei, and Kish, the latter of whom was taken into Babylonian captivity (2:5, 6)—is referred to as "the Jew." His father Kish is said to have left Jerusalem with King Jeconiah (Jehoiachin) at its fall, in 597 B.C. Hence, we may assume that the unknown author lived after that time. One clue suggesting that the book of Esther was written closer to the time of Christ is that the apocryphal book Ecclesiasticus, or Sirach, believed to have been written about 180 B.C., includes a long list of Israelite heroes and heroines but does not mention either Mordecai or Esther.

The omission of the name of God from the romance of Esther is decidedly more than a point of passing interest. The omission, observes John L. McKenzie, S.J., "is so singular in the Hebrew Old Testament that it demands some explanation; but scholars are unable to assign a cause." The prayers and other references to God, added in the Greek translation, McKenzie speculates, "most probably are intended to render the book more acceptable as sacred." The reader may be shocked at this instance of deceptive editing "for a good cause."

If the book was intended as history, it cannot be accepted as such. "While Ahasuerus (Xerxes) is an historical character," McKenzie notes, "and the writer exhibits some knowledge of the city and palace of Susa and Persian life and customs, there are a number of improbabilities in the book which lead most modern scholars to consider it an historical romance . . ." Nothing like the story of Queen Vashti (Chapter 1) can be found in Persian records. Furthermore, a decree which actually permitted the Jews to kill all their enemies is most improbable, and would undoubtedly have left some trace in nonbiblical records.

As Jews do not have to be told, but as most Christians are unaware, the story of Esther—whether fact, myth, romantic novel, or fable—is commemorated in the Jewish feast of Purim. This feast itself, though it has charming and touching aspects, is one of the odder instances of Jewish observance, in that it involves the reading of the story of Esther and Mordecai to the accompaniment of laughter, stamping feet, good-natured booing—at the mention of Haman's name—the wearing of playful attire, and the baking and eating of little pastries, which are called *hamantaschen* or "Haman's ears." The *Encyclopedia Britannica* comments that Esther was probably included in the canon for the sole purpose of sanctioning the celebration of Purim.

The drama itself can hardly be said to be morally edifying. It relates that in the third year of his reign, the king of Persia gathered together leaders of his domain at Susa, his capital, and entertained them with a great feast. After a week of this, the king—somewhat drunk—instructed his aides to fetch his queen, Vashti, so that his visitors could enjoy her beauty. Although there might have been a thousand and one valid reasons for her majesty declining to accept the king's invitation to be publicly exhibited, Ahasuerus wasted no time in determining the reason for her refusal. Encouraged by his counselors, he decided to ban the unfortunate woman from his presence and take for himself someone worthier. Men being what they are, this led to a search for a young and beautiful replacement.

In the capital city at the time lived a wise man, "Mordecai, the Jew." His young cousin Hadassah, adopted as his daughter, was brought to the palace as part of the ongoing talent search. To no reader's surprise, she was the one selected to become queen of the Persian empire.

Mordecai himself was given a position at the court. One day he overheard two of the palace chamberlains plotting to assassinate the king. He asked Esther to warn the ruler, who ordered that the conspirators be seized and killed. Not long thereafter, the king appointed Haman as his chief minister and issued an order that all officials were to prostrate themselves before his new aide. Mordecai, for reasons unclear, refused to follow such an instruction. From this one affront, Haman proceeded immediately to despise the entire Jewish race. Furthermore, he spoke against the Jews to the king and suggested that they should not be tolerated (3:8). Since the ruler did nothing to frustrate Haman's evil intentions, the vizier drew up plans to have the Jews slaughtered and their possessions confiscated.

Mordecai asked his ward—now called by the Persian name Esther—to appeal to the king for justice for their people. The king then perceived Haman as evil and had him executed on the very gallows the vizier had erected for the execution of Mordecai.

Another fascinating plot twist introduced at this point is that inasmuch as the laws of Persia stipulated that no royal decree could ever be countermanded—even by a ruler who changed his mind—another decree would be issued permitting the Jews to defend themselves. Once armed and feeling that only the complete annihilation of their enemies was a suitable defense, they committed one more of the Old Testament's all too common mass slaughters.

I shall have no reason to speak irreverently of many inspiring portions of Scripture. Such passages, alas, constitute a small portion of the Bible. But others, it turns out, are so shameful, so morally loathsome that they deserve to be criticized, in the plainest possible language, so that readers who are uninformed will not fall into the error of assuming that all passages of Scripture are of equal merit, whether judged by the standards of literature, history, or moral education.

EVOLUTION. Just as it is absurd for the fundamentalists, who interpret the entire Bible literally, to deny the existence of evolution, given that the reality of that process is readily observable, it is equally erroneous to suggest that if evolution exists, the mere fact of its existence rules out the possibility that there is a God. In reality, there is no necessary connection or disconnection, between evolution and God. The majority of well-educated

Christians and other religionists believe, in fact, that evolution has been God's practical method of creating and developing all aspects of nature that are alive, which is to say, plants and animals. It is apparently only fundamentalists who are confused about this.

If we consider the history of the controversy on the question, we observe immediately that the present view of educated churchgoers is a fallback position, since the initial reaction of Christians, among other believers, was total hostility to the views of Charles Darwin and other early evolutionists. Nevertheless, it is reassuring that, as regards at least some controversies of long standing, common sense has in the end prevailed.

The better-informed evangelicals, fortunately, no longer tend to deny that evolution exists or has occurred, but they do continue to draw the line as regards one point. They say that evolution does, in fact, explain the very wide variety of forms that particular animals take. They recognize, for example, the obvious biological fact that there is simply not one creature known as the owl, the fox, the bear, the horse, etc., but that, within such sharply defined categories, there are many separate forms that such creatures take. They continue to deny, however, that the separate species evolved from more primitive forms. While there are specific questions that still may be responsibly debated, one fortunate result of recent chapters of the evolution controversy is that both sides are more sharply refining their arguments. (See also AGE OF THE EARTH AND THE UNIVERSE.)

EXODUS. Sir James Fraser and other scholars have shown that many stories in the Bible, chiefly those in the Old Testament, are not encountered there for the first time, but are also to be found in *older* religious literature, myth, and legend. Some people have had their faith in the divine authorship of such accounts greatly weakened upon learning that the stories were not original. But it would be easy to make the error of assuming that, if it can be demonstrated that one or another of the stories *is* original, the likelihood of its being true is therefore increased. This is by no means the case. If a given story is outlandish, then that fact carries its own weight.

The entire opening section of the book of Exodus, which recounts the escape of the Israelite tribes from EGYPT, is patently preposterous. This is not stated on the grounds that miracles cannot occur—perhaps they can and have—but rather that the details of the story, if separated and considered as fair-mindedly as possible, will strike many people as unlikely and certainly insulting to any modern conception of an all-wise, all-powerful, and all-loving God. (For comment on Chapters 2–14, see MOSES.)

Chapter 15. Moses and the people of Israel sing a triumphal song, praising the Lord for their deliverance from Egypt and the utter destruction of Pharaoh's army.

> 2. The Lord is my strength and my song, and he has become my salvation; this is my God, and I will praise him, my father's God, and I will exalt him.

In Verse 3, the Lord is called a "man of war"—a strange appellation for the Deity, but one which will increasingly seem appropriate for the God described in the Old Testament. Most often Yahweh will be depicted as a bully, who cares only for the fortunes of the Israelites, rather than the other 99+ percent of his children. Actually this "personage," far from being a universal God, is nothing but another of the hundreds of tribal deities that were worshiped throughout the Near East. Presumably, all of Israel's "enemies"—who just happened to be other people trying to survive and build their own civilizations in that part of the world when the Exodus is said to have occurred (about 1280 B.C.)—sang similar songs of praise and felt encouraged by *their* gods, who were termed "idols" by the Hebrews. One man's god was another man's idol in those days.

There is no evidence in Exodus that Moses, or the authors who much later wrote about him, conceived of a sole, universal Deity who watched over and cared for all people everywhere. Rather, in this song, Yahweh is just the opposite, loving only the "people of Israel" and helping them destroy anyone who gets in their way: Philistines, Edomites, Moabites, and Canaanites. Because so little of the literature of their contemporaries has survived (although much evidence of their cities, pottery, and gods has been excavated), we do not know if their gods were as xenophobic as Yahweh was.

In Chapter 16, the children of Israel are hungry, wandering in the Sinai desert, so the Lord provides a flock of quail and "a fine, flake-like thing, fine as hoarfrost on the ground." They call this manna. No scholar has ever been able to explain what manna is—or Moses either. He tells the people that it is "bread which the Lord has given you to eat." "It was like coriander seed, white, and the taste of it was like wafers made with honey." There was such a remarkably plentiful supply that we are told the Hebrews survived on manna for 40 years.

In Chapter 17, the people are thirsty after all that manna and demand that Moses produce water. Since "they are almost ready to stone" Moses, the Lord tells him to strike a rock with the rod that earlier parted the Nile waters. A spring appears. Later, in a battle with Amalek, just by holding up his arms Moses was able to win a victory for the Israelites.

(For Chapter 20 commentary, see COMMANDMENTS, TEN.)

Chapter 21. The next several commandments are such that to attribute the most extreme moral relativism to the deity is insulting. Study them carefully.

> 1. "Now these are the ordinances which you shall set before them.
> 2. When you buy a Hebrew slave he shall serve six years; and in the seventh he shall go out free, for nothing.
> 3. If he comes in single, he shall go out single; if he comes in married then his wife shall go out with him.
> 4. If his master gives him a wife and she bears him sons or daughters, *the wife and her children shall be her master's and he shall go out alone.*" (IA)

The passages clearly justify the vulgar and evil practice of slavery, which was common in those days. But one would have thought that the true God, thought to have produced the Commandments, could have stopped that barbarous practice then and there. However, Exodus does not criticize it, even when the slaves are themselves Hebrews. Note the cruelty of the "divine" commandment given in Verse 4 that, *if* a slave is *permitted* to marry and subsequently has children, he must leave them behind when he is given his freedom at the end of his six-year period of servitude. *So much for the Old Testament's concern for the sanctity of home and family.* Obviously, slaves were not considered fully human, even by the God who supposedly created them. No Christian or Jew today pays the slightest attention to such nonsense.

It is perfectly reasonable to wonder what Almighty God—or his human ghostwriters—might recommend in instances when a slave doesn't want freedom at the price of giving up his wife and children. The answer is immediately forthcoming:

> 5. "But if the slave plainly says, 'I love my master, my wife and my children; I will not go out free.'
> 6. Then his master shall bring him to God and he shall bring him to the door or the doorpost; *and his master shall bore his ear through with an awl, and he shall serve him for life.*" (IA)

I submit that this one passage of the Old Testament would be enough to cause a virtuous Jew or Christian to question seriously whether or not he had been deluded in his faith in the Scriptures. For here we see the Old Testament plainly asserting—in a context where no one dare mention the weasel words *allegory* or *folk-history*—that an entity asserted to be God *recommends the performing of a violent atrocity on a victim not only totally innocent of any crime, but "defiant" out of love of family.*

131

Let no mealy-mouthed theologian suggest that this vile passage is merely a now-embarrassing fragment testifying to the primitivism of the 13th century before Christ, for precisely these verses were used to "justify" the hideous tortures inflicted on African Americans when, in the 17th century, some revolted and tried to leave their cruel masters in the American colonies. The good Christians of that day used this very commandment of God to support their own sadism and did, in fact, drive nails and spikes through the ears of defenseless Negroes, whose only offense was to say that they were no longer willing to be slaves. Until after the Civil War there was no federal law that protected them from gross physical abuse.

> 22. "When men strive together, and hurt a woman with child, so that there is a miscarriage, . . .
> 23. If any harm follows then you shall give life for life, eye for eye, tooth for tooth, hand for hand, foot for foot, burn for burn, wound for wound, stripe for stripe."

It is, first of all, strange that the Lord would issue a special commandment applying to those cases, fortunately rare, when men struggling with each other accidentally bump into a pregnant woman so that she suffers a miscarriage and perhaps more serious injury or even death. (See ABORTION.) All those over the centuries who have quoted Exodus 21:23 as justifying their revengeful sadism seem not to have perceived that it applies only to the rare case described in Verse 22.

Some revenge-seekers, of course, have also quoted the 24th chapter of Leviticus, Verses 17-21, in which pound-for-pound revenge is urged. In a case where a man causes a disfigurement to someone else, Deuteronomy 19:21 goes farther and recommends against pity, flatly insisting that "it shall be life for life, eye for eye, tooth for tooth, hand for hand, foot for foot." Modern societies have generally dispensed with all these dreadful punishments, though not with torture, which is on the rise.

CAPITAL PUNISHMENT has become a big issue in the U.S. today. It is curious to note that far more people demand execution when black youths attack a white person than when whites pursue a black man to his death. All Western nations but the U.S. have abolished the death penalty, and find that this does not increase crime. Even in South Africa, the death penalty is on hold.

Chapter 22 is of interest chiefly because of the following verses:

> 18. "You shall not permit a sorceress (witch) to live.
> 19. Whoever lies with a beast shall be put to death.

20. Whoever sacrifices to any god, save to the Lord only, shall
be utterly destroyed."

Verse 18 led to the slaughter of thousands of defenseless people in
Europe and elsewhere during the past thousand years or so. In Salem,
Massachusetts, before the American Revolution, women accused of WITCH-
CRAFT were killed with the justification of this bloodthirsty verse of Scripture,
often without the establishment of guilt by evidence.

Verse 20 is of interest because it apparently justified the slaughter which
the ancient Israelites were accustomed to inflict on neighboring tribes, most
of whom quite naturally worshiped their own gods. This vile passage would,
of course, have "justified" the extermination of practically all the Greeks
and the Romans—and almost everyone else—in ancient times had the early
Hebrews had it in their power to inflict such punishment.

It must be understood that such passages not only permit or authorize
the executions referred to but they also explicitly *command* them. The
verse was also used later by Christians to justify European religious wars,
Crusades, and cruelty to non-Christian peoples everywhere.

In the Old Testament, a variety of sins is referred to. One of these
passages, as every schoolchild knows, is "Thou shalt not kill," sometimes
rendered as "Thou shalt not commit murder." Despite the honor paid to
this commandment down through Jewish and Christian history, as often
in the breach as in the observance, there are few pages of the Old Testament
in which one does not find a reference to killing.

Quite a surprising portion of the killing, we are told, is done by *Almighty
God himself*. The rest of it, for the most part, is left to his devoted children,
although a good deal was also inflicted upon the Hebrews by their various
enemies down through the centuries covered by the Old Testament. They
always seem surprised when their enemies attack and kill them, apparently
preferring to believe that their God gave them unique permission to wreak
vengeance. We find that little reference is made, later in the Old Testament,
to the original Mosaic prohibition against killing.

There is, however, one sin that looms as the most heinous in the eyes
of Yahweh. That crime is the Hebrews' *worship of pagan gods*. Yet this
is absurd in the light of the polytheistic customs of not only the ancient
Israelites but apparently of every tribe and city-state with which they came
into contact, either violently or socially. All the endless murders, the taking
of concubines, the visiting of prostitutes, lying, stealing, vandalism, pillaging,
rape—all the acts, in other words, counted as crimes by every civilized
culture known to history—seem minor compared to idolatry, so far as
one can learn from the PENTATEUCH.

The one dominant moral atrocity is polytheism. Again and again (the ancient Hebrews were apparently a remarkably forgetful tribe) the people "went a-whoring after false gods," or "the people did what was evil in the sight of the Lord." This last, of course, often meant that the people worshiped pagan deities.

Verses 29 and 30 are of interest in that they refer to human sacrifice, which is not unknown in primitive societies.

> 29. ". . . the firstborn of your sons you shall give to me.
> 30. You shall do likewise with your oxen and with your sheep: seven days it shall be with its dam; on the eighth day you shall give it to me."

It is a marvel to see how far modern Jews—a remarkable people— have come in 3,000 years, considering that long ago their ancestors were, at least so far as one can judge by their own religious documents, a thoroughly bloodthirsty, fanatical, and dangerous tribe. Today, in the United States, they include some of the most literate and accomplished people on earth.

Chapter 24 provides a surprise for the earnest student of Scripture:

> 3. Moses came and told the people all the words of the Lord and all the ordinances; and all the people answered with one voice, and said, "All the words which the Lord has spoken we will do."
> 4. And Moses wrote all the words of the Lord.

So it was Moses, not God, who inscribed the Commandments.

Elsewhere in the Scriptures we are told repeatedly that it was the belief of the Israelites that if they saw God face to face they would die. To most people this would seem a strange punishment for those given the highest honor which could befall man, namely, seeing the face of God. It is tempting to suggest that this ancient belief partly explains why the Jews could not accept the claims for JESUS for if, as most Christians believe, he was God Almighty, it follows that thousands of Jews saw him face to face throughout his thirty-some years of life, and not one of them dropped dead as a result.

If the student was surprised by the earlier portions of Exodus, he will be stupified at what the next several chapters reveal. Here are Moses and God, alone together, at the top of a mountain; the 18th verse of Chapter 24 states that "Moses was on the mountain 40 days and 40 nights." Since God could have inscribed the tablets of stone in a fraction of a second, it has never been clear as to why Moses spent almost six weeks on the mountain top.

The point becomes somewhat clearer, however, as one reads Chapters 25 through 31, which contain a seemingly endless description of how to build a temple, how to dress priests, how to conduct religious services, etc. After interminable details about furniture, utensils, lamp stands, oil, washing bowls, etc., the Lord finally returns to what would surely—to the rest of the world—seem of greater importance: a stern command to observe the Sabbath, with death to nonobservers.

Chapter 25. Let the reader, if he or she is a Protestant, imagine that a remarkable archaeological discovery is made, at which time, let us say, a 1,000-year-old document is unearthed in eastern Europe. Assume that after the necessary restorations and translations have been made, it turns out that the document is chiefly a detailed description of Roman Catholic priestly custom and practice. There are details as to the sizes and specific dimensions of priestly vestments, descriptions of the colors considered proper for them, instructions as to which portions ought to be made of silk, wool, cotton, or linen, the recommended physical proportions of churches, chapels, and sacristies, recommendations for the purchase and burning of incense, records pertaining to the purchase and storage of holy oils, etc.

Now all of this would be of great interest to Catholic historians but of little interest to almost everyone else. Scholars would naturally be grateful for such a discovery, since there is no fragment of a vessel, no tatter of papyrus, no broken arrowhead of a past civilization that does not play its role, however modest, in the construction of the grand mosaic of ancient history. It would hardly be assumed, however, that the unearthing of this hypothetical ancient document would lead to its being considered a proper instructional guide for present-day priests. It would simply be an ancient document, of considerable interest to a few and of no interest whatever to most. It might be instructive to examine Chapters 25-31 of Exodus in such a light.

Chapter 34.

1. The Lord said to Moses, "Cut two tables of stone like the first, and *I will write upon the tables the words that were on the first tables, which you broke.* (IA)
2. "Be ready in the morning, and come up in the morning to Mount Sinai, and present yourself there to be on the top of the mountain."

As prepared as I had become by now for surprises in the early chapters of the Old Testament, I was totally unprepared for the messages that the Lord now conveys to Moses. It would be reasonable to expect—if not from a reading of the prior chapters of Exodus, then at least from years of Christian indoctrination—that the Lord would now inscribe the Ten Commandments on the tablets.

The manner in which he proclaims himself to Moses is at total variance to what follows. He begins by saying that he is:

> 6. ". . . a God merciful and gracious, slow to anger, and abounding in steadfast love and faithfulness.
> 7. Keeping steadfast love for thousands, forgiving iniquity and transgression and sin . . ."

The Lord does give commandments to Moses, and then some. But they are not the Ten Commandments at all. After a bit of peculiar bragging and threatening, God at last gets down to business:

> 11. "Observe what I command you this day: behold, I drive out before thee the Amorite, and the Canaanite, and the Hittite, and the Perizzite, and the Hivite, and the Jebusite.
> 12. Take heed to thyself, lest thou make a covenant with the inhabitants of the land whither thou goest, lest it be for a snare in the midst of thee:
> 13. But ye shall destroy their altars, break their images, and cut down their groves:"

Is it possible that, at least for some ultraorthodox Israelis, these verses are used as justification for injustice to Palestinians today?

As we are seeing, there is much in the Testaments, Old and New, that causes confusion in the heart and mind of any true believer who possesses intellectual and ethical integrity. But concerning many passages of Scripture, there is no doubt whatever as to their meaning. The next verse, for example, is very explicit about the jealousy of God:

> 14. "For thou shalt worship no other god: for the Lord, *whose name is Jealous,* is a jealous God. (IA)
> 15. Lest thou make a covenant with the inhabitants of the land, and they go awhoring after their gods, and do sacrifice unto their gods, and one call thee, and thou eat of his sacrifice;
> 16. And thou take of their daughters unto thy sons, and their daughters go awhoring after their gods, and make thy sons go awhoring after their gods,
> 17. Thou shalt make thee no molten gods."

There are various places in the Scriptures where the jealousy of the Old Testament God is stressed, but when he is quoted as saying that his name is Jealous, we can no longer maintain that the point is unclear or ambiguous. Perhaps, to add variety to our prayers, we should not always begin them with the phrase "Dear God," but rather occasionally attract the Deity's attention by saying "Dear Jealous One."

Earlier in Chapter 34, after proclaiming to Moses what was quoted in Verse 6, the Lord says:

> 7. ". . . forgiving iniquity and transgression and sin, but who will by no means clear the guilty, visiting the iniquity of the fathers upon the children and the children's children, to the third and the fourth generation."

Note this emphasis on God's loving and forgiving qualities, juxtaposed against a threat against the innocent. It may be instructive to estimate the general number of innocent little ones likely to be affected by this warning.

Heads of families in the ancient Hebrew culture often had several wives. The Bible repeatedly mentions individuals having 40, 50, or more children, which if one has, say five wives, might not be that unusual. A second generation then might number 50. If all live to maturity and half of these are men and each of them has—say, just 30 children apiece—this means that the original offender would be grandfather to some 750 in the third generation. If less than half of them, 370, fathered only 20 children each, this would mean that in the fourth generation some 7,400 innocent children, born to sons only (I have not counted the offspring of daughters), might be subject to some sort of violent attack by the God they were otherwise taught to worship and love, for an offense they would likely never have heard of, committed by a man of whom they would have no memory and probably very little knowledge. I wonder—does anyone really believe this today?

The "schizophrenia" of Verse 7 can only be explained by suggesting that perhaps one part of that verse was an interpolation, but who can say which part—or even whether this ever happened?

Perhaps, if there ever was a Moses, he wanted to gather into his own hands an enormous amount of power over these wandering tribes, and thus simply made up a story about what God told him to tell his followers. It would not be the first—or last—time in history that a religious leader has been certain he "heard" the word of God, but it is strange that that "word" nearly always requires people to obey the prophet while he violently brandishes the name of God to produce obedience. (This is the explanation given by Paul Kurtz in *The Transcendental Temptation,* Buffalo, New York: Prometheus Books, 1986.) If Moses never existed, then we do not know why a later Hebrew author made this fictional character seem power-crazed—unless to set him against real foreign rulers, who cruelly dominated their subjects (including, often, the Hebrews).

The intellectual difficulties we encounter in Exodus are troublesome, of course, only to those who believe the Bible is the literal word of God. They are of no concern to atheists or agnostics. Nor are they of any interest to Deists, Unitarians, Universalists, and other Protestants, Catholics, and Jews who have such a deep respect for God that they refuse to believe that the sadistic Yahweh described in the Old Testament can possibly be the same God they worship.

What Are We to Make of the Bible's Cruelties? It is certainly one of the strangest ironies of religious history that it has often been men classified as heretics and unbelievers who have been most shocked at the atrocities, murders, and crimes of other sorts attributed to God in the pages of the Old Testament. Surely this would look most peculiar to the proverbial observer from another universe. He would note that those who claim to be closest to God insist that the Almighty has committed crimes comparable in viciousness and destructiveness with those performed by few men in history, whereas writers and scholars who argue that an all-good, all-loving Deity could not possibly be guilty of such atrocities are considered impious, irreverent, and socially dangerous.

The paradox is a telling one indeed. The explanation of this mystery is easy to come by. Churchmen have been trapped into insisting that God was guilty of the worst crimes imaginable, because they had already personally decided and publicly announced that the Bible was, through and through, the authentic word of God. The only intelligent way they could extricate themselves from endorsing divine criminality was by giving up their faith in the inerrancy of the Scriptures. But again, the impartial observer from another realm would be struck by the fact that these sometimes distinguished gentlemen repeatedly made it clear that, when it came to a choice between faith in a credible God and faith in a bizarre and jumbled collection of ancient books, they unhesitatingly made their choice in favor of the books.

If we then ask why such a puzzling choice was made, the answer to that question lies readily at hand. Christian and Jewish scholars, rabbis, and clergymen perceive that, if they were now to give up their centuries-old reliance on the authority of Scripture, they would have no recourse but to immediately disband or drastically modify their religious organizations, and in some cases their political agendas. There are, of course, many who would see this as one of the greatest steps forward in moral history, vastly surpassing, in moral importance, the collapse of Communist authority in Europe in late 1989. Unknown numbers of people have individually made such a choice; a good percentage of these have not felt a philosophical void but have, on the contrary, been emboldened and encouraged by their new-found freedom. A few have proceeded to atheism but a greater number have moved through different sectarian experiments of the Protestant Reformation. Some have become Quakers, some Unitarians, some Humanists, and some Reform Jews or members of New Jewish Agenda.

The average American, parenthetically, has not the slightest idea about the dominance of the Unitarian, Universalist, or Deist religious philosophies among the Founding Fathers and other gentlemen of distinction during the first century of U.S. history. These were high-minded and virtuous men, both personally and civically. They continued to believe in God and in the profound importance of moral behavior, but they could no longer accept what they considered the dangerously anti-God horror stories common in the Old Testament.

To sample the range of God's purported commandments to the Israelites, I suggest the reader look at Verses 18–26 in Chapter 34. Again, there is a suggestion of human sacrifice (v. 20).

> 27. And the Lord said to Moses, "Write these words; in accordance with these words I have made a covenant with you and with Israel."
> 28. And he was there with the Lord 40 days and 40 nights; he neither ate bread nor drank water. And he wrote upon the tables the words of the covenant, the ten commandments.

Note that we are asked to believe that Moses had not taken so much as a sip of water for 40 days, although we have earlier been told that his assembled party ate and drank while sitting and looking directly into the face of God. Since, no one can live for as long as two weeks without liquid, it follows then that we have here either another lie or another miracle.

When Moses descends to the bottom of the mountain, he spends little time offering moral instruction to his waiting flock but instead runs through many of the interminable details concerning the making of clothing and holy furniture, as a result of which the tabernacle is finished and erected.

St. Jerome, in translating the Bible into Latin, in Verses 29, 30, and 35 made the error of translating the Hebrew word *garan* as "horned." The correct translation of the verb was "to shine, or to emit rays." As a result of this mistake a number of Renaissance artists, including Michelangelo, actually show Moses with horns, which in time would find its way into the ugly stream of Christian anti-Semitism. The Catholic Bible retains an image of Moses with horns on his face, but the correction was made for Protestants as early as the King James Bible.

The *Catholic Biblical Quarterly,* a superb example of ongoing scholarship, had in its April 1989 issue (vol. 51, no. 2) a review by Dale Launderville, O.S.B., of John I. Durham's *Exodus* (Word Biblical Commentary Three. Waco, Texas: Word Books, 1987). Launderville explains first that Durham takes a canonical approach to the interpretation of Exodus, and then adds, quite casually, "He contends that Exodus is *first and foremost a theological rather than a historical work."* (IA)

On the next page of his review Launderville says, "He [Durham] recognizes that the canonical text of the Ten Commandments is *the end product of a developing oral and written tradition . . ."* (IA) Both Launderville and Durham are right. But what they have agreed to would have caused them to be burned alive in earlier centuries, for they are saying—among other things—that the text of the Ten Commandments, in the only form now available to us, is *not* a version imparted to Moses on Mt. Sinai.

EZEKIEL. The basic documents comprising this book appear to have been written not long after the book of JEREMIAH, primarily in the 6th century B.C. The prophecies probably occurred from about 593 to 571 B.C. Scholars believe the book was written by Ezekiel himself and one or more editors of his "school."

Ezekiel, both priest and prophet, was one of some 10,000 Jewish captives taken into Babylonian territory in the year 586, eleven years before the destruction of Jerusalem, when a second group of exiles was force-marched to Babylon. He was probably a leader before Nebuchadrezzar's conquest of Judea, and was undoubtedly of high priestly caste. In captivity, without a temple, he nonetheless continued as a spiritual leader, stating that he had received a vision and call to prophesy in 593.

One of the notable visionary descriptions of Ezekiel concerns the rebuilding of the Jerusalem Temple. The book contains a variety of literary forms: oracles, mythological themes and allegory, historical narrative, proverbs, folk tales, lamentations, and the sort of threats and promises supposedly originating with God and directed at his "chosen people."

Although Ezekiel often exhibited bizarre behavior, he was considered a masterful orator and leader of the Jewish exiles, thereby helping shape Judaism for the time that the Jews would be able to return to Judea. (That began to occur in 538 B.C. although not all Jews, by any means, returned.) According to the *Encyclopedia Britannica,* Ezekiel also:

. . . initiated a form of imagery and literature that was to have profound effects on both Judaism and Christianity all the way to the 20th century: *apocalypticism* (the view that God would intervene in history to save the believing remnant and that this intervention would be accompanied by dramatic, cataclysmic events). (IA)

Chapter 1. The opening portion of this prophetic book is bizarre in the extreme, though it has the virtue of containing some striking imagery, which might, of course, be said of almost all science fiction. Except for a reference to "the glory of the Lord," it displays nothing related to religion or morality. The third verse refers to Ezekiel in the third person, although earlier and then in verse 4, the first-person pronoun is used, a confusing switch, which suggests that at least two people worked on the text.

In any event, this chapter describes a vision—never represented as a physical reality—of "four living creatures" that look like a man, but with four faces and a total of eight sets of wings, feet like a calf's, and—but wait—having been first informed that all the creatures look like men we are told, in Verse 10, that they also have "the face of a lion on the right side and the face of an ox on the left." They also have the face of an eagle. These phantasmagoric creatures were somehow connected to a wheel. At the end of the chapter, the writer reports that when he saw all of this he fell upon his face. Little wonder. The author's point is that the strange creature "was the appearance of the likeness of the glory of the Lord."

At this point in the development of the Scriptures, one might have trouble perceiving what is an extremely simple idea—that of God. The Jews in Babylon perhaps thought that the idea of God required colorful but nonsensical imagery to impress upon the wavering or discouraged among them the idea of the majesty of the divine. It is curious, however, that in a religion that permitted no "graven images," the visions of its prophets contained figures that resembled the great stone monuments or bas-reliefs of monsterlike creatures that were prevalent in Egypt, Assyria, and Babylon.

Chapter 2. The Lord—or the wondrous creature—tells Ezekiel to go talk to "the children of Israel," whom the speaker then describes, to the point of monotony, as "a rebellious house." They are referred to as impudent, stiff-necked, hard-hearted, and wicked. There is, in fact, so much of this in the Old Testament that it could be construed as a profoundly anti-Semitic document were it not honored by the descendants of the tribes that, several thousand years ago, gave rise to it. (It is interesting to compare this prophet's words with the speech of Stephen in Acts 7:51-53, a condemnation of the Jews similar to Ezekiel's, which cost Stephen his life.)

Chapter 3. The most interesting portion of this chapter is Verse 20, which attributes theological nonsense to the Deity. It is precisely the sort of comment on the basis of which the churches have, over the centuries, consigned thousands to dungeons and flaming stakes. The verse, first of all, quotes God as saying that he purposely lays stumbling blocks before men who commit iniquity, causing them to die. Secondly, he blames Ezekiel for such deaths since, in some cases, he has not given personal warning to the unlucky sinner.

We know that even in the last decades of the 20th century, when it is possible to address millions of people in an instant and to endlessly repeat such messages, by no means everyone with a television set or radio actually receives these messages. At the time of Ezekiel, speakers rarely addressed more than a few score people at any one time, which meant that the great majority never heard any one specific message.

It is clear that if any human made one-tenth of the sadistic threats of horrible violence which this book attributes to God, he would be viewed as a dangerous psychopath. Why we are supposed to obey and worship an entity that threatens—and, alas, frequently is depicted as committing—depravities that far exceed in viciousness the enormities of Jack the Ripper and Charles Manson is not self-evident.

Let us recall that all these threats of sword, famine, and pestilence are directed against a people that in other contexts we are told have been specifically chosen. Since God would naturally be expected to treat such a favored tribe at least somewhat better than those who were never so honored, the overall picture is bleak indeed. Ezekiel does nothing whatever to stimulate the natural and beautiful emotion of love in any human heart. The emotion to which his passages give rise is that of abject fear. There are, consequently, millions who have rejected, if not God himself, then certainly the image of him projected in the Old Testament.

Millions of others apparently "worship" a God of viciousness and behave accordingly. I am thinking here of those prime ministers and dictators in the 20th century who have called themselves religious men yet who tyrannize and murder those who do not accept their absolute rule.

Chapter 4 is distinguished by what is perhaps one of the most scatological messages in world literature.

The brilliant agnostic Robert G. Ingersoll could not bring himself to defile the ears of his lecture audiences with direct quotations of such passages. Today, for better or worse, almost all cards are face up on the table, and it can scarcely be argued that it is offensive to set down on paper what is, after all, already in the Bible.

12. And you shall eat it as a barley cake, baking it in their sight on human dung."

13. And the Lord said, "Thus shall the people of Israel eat their bread unclean, among the nations whither I will drive them."

It is not entirely clear whether the Lord meant that the barley cake would be baked over a fire that used dried human dung as fuel (as the Revised Standard Version quoted above has it), or mixed with the dung and then baked (according to the King James Bible), or as the New American Catholic Edition (1950) puts it: "And thou shalt cover it in their sight with the dung that cometh out of a man." Whatever the translation, one' is permitted to wonder why human dung had to be introduced into the preparation of bread, if not as a disgusting punishment visited by the Lord on his people.

It makes as much sense to express prayers of thanks to a psychopathically and personally vindictive God because one has escaped a given disaster, as it would be for that remnant of European Jews who survived Nazi murders and atrocities to send letters of gratitude to Adolf Hitler's followers for being spared—that is, it makes no sense at all.

And let us reconsider, for another moment, the reality of the experience of those who, Christians claim, worship "false gods" in our own day—the Chinese, Japanese, many Africans, primitive Indonesians and Malaysians, Australian aborigines, Native Americans, and others. If we perceive such people as individuals, we realize that, in many cases, their piety and faith are as sincere as our own and in some cases a good deal stronger. They are, in general, as well-intentioned as Christians and are fellow human beings trying to do what is right, making earnest attempts to live by whatever moral code their upbringing and accident of geographical residence have made them aware of.

That being the case, it follows that the same, generally speaking, must have been true of the so-called pagan worshipers who lived in the periods during which the Scriptures were written. The Old Testament would have us believe that all "pagans" were evil, sinning brutes. This is certainly not to suggest that pagan religions were entirely edifying or wise, or that all the acts committed in the name of such religions were decent and constructive. But since exactly the same thing may be said about Judaism and Christianity, little is gained by raising the point. Sexual excesses, for example, committed in the name of religion by ancient peoples no more prove the total error of such ancient philosophies than references to the horrors of the Inquisition prove that the Catholic form of Christianity is a vast tissue of falsehood and cruelty.

EZEKIEL

Ezekiel recounts his visions of abominations taking place in Jerusalem and of the siege of the city (which he probably learned of from later exiles who came to Babylon after Jerusalem's fall), of the slaughter of those guilty of worshiping Babylonian gods, and cherubim. False prophets are condemned and a promise of restoration and renewal is given. Up through Chapter 24, the prophecies relate to Judea and Jerusalem. Ezekiel's purpose is to try to keep the suffering Jews faithful to the idea of monotheism in the land of many gods, especially with the promise that if they will but repent and follow the law, God will restore them to Judah.

In Chapter 17, Ezekiel begins to relent somewhat and promises that the Lord remembers his covenant with the people of Israel. And then in **Chapter 18,** there is a promise of justice for the righteous individual. In a passage that stunningly runs counter to previous Old Testament passages, such as Exodus 34:7, and to the Christian doctrine of ORIGINAL SIN, God is quoted as saying:

> 14. "But if this man begats a son who sees all the sins which his father has done, and fears, and does not do likewise,
> 15. who does not eat upon the mountains or lift up his eyes to the idols of the house of Israel, does not defile his neighbor's wife,
> 16. does not wrong anyone, exacts no pledge, commits no robbery, but gives his bread to the hungry and covers the naked with a garment,
> 17. withholds his hand from iniquity, takes no interest or increase, observes my ordinances, and walks in my statutes; he shall not die for his father's iniquity; he shall surely live.
> 20. The soul that sins shall die. *The son shall not suffer for the sins of the father, nor the father suffer for the iniquity of the son;* the righteousness of the righteous shall be upon himself, and the wickedness of the wicked shall be upon himself." (IA)

This seems to be such a clear statement of individual and personal responsibility for one's actions when brought to account before God that it is remarkable that the Christian theologians who formulated, and continue to insist on, original sin were able to ignore it. But then they probably believed they could pick and choose—and sometimes greatly alter the meaning of—passages in the Old Testament.

In Chapters 33–48, according to the *Encyclopedia Britannica,*

> ... Ezekiel proclaimed, in oracles that have become imprinted in theological discourse and folk songs, the hope that lies in the faith that God cares for his people and will restore them to a state of wholeness. As the good shepherd, God will feed his flock and will "seek the lost,"

"bring back the strayed," "bind up the crippled," and "strengthen the weak." He will also "set up over them one shepherd, my servant David, and he shall feed them."

Chapter 35 contains a lengthy quotation, again attributed directly to God and consisting of a condemnation of Mount Seir.

There is no way that a Christian or a Jew of the 20th century, reading this chapter, can know why, given the million and one more serious matters that might have concerned him, the Lord nevertheless chose to issue a thunderous denunciation of the inhabitants of a particular mountain in Edom, which lies south of Judea. The point is clear enough that whoever they were, they had "shed the blood of the children of Israel by the force of the sword," but why this tragedy should be of special concern to the human race thousands of years later is not self-evident.

Chapter 36. These passages are of interest for a number of reasons. The Lord, we are told, speaks of his "jealousy" and "fury." Why such violent emotions? Because the people of Israel have shed blood in the land and defiled it with idols. "But I had concern for my holy name, which the house of Israel caused to be profaned among the nations to which they came" (v. 21). At one point the Lord promises that the mountains of Israel will be fruitful. But a few verses later, he is again critical of Israel. Such benefits as he will bestow, he makes clear, will not be given "for your sake, O house of Israel, but for my holy name's sake, which ye have profaned among the heathen, whither ye went" (v. 22).

Finally, however the Lord promises to clean the land, clean the people of Israel and says:

> 26. "A new heart I will give you, and a new spirit I will put within you; and I will take out of your flesh the heart of stone and give you a heart of flesh."

Chapter 37. We have all heard the old spiritual, the lyrics of which go: "Dem bones, dem bones, dem dry bones . . . the head bone connected to the shoulder bone, the shoulder bone connected to the backbone . . ." etc.

The song is based on the imagery of the vision in this chapter, in which we are told that the prophet was lifted up in the air and set down in a "valley which was full of bones." The Lord instructs Ezekiel to speak to the bones and tell them to "hear the word of the Lord." Ezekiel does so, and in Verse 7 we read: "There was a noise, and behold a shaking, and the bones came together, bone to his bone." This is obviously not to be taken as reality.

Chapter 38. This section of Ezekiel is a violent diatribe against Gog, Gomer, and assorted tribes, not to mention Persia, Ethiopia, and Libya. All of these, it is predicted, shall attack the people of Israel. In the last few verses of the chapter, God—referring to his own jealousy and "the fire of my wrath"—promises to create mighty earthquakes and wars so terrible that "every man's sword shall be against his brother." The Lord also threatens pestilence, rain, hailstones, fire, and brimstone. For what reason?

> 23. "Thus will I magnify myself, and sanctify myself; and I will be known in the eyes of many nations, and they shall know that I am the Lord."

Well, the world has seen many an earthquake, flood, war, and pestilence since that time, and yet only the Jews, Christians, and Muslims, adhere to religions that developed from the Old Testament.

Chapters 43 and 44. *The Lord said unto me: "Thou shalt turn away from sinful ways, for after the brief pleasures of the moment there will be longer times of suffering. But even in avoiding sin and embracing virtue, be not moved by love of self. Rather do God's work by loving your fellow creatures who, like yourself, are children of God.*

If you demand that God love you, you must wish him to love all others as well. And if he does that, how could you dare oppose his will by hating any of his children?

Nor should you imagine that you have satisfied the Lord's requirement by loving only those who are easy to love, the beautiful children, or those who speak with beguiling smile and soft voice, those blessed with beauty.

But rather say I unto you that you shall love those who are hard to love, those who scorn you and turn their backs upon you. These, too, thou shalt love and, lest men fail to see the witness of your love because you keep it within your heart and mind, rather show it to all the world by acting in a manner consistent with the compassion you claim to feel in your heart.

Lift up the fallen, visit the sick, bury the dead, comfort the afflicted, give water to those who thirst, food to those who hunger, clothing to those who suffer in nakedness from the cold.

For otherwise the heart may fool itself, letting the word love *fall easily from the lips but living not in such a way as to make that love a reality.*

For the very things for which you pray to God, you have within your power to grant to others. Because it is a Godlike power it must therefore be dispensed in a Godlike manner."

I ask the reader to compare these passages—composed by myself in a few short moments in a more or less scriptural style—with the actual contents of these chapters of Ezekiel. Try to approach the moment of choice with as little bias as possible. Ask yourself which of the two sorts of instruction an even moderately sensible God, much less one who is *all*-wise, *all*-knowing, *all*-powerful, *all*-loving, would choose to transmit to his creatures.

It occurred to me while reading Ezekiel that no fanatical anti-Semite who ever lived has written harsher or more vile criticisms of the Jews than the authors of many passages of the Old Testament. If Nazis, anti-Semitic Catholics or Protestants, anti-Jewish Russians, or any other enemies had said or published many of these same accusations and criticisms, the entire Jewish population of the world would protest—and properly so. It is remarkable that the most incredible insults are accepted if criticism is closed off at its source.

In Conclusion. One of the most brazen insults ever offered to God was in the preaching, which persists to the current day, that the threats found in the book of Ezekiel are, beyond question, the words of the Lord. If they are, then humans on the planet earth live in the most detestable world imaginable, under the daily vengeance of a vicious Supreme Being whose acts are, in fact, far worse than those commonly attributed to the Devil. Perhaps only Hitler, of all the oppressors of the Jews down through history, has perpetrated such outrages against them as the Lord is said to guarantee in the book of Ezekiel.

It is the simplest of matters to perceive why primitive man thought God capable of the kind of bloody destruction attributed to him in hundreds of instances in the Old Testament. Almost everyone, from the loneliest, most ignorant caveman of long ages ago to the best-educated sophisticate of the present day, is inspired to respectful awe at simple contemplation of the natural universe. Its vastness, its complexity, the mystical questions of its beginning—all of these are enough to make the observer humble. But add to this the fact that primitive societies invariably identify God with nature—or confuse the two, as the case may be—and it is not at all difficult to see where the idea of the Deity as a savage avenger comes from. Nature, on the one hand, provides numerous blessings, benefits, and beauties; it is also violent and dangerous, as we see from floods, hurricanes, typhoons, tornadoes, earthquakes, lightning-induced fires, droughts, plagues, and diseases. To identify God with nature is inevitably to conclude that, although at certain moments he may have tender regard for his creatures, he will at other times treat them with no more loving care than an elephant blindly trampling upon insects.

It seems obvious that the raging god of the Old Testament is simply a carryover from a far more primitive time when man "worshiped" evil spirits—in the sense of performing rites of propitiation to them. Although he may seem horrible and primitive to us, the Old Testament's portrayal of YAHWEH was probably a step forward in mankind's notion of deity, from evil spirit to vengeful god, which would later give way to the idea of a loving, just god.

F

FALL, THE, the theological concept that because ADAM AND EVE disobeyed God in the Garden of Eden, all future generations would be tainted with sin, from which they could be redeemed only by Jesus' sacrifice of his life.

It seems highly unlikely that the concept could have come about in the purely irrational way that some intellectuals of the past five centuries have assumed, but that it was, on the contrary, a result of rational speculation. The reasoning process might have gone as follows:

1. God is perfect and all-powerful.

2. Human behavior, by way of contrast, is characterized by anger, cruelty, cowardice, lying, thievery, war, inability to subject sexual behavior to rational control, and other destructive forms of behavior.

3. A perfect God can hardly have made so dramatically imperfect a creature.

4. The blame for the low estate of man, therefore, must be placed elsewhere.

5. Only two alternative explanations suggest themselves: (a) Either a very powerful but evil "God"—a devil—must have had a hand in the matter; or (b) man himself, being by nature less than perfect, must have been led by his imperfection to make a conscious decision in favor of evil.

That the theoretical structure is hardly watertight is self-evident. I am concerned only to demonstrate that it is at least the product of reasonable theorizing and not simply a random leap into irrationality.

The primary reason why the cause for the Fall, as described in GENESIS, remains unconvincing, however, at least in rational terms, is that there is no way to demonstrate that a decision made by one human—whatever his name—would inescapably be transmitted "genetically" (or any other way) to any or all of the other billions of members of the human race.

I do not believe it possible, or at least very likely, for someone to grasp the obviously mythical component of the account of the Fall in Genesis without also being aware of the literature of other early cultures. Even the most poorly educated Christian would not have the slightest difficulty in identifying the myths of other early peoples as such. He would certainly never dream of confusing them with actual history, or with any kind of science. The reason his judgment would come so readily, and so accurately, is the obviously preposterous nature of the stories.

Talking animals are extremely common in myths and legends. Everyone over the age of three or four is perfectly aware that animals are incapable of human speech; they have neither the vocal equipment nor the degree of intelligence required. Therefore, to have built an entire theology on a story that involves a talking snake seems the ultimate in absurdity. Even if it is argued that the serpent in the Garden only *represents* Eve's "bad" urges—her will to disobey God and tempt Adam into doing the same— *where did such an urge come from before the reported moment of her moral contamination?*

There is probably scarcely a thoughtful Jew, Christian, or Muslim to whom it has not occurred that there is something odd about blaming the entire human race—innocent children, saints, and all—for the single sin of two people, Adam and Eve. Indeed in Numbers 16:22, we find the same thought—which is, indeed, a mere matter of common sense—occurring to the esteemed MOSES and Aaron. "O God, the God of the spirits of all flesh, shall one man sin, and wilt thou be wroth with all the congregation?" Apparently, in the one instance God's anger prevailed and in the other it did not, one more example of inconsistency in the Scriptures. (See also DEATH; EDEN, GARDEN OF; ORIGINAL SIN.)

FLOOD, THE. Although mankind was said to be still in its infancy in NOAH's time, God, we are told in GENESIS 6, had decided that his experiment of creating a planet and inhabitants for it had gone badly awry:

> 5. And God saw that the wickedness of man was great in the earth, and that every imagination of the thoughts of his heart was only evil continually.

This verse does not say merely that man was prone to evil, which everyone is aware of, or that even the best men and women do a certain amount of evil, which is true enough, but that "*every* imagination of the thoughts of his heart was *only* evil, continually." This is to say, there was no virtue in mankind whatsoever, except in the case of Noah, a contention which is obviously absurd.

Now, a supreme deity—by every common definition—knows all things. It therefore inescapably follows that the Lord was well aware, throughout all of measureless eternity, that mankind would perpetrate evil. It is therefore impossible to understand the Lord's reported surprise on this score. Nor is there any way that reason can be harmonized with stories about an all-perfect deity *repenting* of something he has done and feeling sad at heart. Repentance and sadness are human emotions, not those of a Supreme Being. This is reason for confidence that human hands and not the hand of God wrote this passage.

In addition, modern archaeology and anthropology can shed light on the Flood story. The narratives of widely scattered peoples, some of whom, like the Maya in Central America, had no contact with the Near East or the Mesopotamian region, have similar accounts of a disappointed creator-god, who destroyed his first attempt to make a human being and started over again.

Perhaps this reflects an extremely ancient consciousness that has persisted into modern man (*Homo sapiens sapiens*) of a premodern species, like Neanderthal man, which died out or was, in some way not yet understood, the precursor of modern man. Interestingly, archaeologists have recently discovered various remains of modern man that appear to be both older than and contemporary with Neanderthal man in the area of ancient Canaan. It is fascinating to speculate that the ancient Semites may have had an even more ancient oral tradition to account for the disappearance of a creature they recognized to be like themselves but whom they may have feared because they could not communicate with it. A natural assumption would have been that it was evil and that therefore God destroyed it in some spectacular way. Of course, this is just a playful fancy to explain the very common myths about a previous "race of men." So far as I know, no research has been done that would suggest this.

Another objection to the Noah story, which surely must occur even to a child of medium intelligence, is the striking unfairness of *killing innocent animal species simply because of the sinfulness of man.* Theologians agree that beasts can incur no moral guilt, and although some of the prophets and authors of the Old Testament did not grasp the simple fact, it has nevertheless been understood for centuries. This is a theme which is repeated in a number of instances in the Bible, and which certainly casts not the slightest credit on this particular view of God.

So not only are we told a ridiculous thing—that God would kill the sheep and foxes and the sparrows, that we are elsewhere assured his eye is always on, simply because of his anger at the evil of which *man* is sadly capable—but shortly thereafter, in Verse 19, we are led to conclude that

Almighty God changed his mind again and decided that not all animals but only the great majority should be killed. This follows from the instruction of God to Noah that he should take two of each kind of animal with him on the ark to preserve the species.

Elie Shneour has pointed out in the article "Occam's Razor," in the Summer 1986 issue of the *Skeptical Inquirer*, that Genesis gives:

> . . . the volume of the three-story ark as 43,000 cubic meters (1 cubit equals 0.46 cubic meter). The Noah team that built the huge ark and gathered all the bulky terrestrial animals (some of them dangerous), together with their monumental and varied food supply for one year, numbered a total of eight persons.
>
> The Bible is silent about the way such a minuscule group of people, with no clearly defined rational means, no pertinent experience, and a critically limited period of time before the Flood was to start, managed the feat.

Another element of irrationality concerns the amount of water that Genesis claims constituted the flood. The text says that ". . . all the high hills that were under the whole heaven were covered . . ." That means that every enormous mountain, all over the face of the earth, was under water. Mt. Everest, which is approximately 28,000 feet in height, and all the lesser great hills, were presumably invisible, in which case the entire earth must have been nothing but one giant ball of water. As Shneour observes, according to the Bible it rained for 40 days and 40 nights, or for 960 hours. Shneour continues:

> To reach [even] 10,000 feet, it must have rained at a rate of 4 1/3 *feet* of water an hour, a precipitation that would have devastated the ability of any small vessel to remain afloat, let alone the survival of its passengers. But assuming that the Ark was able to weather that large a deluge—it took more than 167 days for the water to come down to normal levels—what happened to all that water? It could not find space in the interior of the planet in such a short time without generating awesome Krakatoa-like eruptions. If, on the other hand, it just dissipated into outer space, by a sort of cataclysmic "boiling away," which no living things could reasonably have survived, why and how did it stop just in time to leave rivers, lakes, and oceans behind?

The discovery of 12 cuneiform tablets in Ashurbanipal's library at Nineveh in northern Iraq came as something of a sensation in the field of biblical scholarship. When the first discovery was translated by the British Assyriologist George Smith (*The Chaldean Account of Genesis,* 1876), it turned out to be an Akkadian account of the flood story found in Genesis:

> To the land of Nishir the ship took its course.
> The mountain of the land of Nishir held fast the ship and allowed
>   it not to stir . . .
> When the seventh day came,
> I (Utnapishtim) sent forth a dove and let her go.
> The dove went and returned,
> But there was not resting place and she returned . . .
> Then I sent forth a raven and let her go.
> The raven flew away, and she beheld the easing of the waters.
> And she ate, wading and croaking, but did not return.

The same treasure trove later produced stories about the CREATION of the world, the suffering of a righteous man (such as JOB), certain psalms of repentance, and even a few hymns similar to those encountered in Israelite literature. Needless to say, Jewish and Christian scholars were reluctant to accept the possibility that the Akkadians and Sumerians had originated such stories and that the ancient Hebrews had simply absorbed them in the way that cultures in contact always exchange information and ideas. The theory was eventually advanced that both versions of the material— the Hebrew and the Akkadian—were drawn from a period *before* Genesis was written down.

However, it has been proven conclusively that the Akkadian civilization predated the emergence of the Hebrews in Israel by more than a thousand years. This casts a shadow on the traditional Christian and Jewish view that the authors of the Bible took their inspiration directly from God. (See also ENUMA ELISH AND GILGAMESH.)

In the period 1927-29, an important find was made at Ur, in Iraq. Temples and dwellings connected with Ur's third dynasty, roughly 2,000 years before Christ, were unearthed, as well as an excellently preserved old cemetery. Later, evidence was discovered that an ancient flood had submerged the region. Comments Jean Levie (*The Bible: Word of God in Words of Men*):

> Beneath the layer in which the royal tombs were found, there appeared a wide layer of clay, varying from eight-and-a-half to twelve feet in thickness, without any remains of human habitation. Then, abruptly, below this layer, clear indications of human life and activity reappeared. These were characteristic of an earlier civilization, much inferior to that of the royal tombs . . . What was the meaning of this thick layer

of clay . . . dating from the middle of the fourth millennium? Was it archaeological evidence of a catastrophic inundation that lay behind the Sumerian and Assyrian stories of the flood and which is also recalled in the narrative in Genesis? . . . I shall mention only the hypothesis which A. Parrot, in 1952, described as "the most probable" (*Deluge et arche de Noe,* p. 30): "One of these cataclysms was accompanied by such ravages that made so great an impression that it became a theme in cuneiform literature. This was *the* flood; *legend certainly magnified its violence and destruction for archaeology indicates that not all the towns suffered to the same extent.*" (IA)

"As for the flood itself," says Jacquetta Hawkes in her superb *The First Great Civilizations:*

> . . . although silt deposits have been discovered at Ur and several other Sumerian cities *they belong to different dates and it has proved impossible to establish a single great inundation affecting the whole land.* Presumably floods were a familiar dread that produced in men's minds the myth of the great flood. (IA)

Since true believers have been on the defensive during recent centuries regarding the story of Noah, it is understandable that they would be relieved by archaeological and geological evidence of almost any ancient flood. But it is by no means clear why such evidence cheers them or what it proves. No one has ever denied the existence of floods, if only because in our own century they have inundated vast areas of land and drowned uncounted thousands.

If a major Middle Eastern flood occurred a few thousand years ago, it would be quite understandable that stories about it were passed through succeeding generations in the area where the event transpired. Since the invention of writing is a fairly recent development in human experience and inasmuch as the average man cannot accurately describe on Tuesday an event he witnessed on Monday, it is only to be expected that facts would be omitted from the story, false additions made to it, and mythical elements would creep in over the course of a long period of time.

There are, as biblical scholars are aware, discrepancies in two variant accounts of the deluge in Genesis. In one, the duration of the flood is given as 40 days; in the other it is said that it was 150 days before the waters had subsided. In one version, Noah builds an altar and offers a sacrifice; in the other, a sacrifice is not mentioned.

We see from these few observations, among others that might be made, that no matter how one attempts to be reasonable and sympathetic about

Genesis, no matter how much one is disposed to believe the story of Noah and the flood, *acceptance of it on its own terms is simply impossible.* If this story is not preposterous by every standard of biological science, by every standard of hygiene, of ship-building, of carpentry, of logical consistency, then man and all his works are irrational and absurd.

FLYING SAUCERS. Although, statistically speaking, almost no scientific observers believe that craft flying from other planets or star-systems travel about in the earth's atmosphere, thousands of ordinary people are convinced of the existence of such objects.

The real problem about flying saucers, of course, is not the secondary question as to whether they exist. If they do not, their nonexistence will obviously never be established. If they do, the fact will presumably eventually be discovered. But the truly troublesome factor of this particular media drama is the willingness of so many people to accept the existence of such objects *in the total absence of conclusive or even consistent evidence.*

If such craft are real, the earth's inhabitants can obviously survive the fact, for they have been doing so since the first UFO was reportedly sighted in the early fifties. But it is clear that we cannot long survive in a world where a majority of us are disposed to accept almost any bizarre report or theory, however implausible.

FREEDOM AND RELIGION. I was astonished recently, when reading the last written words of Alan Paton, to learn that years earlier he had been profoundly impressed to hear Reinhold Niebuhr discuss the dangerous possibilities of freedom, the implication being that it was a rare insight indeed on the part of Niebuhr to have realized that freedom means the liberty to choose between good and evil. I mean absolutely no disrespect to Niebuhr, who has undoubtedly left us much wisdom, when I say that the perception that choice flows out of a state of freedom is so obvious that I have always assumed it is one of the first insights to occur to anyone who thinks about the subject in an analytical way.

Indeed those who consciously oppose or severely limit freedom offer the justification that most people will not use it responsibly.

The naive or poorly informed may imagine that in this ancient debate both the Bible and the formal faiths based on it are firmly on the side of freedom. However, an examination of the Old Testament reveals the error of such an assumption. We must view the military conduct of the Israelite kingdom with dismay, for in its day the concept of freedom, in the sense now dear to the West, was totally unknown.

As John Locke observed in his famous letter concerning toleration, the business of civil government is quite distinct from that of religion. The state, properly, is a society constituted only for preserving and promoting the *civil* interests, such as life, liberty, health, and the possession of property.

As early as 1644, John Milton, in his *Areopagetica,* which recommended liberty of unlicensed printing, argued that administrative censorship leads "to the discouragement of all learning and the stop of truth . . . by hindering . . . the discovery that might be yet further made, both in religious and civil wisdom." Knowledge, Milton correctly observed, is increased through the expression of fresh opinions, and truth is arrived at, or at least more closely approached, by means of free discussion.

All of this, now central to Western political thought, was totally foreign to the prophets, priests, and kings of the Old Testament. Since the system of separation of church and state has, over several centuries, shown itself to be far preferable to the union of the two, we are entitled to regard the practice of the latter among the men of the Old Testament as unadmirable and therefore no guide whatever to the moral conduct of modern society's affairs.

Parenthetically, non-Catholic defenders of the church's past cannot be permitted to argue that at least the Protestant reformers—John Calvin, John Knox, Martin Luther, and others—were defenders of religious liberty per se. Any such assertion would be a lie. It is obvious enough that the reformers wanted freedom for their own beliefs, but since everyone wants that, there is nothing remarkable about it. The first European thinkers creative and courageous enough to suggest, however modestly and circumspectly, that political and intellectual freedom were virtues in and of themselves were regarded not merely as erring brothers but as dangerous heretics, and therefore criminals.

Again, although in the American context at least, the churches have both consciously and unconsciously identified themselves with the concept of freedom, a well-focused perception of the social reality of the past several centuries compels the realization that, with few exceptions, the churches have been opponents, not proponents, of freedom. Contrary to what freethinkers might suppose, this is not because of any inherent hardness of heart or hypocrisy on the part of true believers, but has issued from a factor which is one of the basic building-blocks of religious faith. I refer to the feeling of *certainty*, which is found far more often in the realm of religion—where surprisingly little can be established with certainty—than in the field of science, where persuasive evidence of concrete, observable matters is easier to come by.

It might be simpler for the nonreligious reader to understand the background of this point if he entertains, for the moment, the following fantasy. Let us suppose that next Thursday morning God Almighty appears in the private chambers of the Pope. Suppose he says, "Your Holiness, I have decided to make this personal visit because I sense that in the modern, secularist, scientific age, an age when the church has suffered many setbacks, it is conceivable that even the Vicar of Christ may experience fleeting moments of doubt as to whether I am still the support of the Catholic church. To get to the point, I am indeed the Lord God Almighty, and the Catholic version of the Christian religion is the one true faith, personally founded by my only son Jesus. Of this you need no longer have the slightest doubt."

Can the reader doubt that from that moment the Holy Father and his aides could possibly agree that the Seventh-Day Adventist, the Mormon, the Baptist, the Methodist, the Presbyterian, the Jehovah's Witness, the Jew, the Muslim, or the atheist really had *rights* to preach what would then be clearly heretical and therefore morally deviant views?

Freedom has its obvious emotional attractions and even, in some limited social contexts, its utility. But just as no government would permit the promulgation of a school of mathematics which taught that two and two add up to seven and a half, which would seriously cloud the minds of a generation of children, and just as no society would officially permit a school of medicine in which all the afflicted were to be treated by having their foreheads rubbed for twelve seconds with blueberry jam, so no church or society—if given direct divine assurance witnessed by many—could any longer tolerate toleration itself. One could grant the good faith of George Washington, Thomas Jefferson, John Locke, John Stuart Mill, Thomas Paine, Abraham Lincoln, and other esteemed spokesmen for freedom, but, as a practical matter, one would have to protect the sanity and faith of millions by returning to the ancient Christian doctrine: "Error has no rights."

Quite aside from the position the reader might take in regard to such a turn of events, he or she must concede that once the members of the Catholic faith—or whatever other church one might substitute—had the hypothetical degree of proof I have described above, that they were indeed the one true religion, it would be quite wrong for them to be guided by, say, the American Bill of Rights.

I have asked the reader to accompany me through this brief fantasy by way of suggesting that *precisely the same degree of* certainty *is* felt *by millions of Christians and other believers in practically all churches.* The emphasis is on *felt.*

There is, of course, a clear-cut conflict, a flat contradiction, between this Christian notion on the one hand and the American political ideal on the other. But rationalists should appreciate that it is not innate viciousness that has led to the various infringements on freedom, including wide-ranging atrocities, over the centuries of Christian dominance. It has been nothing more than the comfortable *conviction*—albeit conviction without a shred of proof—that one was in possession of *the* Truth.

So great a mind as that of Thomas Aquinas believed it was perfectly permissible to burn heretics alive because, since it was considered permissible to execute a criminal whose offense was harming the body, it was therefore an even wiser social act to kill a heretic, who was, by definition, guilty of the far more serious crime of harming the soul.

I have long been convinced that a good part of the evil in the world, in addition to coming from criminally psychopathic sadists, also issues from the ranks of the Marvelous Fellows who, once they become convinced of the correctness of a given spiritual or political philosophy, are thereafter quite prepared to authorize the worst sort of cruelties on the grounds that such means are a necessary defense of their society or "democracy."

We must all realize that the American freedoms proclaimed in Fourth of July oratory—if, alas, frequently dishonored at other times—were by no means brought about at the urging of any traditional church. They were achieved, in the majority of instances, over the dead body of the church, though certain individual churchmen were sometimes helpful. That is the reason why, in the American social context among others, lifelong vigilance must be maintained against religious dogmatists.

FUNDAMENTALISM. Fundamentalists often seem not to understand what an inquiry into the Bible, like the present one, means. Consider, by way of illustration, the comment of Rev. K. Owen White, president of the Baptist General Convention of Texas and past-president of the Southern Baptists. When asked about his fervent opposition to such works as *The Message of Genesis* by Professor Ralph Elliott, in which it is merely suggested that parts of the Old Testament be interpreted symbolically rather than literally, White responded, "The average man cares nothing about the modern theological trends, but he knows he has problems in his heart. What shall we preach if we do not preach the Word? *This is no day for raising questions concerning the reliability and authority of God's word.*" (IA)

Professor Elliott was fired from his position at Midwestern Baptist Theological Seminary as a result of such a critique. White does not understand that *every* day is appropriate for raising questions concerning God's word. A certain amount of the fundamentalist defense of tradition, even to the present moment, is irrationality protective of irrationality.

A. C. Gaebelein, for example, in his interesting booklet *What the Bible Says About Angels* (Grand Rapids, Mich., Baker Books, 1987), forthrightly expresses his displeasure with even the most prestigious Bible scholarship. Formal criticism originating from unimpeachable sources he describes as "destructive criticism," adding, "We do not follow the so-called 'scholarly' inventions *which are aimed at the destruction of the Bible as our only authority*. Over against all these denials we put but one witness, the Son of God, Our Lord Jesus Christ." (IA)

Since JESUS cannot or has not returned to tell us everything that he meant, the only approach we can take to his teachings is precisely the same we would take in the case of accounts about any other deceased person, which is to say, literary comment. Jesus himself never wrote anything. We have available only material *about* Jesus, written long after his death by others.

Gaebelein is dishonest in suggesting that biblical criticism comes from outside the churches when, in fact, the great bulk of it comes from within one sectarian fold or another. He says, "We cannot be in doubt as to the source from whence these infidel theories emanate." Gaebelein apparently means that modern scriptural scholars, engaged in the professional act of perfectly respectable criticism, are in fact provided by the Devil with their theories!

It would, however, be a mistake to assume the fundamentalist camp consists very largely of dunces, whereas their scholarly opponents are largely intellectual. In fact, there are intellectuals in both camps, though by far the greater number are found among the modernists, to whom we are indebted for intelligible Bible commentary.

Literalists can point to such early geniuses as St. Augustine, who insisted that "Scripture gives no false information." (Since not even Catholics are obliged to accept anything purely on Augustine's authority, there is no real problem with the assertion itself, though it is remarkable how many imaginary difficulties have been treated, over the centuries, as if they were legitimate.) The answer is simply that on this point, Augustine was badly mistaken; the Bible contains an enormous amount of false information and myth.

I have noted that fundamentalists argue unfairly. For the most part they deny problems of interpretation, simply asserting that the Bible says what it means and means what it says. When, however, it is demonstrated that portions of Scripture flatly contradict each other, then the fundamentalist promptly qualifies his original assertion and interprets to his heart's content.

When fundamentalists encounter almost any criticism of either the Scriptures or their church, they also respond by interpreting the observations as anti-God. "How dare you," they ask, "presume to pit your merely human intellect against that of God?"

The answer, of course, is that (1) if there is a God and (2) he did indeed share with us the benefits of his all-wise mind, then (3) it would be the height of insanity to contradict any aspect of the divine philosophy. But when the fundamentalist is asked how he *knows* that *one* particular opinion or another represents the view of God, he responds by saying that the divine message came to us in the form of the Bible. The entire Bible? Yes, beyond question. His entire case rests on the Bible being the literal word of God. Unfortunately he often attempts to prove this, as regards one portion of Scripture, by referring to some other portion. This puts him in the obviously untenable position of trying to prove the Bible *from* the Bible.

One of the many peculiarities is that millions of fundamentalist Christians consider themselves especially patriotic Americans, though in reality it is quite impossible to reconcile the views of the Founding Fathers with those of the Bible on a number of important questions.

To give only a few examples:

1. The Bible implies in many places the *union* of church and state, whereas the American system is based on the *separation* of church and state. (See FREEDOM AND RELIGION.)

2. The Bible generally teaches that civil power comes from *God,* whereas the Constitution asserts that it derives from *the consent of the governed.*

3. The New Testament preaches that there is *one* true religion and that all others are an abomination, whereas the American system tolerates *all* religions and permits none to attain dominance.

4. The Old Testament *condones* slavery and bigotry against outsiders, whereas the American system *outlaws* slavery and discrimination.

G

GENESIS. The simple word *genesis* refers to origins, to the beginnings of things. It is important to acknowledge what to philosophers is obvious enough—that after thousands of years of conjecture by the very best minds, there is little that can be accurately described as certain knowledge about the origin of the universe, of life, and of humankind. Primitive peoples, however, are unaware of their ignorance. These tribes respond to questions about origins by the development of myths and legends to explain them.

Although well-established items of scientific fact that contradict the simplistic assertions of Genesis are numerous, let us, for the moment, consider but one example: the discoveries in the spring of 1989 by astronomers Martha Haynes and Riccardo Giovinelli. Quite by chance they picked up a signal pattern much like that known to be emitted by galaxies. The first staggering fact that presented itself was that their discovery was several times as large as the Milky Way. The fact that it was *65 million light years* from earth means that what the astronomers were actually seeing was the mysterious cloud as it had existed 65 million years in the past!

The remarkable collection of legend and error we call Genesis, rarely mitigated by a single accurate fact about the physical universe, did not come about because the ancient Hebrews were inherently less intelligent than we are. It happened because they depended on a combination of sensory observations and theological assumptions. The evidence of the senses alone would have inevitably led to a great deal of error, but when speculation about God was added to the mix, the results could hardly have comprised an account of the universe's and man's origins that squared with what would be slowly learned down through the centuries. Astrophysicists are still making discoveries about the beginning and extent of the universe, and physical anthropologists are all evolutionists though they hold conflicting theories about the emergence of *Homo sapiens sapiens* from earlier humanoid forms, as new fossil evidence is unearthed.

No, not only were our ancestors no more unintelligent than we are, but it is quite possible to make a strong case for the reverse. Consider: We have had the benefit of many centuries of scientific speculation and observation about the relevant physical questions. Our astronomers, geologists, physicists, anthropologists, and archaeologists have provided us with remarkably sophisticated devices, information, and theories about our world.

What is incredible is that in the presence of all the scientific information now available—disseminated in millions of books, journals, magazines, films, and tapes over much of the face of the earth—a portion of mankind still clings to notions about the physical universe that are closer to primitive beliefs.

Since it is easier to perceive the absurdity of erroneous ideas to which we have no particular connection, it might be instructive to consider non-Judaic ways of regarding the physical universe, during what might be described loosely as Old Testament times. Observes Patrick Moore in his fascinating and lucid study *Watchers of the Stars:*

> The Egyptians believed the universe to be shaped like a rectangular box, with the longer sides running north-south. There was a flat ceiling, supported by four pillars at the cardinal points, and the pillars were linked by a chain of mountains, below which ran a ledge containing the celestial river Ur-nes. Along this river sailed the boats which carried the Sun and other gods, and there seemed to be no difficulty whatever in turning corners. In parts of the Nile Delta it was thought that the heavens were formed by the body of a goddess with the rather appropriate name of Nut, who was permanently suspended in a position which was as uncomfortable as it was inelegant. In India, the Vedic priests taught that the flat Earth was supported on twelve massive pillars, and that during night-time the Sun threaded its way between these pillars without bumping into any of them. And we also have a Hindu theory, according to which the Earth was carried on the back of four elephants standing on the shell of a tortoise which was itself supported by a serpent floating in a boundless ocean.

If the reader can grasp the fact that the concept of the universe in the early chapters of Genesis is just as nonsensical as those of the early Egyptians, Indians, and other ancient peoples, the air will have been cleared to a degree. (See AGE OF THE EARTH AND THE UNIVERSE.)

It might be instructive to quote Father Bruce Vawter, a respected Bible scholar and devout Christian, who says of the Genesis creation: "Scientifically speaking, this is obviously a pathetic notion of the universe." In the next paragraph of *A Path Through Genesis,* he refers to it as "this erroneous conception of the universe."

One is tempted to ask our fundamentalist friends who insist on Creationist "science": Since God ultimately "permitted" mankind to discover that the world was not created in six days, that there are worlds beyond our solar system, and that man was not created in his present form in one day, why didn't he tell the author(s) of Genesis those facts? If he could part the waters of the Red Sea and perform other miracles, why did he not just endow Moses with the intuitions of a Galileo, a Copernicus, a Magellan, or a Darwin?

Despite the good intentions of most fundamentalists, their case is hopeless. If I could single out any one fact that establishes this, it would be that not one individual of the hundreds who contributed portions of Scripture, from the original writers—whoever they may have been—to a larger number who edited, revised, added, deleted, and otherwise altered the original messages before the 16th century, had the slightest idea that the earth was spherical. They all believed it to be flat.

Chapter 1.

1. In the beginning God created the heavens and the earth.
2. The earth was waste and void. Darkness covered the abyss, and the spirit of God was stirring above the waters.
3. And God said, "Let there be light," and there was light.
4. And God saw that the light was good. God separated the light from the darkness.
5. God called the light Day and the darkness Night. And there was evening and morning, the first day.

The statement "darkness covered the abyss" is flatly at variance with the previous creation of the heavens that contained the sun and stars, millions of which give off light. Light is, of course, observable even on the cloudiest days. Therefore, the earth could not have been in darkness, and Verse 3 is unnecessary.

It is also puzzling to be told that God saw that the light was good, as if this were a surprising and happy discovery by the Almighty. It is a typically human observation, not one we would expect from a deity. Nor is it enlightening to be told that God *separated* the light from the darkness. Light and darkness are inescapably separate, in accordance with nature's physical laws.

For centuries there has been debate about the meaning of the word *day* in the creation story. Honest Jews and Christians of the past interpreted the word to mean a period of 24 hours. Indeed, it is difficult to know how they could have understood it differently.

For a long time only freethinkers, rationalists, and other skeptics were at pains to point out that, since our planet was of very ancient origin, it was difficult to accommodate the emerging *facts* of science with the traditional biblical *account* of creation. Defenders of the True Faith were then forced to interpret the word *day* in a sense so loose as to deprive it of any real meaning.

> 9. And God said, "Let the waters under the heavens be gathered together into one place, and let the dry land appear." And it was so.
> 10. God called the dry land Earth, and the waters that were gathered together he called Seas. And God saw that it was good.

One does not have to be a geologist to know that the waters of the earth are *not* gathered into one place. There are five oceans and many seas, gulfs, bays, fiords, rivers, lakes, ponds, and puddles.

> 11. And God said, "Let the earth put forth vegetation, plants yielding seed, and fruit trees bearing fruit in which is their seed, each according to its kind, upon the earth." And it was so.

It took a long while for the newly formed earth, millions of years ago, to produce plant life. And whatever vegetation did first appear on the planet was under water or along seashores; it took another long while for tomatoes, citrus fruits, pomegranates, dates, apples, etc. to evolve. Of course, the author of Genesis could not have known this, so he simply referred to what he saw around him.

> 14. And God said, "Let there be lights in the firmament of the heaven to divide the day from the night; and let them be for signs, and for seasons, and for days, and years.

The problem here is that if we are to believe the earlier information in Verse 4, "God separated the light from the darkness," then it is absurd to believe that God later said, "Let there be lights in the firmament . . . to divide the day from the night."

> 16. And God made the two great lights, the greater light to rule the day, and the lesser light to rule the night; he made the stars also.

Having already made the sun, stars, and moon, why would God have troubled to create them again, just a few days later? Vawter (*A Path Through Genesis*) tries to defend the unknown author by saying:

Here again we have *the non-scientific mind* at work, of course, which did not necessarily see a causal connection between the sun and daylight, and which certainly was unaware that the light from the moon was a reflection, and that there is a difference of the same kind between the planets and the stars. (IA)

To which one can respond that Genesis would be a much more instructive and reliable document had Father Vawter written it.

The litany of contradictions continues with Verses 26 and 27, in which man is made and then given dominion over all animals. We are told that "man is made in the image of God." Theological authorities specify that God is pure spirit and therefore has no physical image whatever. (See IMAGE OF GOD.)

We are told that "male and female created He them." This is all very well except that the compilers of Genesis were careless. In Chapter 2 we are told that after the seventh day, the Lord formed man of the dust of the ground, and afterwards (at a later but unspecified time) he gave ADAM, the first man, clear instructions that he must not eat the fruit of a certain tree, and only *then* said, "It is not good that the man should be alone; I will make a helper fit for him" (2:18).

Note that in Verse 26, God uses the plural pronoun for himself, saying "in our image, after our likeness." Some scholars have suggested that the use of the plural in early portions of the Bible is consistent with the *polytheistic beliefs* then common all over the world and *to which the Israelites were no exception*. Indeed, the Hebrew prophets, though hewing to a monotheistic line, constantly fulminate against the worship of "false gods," by which they mean local or national gods of the peoples they lived near or among.

> 30. "And to every beast of the earth, and to every bird of the air, and to everything that creeps on the earth, everything that has the breath of life, I have given every green plant for food." And it was so.

It is interesting to observe that God at this stage apparently did not contemplate that man or any other animal should eat meat. Whatever happened to man's original vegetarianism? And what did tigers, lions, and sharks eat at that time? Incidentally, modern studies show that we would live longer if we ate far less meat and more vegetables and fruit.

> 31. And God saw everything that he had made, and behold, it was very good.

Whether all those who have been poisoned by venomous snakes, scorpions, and other crawling creatures, bitten and mauled by large animals, devoured by alligators and sharks, etc., would be prepared to describe all of this handiwork as "very good," we do not know. Surely we cannot retire behind the defense that God had it within his power to create only plant-eating animals but somehow failed in the attempt to do so.

Elizabeth Cady Stanton, in *The Woman's Bible,* has dramatized the fact that two authorial strands, the ELOHIST and the YAHWIST, appear beside one another in the Genesis account of creation. Since they contradict one another on several very important points, which she lists, are we to understand that the early compilers of the Old Testament were working with distinctly separate materials and could not make up their minds which account was true? That may have actually been the case, although historically it could not be admitted, if indeed it had been perceived. Did the compilers decide to include both versions because each had been important to different groups of Semitic speakers?

What is important to note, according to Stanton, is that the Elohist version in Chapter 1 is positive about the creation, especially as regards the position of woman, whereas the Yahwist version becomes punitive in Verse 17 of Chaper 2. And from then on in the Old Testament, God is depicted more as threatening the people he has created than as behaving lovingly toward them. What a heavy burden Jews and fundamentalist Christians have had to carry around with them, cowering before the angry God of the Old Testament.

ELOHIST	YAHWIST
Order of Creation:	Order of Creation:
First—Water.	First—Land.
Second—Land.	Second—Water.
Third—Vegetation.	Third—Male only.
Fourth—Animals.	Fourth—Vegetation.
Fifth—Mankind: male and female.	Fifth—Animals.
	Sixth—Woman.
In this story male and female are created simultaneously, both alike, in the image of the gods, *after* all animals have been called into existence.	In this story the male is sculptured out of clay, *before* any animals are created, and *before* the female has been constructed.
Here, joint dominion over the earth is given to woman and man, without limit or prohibition.	Here, woman is punished with subjection to man for breaking a prohibitory law.

Everything, without exception, is pronounced "very good."	There is a tree of evil, whose fruit is said by Yahweh to cause sudden death, but which does not do so, as Adam lived 930 years after eating it.
Man and woman are told that "every plant bearing seed upon the face of the earth and *every tree* . . . To you it shall be for meat." They are thus given perfect freedom.	Man is told there is *one tree* of which he must not eat, "for in the day thou eatest thereof, thou shalt surely die."
Man and woman are given special dominion over all the animals—"every creeping thing that creepeth upon the earth."	An animal, a "creeping thing," is given dominion over man and woman, and proves himself more truthful than Yahweh or Elohim. (Compare Gen. 2:17 with 3:4, 22.)

Since it is obvious that both of these stories cannot be true, intelligent women may decide which is more worthy of an intelligent woman's acceptance. Paul's rule is a good one in this dilemma, "Prove all things: hold fast to that which is good." Both stories probably come from Mesopotamian CREATION accounts. My own opinion is that the Yahwist version of the Bible was devised in a manipulative endeavor to give "heavenly authority" for requiring a woman to obey the man she married.

Any average reader assumes that the first chapter is so situated because it was written first. On the contrary, Christian scholars now know that it was written down approximately halfway through the Old Testament's growth, although the material itself had a more ancient origin.

Chapter 2. Concerning the observation in Verses 2-3 that "on the seventh day God rested," scholars point out that the author was misleading in attributing the human sensations of physical and mental exhaustion to God. It is more likely that this was inserted to enforce the authority of the commandment about not working on the Sabbath.

In conceding the obvious, that the Scriptures are often confusingly worded, we are led to two important questions. Why would Almighty God communicate so imperfectly? Or, if he did not, then how did such error creep into the divine record? There seems little doubt that many of the discrepancies and contradictions are attributable to the fact that the creation story and other early narratives were obtained from other related peoples and were then handed down through many generations *orally,* long before any of them were written down by the Hebrews.

It is unnecessary, in the light of the biological science now taught at almost every Jewish and Christian university, to comment on the story of the creation of woman out of a rib bone of Adam (v. 21). A new theory has emerged recently that posits that all people on the earth today are descended from one woman who lived in East Africa millions of years ago. It is a complicated theory, developed by genetic and computer science, and is by no means accepted by all paleoarchaeologists. I mention it here only to point out the irony that although it would seem to credit the notion of an Eve as the mother of all humankind, it plays havoc with the notion of Adam being created first and of the Garden of Eden being located "in the east."

> 24. Therefore shall a man leave his father and mother, and shall cleave unto his wife: and they shall be one flesh.

This sounds like a holy endorsement of monogamy. Despite this nice sentiment, the ancient Hebrews practiced polygamy and kept concubines, as did other tribes surrounding them. God, although he was depicted as constantly instructing his chosen people in morality, apparently was not in the least disturbed by polygamy and concubinage. (See also EDEN, GARDEN OF.)

Chapter 3. The story takes a more interesting turn as we learn what is happening in the garden.

> 1. Now the serpent was more subtle than any beast of the field which the Lord God had made. And he said unto the woman, "Yea, hath God said, 'Ye shall not eat of any tree of the garden'?"

It is instructive to be reminded that God *created* that serpent which is about to "tempt" Eve to "sin." Many have raised the question as to how a serpent could speak at all. A miracle? But only God can produce miracles, and we don't like to think his power is ever used for evil.

Eve, in any event, enters into a conversation with the serpent. Modern women may wonder why Eve seems not in the least surprised that a snake could speak her own language fluently, but modern women are accustomed to using reason, whereas there seems to be little evidence in Genesis that rational considerations were of any importance to anyone. Eve explains, without telling how she came by the knowledge, that God had personally warned Adam, before she was created: "You shall not eat [the fruit of a particular tree] for in the day that you eat of it you shall die" (2:17). This sounds like a typical taboo found in many myths.

The serpent says the first intelligent thing, when he remarks, "Surely ye shall not die" (v. 4). The serpent turned out to be right about this, for no one died from eating the forbidden fruit. It is no answer to respond that Adam and Eve did eventually die, since that appears to be a condition of God's creation. (See DEATH.)

Some plants do bear poisonous fruit. Could this story have originated as a simple parable told by tribal elders warning children not to eat a particular species of poisoned berry or fruit? If so, that would be ironic, since the story was greatly inflated to explain the origin of sin and evil, and the very foundation of Christianity rests upon its being true as reported in Genesis. (See FALL, THE.)

The serpent raises an interesting possibility when he indicates familiarity with the mind of God, saying that the Deity knows that if Adam and Eve eat the fruit, their eyes shall be opened and they "shall be *as gods,* knowing good and evil" (v. 5). Note the reference to plural gods.

In any event, the fruit was eaten. The immediate result was that Adam and Eve experienced guilt at their nakedness and quickly sewed fig-leaves together to make aprons. How they were able to sew anything, living in such primitive circumstances, is not explained. Societies differ very widely concerning attitudes toward nakedness, and in hot lands primitive people go almost completely naked with no shame.

The next few verses relate how Adam and God engage in pointless verbal fencing. Like a detective in a television drama, the Lord conducts an investigation to determine the guilty parties, although most people have always believed God was all-powerful and all-knowing. Adam, ungallantly, puts the blame on Eve, though he was equally at fault. Eve passes it along to the snake.

One is curious to know if a meaningful punishment will be meted out to the serpent, since he corrupted Adam and Eve and hence, we are told, *the entire human race for all time!* Yes, "upon thy belly shalt thou go, and dust shalt thou eat all the days of thy life" (v. 14). But snakes have never moved in any other way, so that is hardly a punishment. The statement that serpents eat dust is false.

> 15. "And I will put enmity between you and the woman, and between your seed and her seed; he shall bruise your head and you shall bruise his heel."

There is no *natural* enmity between humankind and *any* animal species, including snakes, although primitive man must have felt vulnerable to large beasts of prey and to *poisonous* snakes. There were probably several species of deadly snakes in the lands where the Israelites wandered.

16. "I will greatly multiply your pain in childbearing; in pain you
shall bring forth children; yet your desire shall be for your husband,
and he shall rule over you."

It is by no means clear to what extent Christian couples today are guided
by what is here represented as the clear instruction of God: that a married
woman should subject herself to her husband. Certainly, men—whether
Christian or not—have tried to dominate women for thousands of years,
most often succeeding. I have heard of fundamentalist cults that quote
this verse to justify an extreme amount of male dominance and even cruelty
to women, and children as well.

We do know that, as regards the warning "in pain you shall bring
forth children," women were denied anesthesia when pain-killing drugs were
first introduced into European medical practice, purely on the grounds of
this verse. Common sense and compassion eventually prevailed over this
cruelty, and one more foot was yielded by believers in Bible inerrancy to
the march of science and Humanism.

The Lord was certainly in a vengeful mood, and yet in Verse 21 he
actually paused in his angry outburst to do a bit of tailoring, to make
coats of skins to clothe Adam and Eve.

The next two verses raise troubling theological questions:

22. And the Lord God said, "Behold, the man is become as one
of us, to know good and evil: and now, lest he put forth his hand,
and take also of the tree of life, and eat, and live forever:"
23. Therefore the Lord God sent him forth from the garden of
Eden, to till the ground from whence he was taken.

Now we learn that there was a second tree, the Tree of Life, a familiar
term in many folk mythologies. It was probably included by virtue of its
prevalence in Semitic myth and Mesopotamian art. To the Celts, the Tree
of Life was the apple tree, to the Chinese the peach, and to Semitic peoples,
the date palm. There is even in Latin American native folklore, among
several Indian tribes, a marvelous tree that bears all edible plants or, in
another version, many kinds of fish.

Incidentally, the serpent is also found widely as an important feature
of worship (especially as the Plumed Serpent) among North and South
American natives, where it is associated with fertility rites and prayers for
rain, especially among the Hopi, Aztec, and Maya. It is also a character
in some tales, just as the dragon is important in North European folklore.

Apparently it occurred to God that either Adam or Eve, or perhaps one of their children, might come nosing around the garden and attempt to get at those two remarkable botanical specimens, the Tree of the Knowledge of Good and Evil and the Tree of Life. Therefore, he resorted to the dramatic solution of placing "at the east of the garden of Eden Cherubim and a flaming sword which turned every way" (v. 24). (See also ORIGINAL SIN.)

Chapter 4. In this chapter we are told that Adam and Eve had two sons, CAIN and ABEL. It is therefore inescapably clear from the record of Genesis that the Hebrews believed that there were exactly four humans on the newly created earth. After we learn the occupations of Cain and Abel, we come upon the two young men making appropriate offerings to God from their possessions, although how they knew they were supposed to do so is not disclosed. God, after all, can have no need of anything produced by humans.

Elsewhere in the present study I shall deal with the essential absurdity of the ancient custom of burning dead animals, grains, and fruits (destroying good food, in other words) in the context of the belief that such ritualistic acts could have been of the slightest interest to pure intelligence (God). Such acts are no better or worse than similar functions performed for similar purposes by other primitive peoples of the earth.

If we pretend to assume for the moment that God, who is supposed to be all-fairness and all-justice personified, nevertheless was pleased—or even interested—in the slaughter and burning of innocent animals and "their fat portions" on the one hand but displeased by the offerings of the grains and fruits Cain brought, we immediately perceive the utter unfairness to Cain of such a divine response. Cain was, after all, only a farmer. He therefore offered up the only sorts of things he could possibly give. When, therefore, we are told that "Cain was very angry and his countenance fell," we can easily understand his emotions.

The only explanation of this story that approaches plausibility is that the Israelites wanted to think that God would be more pleased by their offering of animals (since they were then pastoralists) than by their enemies' offering of grain (since their rivals for God's favor were settled and successful agriculturists.) The rest of the account is equally inane.

8. Cain said to Abel his brother, "Let us go out to the field." And when they were in the field, Cain rose up against his brother Abel and killed him.
9. And the Lord said to Cain, "Where is Abel, your brother?" He said, "I do not know; am I my brother's keeper?"

We are asked to believe that Cain was stupid enough to think he could lie to a divinity who addressed him personally and directly. (Parenthetically, the belief encountered later in the Old Testament—that if one sees the face of God one will surely die—was obviously unknown at this stage of the development of Hebrew religious stories.)

After the Lord punishes Cain,

> 17. Cain knew his wife, and she conceived and bore Enoch; and he built a city and called the name of the city after the name of his son, Enoch.

Who on earth was Cain's wife? At that time only Adam and Eve and their remaining son Cain were alive, if the earlier chapters of Genesis are to be trusted. If Cain fathered a child, one possibility is that the mother was Eve. But this is incest and is therefore hardly acceptable as the solution. Another explanation is that Adam and Eve might have had a daughter after Cain, but if Cain impregnated her he would still be guilty of the crime of incest.

The best explanation lies outside the Bible. For several millenia there had been many individuals of both sexes to propagate the human species and never only three individuals living on earth. Obviously, if Cain existed, he took a wife from some group of people unrelated to his family. The later Hebrew authors wanted to make themselves seem so special that they didn't give this explanation or even the name and tribe of Enoch's mother, even though it would have appeared to the Hebrew audience that Cain had committed incest.

After Cain killed his brother it occurred to him to say to God, "everyone that findeth me shall slay me." The Lord set "a mark upon Cain, lest any [who are these "any"?] finding him should kill him" (v. 15). Now what possible sort of a mark could there be on a man that would prevent his being killed? The answer is none at all. Leonardo da Vinci himself could not have devised a mark that would prevent someone bent on murderous business from assaulting a luckless victim. Since the story is so absurd, we are not surprised that down through the centuries subsidiary inanities have followed, including the common belief that the "mark of Cain" is the dark skin of the Negro race.

Has anyone ever drawn back from killing Negroes? No. Fundamentalist Ku Kluxers, claiming to be God-fearing, killed Negroes with remarkable freedom in the American South for almost 100 years. And let us not forget that in Verse 15 the Lord is quite clear about what might happen to anyone who does kill Cain. "Vengeance shall be taken on him seven-fold."

> 20. And Adah bare Jabal: he was the father of such as dwell in tents, and of such as have cattle.
>
> 21. And his brother's name was Jubal: he was the father of all such as handle the harp and organ.

There is absolutely no sense in which it may be said that the millions of tribesman scattered around the earth today are descendants of Jabal. It is equally absurd to suggest that someone named Jubal was the actual ancestor of Harpo Marx, Albert Schweitzer, and jazz organist Jimmy Smith.

Chapter 5 gives the clear impression of having been written by someone else. It starts by offering a brief account of the creation of man, repeats the birth of Seth (4:25), but does not mention Cain and Abel.

> 1. This is the book of the generations of Adam. When God created man he made him in the likeness of God.
>
> 2. Male and female he created them, and he blessed them and named them Man when they were created.
>
> 3. When Adam had lived a hundred and thirty years, he became the father of a son in his own likeness, after his image, and named him Seth.
>
> 4. The days of Adam after he became the father of Seth were 800 years; and he had other sons and daughters.

Except for the preposterous details about men living for many centuries there is nothing of interest in Chapter 5. Does any modern theologian seriously assert that in the very first pages of *what must be the most important book ever written, if God is its true author,* there would actually be a chapter containing nothing in the way of moral or religious instruction, but merely a listing of men's names and their ages?

(For Chapters 6-9, see FLOOD, THE; NOAH AND THE ARK. For Chapter 11, see BABEL, TOWER OF.)

Chapter 12. If the reader has two Bibles available, I recommend that at this point he open the second book to Chapter 26. By such a comparison we discover one more instance of the confusion that is inevitable when long-held oral traditions are finally reduced to written form, for the stories told of ABRAHAM in Genesis 12:10 ff. and 20:1-7 are repeated in Chapter 26. In the third instance it is said to have happened to ISAAC. Even the name of the king, ABIMELECH, to whom the two Hebrew patriarchs offered their wives, SARAH and Rebekah, is the same.

Chapter 13. Verses 14 to 16 contain a prophecy which has never come true, for there is no land which the Jews have occupied in perpetuity. (See CANAAN; PALESTINE.)

Chapter 19 opens with an exceedingly strange story. Two angels, we are told, came to the city of Sodom, where they met a man named Lot, who happened to be sitting at the gate of the city. Lot invites the two strangers to spend the evening at his house. They decline his invitation saying, "No, but we shall spend the night in the square."

> 3. Yet he urged them strongly, so they turned aside to him and entered his house; and he prepared a feast for them, and baked unleavened bread and they ate.

It will surely occur to even the most inattentive reader to wonder why angels—who are pure spirits—would need to eat anything, but such commonsense questions present difficulties at a thousand and one places in the scriptural record.

At this point the story becomes more bizarre. We are told that the two angels are about to "lie down," which can mean only that they required rest or sleep. Why an angel would need physical rest is certainly not self-evident. But suddenly Lot's house is surrounded by *all* "the men of the city . . . both young and old, all the people from every quarter."

Although there is no way in the world to know what the total population of the community of Sodom was, it is reasonable to assume that the crowd that surrounded Lot's dwelling numbered at least a few hundred. The story relates that they demanded of Lot to know "where are the men who came to you tonight?" The crowd insists that the visitors be sent out of doors "that we may have relations with them." (v. 5)

Does it have to be pointed out that 300 or 400 men can hardly have been planning to have sexual relations with two male strangers? Lot, in any event, steps outside, shutting his door behind him, and asks the troublemakers not to behave so wickedly. Note carefully what he does next. If the reader projects himself into this kind of a situation, it would ravage reason to suppose that in the very next breath he would say:

> 8. "Now behold, I have two daughters who have not had relations with man. Please let me bring them out to you, and do to them whatever you like, only do nothing to these men, inasmuch as they have come under the shelter of my roof."

Certain instances of Christian apology for this revolting story are nothing short of embarrassing. In *U.S. Catholic* (September 1989) a writer states that the point of the shocking account is that "nothing is more important than the guest. Not your own family. . . . The sanctuary movement, in which people risk their family's well-being to protect refugees, illustrates the positive values that arise out of this Bible story."

It is nowhere a building-block of Christian, or any other form of belief that I know of, that *"nothing* is more important" than the well-being of a guest. Obviously one should be cordial to guests. One should not take advantage of them, but if there is any Christian reader who would insist on sending out his dearly loved, teenage virgin daughters to be raped by a band of bisexual ruffians, deliberately choosing that option over inconveniencing two perfect strangers, or devising some third alternative, I would be interested in hearing from him. The incident is inexplicable; nor can we know why it was put in the Old Testament.

And the two strangers, remember, were angels who, since they were gifted with superhuman powers, would not have had the slightest trouble in defending themselves, or simply vanishing.

Chapter 19 is also infamous for one of the vilest incidents in the Old Testament.

> 30. And Lot went up out of Zoar, and dwelt in the hills with his two daughters, for he feared to dwell in Zoar: and he dwelt in a cave, he and his two daughters.
> 31. And the firstborn said unto the younger, "Our father is old, and there is not a man in the earth to come in to us after the manner of all the earth."

For the reader who might not be familiar with the common Bible phraseology pertaining to sexual acts, it should be explained that "to come in unto" refers to sexual intercourse. Lot's daughter was speaking nonsense when she gave the excuse that there was no other man on the entire planet with whom she and her sister could have physical relations, but whoever authored this absurd story was clearly not familiar with human sexuality. The woman urges her sister.

> 32. "Come, let us make our father drink wine, and we will lie with him, that we may preserve the seed of our father."
> 33. And they made their father drink wine that night; and the firstborn went in, and lay with her father; and he perceived not when she lay down, nor when she arose.

The author of this unedifying account is clearly deficient in knowledge about both alcoholic intoxication and sexual intercourse. If a man were falling-down-drunk, he would be incapable of having an erection. If we start with the questionable assumption that a man is able to have sexual intercourse although deeply intoxicated, it would seem that he would at least be aware that he was engaged with a female. It is conceivable that a man in a dark room might not be able to identify the woman, but this cannot be the case with Lot, since he lived alone with his daughters in a hillside cave. If he had discovered a woman copulating with him in the night, he would have known that it could only be one daughter or the other.

To flesh out this absurd fantasy the detail is added that both women become pregnant,—meaning that the drunken sot was able to have at least two orgasms—thereby begetting the Moabites and Ammonites. Scholars now suspect that this story was put into Genesis to justify the Hebrews' hatred for the Moabites and Ammonites, although these groups were related, Semitic-speaking tribes who lived east of the Jordan River. The article on JACOB explains this. I also recommend the remarkable archaeological study, *Out of the Desert?* by William H. Stiebing, Jr. (Buffalo, N.Y.: Prometheus Books, 1989). It could be argued that the calamity that befell Canaan in the 13th century is suggested by the "fleeing" of Lot's family and other details (19:15-30).

Since fundamentalists are now active in censorship campaigns, it would be an interesting experiment to retell the erotic story of Lot and his daughters by putting it in "modern dress." Let us say that Lot was a resident of Chicago, that his name was James Nelson, that his two daughters were named Joan and Dorothy, and that fearing they might go through life as virgins they contrived to get their father heavily intoxicated and then got into his bed and engaged in whatever sort of foreplay was necessary to stimulate the old fellow to—well, it is not necessary to give all the details. But the point is that if a collection of such stories were to be published, there would be an immediate angry outcry from fundamentalist Christians, and perhaps other religious believers as well.

Chapter 21. If the Bible were always reliable as history, we could be quite certain that the Canaanites or the Philistines—claimed by some of today's Palestinians as their ancestors—occupied the general area of the Holy Land, or Israel, *before* the followers of Moses, inasmuch as Verse 34 says that, "Abraham sojourned in the land of the Philistines many days." Archaeologists have found many remains of Late Bronze Age occupation by Canaanites but no evidence of an incursion by outsiders. Indeed, modern Palestinians can refer to this portion of Scripture as establishing their claim to prior occupation. But since scholars believe that the story of Abraham was written a long time after the days of the patriarch, some suggest that the term *land of the Philistines* was a matter of geographic identification for later readers.

Chapter 22. Father Bruce Vawter raises a fundamental question in his chapter on Abraham in *A Path Through Genesis*.

Throughout Israel's long history its deepest thinkers forever ask themselves, in wonder and in awe, why it was that God had chosen this people to be his own. The answer they gave was the only one that could be given:

It was not because you are the largest of all nations that the Lord set his heart on you and chose you . . . it was because the Lord loved you.

But why did he love them the most? Since all primitive peoples have myths about a god creating—and often watching over—them and since the Hebrews wrote the Old Testament, the answer seems obvious. This means that people today do not have to accept the Jews' word for it that they actually were, or are, the CHOSEN PEOPLE. To say as much neither smacks of nor condones anti-Semitism. It should be possible for *a believer in one God to also believe that he created all other people and loves all of his creation,* be they Jews, Russians, Palestinians, Americans, Japanese, or tribes of the Amazon interior.

Chapter 34. The story related in Verses 8-29 is sadly typical of those in the Old Testament.

8. And Hamor [the Hivite] communed with them [Jacob and his family], saying, "The soul of my son Shechem longeth for your daughter: I pray you give her to him to wife . . ."

13. And the sons of Jacob answered Shechem and Hamor his father deceitfully, and said, because he had defiled Dinah their sister: . . .

15. But in this will we consent unto you: If ye will be as we be, that every male of you be circumcised;

16. then will we give our daughters to you, and we will take your daughters to ourselves, and we will dwell with you and become one people . . .

25. And it came to pass on the third day, when they were in pain [from circumcision] that two of the sons of Jacob, Simeon and Levi, Dinah's brethren, took each man his sword, and came unto the city boldly, *and slew all the males.*

26. And they slew *Hamor and Shechem his son with the edge of the sword. . . .*

29. *And all their wealth, and all their little ones, and their wives they took captive.* (IA)

We are asked to believe that two men, each armed only with a sword, slaughtered *all* the men in a particular city. Although Simeon and Levi were presumably revenging the rape of their sister Dinah, we are also told that Shechem loved Dinah and wanted to marry her; it therefore seems unusually nasty—and opportunistic—of Jacob's sons to make the promises of Verses 15-16, and then slay every male, only one of whom was guilty, and finally seize their wealth and enslave their families.

If it is argued that those were the standards by which all people in that part of the world lived in those days, why then are Jacob and his sons held up as special men to whom God promised so much? (See also JOSEPH.)

GILGAMESH. See Enuma Elish and Gilgamesh.

GOD.

His Existence. If there is any form of compliment I am strenuously moved to reject, it is congratulations for making the assumption that God exists.

Probably 98 percent of the believers of the world—believers, that is, in a thousand and one forms of religion, many consisting of mutually contradictory claims—accept the idea of the existence of one or more gods. They usually accept their particular form of belief because of social or geographical circumstances. In most cases, they were born into a Catholic family, or one that is Mormon, Jewish, Hindu or some other faith. But if this is so, and if, secondly, there is indeed a God, nothing more can be said about such individuals than that it is fortunate that they believe as they do. To give them credit, to pin medals on them for that belief, is absurd.

As for the remaining small minority of those who have reasoned their way to one form of religious belief or another, here, too, it is a waste of the emotion of admiration to compliment such individuals for the acceptance of that which has appeared to them logically inescapable.

We ought to be impressed by the moral codes that others besides ourselves profess, because if a given code is reasonable, if adherence to it is socially productive, and if an individual lives by it, then compliments are merited. If, purely out of religious considerations, others sacrifice elements of their own well-being to help the poor, the ill, the orphaned, the unfortunate of any sort, as many religions besides Christianity ask their adherents to do, then it is clear that praise is justified. But this is very different from praise for simply assuming or believing that there is a God.

Just as it is absurd to assume that morality depends on the Bible, just so there are no grounds whatever for thinking that other important religious questions stand or fall as the Bible does. Consider, for example, the question of the existence of God. If we assume that there is a deity, it is obvious that it/he has existed through all periods of our planet's history, which scientists now assure us involved a span of many billions of years, whereas the earliest parts of the Bible were written in the form we have them relatively recently, not much more than 2,500 years ago.

The same applies to the question as to whether humans continue to exist, in any form, after the moment of physical death. Either they do or they do not. If they do, then they always have; again, such a state of affairs must have existed for countless ages before the Hebrews/Jews began to compile their oral traditions, myths, legends, prophecies, poems, and ethical preachments in written form.

Does the existence of JESUS Christ depend on the Bible? Absolutely not. The reasoning is the same. We do, obviously, depend on the four Gospels for the little material we have of the events of his life, although they were not written during his lifetime and unfortunately contradict each other. Even the most devout scholars have noted many serious discrepancies, and we have even less information about his childhood and young manhood. But that such a man as Jesus existed and that he must have been a remarkable individual both seem probable. (Whether or not he was also God is not settled by the New Testament.)

Almost 99 percent of the human race was not mentioned in the Bible. Does that mean they did not exist?

Some fear that if confidence in the Bible is destroyed, or even weakened, the inevitable result will be a loss of faith in the existence of God. But this is by no means necessarily the case; the fear is based on a misunderstanding of the equation. If there is no God, it follows that the Bible is almost total nonsense. But if the Bible is largely nonsense, that fact has no effect whatever on the question of the existence of God.

There are time-honored, creative, and intellectually respectable arguments for the existence of God from diverse parts of the world, as well as the reverse. While it is clear that arguments for God have not convinced all scholars, they nevertheless have seemed convincing to many. Debate on the question will continue among both laymen and philosophers. But it is of profound significance, in the context of my case, that none of the arguments devised by history's most able spokesmen for Christianity and Judaism have suggested that humans ought to believe in a deity simply because the Bible suggests such a course.

There are millions who firmly believe in the existence of an all-powerful, all-knowing power, who nonetheless know little or nothing of the Bible, or who consider it totally irrelevant so far as the question of God's existence is concerned. Many of these peoples have their own scriptures as, for example, the Zoroastrians and the Muslims. Philosophers of Islam have also offered elegant proofs for the existence of God, which few Christians have ever heard of.

A careful, unbiased reading of the Scriptures is as likely to lead to agnosticism or atheism as to unquestioning belief. There is no purely logical reason why this should be the case, but it happens nevertheless because of the unremitting indoctrination, usually by Christian fundamentalism, that the Bible is the source of all necessary knowledge about God, including the fact of his existence.

If we must believe that God's Word cannot contain even one modest instance of error, then the undeniable existence of hundreds of mistakes and inconsistencies demolishes the claims of the literalists. However, it does not follow that, because of its errors, the Bible is totally without merit. It is, in fact, a profoundly important document; it has been a mighty influence on Western culture and is well worth scholarly study by every thoughtful person. (See BIBLE, MYSTERY OF THE.)

However, by exaggerating the virtues of the Scriptures and either dishonestly or fanatically denying its obvious faults, our literalist brethren stake out a position that it is easy to prove is untenable.

Nature of God. One of the most disturbing scriptural contradictions is the two pictures of God: one in the Old Testament and a different one in the New. We are told that Jesus, the perfect man, was such because he was not only the Son of God but—by a process that even the most learned Christian theologians are unable to explain and hence simply define as a mystery—also personally God himself, as the second person of the Trinity. It is the essence of this Christ-God of the New Testament that he returned good for evil, that he preached love and commitment to a higher law than the state's. This is certainly a beautiful pacifist philosophy; the world would clearly see a great deal less bloodshed and other suffering *if even a detectable percentage of Christians* had ever given the slightest evidence that they were guided by it.

But the point at issue is scriptural contradiction. There is not the slightest question but that the God of the Old Testament is a jealous, vengeful God, inflicting not only on the sinful "pagans" but even on his CHOSEN PEOPLE fire, lightning, hideous plagues and diseases, brimstone, and other curses. The reader is advised not to waste time consulting scholarly works in the hope of finding a resolution of the contradiction. No such resolution is possible unless reason itself be cast aside.

Of one thing our intelligence absolutely assures us: laws made by God are not subject to revocation. And if they are not subject to change by divine wisdom itself, it is an even greater absurdity to suggest that they can be changed by one man or a group of men. Practically everyone will agree to this in principle, but the going gets sticky when such obvious sense is applied to particular cases.

For some 26 centuries or more the prohibition against doing work on the Sabbath stood inviolate; this gradually changed. The Mormon church, the Church of the Latter-Day Saints, a century ago was absolutely certain that the Lord had personally authorized the practice of polygamy, which had prevailed in Old Testament times. But when Mormon leaders perceived that to persist in their polygamous customs would prevent the entry of the state of Utah into the United States, not to mention scandalizing the rest of the world's Christians, they shortly arranged to convince themselves that God had changed his mind about the issue, as if divine wisdom were subject to the sort of flightiness that characterizes human thought.

Knowledge of God. A problem which has been particularly troubling to the Christian conscience over the centuries has involved the proper means of "knowing God." I put the phrase in quotation marks by way of suggesting that we have no way of determining—in a scientific sense—whether *knowledge* of God can in fact be acquired. It is perfectly reasonable to argue that everything one might say about God is theoretical, speculative, and hypothetical in the sense that there seems to be no general statement about the Deity whose truth is self-evident to all. The two simplest statements that one can make about God are (1) God exists, and (2) God does not exist. But these two dramatize the point perfectly, for though one or the other would seem to be true—while its opposite would be false—there has never been any agreement, whether in schools of philosophy or on the street, as to which of the two may be held with that degree of certainty common to scientific propositions.

But in the history of theology, it has nevertheless long remained a perplexing question as to *how* man might acquire knowledge of the divine, forgetting the question as to *whether* such a thing is possible. Lefevre d'Etaples, a 16th-century French Catholic scholar, said, "One ought to affirm of God only what the Scriptures teach us about Him," which, in time, turned out to be the Protestant rather than the Catholic position. However, then we are back to the serious problem that the Bible contains several views of God, some of which clash violently with others.

God's Goodness. Let us now ask the question: Which is superior, Almighty God or the Bible?

The question is one about which there could not possibly be a choice, nor any debate, except among madmen. By definition, an all-good, all-powerful, all-loving God is superior to any physical object in his universe. Thus, while one might praise certain pages of the Old and New Testaments very highly, no one could seriously claim that these pieces of paper and the words printed on them are either superior to God or the equal of God.

Having agreed on that, let us proceed to a second question. In situations where there is a flat contradiction, and thus the necessity for choice, between (1) the concept of an all-virtuous God on the one hand, and (2) a vengeful, punishing Deity described in an ancient document, which concept of God will the intelligent individual regard as more worthy of respect? Again there can be no debate; the mind leaps immediately to the conclusion that it is the all-good, all-knowing, all-loving God that is worthy of respect and love.

I have assisted the unsophisticated reader through these simple steps by way of demonstrating that it is by no means the purpose of this study to destroy belief in God. I have known agnostics and atheists and am familiar with their writings, and I respect both. Some of the wisest and most intelligent men who have ever lived have been atheists or held a philosophy that was not deism or theism. I am thinking of Chinese and Greek philosophers in particular.

But the validity of the case against the possibility of God is not relevant to the present inquiry. This inquiry finds me willing to begin with the assumption that the God of classical theism does in fact exist. It is within the context of that assumption that I have found myself faced with certain puzzling questions, since I commenced the present study with the common supposition that the Bible has always been of morally uplifting validity. (That my initial belief has been greatly shaken is self-evident in many articles in this volume, especially those dealing with Old Testament subjects.)

I am, as a result of the present study, now of the firm opinion that *to the extent that the total goodness of God can be defended as a philosophical proposition, the last place to which the devout believer should turn for supporting evidence is the Bible.* There is better evidence in Nature herself—in the inherent order, enormous scale, largesse of air, water, food, sunlight, breathtaking beauty, in the human capacity for love and virtue— than in the familiar accounts of assorted slaughters, sex crimes, atrocities, murders of infants, tortures, and other abominations we read about in the Old Testament. If all such crimes were committed by men the scriptural authors pointed to as evil, if they were condemned in some manner, some enlightening moral might be drawn. But a great many, the devout believer is told, are performed *either by God himself or by esteemed leaders and kings on his personal, clear-cut instruction!*

Although I, like most believers, interpret the word *God* as implying perfection, it is more than understandable that atheists such as Kai Nielsen, professor of philosophy at the University of Calgary, would raise the following question, in his essay "Morality and the Will of God":

> What grounds have we for believing that God is good? Naive people, recalling how God spoke to Job out of the whirlwind, say that God is good because He is omnipotent and omniscient. But this clearly will not do, for, as Hepburn points out, there is nothing logically improper about saying 'X is omnipotent and omniscient and morally wicked.' Surely in the world as we know it there is no logical connection between being powerful and knowledgeable and being good. As far as I can see, all that God proved to Job when He spoke to him out of the whirlwind was that God was an immeasurably powerful being; but He did not prove his moral superiority to Job and He did nothing at all to exhibit His moral goodness. (One might even argue that He exhibited moral wickedness.)

Parenthetically, the serious student of religion will find most instructive *Critiques of God,* P. Angeles, ed. (Buffalo, N.Y.: Prometheus Books, 1976), a collection of statements of the case against belief in God by such respected philosophers and psychologists as Sidney Hook, Paul Edwards, Michael Scriven, Walter Kaufmann, Sigmund Freud, Erich Fromm, John Dewey, and Bertrand Russell.

But again, it is not from the ground of atheism that my questions are addressed but from the assumption of the existence of a purely virtuous God. I am by no means deluded that the existence of God can be proved in the sense that a physical proposition can be proved. Nor can the *non-*existence of God be proved. I can personally advance arguments suggesting the inherent preposterousness of each of the two mutually contradictory positions. I *assume* the existence of a Supreme Being; therefore, on grounds that will no doubt seem peculiar to some rigorous scholars, belief in God seems to me slightly less preposterous than its opposite.

The Problem of Evil. The presence of "just" and "unjust" evil in the world, oddly enough, does not loom as a problem in certain forms of paganism, many of which, being polytheistic, encompass belief in evil gods or spirits, as well as good ones. By attributing practically all evil, destruction, and calamity to such entities, the total goodness of the chief god may be maintained.

Comments Yehezkel Kaufmann, in his scholarly *The Religion of Israel From Its Beginnings to the Babylonian Exile* (Chicago: University of Chicago Press, 1960; first published in Hebrew, 1937–1956):

> It was otherwise in Israel. On the one hand there was no evil principle; good and evil came from Yahweh. On the other hand, Israelite religion tolerated no fault or blame in God. He was altogether good and just. When harsh reality challenged the conventional view of divine justice, concern for the honor of God violently disturbed the devout. They could not break out in insults or surrender to despair; they could only complain and question and go on seeking an answer. At that, it is not so much the human side of undeserved suffering that agitates the Bible as *the threat it poses to faith in God's justice.* (IA)

So it seems that the ancient Israelites, one among other "primitive" people, interpreted evil as a punishment from their one God. It is curious, however, to find a scholar such as Kaufmann maintaining that Israelite religion had an "altogether good and just" God.

As for the once assumed historical validity of the story of JOB, it is summarily dismissed by Kaufmann, who in his excellent history of Israelite religion states:

> The legend of Job's trial at the instance of Satan is surely early. The story belongs—with the stories of the Flood, Sodom and Gomorrah, and Jonah—to the ancient moralistic literature of Israel. Job is a righteous non-Israelite, a hero of popular legend mentioned together with Noah and Daniel in Ezekiel 14:14 ff. The Wisdom author of the book of Job utilized this early story for his own purposes. Hence, there are two elements in the book, *one legendary,* the other sapiential. (IA)

Gender of God. If there is a God, it strikes me that it is nothing more than a convenience of common speech to refer to that divine being as a masculine entity. Perfectly orthodox theologians invariably describe God as pure spirit. It is obvious that such a spirit can have no physical characteristics whatever, and since masculinity and femininity are physical characteristics, that would seem to settle the question.

It is no proper objection to argue that Jesus Christ was God and that he was clearly a male. Again, if there is a divine being who has all power, it inescapably follows that he can physically manifest himself to his creatures in the guise of a man, a dove, a snake, a Chevrolet convertible, or in any other form he might elect; but none of that has any relevance to the question as to whether a divine spirit may be said to have gender characteristics.

God the Father. We know, to our sorrow, that every day on planet earth thousands of children, as well as adults, are burned, assaulted, knifed, strangled, raped, brutalized in all too many ways; yet the Heavenly Father, who we are absolutely assured by the Bible has the power to alter such hideous circumstances, does not employ that power to do so. Nor do many of his ministers, priests, and rabbis on earth call upon legislators to cease and desist supporting or voting funds for the use of military weapons against the innocent and helpless.

It is, indeed, a large part of the appeal of the combined reality and/ or image of Jesus that he spoke out against the monstrous wrongs inflicted by man and that he urged others to follow his religion of love. Jesus, many believe, did heal the sick, restore the dead to life, and comfort the afflicted. Whether the story of Jesus be perceived as history, myth, or a combination of the two, he is lovable primarily because he loves. There is no record that he turned his back on anyone in need.

How immeasurably does it add to the mystery of the Old Testament that the supreme Heavenly Father is not only sparing indeed of personal intervention for the purpose of alleviating suffering, but in countless instances makes it his business to inflict it? To this it may reasonably be objected that it is no fault of God's if men have painted such hideous portraits of him. On this realization, let us reflect deeply.

H

HEAVEN. Christians apparently hold mutually contradictory opinions as to what sort of reality is conveyed by the word *Heaven*. From my own early training, I can attest that most Christian children perceive Heaven as having an actual physical location, in the same sense that New York and Chicago do. Later the idea that Heaven is not, in fact, a concrete location somewhere out in space, but is a spiritual state, becomes more widely held.

This interpretation of the word, far from clarifying the issue, unfortunately, plunges it into philosophical puzzlement. Not all adult Christians have abandoned their original, simplistic notions about Heaven, and they have scriptural support for holding to it. It is a dogmatic component of Christian belief that at some future time—or "end of time"—Heaven eventually will house the actual bodies of everyone who has ever lived except, obviously, those consigned to the opposite extreme from Heaven, which is called HELL.

Oddly enough, Christians are much clearer in their minds about Hell than they are about Heaven. Perhaps this is because we have no difficulty visualizing calamitous physical circumstances because we have so often observed them. The various Christian churches have been quite consistent, down through the centuries, in holding to the view that the flames of Hell are just as literal as those we observe on earth.

As for Heaven, many Christians ultimately return to their first form of belief about it since, if countless millions of human bodies are to spend all eternity there, it follows that there must be an actual "there" for them to inhabit.

If ours were a more rational world, this would promptly lead us to ask precisely where Heaven is, but no one has ever been able to provide any information about it. If there is no Heaven, then all speculations about it are wasteful, but if there is a Heaven, then the only important question is how to get to it.

Catholics and some other Christians are taught that at the moment of our earthly death we go at once to one of only three possible destinations: Heaven, Hell, or Purgatory.

We should not be surprised that since Christians have so often differed with each other, they are far from one mind as to who will be permitted to go to Heaven. The predestinationists, inspired by the writings of John Calvin, think that before we are even born God has determined who will be saved to enter Heaven and who will automatically depart for Hell, no matter how good a life he or she may have tried to live. The KORAN says a similar thing, but Islamic thinkers contradict this idea, fortunately and humanely, by specifying that a certain number of good acts will cancel out many bad ones. Since Muslims repeat continuously throughout their lives, in their prayers, the phrase "God is beneficent, God is merciful," one can assume they live in hope of his mercy.

Some Protestants believe that good works, and not just faith or a "confession" that JESUS is Lord, are necessary for Heaven's full reward. A mystical sect of Islam, Sufism, believes that the seeker, an intense lover of God in an almost personal way, progresses through worldly trials of increasing difficulty, until he or she finally enters the presence of God and is somehow merged into his being.

Another problem is posed by John 3:13, which says, "No one has gone up to Heaven except he who came down from Heaven, even the Son of man whose home is Heaven." The perfectly clear meaning of that is that no mere mortal had ever gone to Heaven as of the 30th year of the earthly life of Jesus. But this is flatly incompatible with the long-held Christian belief that the highly virtuous go to Heaven as soon as they die, and that millions of others go to Heaven some time thereafter, after spending a period in Purgatory.

We seem to be more clear, however, about who will *not* go there.

23. And Jesus said to his disciples, "Truly, I say to you, it will be hard for a rich man to enter the kingdom of Heaven.
24. "Again I tell you, it is easier for a camel to go through the eye of a needle than for a rich man to enter the kingdom of God." (Matthew 19)

The Koran makes it clear that neglect of the poor and orphaned is a grave offense, and two of the five major obligations of the Muslim faith concern the poor: to give a tithe to take care of them and to fast so as to understand how painful it is to go without food.

There is one curious thing I have noticed about some elderly, devout

Christians. They appear to fear death—not the moment of death, which cannot be as painful as some of their earthly ailments—but perhaps they fear that the belief in Heaven, which they have based their lives on, may not be valid, that death may be final with no afterlife. This is perhaps the reason that Christian funerals consist partly of reassurances that the dearly beloved has departed for a better life, which the survivors will share one day when they are reunited with the deceased.

The New Testament does not tell us much about what Heaven will look like, for this was not an especially vivid concept to the Jews up to that time. However, coming about 600 years later, the Koran sets forth an appealing and rather specific picture of Paradise. It is a land of flowing rivers, appetizing food, and beautiful young maidens who will sing, entertain, and presumably perform other services for the gentlemen who go there. No such vision of handsome young men is promised to women; one wonders what a devout Muslim woman thinks she will be doing while her husband is enjoying the company of a voluptuous woman.

A vitally important question about Heaven concerns what happens there. A great many Christians are vague in their own minds, presumably because they have not received precise instruction on the point. If we start with the assumption that there is indeed a Heaven, then it is reasonable to imagine that life there will be perfect. It is often assumed that there will be considerable singing, but we don't know if traditional, earthly music will be sung there. It is pleasing, given American and Western European social conditioning, to imagine heavenly choirs offering beautiful renditions of Bach or traditional spirituals. The vision of a sort of massive Mormon Tabernacle Choir, performing for hours a "day" for all eternity has a certain appeal to some and none to others.

Christians face another problem as regards their belief that families and other loved ones will be reunited in Heaven, for many decent believers have been married several times, due to the death of mates. If we reason consistently about this point, it follows that there will be certain wives and husbands in Heaven who will live in a state of polygamy, in the company of a number of former mates, a situation that would be considered sinful behavior on earth. Will there be sexual relations in Heaven? Maybe we will find there that God approves of a certain amount of good clean sex.

Those who have worked long and hard on earth are naturally attracted by the idea that in Heaven there will be no need for physical labor—indeed, labor of any kind. If we contemplate such practical questions, we might come to an understanding that life in Heaven may be perceived as the Great Retirement in The Sky. Those who are weary of their work on planet earth often spend years longing for retirement but then are dismayed to find that its appeal was largely illusory. There would, of course, be no such problem in Heaven, since no troubling thoughts of any kind could intrude there.

Parenthetically, it might be disastrous for certain economic systems if the masses ever abandoned their belief in Heaven, because down through the centuries, when they have quite justifiably complained about their physical circumstances—often characterized by poverty, illness, the pains of backbreaking labor, the degradation common to life in slums and the poverty of their education, they have been told that while life on earth has been admittedly hellish for them, they can at least look forward to their final reward in Heaven. The overthrow of belief in Heaven might increase the danger of revolutionary uprisings.

Although some fundamentalists are critical of their fellow Christians who do try to alleviate the sufferings of the poor on earth, they would be much wiser if they cooperated in such compassionate efforts rather than oppose them, for if the poor ever gave up their belief in the afterlife they would certainly demand more loving treatment on this earth.

In our own time, Catholic liberation theology and some Protestant clergymen have pointed out that God did not intend for people to suffer on earth just so that they might better enjoy Heaven. This message, however, is received with benign neglect by the majority of churches and churchgoers.

It is important, especially for Christians, to recall that when Jesus and his immediate followers talked of the afterlife, it was in the context of the quite *specific belief that life on planet earth was fast approaching its final chapter.* The first Christians firmly believed that the concluding calamities would occur in their lifetime. In other words, they thought that just 20 or 30 years into their future, earth-time would end. They were not foreseeing long centuries when billions of slaves, serfs, peasants, and nonunionized, defenseless workers would have to struggle desperately every day of their lives.

We now know that the first Christians were mistaken about all this, a fact that leads to the awkward realization that either (1) Jesus himself was in error, or (2) if he was incapable of error, being divine, then the Scriptures paint an inaccurate picture on a matter of the most fundamental importance.

Christians have, of course, been predicting the end of time throughout the almost 2,000 years of their history. Indeed, in our own day we are constantly hearing of small Christian sects giving precise dates on which the curtain will ring down on the drama of human history. Consistent with such beliefs, the members of such churches sell all their belongings, close up their businesses, and often convene in some rural location to await their appointment with the Lord. We shall never know in how many thousands of instances over the last 2,000 years such individuals and groups have suffered the embarrassment of being proved wrong. They, of course, believe this because it is a prominent theme in the New Testament.

It has been dishonest of Christian theologians, when the world did not come to an end, not to revise the notion of the end of time and of Heaven. Not having done so, they permit the haves still to say smugly of the have-nots, "Well, they have Heaven to look forward to," never themselves emulating God as they go about squeezing more work out of some emaciated peasant who has just lost his fourth child to malnutrition.

The spread of communism, meant to be a system of alleviating poverty by equalizing the goods of this world, and which said, "Enough of waiting for the next world," made many churchmen more opposed than ever to a worldly redistribution of the earth's goods. There are few things more morally unattractive than hearing a religious person, well-fed, well-housed, and well-educated, say, "God must love the poor for he made so many of them."

God did not make them poor; he created an earth with an abundance for all, and it is not his fault that greedy landowners seize plots that once fed a peasant's family in order to raise more coffee, sugar, or beef for export to rich nations. And even if we do accept the notion that the poor are going to be rewarded in Heaven, we are justified in asking: "Where will those who made their lives miserable on earth spend *their* eternity?" (See also RESURRECTION.)

HEBREWS, THE LETTER TO THE, is one of the epistles in the New Testament. The reader may be surprised to learn that Christians have never had the slightest idea who wrote this portion of the Scriptures. It is now commonly agreed that the early attribution of the epistle to St. PAUL was an error. In this connection I recommend *Letters That Paul Did Not Write* by Raymond Collins (Wilmington, Del.: Michael Glazier, 1988). A well-written, scholarly work by a Catholic, it naturally stresses that the impossible-to-answer question about authorship is not nearly as important as the essential message of Hebrews. Collins informs his readers—perhaps the first time Christians have encountered such an idea—that not only did Paul *not* write the Letter to the Hebrews, but also he had nothing to do with Ephesians, Colossians, II Thessalonians, I Timothy, II Timothy, and Titus. The first scholar to state this reasonable truth about Hebrews was Origen, who in the 3rd century said, "Who wrote the epistle only God knows for certain."

If we do not know who wrote it, can we at least be sure concerning to whom it was written? No, we cannot. Some scholars believe it was sent to a conservative group of Jewish Christians, but in the Oxford Study Edition of the New English Bible, it is said that "in spite of the traditional title the addressees were probably Gentile Christians." But this is still in dispute. There seems to be broad agreement that it was written sometime between A.D. 80 and 100. It was written in Greek, and its quotations from Psalms and other Old Testament scripture are from the Septuagint, the Greek translation of the Hebrew Scriptures.

To me the oddest thing about the epistle is that, although it speaks movingly and powerfully of JESUS Christ and refers to him again and again as the Son of God, it never clearly states what is, if true, a far more astonishing and powerful assertion made by later Christians: that he was also, as a member of the Trinity, Almighty God. Here, however, in Chapter 10, Jesus is depicted as sitting in Heaven at God's right hand.

It would be irrelevant here to dwell on the mystery of the Trinity. A mystery after all, by definition, is something that cannot be reasonably explained. Indeed, if the anonymous author of the epistle had stressed the divinity of Jesus, he could have written a much shorter and more-to-the-point message, since it is obvious that nothing more complimentary or impressive can be said about a person than that he is the all-powerful Creator and Sustainer of the universe.

Although William Neil, in *Harper's Bible Commentary,* says what many scholars believe—that Hebrews is one of the most important books of the New Testament—he nevertheless opens his exposition by saying, "The letter to the Hebrews is probably one of the least familiar writings of the New Testament, even to those who claim to 'know their Bible.'"

The letter, in any event, has always made sad reading for the actual Hebrews of the world—if they have bothered to read it—since it tells them, in a variety of ways, not only that their traditional religion has been superseded by that of Christ but that they are endangering their immortal souls if they persist in the error of adhering to their ancient rituals and customs. Only in Christ Jesus, they are warned, is true salvation and eternal life to be found.

This is, of course, the central message of Christianity. Until fairly recently all Christian churchmen insisted that those who do not believe Jesus was—is—God would be damned to an eternity of hideous torment in actual flames. More-liberal ministers and priests no longer stress this point, apparently feeling that, despite the New Testament, no one on this earth can be sure of the mind or plans of God.

Another interesting thing about Hebrews is that it cites many figures from the Old Testament. In doing so the author, beyond the slightest doubt, accepts the ancient miracle stories as factual. To be specific, he refers to Enoch, Cain's son, in 11:5, saying that the prophet "was taken up so that he should not see death." This is a truly remarkable assertion in both its original and later forms. Even Jesus suffered death, as did the saints, but we are told that Enoch, like Elijah, was taken directly, while still a living, breathing soul, into the presence of God. It has unfortunately never been clear what the significance of this was meant to be. Surely we are not to conclude that he was superior to or more favored than Jesus, or, for that matter, to other important figures of ancient Scripture. The reference to Enoch's non-death may have been due to a mistranslation of Genesis.

The author of Hebrews also affirms the story of NOAH (11:7), despite the numerous factors which render the tale improbable.

Another Old Testament figure spoken of in complimentary terms is a prostitute named Rahab (11:15), whose story is told in the second chapter of JOSHUA. Elsewhere I take up the subject of "situational ethics," the tendency to consider mitigating circumstances when evaluating moral or immoral behavior. Fundamentalist Christians are very clear about this, a practice they consider modernist and despicable. How they can persist in that view, when Rahab is complimented for lying to defend the two spies that Joshua sent out, is not easy to see. This seems to be a clear-cut case of extreme situational ethics at work in ancient times.

The same puzzle we noted before greets us in Chapter 12 in which, after having just referred to a long list of Old Testament figures who worked wonders simply because of their faith, the writer says:

> 1. Wherefore seeing we also are compassed about with so great a cloud of witnesses, let us lay aside every weight, and the sin which doth so easily beset us, and let us run with patience the race that is set before us,
> 2. Looking unto Jesus the author and finisher of our faith; who for the joy that was set before him endured the cross, despising the shame, and is set down at the right hand of the throne of God.

Again we see that God and Jesus appear to be totally distinct figures in the mind of the author of Hebrews.

The main theme of Hebrews is one that became central to Christianity: that the old Mosaic covenant God made with his people is superseded by the new covenant, of which Jesus was sent to be the instrument; that the Hebrew priest's offer of an animal sacrifice with emphasis on its blood is to be replaced by the bloody sacrifice of Christ on the cross, which *can* be viewed as a regression to human sacrifice.

HELL. The belief in a place of punishment characterized by the most hideous suffering imaginable, that induced by fire and persisting for all eternity, is morally incomprehensible.

A reader socially conditioned to "speak respectfully" of any and all religious ideas—itself an absurdity—may be taken aback by such blunt language. But is *respect* the appropriate response to the idea of Hell, whether the word represents a reality or a mythical fantasy? Hardly. If Hell is real, it is the eternal abode of all the evil people who have ever lived or those who may have sinned once or simply those who don't "accept Jesus as savior." Belief in any such alleged reality must have some sort of point. If there is a God and if he instituted Hell, he cannot have done so in a haphazard and pointless manner. Very well then: What *is* the point of Hell?

It certainly cannot *reform* the billions of poor souls who already inhabit the fiery regions, for if we may trust relevant Christian teachings, they are there forever. Nor, it is reasonable to say, can the flames of Hell ever produce the slightest good for the additional non-Christian billions— many quite decent people—who, according to certain aspects of Christian theory, will endure such suffering immediately upon the cessation of their earthly lives.

Even a child can perceive that if painful penalties are not simply acts of deranged violence, they must be interpreted as a deterrent. We spank Johnny in hope that the next time he is tempted to commit a particular offense, he will avoid doing so simply by recollecting his previous discomfort. The point of Hell, then, should be to provide not only a strong deterrent but the most dramatic one imaginable. Anyone who has burned even the tip of a finger in a flame or touched a hot object is familiar with the excruciating torture of such moments. It requires no special exercise of the imagination, therefore, to extrapolate that brief, passing pain to a situation in which the entire human anatomy is assailed by fire, and *that* not only for a few minutes—which would be maddening enough—not only for a lifetime, but forever and ever.

Very well, then. We have agreed that the whole point of Hell is to serve as a deterrent and that whoever first conceived the place, whether God or man, at least deserves credit for envisioning the most severe punishment imaginable. But what evidence do we have that demonstrates that most Christians, down through the two thousand years in which they have firmly believed in Hell, have been deterred from the commission of one grievously sinful act or another? The answer is inescapable—there is no evidence whatsoever.

Rather, Christians themselves tell us that humankind is totally depraved, naturally sinful, from the very moment of conception. Whether this is true or not, we have no reason to debate it at the present. But if we simply lift our eyes to the world about us, not excluding ourselves from the general judgment, we see that hardly a week passes, in the lives of even morally superior individuals, when they do not commit certain sorts of moral offenses. Since the only possible justification for Hell is to serve as a deterrent, and inasmuch as it has been a resounding failure as such, then we are faced with the inevitable conclusion that an all-knowing, all-wise God has personally instituted perhaps the most massive failure in the long record of human experience.

But since God is perfect and therefore cannot have any connection whatever with failure, we must—if we are determined to preserve our faith in such an appealing deity—renounce our belief in the criminally sadistic hypothesis of Hell.

Christian Sadism. Although I am undoubtedly the inferior of the great Christian saint Thomas Aquinas in a thousand ways, I am bold enough to say that I am his superior in one way. If Hell is real, then even the most depraved and vicious wretches in Hell have my sympathy since, compared to whatever atrocities they might have committed on earth, the punishment that many Christians believe is inflicted upon them by an otherwise merciful and loving God far exceeds the terror of their own deeds. I seek not the slightest credit for the combined emotions of sympathy for the sinner and detestation of his sin, which in other contexts Christians have always insisted must guide the faithful in their contemplation of human evil. But as against this common and compassionate reaction, consider the shocking assertion of Aquinas that he could contemplate the fiery torment of millions of such sufferers with a smile.

In attempting to understand why individuals and groups believe what they do, it is instructive to consider not just each opinion in isolation but rather in the context of a belief-system. It emerged clearly, in the 1950s and 1960s, during which the debate about the morality and military efficacy of nuclear weapons of mass destruction raged with particular heat, that those who were pronuclear were very largely fundamentalist Christians who also believed in Hell. Both sides in the debate have accepted that any and all attacks with such weapons would almost certainly come by surprise. Bear in mind, in this connection, that Catholics and Protestants do not merely hold that sinful members of the Christian faith will be barbecued but that the entire human race, except for those who die in a state of grace, will suffer such a fate.

Suppose now that an enemy country initiates a nuclear conflagration. Scores of millions will be incinerated instantly and thus, if other facets of Christian belief are valid, be plunged immediately into a condition approximating Hell. Moments later, many would proceed to Hell itself. One might think at first that this ugly reality would have led fundamentalist Christians to flock to the antinuclear movement. But quite the reverse has generally proved to be the case, although by and large the mainstream or liberal Protestants have been antinuclear and the American Catholic bishops have flatly stated that nuclear war is morally unacceptable.

To those who wish to punish others—or at least see them punished, if the avengers are too cowardly to take matters into their own hands—the belief in a fiery, hideous Hell appears to be a great source of comfort.

It may, in fact, be the distorted longing for justice that leads to the thought of such retribution, for it is clear enough, alas, that in the only world we know, the guilty not only often go undetected and therefore unpunished but, in fact, may reap rich rewards for their iniquity. It is also troubling to observe that the innocent are sometimes unjustly accused.

The idea of retribution in a future life, incidentally, was not mentioned in the Old Testament through the time of the writing of both books of Chronicles.

Some Christian Commentary on Hell. A Dr. Littledale, reviewing Canon Farrar's *Eternal Hope* in the *Contemporary Review* (April 1878), expressed a view which has come to seem reasonable to a growing number of people.

> The popular theology which teaches that man's doom is irreversibly fixed at the moment of death, and that, if he be unrepentant at that particular instant of time, he is lost forever . . . puts God on a moral level with the devisers of the most savagely malignant revenge known to history—the deed known in Italy as *la gran vendetta.* This differs from ordinary assassination in that the murderer does not strike his victim down at any time feasible, but dogs his steps till he finds him fresh from the committal of some sin accounted mortal in Roman Catholic theology, and then slays him before he has had a moment for repentance, or confession, so as to ensure his damnation as well as his death. . . . The horror with which we read of such a crime ought to make us all careful lest we should give our assent to the teaching which predicates it, only on an infinitely vaster scale, of the just and merciful God.

Professor W. Gleason, S.J., of Fordham University, addressing himself to the knotty question of Hell in a mid-1958 edition of the Catholic quarterly *Thought,* entangles himself in a hopelessly illogical structure of argument by having undertaken to raise the question as to how an all-loving God could possibly create a Hell.

Gleason suggests that the agony of hellfire is not something created by God at all—an assertion that would have had him condemned as a heretic in past centuries—but rather that it arises out of the lost souls' eternal tension between love of self and love of God—perhaps something like the torment of schizophrenia. "It is possible that the soul in Hell," Gleason says, "could feel this inner division with regard to itself and to the God for whom it thirsts with all its being . . . The pain the soul suffers . . . is then the pain of fire and it is the direct result of the pain of loss."

One must observe simply that this makes no sense at all. It would be reasonable to introduce such considerations *if* the Christian idea of Hell over the centuries had had nothing whatever to do with fire but had simply described a place or state where souls, and perhaps bodies, of sinners would languish for all eternity; perhaps in such a place they are driven mad from a sense of loss, sorrow, and disappointment because, having been given the opportunity to behave virtuously, they had instead chosen the path of sin and hence, by their own weakness or depravity, denied themselves the glorious pleasure of being in God's presence in the afterlife. This, as I say—though it would seem to atheists equally as preposterous as the traditional hypothesis—would at least be a conception of Hell which would not ravage both reason and moral sensitivity.

Among the many difficulties about the belief in a literal Hell that have never been adequately resolved—for the very sound reason that they cannot be—we must also add the question as to the response of those fortunate enough to achieve eternal bliss toward the much greater number who are consigned to the eternal flames. If there is a sweet, peaceful HEAVEN, how can those who arrive at its gates remain happy when they make the hideous discovery that many of their own family members, dear personal friends, much-admired acquaintances, and others for whom they had great respect are writhing, for all eternity, in the most painful torment?

Can a woman who was, let's say, a good and caring mother of several children call herself happy when she realizes that some of her dear sons and daughters are among the hundreds of millions in Hell? Can a husband who loved his wife throughout the years of a happy marriage call himself content while knowing that his wife is now a resident of the nether regions? It is obvious that eternal happiness would be totally out of the question in the face of such knowledge.

HERESY. Conservative forces in the churches, as observed in such steaming controversy as that involving the 3,000,000-member Lutheran Church-

Missouri Synod during the 1970s, have frequently been criticized for their tendency to resort to a charge of heresy against more liberal or even quite moderate interpretaters of biblical tradition. Oddly enough, the conservatives are perfectly justified in drawing from their scabbards the ancient accusation of heresy because there is no question but that modern criticism of the literalist position represents a sharp deviance from the orthodox view that has prevailed for centuries.

The progressives, needless to say, are essentially right in acknowledging rational, scholarly critics, who point out that certain passages of Scripture are senseless or anti-God if interpreted literally. But such modification as is taking place clearly tends toward heresy by conservative standards. I am convinced that the world would be a more rational habitat if Western culture had not been so dreadfully short of heretics over the past 2,000 years. There are, of course, sensible and foolish heresies.

Protestants, in any event, present a somewhat semicomic spectacle in sounding this ancient charge, for the reason that Protestantism itself is one enormous collection of heresies in the Catholic view. And so, in fact, is every religion on earth, since they all have come into existence as a deviation from earlier forms of belief.

Although the part of human nature that is largely rational would prefer to have the public debate on questions of philosophical importance always conducted in a dispassionate, scholarly tone, the sad truth must be faced that whenever the questions being dealt with have been religious, even prominent churchmen have often morally disgraced themselves by the spiteful, vituperative coloration of even their most formal pronouncements. Even in the present day, when many open-minded believers and nonbelievers would hope to be able to explore such questions in a fairminded, cooperative spirit, one does not encounter many instances of sweetness and light. It is true, however, that notable progress has been made, particularly among scholarly specialists who have provided an analysis of Scripture in an open and peaceful forum. But as against this, there is still the tragic evidence of centuries in which the debate was conducted in a dangerously combative spirit, even before the time of the Reformation.

It is an interesting question as to why it is chiefly the province of religion, which at its best is concerned with virtue, the dignity of humanity, and the discouragement of evil, which has given rise, for unknown thousands of years, to vicious invective and frequently sadistic and murderous behavior. What we are discussing here is tragedy wrapped in tragedy, for if we make the intellectual attempt to understand the reason for the truly disgusting behavior of millions of fanatics over the long course of recorded time, we see that some—or perhaps much—of it is inevitable, given our pitifully weak capacity for dispassionate reasoning.

Consider: if one is quite convinced that one's own religious philosophy is the only one sanctioned by God, it is, of course, almost inevitable that one will react angrily to even the most dignified criticisms of that philosophy. In situations where there were separate camps competing for the favor of the Creator, or the pocketbooks of his devotees, venomous and certainly unchristian exchanges concerning scriptural commentaries, were inevitable.

In the present Christian age, however, one characterized by an appreciable admixture of ecumenical sentiment, studies of the scriptural record are being produced that are more representative of scholarship than of hateful polemical controversy.

HOSEA, the first of the 12 so-called minor prophets, who wrote, possibly with the assistance of disciples, 14 brief chapters of oracles that both predicted the doom of the northern kingdom, Israel, and by an elaborate marriage imagery, pointed out the possibility of Yahweh's love, mercy, and justice. It is commonplace to refer to Hosea as a troublesome or "a puzzling book with a notoriously corrupt Hebrew text," as a religious writer for *Time* (January 1963) put it. The prophet, whose name means "salvation" or "deliverance," lived in a dangerous time in Israel's history: after a period of economic prosperity and during the last part of the reign of Jeroboam II (786-746 B.C.), when Assyria was threatening its small neighbor.

The people of Israel had either turned from the worship of Yahweh to that of the Canaanite god, Baal, or else were worshiping superficially. Hosea's message, according to the *Encyclopedia Britannica,* "centered on Covenant love" and the prophet "arose to call an apostate people back to their Covenant responsibilities." Also:

> Like his contemporary Amos, the great prophet of social justice, Hosea was a prophet of doom; but he held out a hope to the people that the Day of Yahweh contained not just retribution but also the possibility of renewal. His message against Israel's "spirit of harlotry" was dramatically and symbolically acted out in his personal life.

Chapters 1-3 relate the story of Hosea's marriage.

> 2. . . . the Lord said to Hosea, "Go, take to yourself a wife of harlotry and have children of harlotry, for the land commits great harlotry by forsaking the Lord."

Whether this was an actual marriage, we have no way of really knowing. It may have been the prophet's way of writing a story that would catch his people's attention, much as Dante placed himself into *The Divine Comedy*. No one in Dante's day believed that he actually went to Hell with Virgil as a guide; they understood that he was presenting a poetic vision of the afterlife.

In fact, the naming of Hosea's offspring by Gomer sounds suspiciously as if this first part *was* imaginatively constructed in order to instruct rather than inform. For example, his daughter is named "Not pitied, for I will no more have pity on the house of Israel," (1:6) and there followed a son: "Call his name Not my people, for you are not my people and I am not your God" (1:9). This sounds like a fairy tale; yet we know that the author was concerned with a real place and actual social conditions.

Chapters 4-14 spell out in Hebrew verse why the Lord is angry with the people of Israel. In Chapter 4 we read:

> 1. . . . for the Lord has a controversy with the inhabitants of the
>   land. There is no faithfulness or kindness,
>   and no knowledge of God in the land;
> 2 there is swearing, lying, killing, stealing, and committing adultery;
>   they break all bounds and murder follows murder.

In spite of dire predictions for the future of Israel, the book of Hosea is considerably less bloody than those of some of the other prophets. The Lord holds out the promise that if they "acknowledge their guilt," the Hebrews may be healed and revived, for Yahweh "will come to us as the showers, as the spring rains that water the earth" (6:3). The tribe of Ephraim, which lived north of Jerusalem, is particularly chastised; this would seem to indicate actual knowledge by the author of the idolatrous ways of the Ephraimites. Judah also is admonished.

There is a famous quotation in Chapter 8: "For they sow the wind, and they shall reap the whirlwind" (v. 7).

The Lord is portrayed as having great compassion in Chapter 11, but he makes it clear in Chapters 13 and 14 that he will only be compassionate if the people of Israel repent of their evil ways. Much of the language of Hosea is unusually beautiful and moving for the Old Testament, and foreshadows the more loving God of the New Testament.

Hosea ends on a poetic, triumphant, and quite hopeful note:

> 4 I will heal their faithlessness,
>   I will love them freely,
>   for my anger has turned from them.
> 5 I will be as the dew to Israel;
>   he shall blossom as the lily,
>   he shall strike root as the poplar;
> 6 his shoots shall spread out;
>   his beauty shall be like the olive,
>   and his fragrance like Lebanon.
> 7 They shall return and dwell beneath my shadow,
>   they shall flourish as a garden;
>   they shall blossom as the vine,
>   their fragrance shall be like the wine of Lebanon.

All in all, Hosea is a protest against violence in favor of kindness (4:1–2), a welcome relief from the terrors of the Old Testament.

HUMANISM. Consider the following assertion which, it is important to note, no one seriously denies: that every individual and every social group is not only capable of stupid acts and statements but will, from time to time, commit them. An illustrative instance is the present heated attack on Scientific Humanism by certain fundamentalist religious groups using absurd and unfactual assertions. Needless to say, religious believers are perfectly at liberty to criticize Secular Humanism in all of its aspects. Those societies are most healthy in which debate on important questions continues, albeit in a civilized and rational manner. But the inanity of the present attack lies precisely in the fundamentalist claim that it is Humanism that is largely responsible for the present moral collapse of our society.

The American Humanist Association has an extremely modest membership of fewer than 5,000, the population of a small town. There are no doubt a number of secular humanists not formally affiliated with the organization, but no one argues that there are many. Conservative believers, on the other hand, number in the scores of millions.

It is nonsense to see any connection between the statistically small group of rationalists on the one hand and the ethical anarchy of society on the other. The average drug addict, prostitute, pornographer, alcoholic, juvenile delinquent, street criminal, sexual pervert, compulsive gambler, roué, habitual philanderer, Mafia member, corrupt politician, child abuser, or wife beater would not know a Secular Humanist if he saw one. Secular Humanists, Unitarians, Universalists, academic atheists, and such people are, in fact, generally characterized by a commendable degree of moral restraint. Of the humanists and rationalists I know, practically all are socially admirable. As regards the reason for the collapse of the American social system, some of Humanism's critics might more profitably look elsewhere for clues, perhaps even in their own groups.

To look at their argument another way: God and his enormous flock must be incredibly impotent to be defeated by such a small number of humanists, whom fundamentalists perceive to be in league with the Devil.

Accomplishments of Humanists. Humanists are a somewhat loosely organized group that exists for the primary purpose of civilizing Christians and others—both religious believers and nonbelievers. Inasmuch as, historically speaking, those who have been faced with the necessity of becoming civilized have generally submitted to the process with ill-concealed displeasure, it is hardly surprising that in the modern context, many believers would be quite heated in their reactions to those who are concerned to uplift them. There is the understandable tendency, among those who know little of history, to assume that the degree of civilization presently observable in, let us say, American or Western European Christians, has come about chiefly because of moral pressures arising from within the believer's own philosophy.

Unfortunately this has not been the case. The view, for example, that church and state should be legally separated so that we do not suffer the injustice and excesses of the Inquisition and witchcraft periods in our own history, or the horrors of sectarian violence in Lebanon and of fundamentalist Iran, has been vigorously resisted by believers since it was first put forth by social philosophers of the Enlightenment. Even today, some influential Christian spokesmen insist that what they perceive as the breach between church and state should be healed so that the two might be brought much closer together.

Concerning the modern humanistic political belief in freedom of speech, the same must be said. For many centuries, wherever one sect or another dominated a given society, the right to say whatever one thought reasonable was considered damnably dangerous. The case was even more clearcut as regards freedom of the press since, while it is relatively difficult to inhibit men's tongues, it is a simple matter to destroy printing presses and to consign pamphlets and books to the flames.

There are numerous important questions concerning which people of goodwill honestly differ, but the present issue is not such a one. I refer here to the clear record of history, concerning which even devout believers themselves do not contest the record, although they may be personally uncomfortable when that record is introduced into contemporary evidence.

Another humanistic political virtue which, like the others, is the pride of every patriotic and informed American, concerns the right not to be subjected to cruel and inhuman punishment. Though prisons are severe and bleak institutions, extended residence in which is an ongoing nightmare, they are nevertheless far more civilized than the jails and dungeons of Europe during the centuries in which the power of assorted Christian churches was almost absolute. So vengeful was the dominant mind-set in those ages, in fact, that the mere idea of incarceration by no means satisfied the vindictive desires of judges and prosecutors. Corporal punishment was considered far more important than mere locking-up, and the most excruciatingly painful torture was considered a normal, proper, and perfectly legal part of the larger process of maintaining law and order.

Because such realties are very difficult to harmonize with the more appealing and tender aspects of Christianity, it is painful to contemplate such historical realities. But a failure to be aware of them places modern society in the gravest possible danger. It is difficult to engage in modern debate about, for example, CAPITAL PUNISHMENT without understanding how such punishment was casually employed for thousands of years, especially for political control. We find the same thing in states like Iran, Iraq, Guatemala, and El Salvador that we consider barbaric today. In fact, one powerful argument against capital punishment is that eschewing it gives the U.S. a higher moral standing than countries that abuse it for purely political reasons.

Although capital punishment continues, and is most particularly insisted upon by political and religious conservatives, we can at least say that the situation at present is a great improvement over the state of affairs that prevailed when the church exercised dictatorial powers.

But, to return to our simple theme, the churches never reformed themselves in these and other regards. Reform, moral uplift, civilization itself—all were forced upon them by a statistically small brigade of courageous humanists, freethinkers, Deists, progressives, liberals, including the American Founding Fathers, as well as earlier and contemporary philosophers whose ideas influenced America's colonial leaders.

Needless to say, there were always rare heroic exceptions within the ranks of believers, relatively saintly individuals sensitive and virtuous enough to perceive the moral monstrosities of which the churches were guilty. It is particularly galling that modern churchmen sometimes point with pride to the writings and speeches of such decent and courageous Christian reformers, as if their views were somehow characteristic of earlier religious thinking on such profoundly important questions. They were not characteristic at all; rather, they were rare departures from the norm.

Enemies of Humanism. I find it amusing that the enemies of humanism claim far more influence for that philosophy than it claims for itself. This is, of course, a common fault in human argumentation. We seem not content with an accurate description of our opponents. If they are indeed, let us assume, perpetrating a certain amount of evil in the world, we are likely to greatly exaggerate the degree of that evil. This self-deception in turn serves the purpose of stimulating us to ever higher peaks of righteous indignation by way of fueling our energies for the fight.

Perhaps there should be a convention of the enemies of Secular Humanism. I suspect they would not get along very well, but their confrontations would supply good intellectual entertainment.

Who might be present at such a convention? There would be a sizable representation of Christian and other religious fundamentalists, and it would be a good question as to whether Islamic fundamentalists could set aside their differences with one another and with their Christian counterparts long enough to attend to the business of the moment.

There would be few, if any, astronomers present, although astrologers would be well-represented. So would spiritualists and supermarket-journal prognosticators. There would be frequent squabbles between such quacks and charlatans on the one hand and Christians on the other, since the latter often attribute pseudoscience to the Devil.

(A good many Christians, oddly enough, including Ronald and Nancy Reagan, are ignorant of the fact that it is not intellectually possible, or religiously respectable to hold Christian doctrines on the one hand and also to believe in astrology, numerology, or other pseudosciences on the other.)

Advertising agencies would no doubt send at least a few representatives to the convention, at least as observers, because of their perception that the standards of pure reason are not exactly compatible with their gifts for creative exaggeration and a tendency to ignore contrary evidence, the very essence of the art of advertising.

But perhaps there is no need for such a convention after all, because humanists themselves differ on so many questions. This, at least, has the virtue of making it almost impossible to develop any humanist beliefs that could be described as dogmatic.

And, of course, even if there are certain minimal statements that would be acceptable to almost all humanists, there still remains the problem of interpretation of the particulars of such a canon.

I

IMAGE OF GOD. There are two accounts of CREATION in the book of GENESIS. In the first chapter we read:

> 26. Then God said, "Let us make man in our image, after our likeness; . . .
> 27. So God created man in his own image, in the image of God he created him; male and female he created them.

In the second account however, in Chapter 2, nothing is said about creating a man in God's image. But in 5:1 the idea is repeated.

I confess that I have never understood the assertion that man was made in the image of God. I suspect, moreover, that there are very few who would say they fully grasp it, and of that number it is a separate question as to whether an impartial jury would consider the various interpretations satisfactory. The problem clearly does not arise out of any difficulty in interpreting the separate words that comprise the statement. No one would have the slightest problem in interpreting the statement: *Henceforth all men should be made in the image of Abraham Lincoln.* But when we replace *Abraham Lincoln* with *God,* we are faced with a true puzzle. One awkward factor is that no two human beings, not even so-called identical twins, are identical. We know what, let us say, Dolly Parton looks like, and we know what the famous midget Tom Thumb looked like, and we have no difficulty in grasping that these two are remarkably dissimilar.

We also know that countless children are born in various parts of the planet without arms or legs, as Siamese twins, with bodies misshapen in ways too hideous to contemplate. We are at least safe in concluding, therefore, that whatever the original assertion in Genesis meant, it cannot today mean, to an intelligent person, that a human being looks a good deal—physically speaking—like God.

Given that it has always been an essential element of both Jewish and Christian belief that God is a pure spirit, having no bodily reality whatever, it is no intellectually respectable response to say that a God with all powers could assume human form if he wished. Of course he could.

In my analysis of Scripture, I consider it only fair to reveal such biases as I have rather than pretend to an ideal objectivity. I have no hesitation in stating that I should like to be personally satisfied that humans are more than merely physical beings and that some sort of soul or spirit remains after the moment of physical death—and that in this only, man is like God. There is some comfort in this belief, but, sad to say, there is also a great deal of tragedy, since not everyone will move on to an eternally sublime state (see HEAVEN)—or so we are told by centuries of theologians.

I have tentatively concluded that, inasmuch as Genesis 1:27 was composed in a time and place where almost everyone believed that gods and goddesses had physical forms, as well as enormous power, the author simply accepted the prevailing, so-called pagan view. It is reasonable to assume that this notion did not trouble religious Hebrews of the period.

Another possibility is that the author of Genesis was suggesting that God was not properly represented by statues of snakes, bulls, and other creatures, which were, in ancient times, presented and worshiped as forms that represented pagan deities. (See also GOD.)

ISAAC, favorite son of ABRAHAM. His mother, SARAH, was said to have been aided by the Lord to conceive for the first time at the age of 90, after she had passed menopause. Do we have to be told that a woman so old is past menopause, especially since the Lord plans to cause her to conceive miraculously? There are several veiled hints that Isaac, like Jesus, was conceived (by the Lord?) without the participation of a human male, because Abraham is never said to "go in to" Sarah as he did Hagar, to father Isaac's half-brother ISHMAEL.

Isaac is born, circumcised at eight days, and weaned. After a second encounter with the Philistinian king ABIMELECH, host of Abraham, who "sojourned many days in the land of the Philistines" (Gen. 21:34), Abraham is tested by the Lord, using Isaac as the victim, almost as a laboratory animal is used today. Chapter 22 recounts how Abraham is obedient to God in preparing to murder Isaac, despite the fact that God had previously gone to great effort to produce Isaac for his 100-year-old father and had promised that Isaac's descendants would multiply as the stars in heaven and "possess the gate of their enemies" (22:17).

Concerning this story of Abraham's willingness to plunge a knife into the flesh of his own son, Father John L. McKenzie comments, in his *Dictionary of the Bible:* "It may be the expression of this truth [a criticism of the practice of human sacrifice] by *an imaginary narrative, a parable, or it may preserve dimly the memory of some spiritual crisis in the life of Abraham.*" (IA) Here, we are told, by a competent scholar, that there is great likelihood that an Old Testament story is made up of whole cloth. Many scholars today accept the notion that the PENTATEUCH probably was not even written until during or after the Babylonian Exile in the 6th century B.C., and that stories about a character such as Isaac were legends or were composed at that late date.

There is nothing wrong with reading the Bible to glean spiritual or moral instruction. Intelligence, nevertheless, if consistently applied, will inevitably lead a person to doubt the truthfulness, and eventually to flatly disbelieve, a good many of the more preposterous Old Testament stories. The reader would still be at liberty to draw moral lessons from such tales, just as one may from the fables of Aesop, each of which teaches a sound ethical or practical lesson. The literary and religious process therefore may be accommodated by anyone who combines sensitivity to ethical fundamentals with even moderate intelligence.

The story of Abraham and Isaac seems bizarre unless we interpret it as mythical, as a literary fossil pointing to the once-common practice of human sacrifice. That human sacrifice has been encountered in various cultures is a matter of common knowledge, but not many people are aware that it was also part of the religious practice of the ancient Israelites and other Middle Eastern tribes of prebiblical times.

Finally, in evaluating this story, let the reader ask himself if an extremely old man—of the sort who in the modern day is cared for in a home for the senile aged—could walk for three days, climb a hillside, build an altar, lay out firewood, and then manhandle and tie up a young healthy male with every intention of murdering him.

Before Abraham dies, he asks a servant to promise not to let Isaac marry a Canaanite woman, but to return to the upper Mesopotamian region, the land of his forebears, to find a wife. The servant goes to the city of Nahor and finds Rebekah, a sweet young virgin and a second cousin of Isaac, said to be of an Aramean family. Chapter 24 gives a detailed and repetitive picture of how wives were obtained in the Bronze Age Near East, and Chapter 25 indicates that the Hebrews considered the Arameans to be their close relatives.

Rebekah bore the twins JACOB and ESAU, of whom the Lord had said before their birth:

> Two nations are in your womb,
>> and two peoples, born of you, shall be divided;
> the one shall be stronger than the other,
>> the elder shall serve the younger. (25:23)

A famine occurs and Isaac takes his family off to Gerar in Palestine/ Canaan again, and is treated kindly by King Abimelech. Like his father Abraham, he tells the king the falsehood that his wife is his sister. The Abraham story is repeated in close detail, but Isaac is living u. der a lucky star. Despite his dishonesty and cowardice, he too grows very wealthy in Philistia; finally the Philistines become envious and ask him to leave. (For the story of Isaac's coveted blessing, see Jacob.)

ISAIAH. Even those scholars who find fault with the book of Isaiah nevertheless rarely question its basic thrust: that the Assyrians' savage assaults on the Northern Kingdom were not merely permitted but actually planned by God to punish the sinfulness of Isaiah's fellow Hebrews. William Neil says in his *Harper's Bible Commentary:* "When Yahweh had used Assyria for his purposes he would crush it and humble its pride (10:1-22)." But if one were reading a history of Assyria, it would never occur to the reader that God was directing the Assyrian armies to victory. And what of the other peoples conquered by Assyria? Were they being punished by God also?

I suggest that we step away from this theological interpretation and reflect on the specific reality it obscures. The Assyrians had become a strong, centralized state with many advanced trappings of civilization. It was the kind of nation that generally tried to aggrandize itself by conquering weaker states. By the 8th century B.C. the Jewish kingdom had split into two small, weak kingdoms: Judah and Israel.

Since Israel, in the north, lay closer to Assyria, centered in northern Mesopotamia, it was the one Kings Tiglath-pileser III and Sargon II conquered. The Assyrians defeated their enemies in the way common in that time, which is to say that they plunged swords into bodies, chopped off heads, hands, and feet, pierced with arrows, pillaged, tortured, and raped.

Is the reader comfortable with the Bible's assertion that such atrocities were not just a matter of man's insatiable lust for power and tendency toward violent cruelty but were deliberately instigated by the very same God who, in other contexts, we are taught loves every individual?

Our puzzlement is increased by what appears to be a striking instance of divine injustice. To quote the *Encyclopedia Britannica.* "The king of the Assyrians is described as the rod of God's anger, but Assyria also will experience the judgment of God for its atrocities in time of war." But why? Those very atrocities that Isaiah tells us God has commanded can hardly be held against the Assyrians, if they were doing the will of God.

We are brought uncomfortably face to face with an essential theological problem, one that has never been answered, and for which, in fact, no religion will ever provide an answer: the puzzle of the massive amount of evil that strikes down hundreds of thousands of those we are taught to regard as God's children.

To deny that Isaiah has dealt with the problem of evil when he deals with the Assyrian-Israeli conflict does not, however, suggest that it is a waste of time to study the lessons Isaiah and other prophets have left us. Isaiah is on the firmest possible moral ground when he denounces the social injustices of his place and time. He also deserves credit for speaking in precise terms about the rich who live in idle luxury, indulge in irresponsible sexual behavior and drunkenness, and oppress the poor.

Another aspect of the message of Isaiah to which Christians seem to have paid little attention over the centuries is that when the prophet refers to the city and the people who will finally live in glorious triumph and peace, he is talking, in the most specific terms, about Jerusalem and the CHOSEN PEOPLE. In chapter after chapter he gives precise geographical information, naming various Middle Eastern cities and empires that will be ruthlessly and painfully crushed. The prophet then says: "The Lord God will wipe away all tears and take away forever all insult and mockery against his land and people" (25:8). In other words, God has planned a promising future for the Jews.

It is little wonder that the Jews, to the present moment, have derived comfort from reading this portion of Isaiah, while Christians choose to concentrate on other parts of Scripture.

Authorship. As with almost every part of the Bible, there is considerable confusion as to who wrote which portions of the book long attributed to Isaiah. That an actual prophet by that name, who was also a gifted literary artist, contributed a great deal to the first 35 chapters of the 66 commonly credited to him seems reasonably well established.

There is considerably less agreement as to who wrote Chapters 36-39, which refer chiefly to the Assyrian threat to Jerusalem in 701 B.C. Because this section refers to Isaiah in the third person, there is the general assumption that unknown others, writing in the prophet's name, were the authors.

Starting with Chapter 40, the tone is different, and the events described are those that we know occurred *after* the fall of Jerusalem to the Babylonians in 586 B.C., in other words, *long after Isaiah had gone to his grave.* This section is often termed Second Isaiah. As is often the case in matters of religious controversy, it took a long time for the churches to concede that this portion could not have been written by Isaiah. The debate substantially ended in 1970 when, according to *Who's Who in the Bible,* by Joan Comay and Ronald Brownrigg (New York: Bonanza Books, 1980):

> A lecturer at the Haifa technion obtained his doctorate at the Hebrew University of Jerusalem for a thesis based on a computer analysis of the book of Isaiah. On such criteria as word frequency and sentence construction, the statistics showed odds of 100,000 to 1 against the two parts having been derived from the same author.

Modern scholars consider that the writing of Chapters 56–66 took place in a still later period, during the days of Ezra and Nehemiah. There is a general feeling that we are not looking for "a third or fourth Isaiah" as a specific individual. The chapters are apparently the work of an unknown number of men, writing in Isaiah's name.

I have had the pleasure of visiting, while in Jerusalem, the Shrine of the Book, where the remarkable documents called the DEAD SEA SCROLLS repose. One of these is a scroll of Isaiah in relatively good condition. But even with this fortuitous discovery we are faced with confusion, for among the priceless ancient documents unearthed there was also an admittedly spurious version of Genesis.

Chapter 1. The author of Isaiah was a man of impressive literary talent. He was also possessed of considerable *chutzpah,* because in his opening passages he asks us to listen to what the Lord said to him in a vision:

> 2. . . . . I have nourished and brought up children, and they have rebelled against me.
>
> 3. The ox knoweth his owner, and the ass his master's crib: but Israel doth not know, my people doth not consider.
>
> 4. Ah, sinful nation, a people laden with iniquity, a seed of evildoers, children that are corrupters: they have forsaken the Lord, they have provoked the Holy One of Israel unto anger, they are gone away backward.

There are similar criticisms of the Hebrews in other Old Testament books. A visitor from another galaxy, getting his information about Jews solely from the Judaic Scriptures, might assume that they were among the most evil tribes imaginable. However, we are aware that all peoples are equally prone to evil and, fortunately, also to virtue.

The Lord then states that he is sick of ritualistic sacrifices; he wants no more fat rams, has no interest in seeing blood pouring from animal offerings. "Who," he asks, "wants your sacrifices when you have no sorrow for your sins? The incense you bring me is a stench in my nostrils" (v. 13). (Remember, however, how he provoked Cain to insane jealousy because he preferred Abel's "firstlings of his flock" and "their fat portions" [Gen. 4:4].)

Written with dramatic clarity, these passages make unassailable good sense, whether viewed psychologically or theologically. They represent an enormous advance over the PENTATEUCH's YAHWEH. The Lord holds out hope for those with enough sense to repent, saying, "Come now, let us reason together . . . though your sins be as scarlet, they shall be as white as snow" (v. 18).

Chapter 2 deals with a separate message that Isaiah says he has received. The Lord tells him that in "the last days" Jerusalem and its Temple will become the world's greatest attraction. The prediction is clear: The world will be ruled from Jerusalem, and the Lord personally will settle international disputes. (Would that he did, especially in the blood-stained Mideast of today.) Verse 4 includes the famous prediction that eventually the nations will beat their swords into plowshares and their spears into pruning hooks. Hasten the day and thank you, Mr. Gorbachev.

Speaking in his own voice, Isaiah points a scornful finger at his fellow Hebrews for worshiping their vast treasures of silver and gold and other material belongings. God, he says, will not forgive them for this particular sin. "On that day the Lord Almighty will move against the proud and haughty and bring them to the dust" (v. 12).

Chapter 3. If the Chosen People had the idea that they would receive special favors from the Lord, they were very much mistaken, if we rely on Isaiah.

1. The Lord will cut off Jerusalem's and Judah's food and water supplies,

2. and kill her leaders; he will destroy her armies, judges, prophets, elders, . . .

5. And the worst sort of anarchy will prevail—everyone stepping on someone else, neighbors fighting neighbors, youths revolting against authority, criminals sneering at honorable men.

The poet reserves his and the Lord's particular scorn for the wealthy who have defrauded the poor. Parenthetically, I often marvel at the claims of certain American Christian capitalists, and especially wealthy TV evangelists, who assert that their success is due to the personal intervention of God, since the Scriptures ring with numerous denunciations of the rich.

It is of vital importance to note that in the Bible there are no snide denunciations of the poor such as American conservatives often express today, no references to the equivalent of "welfare chiselers" or "lazy bums." The Lord, it would seem, is aware of what any thoughtful person can perceive: the overwhelming majority of the earth's poor, who constitute the majority of the human population, are by no means poverty-stricken through their own fault.

The prophet also delivers himself of some sarcastically critical observations about "the haughty daughters of Zion, who mince along, noses in the air, tinkling bracelets on their anklets, with wanton eyes that rove among the crowds to catch the glances of the men" (v. 16). Some things, apparently, never change. The prophet gloats that such women shall be made humble, deprived of their beauty.

Chapter 4. In this chapter Isaiah describes a situation which could be interpreted in a comic way, given, of course, that comedy is about tragedy anyway.

1. At that time so few men will be left alive that seven women will fight over each one of them and say, "Let us all marry you! We will furnish our own food and clothing; only let us be called by your name so that we won't be mocked as old maids."

Chapter 5. Isaiah here returns to his ringing attack on the rich. The Lord, he says, "expected righteousness, but the cries of deep oppression met his ears" (v. 7). Further, "you buy up property so others have no place to live. Your homes are built on great estates so you can be alone in the midst of the earth" (v. 8). He also attacks drunkards in very direct language.

Isaiah's confidence that he has been chosen as a messenger to deliver precise, word-for-word messages from Almighty God is apparently not significantly different from the case of those modern Christians who assure us that the Lord has spoken to them in a simple and direct way.

Chapter 6 opens with an impressive vision.

1. The year King Uzziah died I saw the Lord! He was sitting on a lofty throne, and the temple was filled with his glory.

2. Hovering about him were mighty, six-winged angels of fire. With two of their wings they covered their faces; with two others they covered their feet; and with two they flew.

3. In a great antiphonal chorus they sang, "Holy, holy, holy is the Lord Almighty; the whole earth is filled with his glory."

After Isaiah confesses his unworthiness to witness such a spectacle, he reports an act remarkable even in this fantastical context.

6. Then one of the mighty angels flew over to the altar and with a pair of tongs picked out a burning coal.
7. He touched my lips with it and said, "Now you are pronounced 'not guilty' because this coal has touched your lips. Your sins are all forgiven."

Oddly enough, modern Christian apologists do not seem to take Isaiah's account of the incident as factual reporting; but precisely what they do make of it is not clear. The striking imagery of enormous creatures with six wings does not conform to any Christian or Jewish orthodoxy about angels, nor, for that matter, to any known principles of aerodynamics.

Chapter 7. It is this chapter of Isaiah that has given rise over many centuries to controversy as to what particular infant Isaiah was talking about in his famous message to King Ahaz. The prophet told the king that God wanted him to ask for a sign, something that would dramatically prove divine intention in crushing the enemies of the king and his people. But the ruler, we are told, responded that he did not wish to trouble the Lord on the matter. Isaiah, angered, says: "Therefore, the Lord himself will give you a sign. Behold, a young woman shall conceive and bear a son, and shall call his name Immanuel" (v. 14). All scholars are agreed that the child the prophet is referring to is *his own.* This is firmly established in the next chapter.

Chapter 8. The prophet boldly employs the actual words of God as regards the naming of his child. "And I went to the prophetess and she conceived, and bore me a son, and the Lord said, 'Call him Maher-shalal-hash-baz' " (v. 3). The name, Isaiah explains, embodies the prediction that before the child can talk—at about two years—the king of Assyria would invade and conquer both Damascus (Syria) and Samaria, which is precisely what happened in 732 and 722 B.C..

It is impossible that Isaiah was predicting the birth of JESUS (who would not be born until some seven centuries later). There would presumably never have been any difficulty about this simple matter were it not that one of the followers of Jesus, the author of the Gospel of MATTHEW, chose to interpret the reference in Verse 14 as a prediction of the birth of Jesus, because the Hebrew *almah* ("young woman") was translated into the Septuagint's Greek as *parthenos* ("virgin").

Chapter 9. Another element in the controversy is now encountered. The prophet refers to a future time—unfortunately unspecified—when the land of Galilee "will be filled with glory."

> 2. The people who walk in darkness shall see a great Light—a Light that will shine on all those who live in the land of the shadow of death. . . .
> 5. In that glorious day of peace there will no longer be the issuing of battle gear; no more the blood-stained uniforms of war; all such will be burned.

Whatever this refers to, it cannot possibly be any actual historic time, much less the time of Jesus, when Roman legions occupied the Holy Land. In Verse 6, it is clear that the prophet is predicting the coming of a great king whose *earthly* reign will bring peace to the entire planet. This is where the idea of the Jewish MESSIAH is most clearly enunciated.

> 6. For unto us a Child is born; unto us a Son is given; and the government shall be upon his shoulder. These will be his royal titles: "Wonderful," "Counselor," "The Mighty God," "The Everlasting Father," "The Prince of Peace."
> 7. His *ever-expanding, peaceful government* will never end. He will *rule with perfect fairness and justice* from the *throne* of his father David. He will bring *true justice and peace* to *all* the nations of the world. (IA)

Christians, whose familiarity with these lines probably comes more from listening to Handel's *Messiah* than from reading Isaiah, are reinforced in their belief that Jesus is referred to, despite the fact that Jesus did not seek earthly power. Herein also lies the reason for the terrible division between Christian and Jew, with the early Christians insisting that Jesus fulfilled Isaiah's description of the Messiah and the Jews being equally sure that he did not. In this, the Jews are clearly correct, unless one stretches the meaning of almost every word in Verse 7 until they have no meaning at all.

Though Christians have long believed that the prophet was referring to Jesus, we are faced with the troubling fact that when Jesus did live, he did not work to "bring justice and peace to the nations of the world." His message was rather different. First of all, Jesus himself said that he came not to bring peace but a sword, although no one has ever been able to explain why he said that.

If we are to retain faith in the prophetic abilities of Isaiah, it is logically inescapable that we must abandon the view that "a child is born" applied to Jesus. The first instance of a predicted birth, as we have seen, referred simply to the prophet's own son; in the second instance it referred to a great king who would come at some unknown time in the future.

Parenthetically, while claiming the religion was founded by a Messiah of peace, Christianity itself has *never* devoted much time to securing universal peace and justice, even when powerful Christian kings, emperors, and presidents were in a position to do so, rather than fomenting war and conquest.

Those who are only casual readers of Scripture still may not grasp that among those the prophet is excoriating are the people of Israel. In Verses 14 and 15, the prophet clearly states: "The Lord, in one day, destroyed the leaders of Israel and the lying prophets."

The prophet's generally clear thinking here deserts him: "That is why the Lord has no joy in their [Israel's] young men, and no mercy upon even the widows and orphans, for they are all filthy-mouthed, wicked liars . . ." (v. 17). It is obviously foolish to refer to innocent children as "filthy-mouthed, wicked liars."

Chapter 11. How will we recognize the kingdom described in 9:7 when it finally arrives? Isaiah is quite clear on this; again, the day shall be one in which peace—real peace, all over the earth—prevails, even in the animal kingdom. It would have been better if the prophet had simply stressed the virtue of peace among humans; the inclusion of the earth's animals was an awkward mistake. We are told that "the wolf and the lamb will lie down together, and the leopard and goats will be at peace. Calves and fat cattle will be safe among lions . . ." (v. 6). All other creatures, both carnivores and herbivores, shall live side by side. How this will come about without a radical restructuring of carnivores' instincts, teeth, and digestive systems Isaiah does not say—but then he wasn't a zoologist.

Chapter 13. It is a strange anger that is attributed to God in this chapter. "Behold, the day of the Lord cometh, cruel both with wrath and fierce anger, to lay the land desolate: and he shall destroy the sinners thereof out of it" (v. 9).

Since we can readily observe that prophets in the present age are frequently wrong, it should not come as a surprise to note that the same has been true of seers down through the centuries. It has not, fortunately, yet come to pass that the stars, the sun, and the moon have ceased to give light, as Isaiah, in Verse 10, suggests will happen. He has his facts wrong about the moon, since it emanates no light but simply reflects the sun; and it is equally certain that the sun and billions of other stars in the vast universe will always glow until they cease to give light simply because they will have burned up their internal fuel.

Chapter 13 consists, also, of a mighty threat against the empire of Babylon.

> 15. Every one that is found shall be thrust through; and every one that is joined unto them shall fall by the sword.
> 16. Their children also shall be dashed to pieces before their eyes; their houses shall be spoiled, and their wives ravished.

Unfortunately for the idea that the Bible cannot contain error, there is a mistake in the prediction about Babylon: "It shall never be inhabited, neither shall it be dwelt in from generation to generation; neither shall the Arabian pitch tent there; neither shall the shepherds make their fold there" (v. 20). Since *Babylon* did not mean only the precincts inside the city walls, but a great area surrounding the city, we must note that tents and shepherds have *never* been altogether absent from the region, because the area is drained by the Euphrates River and therefore has never been completely infertile. The present capital of Iraq, Baghdad, and many villages lie nearby.

Furthermore, according to *Aramco World,* restoration and preservation work has been carried out in the ancient city since 1978. Describing in *Aramco World* a great celebration that is now taking place on an annual basis, William Tracy and Marjorie Krebs conclude:

> As the Babylon Festival continues into its third and subsequent seasons, these ruins beside the Euphrates, witness to a civilization over 6,000 years old, echo again to the sounds and sights of music, dance and drama. For a few glittering weeks each year Babylon, the splendid, is reborn.

Chapter 27. "In that day the Lord with his sore and great and strong sword shall punish Leviathan the piercing serpent, even Leviathan the crooked serpent; and he shall slay the dragon that is in the sea" (v. 1). Every intelligent person can perceive that the Lord could have no possible interest in punishing creatures of the sea, much less nonexistent creatures such as dragons. Both common sense and moral theologians tell us that animals can incur no moral blame, since whatever destruction they may bring about results either from accident, their need for food, or defense of their young. (See also FLOOD, THE; NOAH AND THE ARK.)

The Leviathan-dragon passage quoted is a clear indication of the extent to which Israelite cosmology depended on that of greater Semitic Mesopotamia, with its emphasis upon battles among gods, demigods, and imaginary creatures. Leviathan is said to represent monstrous evil. If the interpretation is generally agreed to, then it is perfectly acceptable to employ the term to convey such a concept. Isaiah had a remarkable gift for poetic imagery, but there is something risky about communicating the thoughts of God in ambiguous poetic and symbolic imagery rather than in crystal-clear terms.

Chapter 34. The author here asserts that Idumea is inhabited by centaurs, satyrs, and liliths. Since no such creatures have ever existed, the Bible is yet again in error.

Second Isaiah. A number of scholarly studies of Isaiah have been published, among them *Isaiah 40 to 66: A Commentary* by Claus Westermann (Louisville, Ky.: Westminster Press, 1969), *Creative Redemption in Deutero-Isaiah* by Carroll Stuhlmueller, C.P. (Rome: Biblical Institute Press, 1970), and *The Babylonian Captivity and Deutero-Isaiah* by Yehezkel Kaufmann (New York: Union of American Hebrew Congregations, 1970).

Chapter 45. This chapter includes a reference to Cyrus, who ruled Persia in the 6th century B.C. and is important in Old Testament history because he released the Jews from their Babylonian captivity. Gerald Larue explains:

> Because of differences in style, in details reflecting a different historical setting, and in messages directed to people in a different life situation, Chapters 40 onward are believed to be the product of someone living in Babylon *two centuries after the time of Isaiah of Jerusalem.* The Book of Isaiah is, therefore, a composite work. (IA)

ISHMAEL, first-born son of ABRAHAM by his concubine Hagar, whose story is begun in Genesis 16, when the Lord tells her:

> 10. . . . "I will multiply thy seed exceedingly, that it shall not be numbered for multitude."
> 11. And the angel of the Lord said unto her, "Behold, thou art with child, and shalt bear a son, and shalt call his name Ishmael; because the Lord hath heard thy affliction.
> 12. And he will be a wild man; his hand will be against every man, and every man's hand against him; and he shall dwell in the presence of all his brethren."

Abraham implores the Lord, "Oh, that Ishmael might live in thy sight!" (17:18) But the Lord has other plans now and arranges for the ancient Sarah to become pregnant with ISAAC. He relents enough, however, to say:

20. "As for Ishmael, I have heard you; behold, I will bless him and make him fruitful and multiply him exceedingly; he shall be the father of twelve princes, and I will make him a great nation."

The story continues as Hagar returns to Abraham's camp to bear her son and live there. Sarah, seeing the two boys playing together several years later, becomes jealous again. In Chapter 21, she demands:

10. "Cast out this slave woman with her son; for the son of this slave woman shall not be heir with my son Isaac."
11. And the thing was very displeasing to Abraham on account of his son.
12. But God said to Abraham, "Be not displeased because of the lad and because of your slave woman; whatever Sarah says to you, do as she tells you, for through Isaac shall your descendants be named.
13. "And I will make a nation of the son of the slave woman also, because he is your offspring."
14. So Abraham rose early in the morning, and took bread and a skin of water, and gave it to Hagar, putting it on her shoulder, along with the child, and sent her away. And she departed, and wandered in the wilderness of Beersheba.

In reading this passage, one loses respect for Abraham, who will not stand up to his shrewish wife, even though men were assumed to rule the roost in those days; for Sarah, who conspired with the Lord to send Hagar and Ishmael out into the desert to what would have been almost certain death; and for Yahweh, who is described as behaving like an unethical lawyer on behalf of his client, Sarah, even though he makes lavish promises about Ishmael's future greatness three times.

The Lord finally relents, however, when Hagar and Ishmael are near death. Hearing the boy crying, he sends an angel and a well of water; one can imagine which was the more welcome to the much-put-upon Hagar. God, as here depicted, is totally unpredictable, for suddenly "God was with the lad, and he grew up; he lived in the wilderness, and became an expert with the bow . . . and his mother took a wife for him from the land of Egypt" (21:20–21). The wild-man prophecy of Verse 12 has evidently been forgotten.

Abraham disinherited all his "irregular" sons by concubines before he died, but Ishmael was around to help Isaac bury the patriarch, apparently holding no grudge against his father.

The authors of Genesis reveal a curious ambivalence about the fates of Abraham's descendants. As we have seen, the Lord blows hot and cold in respect to Ishmael. Even though Abraham is a coward before Sarah's demands, he clearly cherishes Ishmael, and his son's circumcision at the age of 13 should have placed him among the Lord's convenanted people. It becomes clear, then, that the Jewish people should trace their origins to Sarah, not to Abraham, because if Abraham is to be considered their progenitor, then Ishmael's descendants should also be among the CHOSEN PEOPLE.

The actions of Sarah and the Lord perhaps shed light on the beginning of the fratricidal strife between Jews and Arabs, who trace their ancestry to Ishmael, who incidentally is accorded equal treatment with Isaac in the KORAN.

Anyone who reads the entire Abraham narrative carefully and without a preconceived notion of ancient history must either: (1) discard the entire story as a fiction created by a particular people to glorify their alleged ancestral history—a not uncommon practice in those days; or (2) notice the "sins" of Abraham and Sarah, and conclude that, even in trying to glorify these progenitors, the author(s) were forced to weave in what was a fairly accurate picture of the comings and goings and the relationships of several ancient Semitic-speaking peoples. The Jews and the Arabs obviously were—and are, despite religious differences—related by origin and language. It is tragic that they cannot acknowledge this today and live in peace.

Muslim Arabs take a very different view of the ancient legends about Abraham. The Koran does not have denigrating stories about Abraham and his sons, and pronounces all three great prophets of God.

ISLAM. See **Koran.**

J

JACOB, second-born twin son of ISAAC and Rebekah, younger brother of ESAU. He was a quiet boy, favored by his mother, but he was jealous of Esau, whom his father loved best. Jacob obtained the birthright of Esau —who seems to have been a trusting, perhaps even a stupid man—for bread and a "pottage of lentils." Later Rebekah and Jacob conspired to fool Isaac and receive the blessing intended for Esau. The author of this portion of Genesis (25:27 to 35:29), where Jacob's long and rambling story appears, does not bother to explain why the old man could not bless both sons; even Esau, wising up, asks: "Have you but one blessing?" (27:38). The two brothers become enemies but are later reconciled.

Myth and History. A possible explanation for the hostility of Rebekah and Jacob to Esau may lie in the migrations, alliances, and territorial claims of the Semitic-speaking tribes in the western part of the Fertile Crescent for a millennium before 1000 B.C. Rebekah came from an area lying to the north or northeast of Canaan, in what the Old Testament calls Paddan-Aram, and she sent Jacob there to find a wife. He ultimately takes two wives, Leah and Rachel, and two concubines as well, from the family of Laban, Rebekah's brother. These people were Arameans, whom Old Testament Israelites acknowledged as relatives or allies.

Esau, in the meantime, married wives of Hittite origin, and himself goes to live in Seir (Syria?). He is also called Edom, the name of a land south of the Dead Sea. The Edomites, though of the same stock as the Hebrew-speaking tribes, were later perceived as enemies.

Isaac Asimov provides a possible explanation of the movement of these peoples in southwest Asia, in his book *The Land of Canaan* (Boston: Houghton Mifflin, 1971):

> Some time before 2000 B.C. still another group of tribesmen flooded out of the Arabian peninsula, moving *east* and *west* against *both horns of the Fertile Crescent.* It would seem to be a larger movement of

peoples than had taken place at any time earlier. From the standpoint of the peoples of the Tigris-Euphrates, these wild invaders were coming from the west, and they were called *Amurru* or "westerners." We know that name best in the Biblical form—Amorites. . . . In the west they took over Canaan. When the early books of the Bible speak of the inhabitants of the land of Canaan, it is the Amorites they mean. . . . The Amorites were Semites, and the language they spoke was *an early form of the one we now know as Hebrew.* (IA)

The Amorites settled down in Canaan and became civilized, building cities. They seem to have been hospitable to a later wave of nomadic wanderers represented by Abraham, Isaac, and Jacob, and formed the culture that the later Israelite tribes, said to have been led by MOSES, tried to destroy, if the book of Joshua can be believed. (Historians and archaeologists today discount any notion of a conquest.)

It is ironic to learn that all these people were related to one another, having originated in Arabia. The Amorites or Canaanites built JERICHO, Salem (perhaps the site of the later Jerusalem), Hebron, and Beersheba, cities now disputed by modern Israel and the Palestinians.

Asimov elaborates:

The Egyptian garrisons in the Canaanite city-states found themselves forced to defend their areas against onslaughts from the eastern desert area. Once more *Arabia was stirring and its tribes were seeking haven in the delectable riches of the fertile regions.*

From the outposts came a stream of reports to Ikhnaton [Egyptian pharaoh who ruled after 1379 B.C.] concerning the activities of these "Apiru." This may represent the word which eventually came to be "Hebrew" in our language. This is, in turn, usually derived from a Semitic word meaning "one who is from across," that is, an outsider from beyond or across [east of] the Jordan River.

These Hebrew tribes were of similar origin to the Amorites but *were far lower, at the moment, in the scale of civilization. . . . They went on to adopt the Canaanite alphabet and many other aspects of Canaanite culture.* (IA)

Still later, Asimov says:

The Israelites recognized their kinship to the Hebrew [-speaking] tribes who had preceded them in the attempt to take over Canaan in the time of Ikhnaton, a century and a half before. This was expressed tribally by supposing all the Hebrew tribes to have descended from the family of Abraham. . . .

Thus, the Edomites were supposed to be descended from Edom, who was identified with Esau, a grandson of Abraham, and, therefore, a brother of the Israelites' own ancestor, Jacob-Israel. The people of Ammon and Moab were supposed to be descended from Lot, a nephew of Abraham.

If the people of Edom, Ammon, and Moab recognized this common kinship, we cannot say. None of their historical traditions have come down to us. *Concerning them we know only what the Israelites tell us in the Bible.* (IA)

Thus, it appears that—by being limited to one small tribe's account of this prehistoric time and place, by seeing only their viewpoint and hearing about their needs (translated into religious terms: God gave them the land), and by reading about their constant hatred of all other people nearby (again translated into religious terms: God favored them over their vile enemies)—we have been led by our general ignorance into assuming that there is some special grace and religious authority to be found in the people depicted in Genesis.

Oddly enough, however, what we see—the Old Testament is admirably frank about this—is a continual record of lying, cheating, warring, pomposity, polygamy, concubinage, and intense hatred among blood brothers. All of this is clearly revealed by those who finally wrote down the oral narratives in the PENTATEUCH, in some cases more than a millennium after the events that were supposed to have taken place.

To return to Genesis: Jacob has a famous dream of angels going up and down a ladder that stretches to Heaven. God appears and makes the usual promise that his descendants will spread over the earth and inherit the land of Israel.

Suppose I announced tomorrow, truthfully, that I had had a dream that God loved me more than anyone else in California and wanted me to take over the entire state. Would Californians bow down before me, or clear out? I think neither; they would fight for their land, just as the Canaanites, Moabites, Edomites, Ammonites, Philistines, and Palestinians have done in both ancient and modern times.

In 32:24 we are introduced to a strange little story. Jacob, we are told, is left alone "and a man wrestled with him until daybreak." Who is the man? Having read the story repeatedly and consulted scholars of Scripture, it is my honest opinion that we do not know who it was or even if the story is true. Since the Lord, in 35:10, tells Jacob that his name will be changed to Israel, as the "man" has previously done, are we to assume that the two are the same "person"? But, if so, why is the encounter presented as a wrestling match, and why is the wrestling partner a "man"? Jacob/Israel seems to assume that he had been wrestling with God (v. 30).

Needless to say, neither Jewish nor Christian scholars are likely to concede their ignorance. They therefore advance certain guesses, mention certain possibilities, and try to construct certain explanations.

Although Jacob was tricked into marrying his Uncle Laban's eldest daughter, Leah, he worked a total of 14 years to obtain Rachel in marriage, the daughter he loved more. Oddly, however, God did not favor Rachel at first; instead he gave Jacob numerous offspring by Leah and two concubines: Reuben, Simeon, Levi, Judah, Issachar, Zebulun, and Dinah; Dan, Naphtali, Gad, and Asher. Finally, Rachel bore JOSEPH and, many years later, Benjamin. The last two were Jacob's favorites, which inevitably made the older sons jealous.

As we have seen, Jacob, a nomad, dwelt at various times in Canaan, Aram, and Egypt. Jacob's sons are claimed to be the tribal ancestors of the twelve Hebrew tribes whom Moses is said to have led to the Promised Land. We have no way of knowing, however, whether any of these people ever existed as individuals, or whether their names represent various groups of Semitic-speaking tribes.

JEHOVAH. Since the Old Testament name for God, Jehovah, is found in some Christian Bibles and in much of the fundamentalist literature about it, a word of explanation is required as to why I have avoided using this name. The reason is simply that, properly speaking, there should never have been such a word. The Hebrew language is remarkable in a number of respects but in none so much as the fact that in its early written forms vowels were not included. The written language was a sort of clue or key to the spoken tongue and thus would have been, like most code-ciphers, incomprehensible without familiarity with the common oral pronunciations.

In certain ancient scriptural records the name of God—so holy that one was not supposed to speak it—was written JHVH. Jews, who read Scripture aloud, substituted a phrase meaning "the Lord," since they did not pronounce the name itself. We are grateful to some painstaking scholar for the information that there are 6,823 instances of this in the Old Testament.

Many centuries later, vowel letters were added to written Hebrew. Sometime during this stage a totally arbitrary guess was made that the letters e, o, and a might properly be inserted between the consonants. Later scholarship corrected this error, dropping the o vowel. There is additional confusion in that in many languages the letters j and y are interchangeable, the same being true of the letters *v* and *w*. In any event, the correct pronunciation of the first letter of the divine name is indicated by the use of the letter *y*, hence the modern *Yahveh* or *Yahweh*.

Where this leaves the denomination known as Jehovah's Witnesses is a question I cannot now pursue. (See also YAHWEH.)

JEREMIAH was a prophet who worked as a religious teacher and preacher in Jerusalem about 626-580 B.C., beginning during the reign of Josiah (640-609). He was witness to the fall of the Judean kingdom, the destruction of Jerusalem in 586, and the deportation of masses of his people into slavery in Babylon. He himself, however, was not taken away; instead he was apparently kidnapped by conspirators and taken to Egypt, where he later died.

The prophecies in the book attributed to him are not given in chronological order, and scholars now agree that there is no certainty as to who may have gathered them together. There is common agreement that Jeremiah preached the oracles found in Chapters 1-36 and 46-52, and the *Encyclopedia Britannica* states that he dictated his oracles to his secretary Baruch, who also contributed, in Chapters 26-29 and 33-45, to our knowledge of Jeremiah.

Chapter 1. The first thing that strikes the studious reader is that Jeremiah relates a story we have heard before: the Lord directly addresses a man of modest station whom he chooses to be his prophet.

> 6. Then I said, "Ah, Lord God! Behold I do not know how to speak, for I am only a youth."
> 7. But the Lord said to me, "Do not say, 'I am only a youth,' for to all to whom I send you you shall go, and whatever I command you you shall speak."

Despite a strange conversation about rods of almonds and tipped pots, the message God gives Jeremiah is an extremely simple one, namely that Northern Kingdom tribes will make war against Jerusalem and Judean cities, with whom the Lord is angry for worshiping other gods. One is impressed by the fact that the Lord spoke for a remarkably long period of time—the passages add up to seven chapters—in the form of poetry. The conscientious reader must be perplexed by the ambiguity and haziness with which the Lord often addresses his children, who appear to be notoriously forgetful of his strictures against worshiping "idols."

Chapter 10. Verse 10 says, speaking of God, "At his wrath the earth quakes." I know of no intelligent Christian or Jew who believes that earthquakes are caused by the anger of God. We know exactly what causes earthquakes; the means are perfectly natural. The released and frequently violently destructive energies flow from the shifting of slowly moving rock formations beneath the surface of the earth.

The reader may satisfy himself, simply by consulting records of historically recorded earthquakes, that there is no connection between the personal sinfulness of those killed, maimed for life, or injured by earthquakes on the one hand and the timing or locations of such cataclysmic events on the other. In my childhood, there was a serious earthquake in Long Beach, California, but I should be very surprised if the Christian residents of that community concluded that the disaster struck where it did because the inhabitants of Long Beach were more sinful than those of Sacramento, Bakersfield, or San Diego.

Chapter 50. This chapter is one more biblical assertion of the legitimacy of violence and revenge, chiefly against Babylon. The same point is made repeatedly and is nowhere more clear than in Verse 29: "Call together the archers against Babylon: All ye that bend bow, camp against it round about. *Let none thereof escape. . . .*" (IA)

In the modern world, most people count it an atrocity when any victorious military force determines as a cold-blooded policy to "let no one escape," which is to say to kill all prisoners, including innocent women and children. In many instances, the Old Testament not only recommends such a policy but asserts that the authority for such atrocities is God.

Chapter 52 deals with what is alleged to be history and, for all I know, it may be. It concerns the misfortunes of the Judean ruler Zedekiah, who was defeated by the Babylonians. It contains an inventory of valuable items said to be carried away by a Babylonian captain of the guard: cauldrons, shovels, snuffers, bowls, spoons, basins, firepans, candlesticks, cups, etc. Has any priest, minister, or rabbi ever read these passages to his flock? The last verses tell the exact numbers of Jews taken away to Babylon in different years.

It might be instructive if the reader makes the experiment of imagining himself or herself newly arrived on the planet earth. Let him or her assume that he or she is shown certain religious documents, told that they were inspired by God, and that hundreds of millions of the earth's inhabitants believe that they are genuine, valid, and morally uplifting.

Let us further assume that, when the alien opens the collection of such documents at random, his or her eye falls on a passage in which, let us say, a German prophet describes the future destruction of France. The document includes description after description of specific instances of suffering. These are related with not the slightest suggestion that the author laments the pain and misery he foresees; rather the German speaker quite clearly relishes the predicted suffering of innocent children, the ravishing of Frenchwomen, the burning of French homes, the murderous slaughters of French citizens. Would not the space visitor entertain the possibility that certain inhabitants of earth were suffering delusions of an extremely dangerous nature and wonder why their all-powerful God would not use his power to settle human disputes, not egg on his Chosen People to more feats of violence and revenge?

Dear Christian and Jewish friends, I know thousands of you personally. One of the reasons I love you is that you are personally so much better than many of your professed beliefs and religious ancestors.

JERICHO. The story of Jericho's fall to JOSHUA (Josh. 6:1-21) cannot possibly be defended as accurate history. This is frankly acknowledged by experts on such questions, including Leslie Hoppe, O.F.M. Hoppe, associate professor of Old Testament at Catholic Theological Union in Chicago, an archaeologist and much-published author on scriptural matters, says in the *U.S. Catholic,* September 1989:

> When historical critics look at these narratives they say, "Hmm, this passage about the fall of Jericho doesn't really seem like a military campaign." The Bible says that the Israelite priests put on their vestments, marched around the city, and blew their horns for seven days; then on the seventh day the city fell. That seems to decribe a procession—a liturgy, in fact—not a battle.
>
> So, that's the critics' first clue that *the narrative is not an accurate historical account of the fall of Jericho.* Then the critics look to archaeology to see what was actually found at the excavations of Jericho. They discover that there were walls at Jericho that came tumbling down; but *they came tumbling down in 2300 B.C., which was about 1000 years before the Israelites were on the scene.* When the Israelites did arrive at Jericho, the town was sparsely populated and mostly in ruins. (IA)

Jacob J. Finkelstein, a professor of Near Eastern languages, writing in the Jewish magazine *Commentary* (April 1959) states:

> There are many instances where archeologically provided fact or near certainty has contradicted a Biblical statement. I shall discuss at length only one, possibly the most famous, the Fall of Jericho.
>
> Jericho, or its ruined site, has been the subject of intense excava-

tion, on and off, from the early years of the century down to the present day. One of the results of all this work, known to every student of Palestinian archeology, is the plain evidence that *Joshua could not have fought the famous Battle of Jericho for the simple reason that the site was uninhabited during the only period in which it is possible to fit the story of the conquering of Canaan under Joshua, around the middle of the 13th Century B.C.* (IA)

Dr. Finkelstein later comments:

> . . . the most recent excavations at Jericho have proved that *the violent destruction of the city occurred in the 15th Century B.C. and not in the 14th* . . . The fortifications of Jericho found by the first excavators of the site before World War I . . . are now known to be of the third millenium B.C., that is, *more than a thousand years before Joshua!* (IA)

Adds Finkelstein, "Surely not even the exponents of the new trend will expect archeology to confirm the tradition that the fortifications of Jericho tumbled down at the sound of seven trumpets."

The *Encyclopedia Britannica* notes that the city was "razed at the end of the Middle Bronze Age (about 1550 B.C.)" and probably had *not* been reconstructed by the time the Israelites appeared in CANAAN, about 300 years later. It is not known how the author of the book of Joshua obtained his story, unless the Israelites found some people living at the site, noted massive fallen walls, and simply gave themselves credit for having destroyed Jericho. Then, constant repetition made believers out of hearers of the story, until today, some 3,000 years later, many people still believe that Joshua somehow caused the walls of Jericho to tumble.

Truth, as Jesus suggested, can make us free. Why does conservative tradition resolutely oppose it in so many instances?

JESUS. Most Christians profess to believe that Jesus is not only the Son of God but God himself. No other religion makes such a claim about its founder or recognizes the legitimacy of this Christian claim. But if Jesus is indeed God, much that appears in the four Gospels is puzzling.

First is the matter of the two different genealogies given in MATTHEW and LUKE, the only two Gospels to give an account, also with variant details, of Jesus' conception and birth. Matthew (1:1-16) traces Jesus' ancestry through his "father" JOSEPH back to Abraham, whereas Luke (3:23-38) gives all the male line from Adam through Joseph to Jesus.

Two questions have never been satisfactorily answered. First, if God is indeed the father of Jesus, then Jesus has none of Joseph's genes, and Joseph's genealogy (and we cannot know whether Matthew's or Luke's is correct or even if either one is) is superfluous. Why do the authors so carefully record them? Secondly, if Jesus is indeed God, why did he not personally clarify this supremely important question for his followers?

What Jesus Called Himself. One would think that Christians, professing to believe all the words of Jesus, would regard him as he evidently regarded himself—if we are to believe the four Gospels, which are, after all, the only "evidence" we have for what Jesus said in his lifetime on earth. This leaves aside, for the time being, the question as to how reliable the evidence of the Gospels is, since the Gospels were written many years after the death of Jesus, and they sometimes present contradictory accounts of the same events.

But what is remarkable is that in only a few places in the Gospels does Jesus imply that he is God. One exception may be Matthew 4:7, where Jesus, speaking to the DEVIL, implies that he is God. However, another interpretation could be given, or the verse could be a later interpolation.

How *does* Jesus refer to himself and the Deity? We find that he almost always refers to God as "your Father" or "my Father." "Be ye therefore perfect, even as your Father which is in heaven is perfect" (Matt. 5:48). Does that sound as though Jesus is speaking of himself? When he instructs the assembly at the Sermon on the Mount in the Lord's Prayer, saying, "Our Father which art in heaven . . ." (Matt. 6:9), that does not sound as though Jesus were referring to himself. In fact, the entire Sermon is instruction in how to behave vis-a-vis the Father, which any close, or even casual, reader would interpret as a totally separate being.

When we first meet the adult Jesus in Matthew, after his baptism, he has seen the Spirit of God as a dove but nothing is said about his *being* that Spirit of God, or Holy Spirit, as those who believe in the TRINITY claim that he is. In fact, the voice of another speaking from Heaven says, "This is my beloved Son, in whom I am well pleased" (Matt. 3:17). In Matthew 4, Jesus tells Satan not to tempt the Lord and to worship "the Lord thy God," but the text does not remotely suggest that Jesus expected Satan to bow down to him.

Jesus first calls himself the Son of man in Matthew 8:20, and later in 9:6, when he heals a man afflicted with palsy: "But that you may know that the Son of man has authority on earth to forgive sins." He then said to the paralytic, "Rise, take up your bed and go home."

He prays directly to God—obviously a separate personage—in 11:25:

"I thank thee, Father, Lord of heaven and earth . . ." And in two very clear passages Jesus is obviously talking about two distinct beings: "So every one who acknowledges me before men, I also will acknowledge before my *Father who is in heaven;* but whoever denies me before men, I also will deny before my *Father who is in heaven*" (Matt. 10:32-33) (IA). Then: "All things have been delivered to me by my Father; and no one knows the Son except the Father, and no one knows the Father except the Son and any one to whom the Son chooses to reveal him. Come to me, all who labor . . ." (11:27-28).

In a particularly compelling passage we find: "And behold, one came and said unto him, 'Good master, what good thing shall I do, that I may have eternal life?' And he [Jesus] said unto him, 'Why callest thou me good? There is none good but one, that is God . . .' " (Matt. 19:16-17).

Whatever the reader believes in this matter, every student of Scripture should read the Gospels carefully to learn what Jesus says on this question.

Was Jesus God? There is another way to approach this thorniest of difficulties. Let the reader assume for the moment that Jesus *was* God. Imagine further that he or she is present in the time and place Jesus lived, and is totally convinced of the divinity of Jesus.

Even the most fervent atheist will have no problem in grasping that it would be impossible to engage in mere casual conversation with such a being, however friendly his demeanor. The simple knowledge that one was addressing the Supreme Creator and Ruler of the Universe would reduce any sane person to a state of open-mouthed awe. One could not even bear to take one's eyes off the revered deity; every moment of one's existence would be an ongoing miracle, far surpassing any that has actually occurred or been alleged. That one was actually in the presence of God would be, at all moments, a dazzling, shattering experience.

This is all plausible enough, but do we find extreme awe and reverence in the mostly quite matter-of-fact Gospel accounts of the words and actions both of Jesus and of those in contact with him? Strangely enough, we do not. There is certainly respect, there is love and admiration, but they are precisely the sort of reactions with which millions are familiar from personal experience with esteemed mortals. On the other hand, not only the saints but every leader of even the most irrational and bizarre cult is made the object of docile veneration, but *we find close to nothing in the behavior of his associates that would be appropriate were Jesus considered divine by those who knew him best.*

This is perhaps nowhere so striking as in the few stories that describe his relationship with his mother, Mary. Nothing very remarkable, in either act or word, appears to have taken place between them. Certainly there is nothing in the biblical record before the crucifixion to establish that Mary herself believed her adult son was, in every possible sense, God. Indeed, Jesus even appears to deny his mother in Mark 3:33.

While to millions of Christians the idea that Jesus was not God in human form is abhorrent, the great majority of the inhabitants of our planet—including many who consider themselves good Christians—have felt no need to believe Jesus to be God, in order either to believe in a Supreme Being or to construct a moral code of ethics. Some Christians nevertheless assume that, if Jesus is not God, then the entire Christian religion is groundless and worthless.

But this does not necessarily follow. It is true that many confessions of faith in the various Christian denominations would have to be reworded; pastors of the more flamboyant variety who shout to their audiences about the "blood of Jesus saving us" would have to alter their sermons (which would not be a bad idea); and the words of some hymns would need to be changed; but the God of love, preached by Christianity, would remain unaltered. Indeed, this might free many ministers and priests to teach Jesus' message of brotherhood and peace instead of asking adherents to repeat endlessly the belief that Jesus is God.

Certainly, there have been hundreds of millions of devout believers in the teachings of Confucius, Lao-tse, Zoroaster, Buddha, Moses, Mohammad, and other "prophets" and "saints" who were able to revere these men, without worshiping them or feeling the need to declare them divine. Each inspired people in some part of the world to adopt an admirable code of ethical behavior.

A perfectly sound reason for respect for Jesus, even by non-Christians, is the important service his image provides to mankind. This would be true even if, as a few historians have argued, Jesus is a mythical rather than an actual historical figure. My own belief is that he did indeed live in the time of Augustus Caesar; but whether he did or not, our notions about him serve to set forth the highest ideals. Heroic figures invariably embody ideals, but among human heroes, Jesus is supreme. For he not only preached but apparently demonstrated the virtues of compassion, charity, love, courage, faith, and intelligence. To millions he seems perfection in human form.

If it is the case, as it clearly is, that the Scriptures occasionally depict him in less-than-perfect moments—as, for example, in his rudeness to his mother—he nevertheless approaches the ideal of perfection more closely than anyone else who has ever lived.

The Designation Christ. Among the thousand and one interpretive errors of which the modern age is guilty, one concerns the designation of

Jesus as *Christ*. Young children interpret the appellation just as if it were a surname like Adams or Jones. In origin, of course, the word is not a personal name at all but simply a Greek word meaning "the anointed." The equivalent Aramaic word is *meshiakh*. In pre-Christian times kings and high priests were anointed with oils. Consequently, "the anointed one" became a common expression defining a royal personage. This helps explain why the Messiah awaited by the Jews was perceived not as a humble civilian but as a great, kinglike leader. The Gospels generally—and properly— precede the word with the article *the* so that Jesus, the Christ, is a designation of the same type as Jesus, the King, or Jesus, the Holy One.

Omissions in the Bible About Jesus. Many analysts of Scripture, including devout Christians, have referred to the serious difficulties caused by unfortunate gaps in all the Gospel narratives. None of them, for example, provides the slightest hint as to what Jesus was like physically. None says whether he was tall or short, light-haired or dark, heavy-set or slender, handsome or plain. We are never told whether he spoke with a deep or a high-pitched voice. Nor, for that matter, are we told much about his life at all. After his infancy (described only in Matthew and Luke), there is *a blank of some 11 years* in Luke, after which there is reference to a visit with his parents to the Temple at Jerusalem when he was 12. Luke alone tells this story.

Following this brief report there is *another 18-year period concerning which substantially nothing is known*. The Gospels of MARK and JOHN introduce Jesus as an adult, and even Matthew skips from his birth to his adult baptism. Mark provides information that Jesus' trade was that of carpenter (6:3) and that he had brothers named James, Joses, Judas, and Simon (6:3) and sisters, though the names of the women are not provided. How he can have had any brothers or sisters at all if his mother was a lifelong virgin (as Catholicism, but not all Protestant groups teach) and his father did not take another wife is never explained for the simple reason that there can be no explanation consistent with the dogma of Mary's virginity.

It is especially disturbing to learn that the brothers and friends of Jesus did not personally believe that he had a divine mission or was a divinity. Mark, for example, tells that some of his friends approached him as he preached ". . . to seize him, for they said: he is beside himself."

The promise of Jesus to "be with" his followers until the end of time is not one that can be tested, since there is no common agreement as to its meaning. Very young Christians, particularly Catholics, assume that the quoted statement is a guarantee that the church itself will be defended in such a way that it will triumph, or at least not be soundly defeated in any context characterized by strife or oppression. But such an interpretation dissolves the moment it is tested against the record of history.

The church has suffered serious losses, in various centuries, and in many parts of the world. For example, peoples in the North African region of the Roman Empire, particularly in the area of Egypt, embraced Christianity, becoming Coptic Christians. But when the Arabs invaded the region in A.D. 641, the Egyptians, by and large, abandoned the church and embraced Islam. This was true also of the vast regions we now know as Syria, Israel, Palestine, Jordan, Libya, Morocco, Algeria, Tunisia, and Turkey. The Christian church never prevailed in most of the enormous expanse of Asia and in many parts of Africa. Parts of southern Spain and southeastern Europe were also Muslim in former centuries.

The Efficacy of Jesus' Message. It is simply not true that Jesus merely added to the Old Testament message rather than contradicted it. He in fact did both. It is to his eternal credit that, with the possible exception of a few angry outbursts, he did not speak in the violently vindictive tone that characterizes allegedly divine utterance in the Old Testament. The great tragedy of Western history, however, is that, so far as one may judge Christian behavior over the past 2,000 years, too much of it has been governed by the vast sections of the Bible that glorify violence and mayhem.

Those decent, law-abiding, and warm-hearted Christians who derive comfort from their faith and who apparently are not aware of the historical record sometimes assume, when they encounter criticism of their religion, that it must come from individuals who are essentially evil and wish to do little more than attack the good in the world.

Such a reaction, while understandable, is nevertheless very wide of the mark. It is important therefore for Christians to give careful study to questions and criticisms raised by non-Christians, whether these be atheists, agnostics, Muslims, Hindus, Buddhists, or others. Consider, by way of illustration, some perfectly reasonable questions raised by philosopher Bertrand Russell, in his *Has Religion Made Useful Contributions to Civilization?*

> . . . if we are to judge Christianity as a social force we must not go to the Gospels for our material. Christ taught that you should give your goods to the poor, that you should not fight, that you should not go to church. . . Neither Catholics nor Protestants have shown any strong desire to follow His teaching in any of these respects. Some of the Franciscans, it is true, attempted to teach the doctrine of apostolic poverty, but the Pope condemned them, and their doctrine was declared heretical. Or, again, consider such a text as "Judge not, that ye be not judged," and ask yourself what influence such a text has had upon the Inquisition and the Ku Klux Klan. . . .

To this point, Russell himself sounds rather like an Old Testament prophet, a Christian reformer, or a zealous Catholic who calls his fellow believers to moral account while remaining within the church. No doubt many Catholics and Protestants will agree that he is on solid moral ground in what he has just said, which boils down to the long-observable fact that religious believers often do not behave in accordance with the doctrines they profess.

But now note that Russell points out a process that does indeed exist —though it ought not to—and that has led to corruption in more than one religion over the centuries.

> There is nothing accidental about this difference between a church and its founder. As soon as absolute truth is supposed to be contained in the sayings of a certain man, there is a body of experts to interpret his sayings, and these experts infallibly acquire power, since they hold the key to truth. Like any other privileged caste, they use their power for their own advantage. They are, however, in one respect worse than any other privileged caste, since it is their business to expound an unchanging truth, revealed once and for all in utter perfection, so that they become necessarily opponents of all intellectual and moral progress. The church opposed Galileo and Darwin; in our own day it opposes Freud. . . .

Dissenting Views on Jesus. The ancient question posed by Jesus himself "What think ye of the Christ?" (Matt. 22:42) is still of enormous importance. As we have noted above, some see Jesus as God, others as only the specially loved son of God, still others as both. A fourth group perceive him as a mere mortal, nothing more than a very great moral teacher. The Muslims call him the greatest of the prophets to have preceded Mohammed, but they worship neither Jesus nor Mohammed.

The last two views are regarded as heresy by most Christians, and so the earnest seeker after truth rightly returns to the primary source of information about Jesus, the New Testament itself, in hope of arriving at a rational set of assumptions, if not scientifically firm conclusions, about the large question. The views of Bertrand Russell—who, like most unbelievers, has given far more serious study to religious questions than have a good many Christians—are interesting on this point. In the essay "Why I Am Not a Christian" (1927) he comments:

> I now want to say a few words upon a topic which I often think is not quite sufficiently dealt with by Rationalists, and that is the question whether Christ was the best and the wisest of men. It is generally

taken for granted that we should all agree that that was so. I do not myself. I think that there are a good many points upon which I agree with Christ a great deal more than the professing Christians do. I do not know that I could go with Him all the way, but I could go with Him much further than most professing Christians can. You will remember that He said *"Resist not evil: but whosoever shall smite thee on thy right cheek, turn to him the other also."* [Matt. 5:39] That is not a new precept or a new principle. It was used by Lao-tse and Buddha some 500 or 600 years before Christ, *but it is not a principle which as a matter of fact Christians accept.* I have no doubt that the present Prime Minister, for instance, is a most sincere Christian, but I should not advise any of you to go and smite him on one cheek. I think you might find that he thought this text was intended in a figurative sense. (IA)

Russell is, of course, indulging his justly famed gift for wry humor, but he next takes up, in a more serious vein, the troublesome task of giving specific reasons why he does not believe that either the superlative wisdom or unique goodness of Jesus can be granted. He naturally makes his observations in the context of the Jesus described in the New Testament, and simply sets aside the historical question as to the factual accuracy of the Gospels.

He certainly thought that His second coming would occur in clouds of glory before the death of all the people who were living at that time. There are a great many texts that prove that. He says, for instance, *"Ye shall not have gone over the cities of Israel till the Son of Man be come."* [Matt. 10:23] Then He says, *"There are some standing here which shall not taste death till the Son of Man comes into His Kingdom"* [Matt. 16:28]; and there are a lot of places where it is quite clear that He believed that His second coming would happen during the lifetime of many then living. That was the belief of his earlier followers, and it was the basis of a good deal of His moral teaching. When he said, "Take no thought for the morrow," and things of that sort, it was very largely because He thought that the second coming was going to be very soon, and that all ordinary mundane affairs did not count. . . . *The early Christians did really believe it,* and they did abstain from such things as planting trees in their gardens, because they did accept from Christ the belief that the second coming was imminent. In that respect, clearly He was not so wise as some other people have been, and He was certainly not superlatively wise. (IA)

We might add that if Jesus had truly been God, he would not have made such a mistake about the end of the world.

Russell next addresses himself to a moral question raised by the New Testament descriptions of Jesus:

There is one very serious defect, to my mind, in Christ's moral character, and that is that He believed in hell. I do not myself feel that any person who is really profoundly humane can believe in everlasting punishment. Christ, certainly as depicted in the Gospels, did believe in everlasting punishment, and one does find repeatedly a vindictive fury against those people who would not listen to His preaching— an attitude which is not uncommon with preachers, but which does somewhat detract from superlative excellence. You do not, for instance, find that attitude in Socrates. You find him quite bland and urbane toward people who would not listen to him; and it is, to my mind, far more worthy of a sage to take that line than to take the line of indignation. . . .

You will find that in the Gospels Christ said, *"Ye serpents, ye generation of vipers, how can ye escape the damnation of hell?"* [Matt. 23:33] That was said to people who did not like His preaching. It is not really to my mind quite the best tone, and there are a great many of these things about hell. There is, of course, the familiar text about the sin against the Holy Ghost. *"It shall not be forgiven him, neither in this World nor in the world to come."* [Matt. 12:32] That text has caused an unspeakable amount of misery in the world, for all sorts of people have imagined that they have committed the sin against the Holy Ghost, and thought that it would not be forgiven. . . . I really do not think that a person with a proper degree of kindliness in his nature would have put fears and terrors of that sort into the world. (IA)

Jewish Views of Jesus. We must be compassionately understanding of the Jews of Jesus' time who, but for a few exceptions, found themselves unable to believe that he was not only the son of God—which in a sense all of us are—but also literally God himself. It is easy enough for lifelong Christians or recent converts to assume that if they had been alive 2,000 years ago, they would have recognized the godliness of Jesus upon first sight. Any such belief is nonsense. Practically nobody of his day ever dreamed that Jesus was literally God, even after he created miracles of the most dazzling sort, assuming that we can rely on the record of the Gospels that thousands saw them.

I find it impossible to conceive that, upon meeting any other gentleman— no matter how obviously spiritual, charismatic, handsome, and compassionate—I would immediately perceive him as the Ruler of the Universe. The most I can even imagine doing is accepting such an individual as a saint.

We can, alas, go very little further in reasoning our way through this historically troublesome thicket for, as we have seen—and as hundreds of scholars have recognized—the scriptural record about the life of Jesus, written long after his death, is by no means clear but is characterized by contradictions, puzzles, strange omissions, and stories that are simply nonsensical if the chief player in them is indeed God.

Please understand: I am not saying that even some sort of generally homogenized and simplified version of the story of Jesus could not possibly conform, to one degree or another, to the reality that Jesus lived. Something of the sort may well represent historical reality. All I assert is that if any such sweet, edifying, and uplifting life was ever lived, we cannot prove it from the scriptural record.

There is so little true knowledge of matters scriptural and, for that matter, religious in general, that many sincere Christians appear to believe that if they could somehow establish that Jesus was indeed the MESSIAH, this fact in itself would suffice to confirm his divinity. But as all true scholars of Scripture are perfectly aware, it would do nothing of the sort. It is recognized that the word *Messiah,* as it is used in the Old Testament, is not a synonym for *God.* The original belief in the coming of a Messiah was a conception of the Jews, although it is not much mentioned in synagogues and temples in the present. It is nowhere stated in the older Scriptures that when and if the Messiah comes, he will actually be God himself in disguise.

Whoever Jesus was, he certainly appeared to be a heretic in the context of Jewish tradition and belief. However, there is nothing inherently wrong either with heresy or with resistance to heresy. Those who attempt to change any status quo, whether religious, political, economic, or any other, are *always* mistrusted. It does not require an evil heart to mistrust them; the critical reaction is fully human. It grows, in fact, out of no soil more pernicious than the earnest desire to protect and honor what are perceived as the ancient verities, to guard them against anyone who would tamper with them. There is no reason for Christians to have grown angry and vengeful, as millions have over the centuries, about the failure of the Jews in Jesus' day to recognize that he was God. Even if we take the position that the Jews were mistaken, to be guilty of an error is morally different from consciously committing a sin.

Jews are a small minority of the earth's population, but, among their millions, we find only a handful who accept the divinity of Christ. The Jews, as it happens, are not alone in this. They are, in fact, part of an enormous majority of the human population that does not believe that Jesus was divine. If, therefore, the overwhelming majority of humans alive today are as skeptical as the Jews of 2,000 years ago reportedly were, then there is nothing evil in the failure of the Jews to come to a perception of Jesus as God, and to see him as a mere mortal—and a troublesome one at that, to their way of thinking. (See also CRUCIFIXION; RESURRECTION.)

JEWS, PERSECUTION OF. See **Anti-Semitism.**

JOB. The human heart responds readily to the poetry of the book of Job because it addresses chiefly the God-of-nature or the God-in-nature to which, in a certain sense, even most atheists pay respect. The intellectual atheist is aware of the astounding immensity and grandeur of the physical universe. Even the most casual contemplation of the vastness of space and the multiplicity of enormous bodies moving at incredible speeds inspires awe.

The essential mystery of the Bible is unfortunately not diminished by the book of Job. Its thrust is not historical but clearly poetical. Included with the Wisdom literature (Proverbs, Ecclesiastes) of the Old Testament, Job points to the existence of a superbly gifted poet at some unknown time in the Jewish past.

Unfortunately, even the best scholarship has been unable to determine when that time was. In past centuries authorship of Job was sometimes attributed to Moses, but that error has long been acknowledged. There is now no agreement as to who the author is, nor where he lived. For more than 2,000 years the book of Job was looked upon as the story of a real person, but that traditional view has been abandoned, although it is a fair question as to how many of the faithful are aware that this ancient belief no longer has scholarly defenders.

What Job lacks in facts, it more than compensates for in poetry, of which it is one of the great examples in world literature. The author has expressed himself in a form that was traditional in his time; the early Hebrews, although by no means the only people of their day to create poetry, nevertheless were gifted at it. The blessing of Jacob in Genesis, the songs of Moses and Miriam at the Red Sea in Exodus, the blessing of Moses in Deuteronomy, David's lament over Jonathan in II Samuel, the Psalms, Proverbs, Ecclesiastes, and the Song of Solomon are a few examples of this gift.

As philosophy, alas, the book is markedly less successful. The author sets himself to answer a philosophical puzzle that has perplexed people through all recorded time: the question as to why the innocent and righteous suffer the world's calamities just as frequently as do the corrupt and wrongdoers.

For most of us the mystery first comes to mind at the contemplation of particular incidents: an innocent infant born with AIDS or hideously deformed; a loving father accidentally backing the car over one of his children in the driveway of his house; a decent, churchgoing family trapped by flames in their home. There is no need to recite additional examples; they come painfully to our attention every day in the news. And besides these countless individual tragedies there are larger calamities; for example, the 18th-century Lisbon earthquake, which struck on a Sunday morning when most of the people were in church, killing over 30,000 Christians.

To atheists, there is no philosophical puzzle here; although they view such disasters as sympathetically as do believers, they nevertheless do not ask how it is that such tragedies are permitted by a loving God. Inasmuch as they do not believe in a Great Permitter, they concentrate instead on what practical steps they might take to prevent or respond to such events. But for almost all religious believers the problem is probably the most perplexing philosophical dilemma of all.

The unknown author of Job does not write a philosophical treatise but instead tells the story of a pious man named Job, a resident of the land of Uz. Job's condition, when we first hear of him, seems almost too good to be true. He is successful in almost every way; he possesses wealth and honors, and is loved. The story takes a sharp turn, however, when an incredible series of misfortunes befall the poor man. The literary style, structure, and general tone of the narrative is not typical of biography but is appropriate for the sort of story whose purpose is to explore a moral lesson.

The second point the student of Job must grasp is that neither Bible scholars nor simple believers have any clear idea of its essential meaning. William Neil says in his *Harper's Bible Commentary:* "Even with the help of Moffat's translation it is still not immediately plain what the book of Job is all about."

Although most believers imagine that the present books of the Bible somehow magically came together, despite the fact that they were written by many different authors, over a range of centuries and in different places, the fact is that there was never any moment of decision when the canon of the Bible was established. Scholars know that there were very early differences of opinion among Hebrew editors as to whether Job should be included in their Scripture. The great Jewish philosopher of 12th-century Spain, Maimonides, found it difficult to believe that Job was part of God's word, because he could not harmonize its message with Judaism.

Yet another surprise awaits the Christian reader who studies *Job for Modern Man: Today's English Version* (New York: American Bible Society, 1971). Reviewing this constructive and enlightening work, Richard Clifford,

S.J., makes a concession that may set a fundamentalist's head reeling: "Job is particularly difficult to translate. The poetry is dense and the allusions often obscure. *Almost half of the text is corrupt* [that is, probably not the original] *and hence many renderings must be conjectural.*" (IA)

For making similar observations in the 18th century people like Voltaire were considered agents of Satan. Today's most competent Christian scholars are saying, in effect, that people who thought like Voltaire were essentially correct and their Christian persecutors were mistaken.

Chapter 1. The first several verses are more appealing than most of the Old Testament because they describe a man of remarkable virtue. But it would be too much to hope that such a pleasant account would continue. Shortly, the story becomes confusing.

> 6. Now there was a day when the sons of God came to present themselves before the Lord, and Satan came also among them.
>
> 7. And the Lord said unto Satan, "Whence comest thou?" Then Satan answered the Lord and said, "From going to and fro on the earth, and from walking up and down on it."

We are not told who the sons of God were nor why they came to the Lord. Nor are we told of what must have been their great astonishment to discover that Satan stood among them. It is certainly odd that an all-knowing deity would have to ask anyone anything, but perhaps the question was put to Satan in the hope that his answer would be instructive to bystanders. (See DEVIL, THE.)

In the following verses Satan suggests that Job will not be so God-fearing and God-loving if he is struck with disaster. To test this, God tells Satan that he may thereafter do whatever he wishes in the way of evil to Job, with the exception that he is not to touch Job personally. The Devil, thereafter, causes various sufferings to befall Job and those dear to him. Job's response to this is odd:

> 20. Then Job arose, and rent his mantle, and shaved his head, and fell down upon the ground, and worshiped.

It is not clear why a man, crushed by great tragedy, should respond by shaving the hair from his head. We would understand if the Scripture had said, "Then Job wept freely and cried aloud in his misery and fell into the arms of bystanders." The author makes it clear that Job refuses to blame God for his misfortunes.

In Chapter 2 the would-be believer in Scripture is again puzzled. A narrator interested in consistency would have had Satan continue his cruelties to Job in the hope that the virtuous man's faith in the goodness of God would weaken. In the first chapter God had instructed Satan that he was forbidden to touch Job, but in the second chapter, God, perhaps forgetful, permits Satan to do so, which he proceeds to do with a vengeance.

> 7. So went Satan forth from the presence of the Lord, and smote Job with sore boils from the sole of his foot unto his crown.

We are next told that three of Job's close friends come to visit him.

> 12. And when they lifted up their eyes afar off, and knew him not, they lifted up their voice, and wept; and they rent their robes and sprinkled dust upon their heads toward heaven.

Job's friends, evidently believing that misfortunes are caused by sinfulness, urge Job to repent, but at this he protests that he is innocent of any significant wrongdoing. Up to this point Job and his friends have merely set the stage for posing the theological dilemma; they have in no way resolved it.

Chapter 38. If the problem of evil befalling good people is ever to be resolved, it would presumably be none other than God who could explain the inexplicable. He is therefore now reintroduced into the account. It is in the section of Job starting with this chapter that the gifted poet attributes to God poetry of a sublime order, especially as translated into the formal Elizabethan English of King James I's day.

> 1. Then the Lord answered Job out of the whirlwind and said:
> 2. Who *is* this that darkeneth counsel by words without knowledge? . . .
>
> 22. Hast thou entered into the treasures of the snow? or hast thou seen the treasures of the hail,
> 23. Which I have reserved against the time of trouble, against the day of battle and war?
> 24. By what way is the light parted, which scattereth the east wind upon the earth?
> 25. Who hath divided a watercourse for the overflowing of waters, or a way for the lightning of thunder;
> 26. To cause it to rain on the earth where no man is; on the wilderness, wherein there is no man;
> 27. To satisfy the desolate and waste ground; and to cause the bud of the tender herb to spring forth?

28. Hath the rain a father? or who hath begotten the drops of dew?

29. Out of whose womb came the ice? and the hoary frost of heaven, who hath gendered it?

30. The waters are hid as with a stone, and the face of the deep is frozen.

The rest of the chapter, as well as Chapters 39-41, continues in this high poetic style.

Lovers of poetry are urged to read these passages and others in Job aloud. They resound with a mighty music, presumably in any language. The very shimmering beauty of the words, however, partially obscures the fact that the *Lord never does answer the question at issue.* He says, in effect, "How dare you, puny man, presume to trouble the mighty creator of the universe with such paltry puzzles? Do you think that I could not answer such questions if I wished to? Be quiet and make no more such demands on me." Paul gives the same answer in Romans 9:19-21.

This is all dramatic enough, no doubt, and one may even argue that it is conducive to the development of humility and patient suffering, but it should be generally recognized that even after the Lord speaks, in what is one of the longest addresses attributed to him in the Bible, nothing has been resolved. The believer can, in this context, envy the atheist, for whom the problem does not exist. Theists like E. S. Brightman and Charles Hartshorne deal with the problem of evil by denying that the Deity is omnipotent. (See Hartshorne and Reese, *Philosophers Speak of God,* 1976.)

JOHN, GOSPEL ACCORDING TO ST. It is not now believed that the fourth Gospel, attributed to John, who was the son of Zebedee (Luke 5:10), was written by one of Jesus' alleged apostles. The author, whoever he was, is believed by some scholars to have written the three so-called Epistles of John, but most scholars feel that Revelation, also claimed for a John, was created by someone else. It is not known whether the latter was another individual of the same name or whether the name of the better-known Gospel "author" was simply attached to Revelation as a result of the kind of "pious deception" that was common in the collection and revision of biblical documents during the early centuries when Christianity was developing.

It is interesting to observe the present terms of the long debate occasioned by the uncomfortable discovery that the story of JESUS as told by someone designated *John* is, at numerous points, in flat contradiction with the accounts given in the books of MATTHEW, MARK, and LUKE. For how long a period of time we shall never know, such discrepancies were not always apparent even to the orthodox Christian priesthood.

A good example of the direction of scholarly Christian response to the dilemma of New Testament contradictions is *The Gospel According to St. John: Introduction and Commentary* (London: SCM Press, 1959) by Alan Richardson, a professor of Christian theology at the University of Nottingham. He is a highly respected scholar of impeccable Christian and intellectual credentials. His solution is to sacrifice John in the interests of preserving faith in Matthew, Mark, and Luke. He is in no sense pejoratively against the author of the fourth Gospel; his book is, in fact, a remarkable exercise in apologetics and a ringing defense of John. Nevertheless, he frankly states that in many instances the author "is setting forth the true history by means of *stories which are not in their details intended to be literally true.*" (IA)

Most earnest students of the matter will indeed conclude that certain stories and details given in John certainly are *not* true. But whether they were so "intended"—ah, that is another question. For all of Dr. Richardson's brilliance and piety, he is not, it seems to me, capable of deciding precisely what was intended by a writer in the 1st century A.D. I would give his analysis of John's Gospel high marks except for his repeated use of terms such as *doubtless, no doubt,* and *it is clear,* referring to John's *intentions* in setting forth material that Christian scholars now believe has a large component of fictional detail.

The alternative explanations are troubling to the faithful. Consider: (1) If the author *intended* to present a factual, *historical* record, then he was guilty of a high percentage of mistakes, which hardly argues for divine inspiration. (2) If he was telling stories that he was perfectly aware were *not* true, in the sense that a modern speaker might tell an imaginary story to make a philosophical point, then he failed to take into account that later readers would not understand this. (3) If he deliberately told falsehoods in order to put together a story that would be more impressive to the faithful, then he was guilty of believing that the end justifies the means. (4) Since no manuscript exists written by the hand of an "author" of this Gospel, it may be that the version that survives was not the product of a single author but rather represents a gradual accumulation of documents. Many—perhaps all—portions may have been reworked by well-intentioned, 2nd-century Christians who wished to prepare and distribute one more alleged "record" of the ministry of Jesus for the instruction of the faithful. In any event, Dr. Richardson, in dozens of instances, makes the same point; as we shall see over and over again, the author of John is not concerned with historical details.

JOHN, GOSPEL ACCORDING TO ST.

Rudolf Bultmann is considered by knowledgeable Christians to be one of the most influential New Testament scholars of the 20th century. In his masterly *The Gospel of John: A Commentary* (Louisville, Ky.: Westminster Press, 1971) he perceives a variety of steps in the formation of John. These are summarized by Richard J. Clifford, in a review of Bultmann's study in the November 27, 1971, issue of *America:*

> In stage one the evangelist, quite possibly a Gnostic converted to the Christian faith, drew together material *from three sources,* all independent of one another: a signs-source, a *collection of Jesus' miracles— symbolic rather than historical;* revelation discourses, oriental Gnostic in origin; a Passion-Resurrection account. A *later redactor organized and harmonized the whole with an eye to orthodoxy and sacramentalism.* One of Bultmann's tasks is to continue the work of the redactor by constructing the original order of the evangelist. (IA)

What this means is that, far from being the eyewitness reporter that most Christians assume, an unknown author who may or may not have been named John (which if true is actually irrelevant) read various other works in compiling his own account, a factor which certainly renders his testimony less reliable than would otherwise be the case. Then, at an unknown later stage *someone else (the redactor) rewrote this material and made significant changes in it, including additions.* It is therefore likely that the Gospel of John, as it is presently preached, contains passages that would come as a surprise to its original author(s).

One may be grateful that we have such a book as the Gospel of John available in the modern age. But saying this is something very different from insisting that every word Christians read in John was personally guaranteed by God or written by a disciple of Jesus.

Chapter 1. Verse 18 has an absolutely clear meaning. JOHN THE BAPTIST says: "No one has ever seen God. The only-begotten son who abides at the Father's side has made Him known." Neither simpleton nor sage has the slightest difficulty in interpreting such a plainly worded statement. The problem grows out of the fact that older portions of the Scriptures assert that others have not only seen God but—as in the case of MOSES—seen him face-to-face.

Another sort of difficulty is the fact that if, as millions of Christians insist, Jesus was, in every possible respect, God himself, then it is absurd to say, given that he was seen by thousands, that "no one has ever seen God." If we assume that John was correctly quoted, it inescapably follows that he, at least, had not yet come to believe that Jesus was also God.

There is further evidence of this in Verse 32, in which the Baptist is reported to say that he saw the Spirit come down from Heaven as a dove and remain on Jesus. A moment later, in Verse 34, John says: "I testify that he is the Son of God." It is not necessary to disbelieve that Jesus is the Son of God to perceive that, while it would be the highest praise of a human being to assert that he is, in some unique sense, the Son of God, such a compliment pales into insignificance next to the assertion that a given human was also God. But of this John the Baptist makes no mention.

Chapter 2. At the wedding party at Cana, Jesus says something very puzzling to his mother. Mary, be it remembered, is revered by Catholic and Orthodox millions as semidivine herself, miraculously preserved from all sin—a distinction shared with only one other person, Jesus—and also impregnated miraculously by a divine spirit rather than a man. She is deeply venerated by pious throngs, who sing hymns to her, pray to her, light candles to her, march in procession in her honor, and indeed behave toward her in a manner that scandalizes Protestants, since these devotions are indistinguishable from worship, something forbidden by the First Commandment.

And yet, after his mother tells him their host has just run out of wine, "Jesus said to her, '*Woman, what have you to do with me? My hour is not yet come.*' " (v. 4) (IA)

No one has ever known what this statement means. The obvious message is one of startling rudeness. The reader himself would expect to be chastised if he addressed his own mother in such terms, particularly in front of witnesses at a public gathering, and even more certainly if his mother was the greatest woman who ever lived, the very "mother of God," as Catholics believe. The obvious meaning, therefore, must be rejected, alas by means of utterly unconvincing arguments, in favor of alternative explanations.

The classic mystery concerning Mary's *lifelong* virginity (as claimed by Catholics but not all Protestants) is sharply posed in this same chapter: "After this He went down to Capernaum—He and His mother *and his brethren,* and His disciples; . . ." (v. 12) (IA)

The argument for Mary's virginity is sometimes defended by pointing out that the word *brethren* has two meanings. It may mean blood brothers, sons of the same father and mother, or it may mean colleagues, friends, followers. But the second possibility appears to be ruled out because the text suggests that *brothers* and *disciples* are two separate groups. At any rate, in Mark 6:3 four brothers are named and sisters are mentioned in a context that can only mean blood-related siblings (although presumably JOSEPH is their father).

It is interesting to note that the Gospel of John, along with that of Mark, does not carry the story of Jesus' birth; hence, there is no mention of Mary being a virgin or of Joseph. Both Gospels open with John the Baptist and the story of Jesus' baptism in the Jordan River. Is this a possible explanation of why Jesus could speak to her rudely: because he did not revere her as highly as later Christians would do—as the Virgin specially chosen by God to bear a son in a miraculous manner?

After commenting on Verses 13 through 16, I shall have to explain why, when I began to dictate these notes, I started to laugh. From earliest childhood in the Catholic church I had heard about "Jesus chasing the money-changers from the Temple," but I had never actually read the portion of John in which the details are given. First of all, I was surprised to discover that the pictorial sketches I had seen did not give an accurate picture of what reportedly transpired.

13. And the Jews' Passover was at hand, and Jesus went up to Jerusalem,

14. And found in the temple those that sold oxen and sheep and doves, and the changers of money sitting:

15. And when he had made a scourge of small cords, he drove them all out of the temple, and the sheep, and the oxen; and poured out the changers' money, and overthrew the tables;

16. And said unto them that sold doves, "Take these things hence; make not my Father's house a house of merchandise."

It was, then, a considerable number of business people whom Jesus chased out of the Temple. This suggests—assuming the story to be accurate—that he must have been physically formidable, although there is no indication anywhere in the Scriptures as to what his physical dimensions were. If he were short of stature, the first fellow he approached with his whip raised would have simply counterattacked and driven Jesus from the premises rather than the other way around.

John also gives no indication that, at the time the incident occurred, Jesus had any particular standing in the Temple, no authority which might have inclined those chastised to obey him. Indeed, the next several verses give precisely the opposite impression.

The incident is puzzling in a number of other respects as well. It would have been understandable, assuming there was anything improper about the selling of farm animals on the Temple grounds, if Jesus had simply admonished the sellers and peacefully sought to shame them. But he did nothing of the sort. That his temper, in this instance at least, was violent is demonstrated by the fact that he tipped over the sellers' tables.

The reason all of this moved me to amusement was that in one of the churches I attended for several years during my childhood in Chicago, St. Thomas the Apostle, on the city's south side, there were *literally* money-changers—if not sellers of cows and sheep—inside the church. Since most members of the parish in those Depression days were either poor or in lower-middle-class circumstances, it was rare to see paper money in the collection plates. My own family felt particularly generous if we could spare 50 or 75 cents when the basket was passed. The pastor, knowing this, positioned a couple of men seated at card tables at the entrance to the church and provided them with stacks of nickels, dimes, and quarters so that no one could later say, "I would have made a contribution but all I had in my pocket at the moment was a five-dollar-bill."

Chapter 3. Verse 13 presents a serious difficulty. "No one has gone up to heaven except he who came down from heaven, even the Son of man whose home is heaven." The meaning here is clear, not in the least ambiguous. The problem grows out of the fact that, if the assertion is taken as literal truth—which for Christians it must be since its source is considered to be sacred—then other portions of the Scripture that refer to other individuals as having gone to Heaven must be in error.

Christian leaders of the modern day have been frequently embarrassed at being asked, publicly, to comment on the long-standing Christian teaching that those who do not accept Jesus Christ as their Lord and Savior cannot possibly be welcomed into the divine presence following their death. There was a day when Christianity had no trouble at all with the forth-right assertion of this fundamental belief, but in a pluralistic society such as the United States, it is hardly "good public relations" to go about telling fellow citizens who are not Christians—and who, we must never forget, constitute the majority of the human race—that there is not the slightest possibility they will get to Heaven.

The difficulty here would appear to be one that Christians are going to have to live with, given that the New Testament is not in the least ambiguous on the point.

> 18. He who believes in him [his only Son] is not condemned;
> but *he who does not believe is already condemned because he has not believed in the name of the only begotten Son of God.* (IA)

If Jesus has been quoted correctly in this instance, it inescapably follows that the overwhelming majority of the human race always has been, and will continue to be, consigned to the flames of HELL. However, if the author of this Gospel simply made up the point, millions of smug Christians will be jarred out of their smugness that God favors their religion over all others.

There is some confusion in Verse 32, in which John the Baptist, speaking of Christ, is quoted as saying, "He testifies to what he has seen and heard, yet nobody accepts his testimony." Whatever one's biases for or against the Scriptures, all parties will agree that it is a mistake to say that in the time of Jesus "nobody" accepted his testimony. Any editor, even one prejudiced against Christianity, could easily recommend a revision that might read "yet few accept his testimony."

Chapter 8. The tale containing the famous passage "Let him who is without sin among you be the first to throw a stone" is now recognized by all scholars as of unknown origin. In some ancient manuscripts the story of the adulteress (Verses 1-11) appears after Luke 21:38. In the Revised Standard Version it is printed as a footnote in John.

Its moral is edifying enough, and there are obvious reasons for wishing it to be authentic since it is consistent with the image of Jesus as compassionate, tolerant, forgiving. Because it accords with modern social impulses, it is difficult for us to perceive what an astonishing lesson the story was intended to convey when it was first told, whether Jesus told it or not. As it is said, those who brought the woman to Jesus themselves stated: "Moses commanded us to stone such."

To those so intellectually careless as to base their endorsement of CAPITAL PUNISHMENT on the frequent references to it in the Old Testament, one can only say that if strictures against adultery (and many other ancient "sins") were consistently carried out in the present, more than half of the American population—including, no doubt, millions of defenders of capital punishment—would have to be carted off to gallows, gas chambers, electric chairs, and firing walls.

Chapter 11. Peter Somerville-Large's charming *Irish Eccentrics* (London: Hamish Hamilton) tells of John Asgill, a 17th-century British lawyer who became convinced, in reading the Gospel of John, that he would not die. He concentrated, understandably, on the following passage:

> 25. Jesus said to her, "I am the resurrection and the life; he who believes in me, though he die, yet shall he live,
> 26. and whoever lives and believes in me shall never die.

Asgill preferred to interpret the God-man relationship, explains Somerville-Large,

. . . by ordinary English law. Thus, as death was the penalty for Adam's sins, and as Christ had suffered this penalty, death could no longer be inflicted on those who claimed their rights. "Man died simply because he wanted [i.e., lacked] perspicacity to see, courage to rely on it as all-sufficient, and wisdom to plead it against the common enemy, death."

Chapter 21. The mystery of the identity of the beloved disciple presents itself at the point in the story when Jesus appeared after his crucifixion. Says Alan Richardson (*The Gospel According to St. John: Introduction and Commentary*):

> Seven disciples were present, though it is difficult to find particular significance either in the number or in the composition of the group. The two "Johannine" disciples, Thomas (see on 11:16) and Nathanael (see on 1:45), were there, and also the fishermen trio, Peter, James and John. There were also two unnamed disciples. According to v. 7 one of the seven was the Beloved Disciple, but his identity is tantalizingly undisclosed. He might be the son of Zebedee or he might be one of the two other of his disciples. It is hard not to think that the writer is deliberately concealing his name for the very good reason that he was never an historical character at all.

Richardson makes an astonishing admission in respect to Verses 18-19, in which Jesus is said to predict the crucifixion of Peter.

> Since it is virtually certain that *the "prophecy" had been fulfilled by the time this chapter was written,* we have here first-class historical evidence for the mode of the martyrdom of St. Peter. (IA)

Because the reader is possibly unfamiliar with the technicalities of Bible analysis, it needs to be stressed here that the unknown author(s) of these verses practiced deception in treating as a prophecy a statement written not before but *after* the event it pretended to predict. Let us suppose that at the present the alleged seer Jeane Dixon hears the announcement of some important tragedy on the CBS evening newscast and that she then writes an approximate description of the unhappy event, expressing it in the future tense, seals it in an envelope, dates it six months earlier, and then calls a press conference to announce that she had predicted the event. Anyone knowing the sequence as here outlined would have nothing but contempt for Dixon's shameless dishonesty.

Because of the many difficulties we have studied, we are, like it or not, brought face to face with the reality that there is simply no way at

247

all for any person, saint or atheist, to have any degree of *certainty* as to precisely what Jesus, or anyone else quoted in the Bible, actually said.

For a truly outstanding treatment of recent *literary* criticism on the Gospel of John, consult *Anatomy of the Fourth Gospel: A Study in Literary Design* (Philadelphia: Fortress Press, 1983) by the noted Baptist scholar R. Alan Culpepper. Culpepper is a careful student of the composition of novels and fiction.

JOHN THE BAPTIST, a highly respected predecessor of JESUS, who lived about 7 B.C.–A.D. 28. He appears in the Gospels of MATTHEW, MARK, and JOHN, but it is only LUKE that provides a detailed account of John's parents, Elizabeth and ZECHARIAH, a priest. The story of the elderly and barren Elizabeth's conception closely parallels that of SARAH in the Old Testament, and both resemble the story of the intervention of the Holy Spirit in causing Mary to conceive Jesus. In fact, it is said to have been Mary's greeting to Elizabeth, when the latter was five months pregnant, that caused the babe to leap in her womb (Luke 1:41).

Some people have found John—despite the sketchiness of his story— a more in-focus character than Jesus. Matthew describes him in Chapter 3:

> 4. Now John wore a garment of camel's hair, and a leather girdle around his waist; and his food was locusts and wild honey.
> 5. Then went out to him Jerusalem and all Judea and all the region about the Jordan,
> 6. and they were baptized by him in the river Jordan, confessing their sins.

John was a classic hermit, and he was humble before Jesus, whom he called, in Mark 1:

> 7. ". . . he who is mightier than I, the thong of whose sandals I am not worthy to stoop down and untie.
> 8. I have baptized you with water; but he will baptize you with the Holy Spirit."

John fulminated mightily in Matthew against the Pharisees and Sadducees, refusing to baptize them—but we are not told why. Since he lived in the Judean wilderness, scholars have suggested he may have been a member of the Dead Sea community (see DEAD SEA SCROLLS) or at least had contact with it. This group did not like or respect the Pharisees and Sadducees, so if John were a member of the Qumran community, that would explain his hostility to traditional Jewish groups.

Mark and Luke both tell about John's problems with Herod. Luke explains, saying in Chapter 3:

> 19. But Herod the tetrarch, who had been reproved by him [John] for Herodias, his brother's wife, and for all the evil things that Herod had done,
> 20. added this to them all, that he shut up John in prison.

Shortly before this happened, John had preached an inspiring message about sharing the wealth—never an appealing idea to the wealthy—and to tax collectors and soldiers he said, "Collect no more than is appointed you" (Luke 3:13) and "Rob no one by violence or by false accusation, and be content with your wages" (v. 14). It is easy to see why the preachings of John the Baptist, in the corrupt court of Herod, might have gotten him arrested.

Some people wondered if he were the MESSIAH for whom the Jews had been waiting, but he disclaimed this, saying, "I am the voice of one who cries in the wilderness, 'Make straight the way of the Lord.' "(John 1:23).

Paul—very strangely—never mentions John the Baptist, but the latter's apparent historicity is confirmed by the Jewish historian of the 1st century, Josephus. However, his explanation for John's arrest and execution differs from that of Mark, who recounts the familiar story of Salome's asking for his head (6:16-29).

JOSEPH, in Genesis, the second-youngest son of JACOB. He was sold into slavery to merchants traveling to Egypt. Since he was the favorite of his father and had reported on his brothers' lapses as shepherds, had received a beautiful coat, and could interpret dreams, they were jealous and hated him, as recounted in Genesis 37. In Egypt he was sold to Potiphar, the captain of the pharaoh's guard, but because the "Lord was with Joseph . . . he became a successful man" (39:2), rising to become an overseer and later a powerful figure in the pharaoh's court.

Concerning this narrative, Jean Levie, S.J. (*The Bible: Word of God in Words of Men*), observes:

> The period of the Hyskos invasion [of Egypt from the northeast] suggests a possible setting and an approximate date for the preponderant role of a Semite Joseph, in the administration of the country and the

establishment of his kinsmen in Goshen, but no trace of these events recorded in Genesis has to date been found in Egyptian historical documents. (IA)

In 1852 scholars located the Egyptian Orbiney Papyrus, preserved in the British Museum in London. It relates the story of two brothers who lived under the same roof. One day as they were working in the fields the elder, who was married, sent the younger back to the house to fetch a supply of seed. When he reached the house, however, he was approached by his brother's wife, who wasted no time in inviting him to have sexual intercourse with her. "Come," she said, "let us lie together for an hour. That will be pleasant for you and I will make fine clothes for you." The young man, shocked, refused—by which the Egyptians obviously intended that an important moral should be taught.

Fearing that the youth would reveal her unseemly proposal, however, the wife accused him of having tried to seduce her. When her husband came home she libelously quoted his brother as having said to her, "Let down thy hair and let us lie together for an hour." Enraged by this news, the man killed his younger brother on the spot. In Genesis 39, in which Joseph is tempted by Potiphar's wife, Joseph was not killed, though he was imprisoned for a time.

Joseph reportedly used his ability to interpret dreams to find favor with the pharaoh, so that when his father and brothers had to go down to Egypt during a famine, he was able to help them, having been so overjoyed to see his family again that he was reconciled with his brothers.

It is possible that the elements of this story that relate to reality concern a famine that caused the ancient Hebrew tribes to migrate in the direction of Egypt, since they were still nomads at that time. What is now the Sinai— and even parts of southern Canaan—were Egyptian territory then. So it was not necessary for the tribes to move all the way into the Nile Delta— where they would have been unwelcome in any case—for the unknown writer of the biblical story, many centuries later, to have used the term *Egypt.* It is important to note, however, that there is no historical evidence that the ancestors of the Jews were prominent in Egyptian society at any time, nor that the stories about Joseph and MOSES relate to real people.

JOSEPH, the husband of Mary, the mother of JESUS. Whether he was also the father of Jesus is one of the many questions that have never been settled. In my own early religious training Joseph loomed as a large and important figure. As head of the Holy Family, he served as an ideal father against which the real fathers of the world might be held to account. It has always seemed perfectly reasonable to me that there be an ideal of family life—quite aside from the question as to whether Mary, Joseph, and Jesus ever existed. The reason, obviously enough, is that it is within the context of families that human beings come to exist and, unless their circumstances are extremely unfortunate, develop to maturity.

Considering, then, that the well-being of individuals and the prospering of a family over generations depend upon the warmth and stability of their upbringing, it seems wise for the churches to emphasize the ideal exemplified by the Holy Family. It comes as quite a surprise, however, when one consults the Gospels, to see that Joseph is actually a minor and shadowy figure and to realize that it is only church art and legend that have contributed to our picture of him. MARK and JOHN do not mention him at all. Parenthetically, they also refer to Mary only in passing, but the total absence of references to Joseph came as a shock when I first realized it.

MATTHEW and LUKE speak of Joseph, since they include details of Jesus' birth and infancy. The esteemed Abingdon Press' *Interpreter's Dictionary of the Bible* (1976), a seven-volume encyclopedic work, refers to these accounts by Matthew and Luke in a way that will no doubt startle many of the faithful:

> They are not primarily historical records, though they contain valuable historical data. To insist too narrowly on the accuracy of the stories is to misunderstand their nature and purpose. *No fully historical account of Joseph's career, or any part of it, is possible.* (IA)

For centuries church scholars have been aware that of the two genealogies of Joseph that are given—one by Matthew (1:1-16) and the other by Luke (3:23-38)—it is not possible that both are correct, since they differ. The obvious purpose of them is to demonstrate that Jesus belonged to the line of DAVID. This detail, however, adds rather than subtracts confusion since we are also told that Joseph was not the actual father of Jesus. It has never been possible to resolve this puzzle except by assuming serious error in the Scriptures.

Another difficulty concerns the fact that, according to Matthew, Joseph was a resident of Bethlehem who moved to Nazareth, as the *Interpreter's Dictionary of the Bible* puts it, "because conditions were not propitious in Judea under Archelaus" (2:22-23). Luke, however, tells quite another story, that Joseph lived in Nazareth before Jesus was born.

If we start by reading Matthew, then it is difficult to grasp that Luke, or whoever the author of his Gospel was, was writing about the same couple. Luke makes no mention of a dream by Joseph, refers to no angelic visitation, and writes nothing of a hurried trip by night into Egypt. In Luke's version Joseph and Mary merely take their son to be circumcised and then to the Temple in Jerusalem to be consecrated. It is at this point, in Luke, that Joseph loses his importance and disappears from the story. Some scholars have hazarded the guess that the reason so little is said in the New Testament about Joseph is that he died sometime during Jesus' childhood. This is nowhere borne out by the scriptural record although it may well have been the case.

Another problem, which I assume is classically recognized since it occurred to me on a casual first reading, presents itself in Matthew 1:25, where it is stated that Joseph "knew her not until she had borne a son." Both the Old and New Testaments frequently use the verb *to know* to refer to sexual intercourse. If in this specific instance we adopt a literal interpretation of the passage, it is suggested that, *after* Mary had given birth, then Joseph did have physical relations with her. But of course such an interpretation cannot be accepted by the millions of Catholics who believe that Mary was a virgin her entire life. Nor do they acknowledge the existence of Jesus' siblings, as related in Mark 6:3 and John 2:12.

In this connection, we owe to the esteemed church father Origen the particulars of a version of Jesus' parentage that existed in pagan and Jewish tradition. It suggested that Jesus was conceived in a perfectly natural way and that his father was a Roman soldier named Panthera. The Greek Platonist philosopher Celsus, writing in about 180, not only recounted the story but also shared the detail that Mary, having become pregnant and beginning to show signs of it, was convicted on a charge of adultery and driven out by Joseph, after which she gave birth to Jesus secretly. Oddly enough, the modern world would probably have known nothing of this had it not been for the fact that Origen was concerned to refute it.

Matthew, in any event, describing Joseph as a just man, added that he was "unwilling to put her to shame although it did enter his mind to divorce her quietly when he learned of her pregnancy" (1:19). This is the difficulty for Joseph that was resolved by the dream in which an angel explained that Mary's pregnancy had been achieved by miraculous means.

It is fascinating to learn that early documents circulating in the Christian community drew a picture of Joseph considerably different from that in the Gospels. In the 2nd century, for example, a religious story called *The Book of James* and another called *The History of Joseph the Carpenter,* or *The Death of Joseph,* produced in the 4th century, describe Joseph at the time he became betrothed to Mary as a widower with children. The latter book also provides considerable detail about the death of Joseph at the age of 111.

Another Christian account, the 2nd century's *Gospel of Thomas,* also tells stories about both Jesus and Joseph, which the *Interpreter's Dictionary of the Bible* describes as "fanciful."

One extremely odd aspect about the fundamental Christian belief in the virgin birth is that, so far as we can tell from the Gospels, Jesus himself never mentioned the subject.

JOSHUA. After the PENTATEUCH, or Law—the first five books of the Bible—come the Prophets, consisting of 21 books, the first of which is Joshua. However, Joshua is written as though it were history rather than prophecy, nor was Joshua ben Nur a prophet.

Fictional Nature of the "Conquest." Untold generations of Jews and Christians have believed, understandably enough, that the book of Joshua was written by Joshua. It was not, and it was written many centuries after the events it describes are alleged to have happened. It is not enough, however, merely to become aware that this error has now been recognized; it is important to perceive the long and frequently controversial process by which such errors are corrected.

For example, as late as 1952 the Revised Standard Version of the Bible (Philadelphia: A. J. Holman Co.), which incorporates revisions of the most competent scholars up to that date, explains in an introduction by Charles F. Pfeiffer:

> The title of the book implies that Joshua is its principle character. The book itself is anonymous, although there is strong internal evidence that it was written by an eyewitness to many of the events which it describes.
>
> In its present form, however, the book is later than Joshua, whose death it records. The conquest of Debir by Othniel, and of Laish (Leshem) by the Danites took place after the death of Joshua.
>
> The book may be the work of one of the "elders that outlived Joshua," who made use of material written by Joshua himself.

This introduction is almost as misleading as the book of Joshua itself. It is wrong to say that there is "strong internal evidence" that Joshua was written "by an eyewitness to many of the events which it describes." Just the opposite is the case. Archaeologists have not been able to come up with a shred of plausible evidence that Israelite tribes entered CANAAN and defeated its powerful cities in the manner that the book of Joshua claims.

Archaeological evidence of a major upheaval in Palestine in the last half of the 13th century B.C. lets us place the beginnings of the Israelites at that time. However, archaeology does not corroborate the main account in Joshua 1-12. There was no sudden, complete conquest; rather it may have been a long, drawn-out affair in which the Israelites slowly moved west across the Jordan in small groups—families, clans, and groups of clans—perhaps sometimes occupying vacant land and building new villages, perhaps at other times battling the Canaanites for possession of long-established settlements, such as Lachish, Debir, and Hazor.

However, in a provocative book by William H. Stiebing, Jr., *Out of the Desert?* (Buffalo, N.Y.: Prometheus Books, 1989), many theories about the so-called Exodus and the misnamed Conquest are examined, along with an enormous amount of archaeological material. Stiebing concludes that the Israelites did not "enter" Canaan as a separate people; rather the various tribes developed out of populations of Canaanites who fled to the hills when the cities declined because of drought, internal fighting, and neglect. It is stunning to realize that six or more books of the first part of the Hebrew Scriptures may have been fictional, *and* that this fiction may not have been created until *after* the Babylonian Exile.

Many contemporary biblical experts have already accepted the thesis of the German scholar Martin Noth that the book of Joshua was the second in a group of no-longer-existing historical scrolls (Deuteronomy, Joshua, Judges, Samuel, and Kings), which were written after the fall of Jerusalem in 586 B.C. This theory too would place at least 600 years between the alleged events and the first recorded accounts of them.

Chapter 1. It was a common convention in the time of the Israelites to portray God as speaking directly to an important leader; this served as a justification for Joshua's doing what he did and a rationale for the people's incursion into someone else's land. Almost all religious leaders down to the present—and many political ones as well—rationalize their behavior, whether decent or shameful, by claiming that God told them to do thus and such.

Once one begins to question whether Joshua wrote this book, whether these events happened, and whether the Lord really spoke to a real person named Joshua, then we must wonder why the Israelites claimed they received a mandate to expand into an area described in Verse 4 as already occupied by others. Did God create the Canaanites, the Hittites, etc. (see 3:10), let them live for awhile in places where the Israelites found them, and then change his mind in favor of the Israelites? The Bible never tells us so, although it is implied that, for some reason never made clear to Gentiles, he "chose" the Israelites to occupy this particular piece of real estate, although he could as easily have made the Sinai desert bloom and established them there.

Nevertheless, the first chapter of Joshua claims that the Hebrews were given divine title to an area stretching north to Lebanon, west to the Great Sea (the Mediterranean), and east to the Euphrates River, with which the writer was probably familiar from the Babylonian Captivity. (Oddly, God does not supply a southern boundary.)

It is curious that *at no time in Hebrew history* are we certain that *any* of their leaders or kings controlled this vast an area, which would have included present-day Jordan, Syria, a small part of northern Saudi Arabia, and western Iraq. The historian John Bright, in *A History of Israel* (Louisville, Ky.: Westminster Press, 3rd ed., 1981), believes that at a maximum King David's

> . . . frontier ran northward with that of Tyre along the back of the Lebanon range to a point near Kadesh on the Orontes River, where it bent eastward with the frontier of Hamath (which may itself have been tributary to David) in the desert. David probably exercised a loose control, as Hadadezer [king of an area north of Damascus whom David defeated] had, over Aramean tribes to the northeast as far as the Euphrates valley; . . . (p. 200).

It is not clear how Bright can make the claim that David's hegemony extended to the Euphrates, unless by using the term *valley* he means "area watered by the Euphrates and its west bank tributaries." This assumes, of course, that there was a historical King DAVID.

Even so, the Hebrews, under rulers down to the Assyrian conquest, were seldom in complete control of the two narrow strips along the Mediterranean known as Philistia (roughly the present disputed Gaza Strip) and Phoenicia, which began north of present-day Haifa and ran far up into Lebanon.

But it is hardly necessary to argue the extent of King David's rule. The point is that, if his reign is not a fiction, his kingdom became divided after his son Solomon's death and was later curtailed and then completely conquered by the Assyrians and, still later, by the Babylonians, Persians, Greeks, Romans, and others. We never see a long, continuous domination of the entire northern and western part of the Fertile Crescent region by Hebrew-speaking peoples, which the Old Testament so often claims God promised them.

Joshua 1:5 is clearly in error when it states: "No man shall be able to stand before you [that is, remain unconquered], all the days of your life; . . . I will not fail you or forsake you."

6. Be strong and of good courage; for you shall cause this people
to inherit this land which I swore to their fathers to give them.

There is more of the same in Chapter 1. We see in later Old Testament
books, however, that no matter how strong and courageous the Hebrew
children were, they did not conquer what God had allegedly promised them
in the book of Joshua.

In Verses 12-18 Joshua instructs all the tribes to cross the Jordan,
from east to west. The women, children, and cattle of the tribes of Reuben
and Gad and half of the tribe of Manassas are to be left east of the Jordan
in lands called Sihon and Ammon, while the men help the other tribes
take the land west of the Jordan. Then the men are to return to their
families on the east bank.

Chapter 2 recounts the story of two spies whom Joshua sent to re-
connoiter JERICHO. They lodged with a harlot named Rahab, who agreed
to help the Hebrews in exchange for a promise that her family would
be spared. She assured them that all of Jericho feared them and that the
land would be theirs for the taking.

Chapter 3. God is said to have miraculously parted the waters of the
Jordan, and the Levitical priests, carrying the Ark of the Covenant, led
the people into Canaan. Incidentally, the fact that the writer always speaks
of "the people" and mentions families and flocks seems to reveal that there
was no military conquest by the Hebrews, thus providing internal con-
firmation of what archaeologists have elucidated. No group intent on armed
conquest would have dragged all that impedimenta along.

Chapter 4. This contains a curious account of the dragging of 12 stones
from the Jordan to a place called Gilgal, near Jericho, to mark the spot
where the Lord dried up the Jordan. Forty thousand armed men were
said to have been present, but the writer is unlikely to have known any
accurate numbers 600 years after the event.

Chapter 5. For some never-explained reason, the Lord decided to halt
the invasion to get everyone circumcised, a curious thing to do on the
eve of battle, since I doubt if such a painful procedure would make any
soldier eager to race into the fray against men who had *not* just had their
foreskins cut off. Would 40,000 already painfully wounded men be likely
to storm into battle? And didn't the other side's spies see the invaders
mutilating each other?

The writer does note that they rested while they healed. In all seriousness, however the practice of CIRCUMCISION actually began, this chapter
serves to remind the Hebrews once again that they are special and different
from other peoples in the Middle East: Arubu (Arabs), Moabites, Edomites,

Philistines, etc.

The Hebrews also stopped to eat. The manna that had sustained them during their wandering in the Sinai desert "ceased on the morrow, when they ate of the produce of the land . . ." (v. 12). The writer reveals what it was that actually drove the Hebrews inside Canaan, which, since it lay in the Fertile Crescent, was far more luxuriant than the region east of the Jordan and south of the Dead Sea. The Sinai, the Negev, and much of Transjordan are still harsh lands, where only small numbers of nomads and their flocks of sheep or goats can thrive. One cannot raise grain, fruit, or cattle in such arid conditions, and the Jordan does not supply much water for irrigation, as do the Nile, Tigris, and Euphrates. One can easily imagine a very hungry—perhaps starving—people coveting the rich lands of PALESTINE, a phenomena known to anthropologists as population pressure.

Parenthetically, many Palestinians of pre-1948 Israel lived mainly as did agricultural people from biblical times: growing olives, dates, fruit, and grain, and tending flocks. Some however were educated and of a professional or merchant class. Ottoman Empire maps (pre-1918) show a land covered with towns and villages; it was not an empty or unfertile area waiting to be brought to life by European immigrants, as has been claimed, though modern Israel has much improved it.

Although all branches of Judaism and Christianity teach that absolutely no one may be worshipped except God himself, the Old Testament contains many instances of idolatry. I do not refer to the many pejorative references to the adoration of false gods but to the apparently acceptable worship of non-gods. Such an example comes in Verses 13-14.

13. When Joshua was by Jericho, he lifted up his eyes and looked, and behold a man stood before him with his drawn sword in his hand; and Joshua went to him and said to him, "Are you for us, or for our adversaries?"

14. And he said, "No; but as commander of the army of the Lord I have now come." And *Joshua fell on his face to the earth and worshipped* and said to him, "What does my Lord bid his servant?" (IA)

It is naturally to be understood that the strange apparition was an angel; nevertheless it is contrary to Jewish and Christian theology that angels should be worshiped.

Chapter 6. One of the most striking—indeed most typical—characteristics of YAHWEH, from what one may learn about him in the Old Testament, is his savagery and bloodthirstiness. In the Old Testament he is often an utterly ruthless mass-murderer, a military strategist and tactician as violent as any human tyrant known to history. Since I do not perceive God as bloodthirsty—though there is the problem of the fang-and-claw factor in the nature he created—it follows that I cannot accept the accuracy of the Old Testament, except as a record of what the Hebrews believed at the time it was written.

Again and again, in chapter after chapter, book after book, we are told of two categories of atrocities committed by God: (1) those he performed directly, by his own hand, and (2) those he commissioned the Israelites to perpetrate. The story of his personal command of the troops of Joshua in their assault on the city of Jericho is but one instance.

First, there is a great deal of nonsense about marching around the walls of Jericho a specific number of days. Not five, not seven. Only six days would suffice. God knows why but never explains his numerical predilections. Then we are told that precisely seven priests shall blow seven trumpets, while everyone marches seven times around the city on the seventh day. The Israelites claimed they entered the now defenseless city, where, acting on God's clear orders, they naturally felt no guilt at committing precisely the sort of crimes that rightly brought captured Nazi officials to Nuremburg.

> 21. Then they utterly destroyed all in the city, both men and women, young and old, oxen, sheep, and asses, with the edge of the sword.

Not content with the massacre itself, Joshua reveals his general level of "civilization" by making a solemn oath that whoever, in the future, might be tempted to rebuild the city of Jericho, should be cursed and should suffer the murder of both his youngest and oldest child! It *was* rebuilt and stands today, often said to be the world's oldest inhabited city.

Chapter 7. This chapter relates another horror story. Joshua has instructed that valuable items of gold, silver, and brass shall not belong to those who find them in the destroyed homes, shops, and temples of Jericho but shall go into the general treasury—which is to say where Joshua can keep an eye on them himself. Naturally a few are tempted to disobey this instruction, as soldiers have always done. As a result, it is alleged that one of their armies is routed by the courageous defenders of the small community of Ai. Because of the loss of 36 men out of a force of some 3,000—the kind of loss for which any intelligent commander would breathe a sigh of relief—Joshua throws an incredible tantrum, flinging himself to the ground, tearing his clothing, and pouring dirt on his hair. One wonders if people really behaved so strangely in either the 13th or the 6th century B.C.

God shortly informs on the greedy soldiers. Furthermore, he gives specific instructions concerning the punishment their crime deserves. One luckless family is selected to serve as scapegoat, and all its members are stoned to death.

Concerning the repeated resort to CAPITAL PUNISHMENT in the Old Testament, one is struck by the fact that the imposition of a brutal death penalty in those days seems to have deterred no more criminal conduct than it does in the present.

Chapter 8. We should not now be surprised at what happened to Ai.

> 24. When Israel had finished slaughtering all the inhabitants of Ai in the open wilderness where they pursued them, and all of them to the very last had fallen by the edge of the sword, all Israel returned to Ai, and smote it with the edge of the sword.
>
> 25. And all who fell that day, *both men and women, were 12,000,* all the people of Ai. (IA) . . .
>
> 29. And he hanged the king of Ai on a tree until evening; and at the going down of the sun Joshua commanded and they took his body down from the tree, and cast it at the entrance of the gate of the city . . .

This is a barbarity of the sort we hear about among Stone Age tribes living isolated and fearful lives in the Amazon valley or New Guinea interior.

The slaughter involved the killing of not only warriors but also helpless old men and women, young children and babies, and presumably any invalids or disabled. The Israelites naturally celebrated the event by constructing an altar: "and they offered on it burnt offerings to the Lord and sacrificed *peace offerings*" (v. 31) (IA).

It is interesting how often in the Old Testament we are told about "peace" offerings that must have been submitted to the Lord's attention while the blood of the helpless victims was still moist on the worshipers' hands. Such accounts produce an ambivalence in the modern reader. Whereas we realize that the Hebrews may not have been any more or less barbaric than many other peoples of their times, their writings have been held up to us from our childhoods as being holy. They do not present an edifying view of the Lord or of the religion of the time.

Near the time the book of Joshua was written, the Hebrews of Israel and Judah had been subjected to a fearsome conquest by Assyria and then by Babylon. The Babylonians force-marched them across the Arabian desert to their capital on the Euphrates, a trek which probably rivaled the Bataan death march or the Cherokees' removal to lands west of the

Mississippi River, an event known as the Trail of Tears. Thus the writer is perhaps saying, in effect, "Despite the terrors we have endured, I am here to tell you that *we* once were strong and did the same to our enemies."

It is curious, incidentally, that JESUS never specifically denounced these portions of the Old Testament, remaining a Jew even while teaching a new dispensation based on love and the forgiveness of enemies.

Chapter 9 would seem to offer proof that not all of Canaan was taken by the sword, as most of Joshua would have us believe, although whether the details of the story of a group called Hivites is true, we do not know.

Frightened by the Israelites' successes at Jericho and Ai, the Hivite leaders from Gibeon, a city west of Jericho, "acted with cunning" (v. 4) and prepared a delegation that carried worn sacks and wineskins and moldy bread and presented themselves to Joshua as people from far off. They made a covenant, offering to be servants. Even when Joshua discovered their trickery, he let them live as slaves, as "hewers of wood and drawers of water for the congregation and for the altar of the Lord, . . ." (v. 27).

We can hardly be shocked at the Israelites' behavior, since slavery officially existed in our own country until 1863, and many people throughout the world still work in slavelike conditions for little wages.

Chapter 10. Adonizedek, King of Jerusalem, angered because of the covenant the city of Gibeon made with Israel, unites four neighboring chieftains and plans to make war against Gibeon. (Note that much-disputed Jerusalem is said to have existed before the Hebrews arrived.) When Joshua hears of this, he leads an army against the followers of Adonizedek, which leads to the usual "great slaughter." In this instance the Israelites can take only part of the credit for the killing.

> 11. And as they fled before Israel, while they were going down the ascent of Beth-horon, the *Lord threw down great stones from heavens* upon them as far as Azekah, and they died; there were *more who died because of the hailstones than the men of Israel killed* with the sword. (IA)

Verses 12-14 describe one of the more famous "miracles" in the Old Testament.

> 12. Then spoke Joshua to the Lord in the day when the Lord gave the Amorites over to the men of Israel; and he said in the sight of Israel, "Sun, stand thou still at Gibeon, and thou Moon in the valley of Aijalon."
> 13. And the sun stood still, and the moon stayed, *until the nation*

260

took vengeance on their enemies. .... The sun stayed in the midst of heaven, and did not hasten to go down for about a whole day.

14. There has been no day like it before or since, when the Lord harkened to the voice of a man; for *the Lord fought for Israel.* (IA)

Verse 13 implies that the sun moves around the earth. One wonders why the Lord, who spoke so often to the Hebrews, did not tell them that the earth and nine other planets move around the sun. Now *that* would have been a miracle: a manuscript from the 6th century B.C. describing proto-astronomers of the 13th century who, without the aid of the telescope, had ascertained certain basic facts about the universe.

As it stands the story is an insult to God, for it alleges that he performed his most remarkable miracle for the sole purpose of helping the Israelites slaughter a few thousand Amorites. In time of war, killings occur by day and by night. So, in one more instance, we are confronted with an utterly preposterous story and one that does no credit whatever to the concept of an all-wise, all-loving God. (Precisely the same story of the sun's stand-ing still is encountered in ancient Indian, Chinese, and Mexican legends.)

The remainder of Chapter 10 and all of Chapters 11 and 12 concern the conquest of various Canaanite cities, a saga, of unrelieved brutality. We encounter such repetitive phrases as: "he utterly destroyed every person in it" (10:28 and 39); "smote it with the edge of the sword" (30, 32, 35, 37); "utterly destroyed all that breathed, as the Lord God of Israel com-manded" (40). Chapter 13 acknowledges areas not taken by the Israelites.

Chapters 13-22 are—to the modern reader—tedious accounts of the division of Canaan among the Hebrew tribes. The cities of Hebron, Sche-chem, and Ramoth were made sanctuaries under the cultic influence of the Levites. These "real estate" chapters were probably intended to keep to a minimum squabbles among the tribes over boundaries. Yet the listing of tribal boundaries is as error-ridden as the rest of the book of Joshua. The boundaries, as Isaac Asimov observed in *Asimov's Guide to the Bible: The Old Testament* (Garden City, N.J.: Doubleday, 1968):

> ... were idealized versions referred back in time from the situation as it existed in the period of the monarchy. They could not have existed in the form given at the time of the conquest. Jerusalem was assigned to Judah, for instance, but that town was not conquered by Israelites until the time of David. Philistia was divided between Judah and Dan, but Philistia was not conquered until David's time, too. The tribe of Asher was awarded much of the Phoenician coast which it never, in actual fact, controlled.

Even the esteemed and usually forthright John L. McKenzie, S.J., in his *Dictionary of the Bible,* becomes somewhat evasive in discussing the utter bloodthirstiness of the book of Joshua, although he concedes it is among the less edifying books of the Old Testament. He is frank in saying of the military behavior of Joshua and the Israelites, that "their practice can be justified on no ground whatever, and *their primitive morality is no example for anyone."* (IA)

McKenzie, a Catholic priest, is naturally not at liberty to follow this judgment to its logical conclusion and deny divine authority for such vulgar cruelty as we find in Joshua. He therefore is reduced to the following sort of argument. "The Israelite view of the Charismatic leader as one under the guidance of Yahweh must be understood in Israelite terms and *not pressed into a crass literal sense."* (IA)

Since the present study is not written for scholars, I shall say—quickly, and truly in a friendly tone—baloney, Father! Although McKenzie, like any intelligent modern reader, is perfectly aware that Joshua is not accurate history, the fact remains that *its author intended it to be taken as such.* Secondly, the churches for centuries—and many self-proclaimed religious leaders to the present day—have insisted on both the literal accuracy and the divine authority of Joshua, along with all the other books of the Bible.

It should not be interpreted as a criticism of today's Jews in the United States to assert the obvious: that their remote ancestors of thousands of years ago—if the Bible is accurate—were bloodthirsty brutes. Precisely the same is true of the ancestors of the Irish, the Germans, the Italians, the Poles, the English, the Scots, and indeed practically every other major and minor tribe known to history. But since such behavior is theoretically outlawed today by United Nations decrees and World Court rulings, it is unacceptable that *any ancient society of mass-murderers* be regarded by any modern man as worthy of the highest *moral* respect.

Whether the Lord did in fact "promise" the land of Canaan for the exclusive use of Jewish tribes thousands of years ago and is giving divine guidance to the nation of Israel today, there is no way of ascertaining. One can only observe that the overwhelming majority of the world's peoples and scholars do not perceive this notion as legitimate.

Yet even if, for purposes of argument, we grant the point, the news would still have fallen strangely upon the ears of those whose lands were claimed. The prior inhabitants of that land which is called Holy—although it has seen far more of unholiness than its opposite—were in all likelihood neither better nor worse than humankind generally. It is obvious that they were merely defending their homes, families, and way of life against nomadic invaders. That these invaders, allegedly led by Joshua, chose to say God gave them the land is not God's problem.

An even odder problem to consider is that God had it within his power to create hundreds of more peaceable tribes, as well as adequate room for them to live in. He also had it in his power to prevent the Holocaust. Why he did not do so is another profound mystery raised by the Bible and history.

K

KINGS, FIRST, continues the story of DAVID, second king of Israel, which was begun in I and II Samuel. It also recounts the reign of Solomon.
Chapter 1. The first book of Kings begins with a strange story.

> 1. King David was old and advanced in years: and although they covered him with clothes, he could not get warm.

This is unlikely to have been the case unless he was suffering some sort of severe chill associated with a high fever. The Near East is, in any event, a warm part of the world, and David, as a king, would have had adequate access to warm clothing, fires, hot baths, and warm bedding. The idea that he nevertheless "could not get warm" seems to be introduced simply to lead to a story that the author may have thought sexually titillating.

> 2. Therefore his servants said to him, "Let a young maiden be sought for my lord the King, and let her wait upon the King, and be his nurse; and let her lie in your bosom, that my lord the King may be warm."
> 3. So they sought for a beautiful maiden *throughout all the territory of Israel,* and found Abishag the Shunammite and brought her to the King. (IA)

A moment's study of the preceding verses suffices to demonstrate the unlikelihood that the story is true. Since Israel was a fairly extensive territory during David's reign, the search must have involved a good many men and taken at least a few weeks. This means that we are asked to believe that the old man went on with his nonstop chill until the search was over and Abishag the Shunammite was brought to the palace. In the event that there is a nucleus of truth to the story, the alleged excuse for an old man's taking a beautiful young woman into his bed will have been just that— a half-lie, half-excuse, the sort of thing not unknown then or now.

To the question, "Who wrote the first book of Kings?" the answer is: no one has the slightest idea. There is, in any event, nothing in it any more morally edifying than we find in the remainder of the first chapter. It is more like an adventure story than religious literature, because it deals with the rivalry between David's son by Haggith, Adonijah, who wished to be king of Israel, and David's son by Bathsheba, Solomon, who also had his eye on the throne. David settles the case in favor of Solomon, at which Adonijah, knowing his rival well, says, "Let King Solomon swear to me first that he will not slay his servant with a sword."

I and II Samuel have made it clear that David was murderous, deceitful, adulterous. He had taken Bathsheba to be his wife after spying upon her— like any neighborhood peeping Tom—as she bathed naked. Afterwards, he had arranged to have her husband killed, the type of crime committed in modern times by the New York Mafioso Vito Genovese. We are therefore entitled, in regard to this one act, to have the same opinion of David as we have of the gangster. It is nevertheless the son of David and Bathsheba who next becomes the ruler of all Israel.

We can hardly be surprised, after all that has gone before, to discover that Solomon, too, is a murderous tyrant, whom no modern Jew would tolerate as leader of the state of Israel. His vengeful nature is revealed in the story of his response to a request by his own mother.

Chapter 2. Adonijah, who lost the throne he thought rightly his, requests Bathsheba's aid in securing the beautiful Abishag for a wife. She agrees to speak to Solomon on Adonijah's behalf and goes off to see her son. When Bathsheba appears, Solomon rises to meet her, bows, and places her in an honored position on his right.

> 20. Then she said, "I desire one small petition of thee; I pray thee, say me not nay." And the king said unto her, "Ask on, my mother: for I will not say thee nay."
> 21. And she said, "Let Abishag the Shunammite be given to Adonijah thy brother to wife."

The king, far from honoring his promise uttered a moment earlier, cries out angrily:

> 23. . . . "God do so to me, and more also, if Adonijah have not spoken this word against his own life.
> 24. "Now therefore, as the Lord liveth . . . and set me on the throne of David my father . . . *Adonijah shall be put to death this day.*" (IA)

Adonijah, Solomon's brother, had already expressed the fear that Solomon would try to kill him. We see here proof that he knew his half-brother well. Were it not for the fact that Solomon is referred to respectfully by the authors of these portions of Scripture—written, of course, by members of his own tribe—there is not a sensible reader who would have a more flattering opinion of him than he does of Colombian drug lords. It is curious how often we read of the treachery of one brother against an unsuspecting sibling in the Old Testament. Not much in the way of family values here.

Chapter 3. As for the famous story of the two women claiming one infant and Solomon's method of judging the case, even the most devout fundamentalist must take notice of the fact that it is to be found in the myths of other tribes and religions.

Chapters 6-8 cover the most important event of Solomon's reign which was the building of the first Temple, the supremely holy place in the minds of all Jews. The second temple was rebuilt after the Jews returned from the Babylonian Captivity. The Wailing Wall is all that now remains of the third temple. Solomon's architect was a foreigner, Hiram, a Phoenician from Tyre.

Chapter 11. We have seen that Solomon is devious and murderous. What of his sexual behavior? Was it, at least, perhaps edifying enough to be held up as a moral example to generations of impressionable children?

> 1. Now King Solomon loved many foreign women: the daughter of Pharaoh, women of the Moabites, Ammonites, Edomites, Sidonians and Hittites;
> 2. Of the nations concerning which the Lord said unto the children of Israel, "Ye shall not go in to them . . . for surely they will turn away your heart after their gods:" Solomon clung to these in love.
> 3. And he had 700 wives, princesses, and 300 concubines . . .
> 4. For it came to pass, when Solomon was old, that his wives turned away his heart after other gods: and his heart was not perfect with the Lord his God . . .

Does the Pope himself seriously believe that a man whose rank required him to administer the affairs of the ancient Jews had 1,000 sexual partners?

Solomon's alleged sexual prowess and general style of life is utterly inconsistent with the traditional Catholic view of sex, according to which asceticism and virginity are important ideals. The Solomonic approach, however, is perfectly consistent with the philosophy espoused in modern times by such hedonists as Larry Flynt, Bob Guccione, and Hugh Hefner. But let no one respond that the Bible holds up various forms of evil behavior as bad examples. The Scriptures utter not a single critical word about the amount of time Solomon must have spent abed if he had sexual relationships with 1,000 women.

Also note that the hero didn't eschew the worship of Yahweh by himself; his "foreign'" wives so influenced him that the poor man could not help himself from falling before idols. One wonders also why he did not select 1,000 Jewish princesses for his harem.

Chapter 16 continues a tiresome recital of the names of long-dead rulers of the two kingdoms that came about after Solomon's death, Judah and Israel, concerning whose existence there is otherwise little or no record. They all seem to do much the same thing. They do evil in the sight of the Lord, walk in the way of some already criticized leader, make Israel or Judah to sin and, in time, sleep with their fathers, that is, expire. If this is accurate history, it is no duller than that of any ancient people, but one wonders what it is doing in the Bible and why these kings cannot behave themselves.

The account also leaves much to be desired in terms of simple coherence. We are told that Asa died and was buried, and then later are given more information about him as if he were still alive. We are told of an unedifying character named Zimri, a captain of chariots, who assassinated a man named Elah and reigned in his stead. In reading the following verse, bear in mind that such vulgar language is said to have been written at the inspiration of God:

> 11. And it came to pass, when he began to reign, as soon as he sat on his throne, that he slew all the house of Baasha. He left him *not one that pisseth against a wall,* neither of his kinfolks nor of his friends. (IA) (King James Bible)

Chapter 18. What would the reader think of a religious leader who commanded his followers to murder several hundred rabbis, priests, or prophets of a rival religion? Were this crime to be committed at any time in recent centuries, he would quite rightly be regarded as one of the most fiendish criminals in history. But the leader who committed the atrocity was Elijah, a man referred to in I Kings in the most glowing of terms.

Elijah is said to have performed, with the aid of God, the miracle of having fire consume a bull after the priests of Baal had been unable to perform that magical act, despite repeated entreaties to their god. That Elijah may have contrived to start a fire under the dead animal is certainly within the realm of the possible. But one detail of the story falls strangely on our ears. I have italicized it in the following verse:

> 38. Then the fire of the Lord fell, and consumed the burnt sacrifice, and the wood, *and the stones,* and the dust, and licked up the water that was in the trench. (IA)

Nowhere on the earth's surface does fire consume stones. If it did, it would be impossible to build kilns and ovens.

Chapter 19. This chapter, which the reader should study, relates a number of highly improbable events. In one reported conversation with God, the Deity says that he will leave only 7,000 alive in Israel. If this is to be interpreted at face value, it implies the death of many thousands of Hebrews, apparently willed by their creator.

Chapter 20. Here we read of an evil king named Benhadad, ruler of Syria, who was supported by 32 other kings. The Lord, however, arranges that "all" the people of Israel, now numbering only 7,000 presumably, slaughter precisely 100,000 enemy soldiers in one day. There are very few scholars of the Scripture who accept the stated facts of this case.

A particularly nonsensical story follows.

> 35. And a certain man of the sons of the prophets said to his fellow at the command of the Lord, "Strike me, I pray." But the man refused to strike him.
> 36. Then he said to him, "Because you have not obeyed the voice of the Lord, behold, as soon as you have gone from me, a lion shall kill you." And as soon as he had departed from him a lion met him and killed him.

It is not enough to simply recognize the preposterous nature of such fictions; their content should be pondered. The unidentified prophet has contrived to conspire in the killing, by a wild animal, of a man who had committed no offense more serious than refusing to do an evil deed, that is, physically assault a stranger.

Such stories must be kept in mind when we hear fundamentalists insist, in the present day, that we must teach our children the morality of the Scriptures. Perhaps we should, but *only that portion of it which is sensible.* A good many of the lessons of the Scriptures should be ignored, as, fortunately, they generally are.

KORAN. It is helpful in understanding the Koran if Christian and Jewish readers view it as the Muslim equivalent of our Bible; it has, in fact, parallel material. Jews and Christians are united in agreeing that the billion people who revere Mohammed as a prophet of God are utterly misguided in supposing that theirs is the one, true, or best religion, personally endorsed by the Almighty. The Christian-Jewish view in this matter, moreover, is thought to require no scholarly expertise or any philosophical gifts but is considered merely a matter of common sense. This view holds that it does not matter how personally devout an individual member of the Muslim community might be, or how learned or sincere. He may be an admirable citizen in a number of other important regards, but insofar as he assumes that his religion bears the divine imprimatur, he is thought to be completely mistaken.

The point is that this opinion, which seems so obviously reasonable to Christians and Jews, is of course, considered dangerous nonsense by the followers of Mohammed. They, in fact, make a similar evaluation of other religions, considering it absurd that non-Muslims imagine that theirs is the one true faith.

Muslims believe that God—or Allah, in Arabic—first established monotheism by means of a "book" (the Old Testament) and sent all the revered Jewish prophets and kings to teach mankind monotheism. They believe these Scriptures were then altered or corrupted and that God sent JESUS, who they believe was not his son but rather an especially important prophet, to do the same. Finally, still unsatisfied, God sent Mohammed to purify the faith and spread it throughout the world.

Mohammed is considered to be the last true prophet, and anyone within Islamic lands claiming subsequent prophets, as the Bahais do, are considered to be heretics. Fundamentalist Muslims, in a country such as Iran, have often executed the peaceful Bahais for their "heresy," when they held the political power to do so.

The Koran is said to have been revealed word for word by the angel Gabriel to Mohammed on many different occasions. Mohammed, who could not read or write, then dictated the surahs (chapters) to family or friends, who set them down precisely as the Lord wanted them recorded. Hence, Muslims are not permitted to change a single word of the Koran. Moreover, the Arabic Koran is supposedly not open to individualistic scholarly interpretation and is considered the only true Koran, although it may be issued in "less authentic," translated versions for people who do not read Arabic.

It is a simplistic notion of language indeed to assume that every word or phrase has only one possible meaning and therefore does not require interpretation. In reality, the great majority of statements are subject to a number of interpretations. In fact, down through the ages Muslim jurisconsults *have* interpreted the Koran and the Hadith, a collection of traditions relating to the Prophet, to solve legal disputes and provide economic, political, and moral guidance to states and individuals. (See Roy Mottahedeh, *The Mantle of the Prophet,* New York, Simon and Schuster and Pantheon, 1985.)

There are two main sects of Islam, Sunni and Shiah. Their views differ on historical points—for example, on the proper succession of leadership after Mohammed died. Within these and other minor sects, there is also a range of practice, as in Judaism and Christianity, from tolerant to fundamentalist. A friend of mine with some understanding of the world's Muslims has pointed out that not all Shiah Muslims are as fanatic as certain Iranian and Lebanese clergymen who became notorious during the 1980s for encouraging the kidnapping of diplomats and political terrorism, recommending the assassination of authors, etc. But if there are Shiite Muslims who are not as fanatic as Ayatollah Khomeini, most seem to have kept their own counsel, perhaps for the same sound reason that Christian critics and heretics of earlier centuries used to express themselves with great care, given that the church sometimes dealt with such doubters by putting them to death in the most painful ways possible.

What could—but does not—unite Islam, Judaism, and Christianity is the common belief in one God, as against many of the world's peoples who are still animists or polytheists, agnostics, or atheists. The Koran teaches respect for many aspects of Judaism and Christianity, but since Islam came later, there is no tradition of respect for it within them. Today we find varying degrees of toleration and intolerance within each religion for the other two, but this is largely based on historical, geographical, and cultural factors.

L

LEPROSY. Although there is a common impression that there are numerous references to lepers in the Old Testament, only three lepers are named. They are as follows:

Namaan, an honorable Syrian captain ("he was a mighty man in valor, but he was a leper," II Kings 5:1), was cured by the prophet Elisha, who told him to bathe seven times in the River Jordan.

Gehazi, a servant of Elisha, was struck by leprosy because he extorted money from Namaan and then lied about it to Elisha (II Kings 5:27).

Azariah, king of Judah, was struck with leprosy by an angry Lord, because he did not prevent the Judeans from sacrificing and burning incense "on the high places" (II Kings 15:4-5).

Jesus cured a leper, a story told in Mark 1:40-41.

Moses and his sister Miriam do not qualify as lepers since they were said to be stricken very briefly.

In any event, scholars now know that the Bible is as unreliable on this subject as it is on many others. According to John L. McKenzie, S.J. in *The Dictionary of the Bible* (New York: Macmillan, 1965):

> It is not certain that the Hebrew and Greek words always refer to leprosy, although it is highly probable that the disease was known; but the words are applied in some cases when no more than some infectious but milder skin disease, it seems, can be intended . . . the position of Namaan in court . . . makes it very unlikely that he suffered from leprosy, and the disease of Gehazi in the story is understood to be the same type.

As for the priestly rules given for the diagnosis and cure of the disease in Leviticus 13-14, McKenzie observes, "Modern medical science can ascertain little from the symptoms here described; they are not the symptoms of leprosy."

LIFE. The most likely emotional response to even the simplest contemplation of the wonder of life is a deep, reverential awe. Viewed optimistically, life seems an enormous magical gift, an absolutely dazzling achievement, whether originating from the blind collision of atoms or designed in every detail by an all-encompassing mind, which is to say, God. But because of its magnificence, there is a tendency to see life in purely sanguine terms, so to speak.

Unfortunately, the relevant realities are so complex as to make us pause in drawing such happy morals, for it is, for the most part, living organisms that attack and kill other forms of life. If cancer cells, or any aggregation of them, could have a mind—in some sort of science-fiction sense—they would be eminently happy and healthy as they flourished and expanded in whatever living tissue they might find themselves. Indeed, the healthier and more vigorous such cells, the worse is the destruction they wreak in the unfortunate organisms serving as host. When this is added to the more obvious reality of the endless daily carnivorous slaughter that is part of the food-chain on planet earth, we can see that life in and of itself is not necessarily either good or bad. It merely exists or ceases to exist. It requires no difficult exercise of the imagination to conceive of many situations in which the cessation of a given life would be much preferable to its continuation.

One philosophical difficulty that immediately presents itself concerns the definition of the seemingly simple term *life*. There is a sense in which "everyone knows" what life is; that sense serves, in quite a practical way, when we distinguish between those creatures that are alive and those which are dead. But when we attempt to pinpoint precisely the moment at which any individual form of life begins, confusion is apparent.

Conventionally, we think that life begins the moment a wriggling cell from a male "fertilizes" the egg from a female, whether the species is cattle, frogs, winged creatures, or humans. But if this is indeed when life begins, then what do we say of the two separate components which have just been united? Do we assert that the sperm or egg was *not* life? Certainly not. If the sperm were not alive, it would lie motionless the moment it emerged from the male organ. Both egg and sperm were separate forms of life *before* uniting.

The pinpointing of when human life begins is virtually impossible to do, both medically and theologically. Certainly, no religious text, like the Bible, specifies the moment. However, this notion—that it can or cannot be done—is central to the debate on abortion. Many deeply religious people believe that a new, potentially human life begins when the sperm connects with the egg and the egg is successfully implanted in the uterus. Others, equally religious or perhaps not professing any religion, do not speak of human life until the fetus is born.

Any woman, menstruating regularly, is aware that her body spontaneously expels each month (except when she is pregnant), for perhaps as much as 40 years, a viable egg. The "accident" of a sperm connecting with one of these eggs in an unplanned pregnancy does not make every woman believe that she is obligated—whether by a higher power, the state, or the views of someone else—to carry that embryo to term. And, daily, nature produces countless millions of "abortions" called miscarriages. In fact, many women do not feel that they are truly carrying a baby until it "quickens," that is, grows so large in the womb that the mother-to-be can feel the fetus moving about.

This is not to argue for the correctness of any single position, but merely to acknowledge that there are different views held by equally sincere people. (See also ABORTION; DEATH.)

LORD'S SUPPER. See **Communion**.

LUKE, GOSPEL ACCORDING TO ST. Chapter 1. It is interesting that the author of Luke opens the narrative by reporting that *many* other stories of Jesus' times had been compiled. Since he means either oral accounts or documents in addition to those of MATTHEW, MARK, and JOHN, it is a great pity that they have been lost. We may hope that such records will ultimately be found, as were the DEAD SEA SCROLLS, but even the most optimistic scholars consider such hopes exceedingly frail.

There is no evidence to suggest that the author of Luke himself ever saw JESUS. Though there is doubt on the point, the author was probably an educated Gentile physician, whose command of Greek was superior to that of the author of Mark, which is demonstrated also in the ACTS OF THE APOSTLES, probably written by the same author.

During my Catholic training, scant as our Bible study was, I was given the impression by well-intentioned nuns and priests—who probably innocently shared the error—that Luke was one of the apostles, knew Christ personally, and was an eyewitness to many, if not all, of the events he reports. This was not the case; the author of Luke never made such assertions, and in fact strongly implies the opposite.

If it is argued that Luke's lack of personal familiarity with Jesus has no importance, given that the Lord inspired him to write his "historical" account, then one must reply that it is well established that he by no means depended solely on inspiration in his work, but, like all sensible writers or reporters, consulted numerous sources and, presumably, individuals. In the first few lines of his Gospel he refers to stories "delivered to us by those who from the beginning were eyewitnesses and ministers of the word."

Chapter 2. Luke plainly states that JOSEPH and Mary (in the ninth month of her pregnancy) were not in their regular home city of Nazareth but happened to be in Bethlehem because that was the place where those belonging to the house of DAVID, as Joseph did, were to be recorded in a census ordered by Augustus Caesar. Whether the actual birth took place in an open field, as births often do in simple agricultural societies, there is no way of knowing. All we are told is that after the infant was born he was "laid in a manger" because there were no quarters available at the nearest inn. We are left to assume that the birth took place in a stable or cowshed, where the manger, a trough from which cattle feed was located (v. 7). Matthew, who says nothing about a manger, notes that the WISE MEN visited the Holy Family in a house (RSV; 2:11).

Note carefully the following passage from Luke:

> 1:32. . . . and the Lord God will give to him the throne of his
> father David,
> 33. and he will reign over the house of Jacob for ever; and of
> his kingdom there will be no end.

This is the prediction that the angel of the Lord, who visited Mary at the annunciation, gave her. However, not only did this prediction never come to pass (nor is it likely to do so) but it never appeared to be part of Jesus' mission to make it come to pass. He never sought a throne, or indeed, any sort of political power. Or if he did, such is not recorded in the New Testament.

It *is* possible, of course: (1) that various of his followers did consider, or wanted him to be, the MESSIAH, which to Jews would have meant an earthly king who would restore the kingdom of David, and that by claiming such they got the innocent Jesus into trouble with the Jewish and Roman authorities; or (2) like many subsequent false claimants to the Messiahship, he did claim to be the Messiah, did attempt political action to overthrow the Romans, and therefore was punished, with his "mission" ending in failure. At this turn of events, his followers converted his "teachings" into talk about an otherworldly kingdom, and made certain that they did not further antagonize the Romans by preaching any such ideas that Jesus may have had.

If the second is the case, then all four Gospels would have distorted the historical Jesus' life, with the result being that those who founded

Christianity may have founded it upon a mythical version of a real person's life. No one can be certain what actually happened.

In Verses 41-45 we encounter a story that has the ring of truth simply because the behavior attributed to Jesus is typical of that of young teenagers into the present. He decides to stay on in Jerusalem while Mary and Joseph return to their home, or else he carelessly forgets his obligation to accompany them and remains behind. The problem here, of course, is that though this is typical and even, in a sense, endearing behavior, it is impossible to accept the account if we also wish to preserve our firm belief that the boy Jesus was far more than a brilliantly precocious human but, rather, was either the specially chosen Son of God or, as most Christians believe, actually God himself.

Of all the complimentary adjectives ascribed to God, the one that is absolutely essential is *perfect*. The imaginary gods of paganism were clearly less than perfect, but this cannot possibly be the case with the God perceived by the world's Christians. So we are faced with a painful choice. Either we must discard our bedrock conviction that Jesus was God in human disguise or we must assume that the incident reported was a figment of someone's imagination and that the report is inaccurate.

Chapter 3. Luke here relates that in the 15th year of the reign of Tiberius Caesar—Pontius Pilate being governor of Judea and Herod being tetrarch of Galilee—a man named John, the son of ZECHARIAH, having received direct divine inspiration, began to preach in the area of the Jordan River. He talked about the baptism of repentance for the remission of sins. (See JOHN THE BAPTIST.)

Of Verse 5 there seems to be no agreement as to its meaning. It is part of a quotation from Isaiah.

> 5. Every valley shall be filled, and every mountain and hill shall be brought low; and the crooked shall be made straight, and the rough ways shall be made smooth.

No one with whom I have discussed this verse knows what it means. It obviously cannot be taken literally since neither during the time of John and Jesus, nor during any subsequent period in the earth's history, has every valley been filled, every mountain brought low, etc. And if such an unlikely thing did happen, what could possibly be the point of it?

It is obvious that over the course of many millions of years the bottom of a valley does tend to rise and that over even vaster periods of time mountains gradually erode, but this self-evident fact can scarcely bring comfort to literalists, since it cannot be equated with the plain meaning of the words of the verse. As for things in the world that are crooked, they are rarely made straight, and the rough ways encountered on the planet, whatever the phrase might mean, seem rarely to be made smooth.

Nor is it clear what is meant by the next verse: "And all flesh shall see the salvation of God" (v. 6). Perhaps at some point in the far distant future that phrase—if it be interpreted as prophecy—shall become truth. But such a thing has clearly not yet come to pass.

We come to a more interesting part of Chapter 3 when the people, having been moved by John the Baptist's exhortations to virtue, ask him what, specifically, he wants them to do. In Verse 11 he gives them precise information indeed, telling them that anyone who has two coats should give one of them to someone who has no coat at all. He gives the same absolutely clear instruction to anyone who has meat, from which it is reasonable to assume that he meant food generally.

This is one of those all-too-rare passages of Scripture where there is no difficulty whatever in interpretation. But if so, more is the pity, for it is clear, as we inspect the behavior of Christians over the last 2,000 years, that only a minuscule number of them have ever acted upon such advice. And we must bear in mind that Christians profess to believe that John spoke on the authority of divine inspiration.

There is also some difficulty with the equally clear-cut advice that John later gives:

> 14. And the soldiers likewise demanded of him, saying, "And what shall we do?" And he said unto them, "Do violence to no man, neither accuse any falsely; and be content with your wages."

We may be quite confident that during the last 2,000 years no Christian soldier has believed that, despite his uniform and lethal weapons, he should never actually do the one thing he has been carefully trained to do, namely, violence.

There are those—and they perhaps merit God's special blessing—who do refuse to do violence, generally citing this verse and especially the commandment: Thou shalt not kill. They are of course gentle saints and pacifists, but they are rarely popular, especially among religious believers, until long after their deaths, if even then. John is not cited either in mainstream or in fundamentalist churches for this admonition. The majority in Christian societies and nations have contemptuously rejected John's advice on this point, even though it is perfectly consistent with the advice of Jesus to turn the other cheek when one is struck.

And what are we to make of John's suggestion that we must be content with our wages? Nothing more than common sense is required to demonstrate that this is a poor suggestion indeed for a large percentage of the human race, since it is apparent that hundreds of millions are unjustly paid pitifully low wages. Certainly none of the heroic Christian social reformers who have tried to help the world's laborers over the centuries have paid the slightest heed to this particular admonition.

A further difficulty with the chapter is that although John has just exhorted his hearers to compassionate, pacifistic behavior, he nevertheless warns them that, as for Jesus, "He will burn with fire unquenchable" those evil-doers who are referred to as "the chaff."

The following verse is tantalizing: "And many other things in his exhortation preached he unto the people" (v. 18). We are, sad to say, never told what those other things are. This is odd because it has already been established that John spoke with divine authority. It was therefore very careless of whoever wrote this chapter of Luke not to share these many other things with us.

Chapter 9. That it was difficult for Jesus to inculcate the ideal now assumed to be one of the fundamentals of Christianity—the loving of one's enemies—is clear from the following verses.

> 51. And it came to pass, when the time was come that he should be received up, he steadfastly set his face to go to Jerusalem.
> 52. And sent messengers before his face: and they went, and entered into a village of the Samaritans, to make ready for him.
> 53. And they did not receive him, because his face was as though he would go to Jerusalem.
> 54. And when his disciples James and John saw this, they said, "Lord, do you want us to bid fire come down from heaven, and consume them?"
> 55. But he turned, and rebuked them, and said, "Ye know not what manner of spirit ye are of."
> 56. "For the Son of man is not come to destroy men's lives, but to save them." And they went to another village.

The quotation is remarkable for a number of reasons. It would appear to be the only instance in the New Testament in which the APOSTLES spoke with absolute conviction that they had the power to perform a theatrical and destructive miracle. Secondly, it is important to consider that the two "saints," James and John, were driven to such fury at a minor offense that they recommended the most hideous sort of punishment imaginable, that by fire. We are not surprised that Jesus rebuked them.

Chapter 14. In the following verse we have one of the most puzzling passages in the entire 66 books that comprise the Bible.

> 26. "If anyone comes to me, and does not hate his own father
> and mother and wife and children and brothers and sisters, yes, and
> even his own life, he cannot be my disciple."

We address here a many-faceted problem. Each factor merits careful consideration.

1. Although Christianity, as represented by hundreds of churches, has long prided itself on being a religion of love, as distinguished from the other major faiths, we are here presented with the spectacle of the founder clearly preaching not love but hatred.

2. It would have been entirely reasonable for Jesus to say that if it ever came to a necessary choice between him and his perceived truth on the one hand and the combined love and loyalty to a close member of one's family, that choice, painful as it might be, would have to be in favor of the Lord and his truth. In fact, Verse 33 suggests just this modification of the point he seems to make in Verse 26. But in 26, he did issue a simple, clearly worded command.

3. Jesus says nothing to the effect that there may be certain situations in which members of one's family are unbelievers or in some other sense impediments to faith, in which case it would be perfectly reasonable to set loyalty to God above loyalty to such erring relatives. Again, this is not what Jesus is quoted as saying. Of course, this may represent mistranslation. If we read *set aside* or *disregard* in place of *hate,* the verse, along with the parables that follow, makes more sense, and then Verse 33 can be seen as summarizing Jesus' meaning correctly. If we are to preserve our faith in the superiority of Jesus, we must assume that he could not have said anything so antithetical to his message of love, and that therefore he has been misquoted.

> 33. So therefore, whoever of you does not renounce all that he
> has cannot be my disciple.

Ideas, as the saying goes, have consequences. The Children of God and other destructive Jesus-movement sects and cults of the early 1970s in the United States appealed to this peculiar warning as justification for turning their backs—often quite rudely—on parents. Most religious cultists are Bible literalists, which is one of the reasons they are considered dangerously fanatical by most observers, whether disinterested or personally concerned.

Chapter 15. There is a strange aspect to the famous story of the lost sheep. If a man owns or shepherds a hundred sheep, Jesus asks, and loses one of them, does he not leave the 99 and go in search of the one that is lost? Jesus then paints an appealing picture of the shepherd finding the little lost animal, placing it on his shoulders, returning home, and calling out to his friends and neighbors, "Rejoice with me for I have found my sheep which was lost."

If the story dealt not with sheep but with a pet dog, its point would be much clearer, given the awkward fact that men raise sheep for two reasons: to rob them of their coats and to kill and eat them. It can be clearly seen, then, that a shepherd's pleasure at locating a lost animal would probably be selfish and have nothing whatever to do with sweet affection for the beast.

M

MAGI. See **Wise Men.**

MARK, GOSPEL ACCORDING TO ST. As a young Christian I was taught that Mark was one of the twelve APOSTLES; the erroneous belief is still common. In reality, modern biblical scholarship has almost nothing in the way of certain knowledge about the person designated "Mark." However, from internal evidence in this Gospel, it would seem that we are entitled to conclude that the writer was a well-educated Jewish Christian, familiar with the Aramaic, Greek, and Latin languages.

Robert W. Funk, Brandon Scott, and James R. Butts, authors of the superb work of scholarship *The Parables of Jesus* (Sonoma, Calif.: Polebridge Press, 1988) say:

> The names attached to the gospels, including those included in the New Testament, are traditional, and *in most cases do not provide any real information about authorship or origin.* When the gospels emerge as written documents in history—when the first copies are made and circulated—author and place of origin have already been lost. The *original composition* of these gospels took place between 50 C.E. and the beginning of the third century C.E. (IA)

If Peter is reliable, "Mark" was his companion and secretary, although modern scholarship considers it more likely that he was a friend of PAUL. It is not established that Mark personally ever saw JESUS, although there is the possibility that he might have while he was still a child. His account is therefore in no sense to be construed as an eyewitness rendition, but it could represent what Mark had been told by Peter and others.

Since the writers of the Gospels attributed to MATTHEW and LUKE depend heavily upon Mark, this means that their accounts are *two* steps away from first-hand knowledge.

The faithful generally assume that, when the same story appears in two or more of the four Gospels, each version of it must be harmonious with the others; this is not, in fact, always the case. Everyone is perfectly aware that if two or more witnesses give an account of the same event, even assuming it is one that they participated in personally, their versions will differ in certain particulars.

When the chief figure in the New Testament accounts is Jesus, and when he is directly quoted, then the fact that the accounts differ is a matter of some awkwardness. In any event, it rules out direct, divine inspiration, since an all-wise God would hardly dictate or inspire three contradictory versions of the same story or quotation in the minds of three different writers.

The fundamentalists, even at this late date, are still insisting that all statements attributed to Jesus in the Gospels represent exact quotations in precisely the same sense that a quotation in tomorrow's *New York Times* of a statement made the day before on television, can be assumed to be accurate. Fundamentalists are, of course, quite mistaken in this. As Funk, Scott, and Butts put it in *The Parables of Jesus:*

> It may be possible to identify some of Jesus' words and the structural outline of the things he said, but *it will never be possible to determine his exact words with absolute certainty since they were transmitted orally.* (IA)

A respected Christian scholar who frankly concedes the New Testament difficulties is William A. Beardslee, in an essay "Literary Criticism of the New Testament" in *Guides to Biblical Scholarship,* New Testament Series (Philadelphia: Fortress Press, 1970). Referring to instances in which the texts of Matthew and Luke are in substantial agreement with each other but in disagreement with Mark, Beardslee states that some of this

> . . . may be explained by independent, parallel editing of Mark by Matthew and by Luke, some by later assimilation of one text to the other. *There was a strong tendency toward such assimilation in the process of copying: Usually Matthew's form, being the most familiar, was inserted into Luke and, for that matter, also into Mark in some cases.* (IA)

The Catholic scholar Ivan Havener observes in his *Q: The Sayings of Jesus* (Wilmington, Del.: Michael Glazier, 1987) that Mark is guilty of errors in quoting from the Old Testament, whereas the authors of Matthew and Luke do not make such errors.

Chapter 2. Some of Jesus' remarks to the scribes of the Pharisees are brilliant. Others are not. It is clever and sensible, for example, when he is asked why he eats with tax collectors and sinners, for him to say: "They that are whole have no need of the physician, but they that are sick: I came not to call the righteous, but sinners to repentance" (v. 17).

But when, a moment later, some disciples of JOHN THE BAPTIST, as well as of the Pharisees, ask him why his disciples do not fast, Jesus' answer is unclear. And in Verse 21, the meaning of Jesus' statement is confusing. He says, "No man also seweth a piece of new cloth on an old garment: else the new piece that filled it up taketh away from the old, and the rent is made worse."

As the reader may know from personal experience, Jesus or whoever created the observation is mistaken about this. All over the world poor people sew new pieces of cloth onto old garments. I have a very old jacket which I have not discarded simply because I am fond of it. When, after some 25 years of wear, the cloth on the elbows wore through, I simply had new cloth elbow patches sewn on the old garment. The rent was *not* made worse. One New Testament scholar suggests that by translating *new* as *unshrunken* and *old* as *shrunken* we can make more sense of Jesus' words.

Then we encounter the famous story of the disciples of Jesus being criticized for picking ears of corn as they passed through a field on the SABBATH. Jesus responds by reminding his questioners that DAVID, whom they revered, in earlier times had done the same thing. In Verse 27 Jesus makes the famous observation: "The Sabbath was made for man, and not man for the Sabbath."

This is all very well, but in making such a statement, if indeed he did, Jesus was not merely casting off an old fragment of ritual that had gradually fallen into disrespect. Instructions about the Sabbath came, according to MOSES—or, more properly, according to the unknown men who wrote about Moses—directly from the lips of the Lord. The instructions are, after all, part of the Ten COMMANDMENTS. If, therefore, Jesus was God, as hundreds of millions of Christians believe, then we are presented with a theological dilemma in that the available evidence compels us to believe that Almighty God changed his mind, as if to say, through the mouth of Jesus: "You know, having rethought the matter, I realize that some of the commandments I gave to Moses on Mt. Sinai about the Sabbath weren't that important after all."

Verses 25-26 present a problem in that the name the author puts in the mouth of Jesus, that of the high priest to whom David went, is Abiathar. When this story was originally told in I Samuel 21:1-3, the name of the priest was Ahimelech. Because both names are foreign to American readers, this may seem an unimportant inconsistency. We must conclude, since obviously both names cannot be correct, that: (1) the author of I Samuel was in error, (2) the author of Mark was in error, or (3) Jesus was in error. None of these alternatives can be accepted by those who believe that Jesus was divine and that every word of the Scriptures was divinely inspired.

Chapter 3. Beginning with a man who had a withered hand, Jesus next

> 10. . . . healed many; insomuch that they pressed upon him for to touch him, as many as had plagues.
> 11. And unclean spirits, when they saw him, fell down before him, and cried, saying, "Thou art the Son of God."

Christians in the present day, when they are ill, wisely go to doctors, not to exorcists, for the required treatments. But if the story is reliable, it follows that *Jesus believed* he had indeed forced evil spirits to leave the body of the sufferers.

When bystanders suggested that Jesus might have been able to remove the demons by working in league with Satan, here called Beelzebub, he responded by an argument that, while spontaneously creative, is nevertheless odd.

> 23. . . . How can Satan cast out Satan?
> 24. If a kingdom is divided against itself, that kingdom cannot stand.
> 25. And if a house is divided against itself, that house will not be able to stand.
> 26. And if Satan has risen up against himself and is divided, he cannot stand, but is coming to an end.

But is it true that a kingdom divided itself will suffer military defeat? No, in simple fact it is not. It is obvious enough that when a nation is under attack, general concurrence among its officials and people is to be preferred over discord. But the fact is we never observe a situation in which a democratic nation at war, or in danger of going to war, is monolithic in its attitudes. Governments that permit freedom of speech have their hawks and doves, and the interests of the poor are unlikely to be identical to those of the rich. And since it is the middle-aged and elderly who force the young to do the fighting and dying, it can hardly be said that they are serving the interests of the young.

What does it mean to speak of Satan being divided against himself? If Satan is—as Christians have always taught—a single individual, then it is not clear in what sense he can be said to be divided against himself, except to the extent that all of us frequently waver and change our minds about things. But if, in a given situation, Satan does something that produces a good result, there should be nothing remarkable about this, since the churches have always taught that the DEVIL will tell a thousand truths in order to make us believe one lie.

Chapter 11. Another awkward quotation occurs in this chapter, when Jesus, extolling the virtue of faith, says:

> 23. For verily I say unto you, That whosoever shall say unto this mountain, Be thou removed, and be thou cast into the sea; and shall not doubt in his heart, but shall believe that those things which he saith shall come to pass; he shall have whatsoever he saith.

This is surely one of the most remarkable claims made by Jesus, who, we are told, worked many wonders and made many promises. The problem, of course, is that such a thing has never happened. Not even Jesus himself moved a mountain. And it is highly doubtful that any of the most devout Christians of the present day would be willing to assert that they personally have the power to cause even a small stone, much less a mountain, to be moved from its normal position into a nearby body of water simply by concentrating on the matter or believing faithfully that it will happen.

It is no defense to argue that we still do not know whether such a thing is possible under the terms Jesus laid down, because no one has ever had the proper degree of faith. Despite the firmness of even the fundamentalists' faith, there is no reason to believe that any one of them has even moved a pebble.

Chapter 12. This is the chapter that includes the famous statement attributed to Jesus, "Render to Caesar the things that are Caesar's, and to God the things that are God's" (v. 17). However, it seems to be rarely perceived that this advice of Jesus indeed contains divine wisdom, that fact is by no means self-evident. Everyone has always known that living in a state, whether it was just or unjust, placed residents and/or citizens under certain obligations; and, of course, those who believe in God automatically assume that their belief places them under certain obligations of a religious nature.

But since both ideas are obvious, this verse can hardly be counted an example of great wisdom as Jesus states the case. What the devout sorely need to be told is how to behave when there is a *conflict* between the demands and laws of the state on the one hand and those of their faith on the other, as has frequently happened down through the centuries. The more firmly the faith of the believer living in an unjust nation is held, the more likely he or she will reject the requirements of citizenship and cast his or her lot with God, which sometimes leads to legal punishment and, in more extreme cases, to martyrdom. That crucial part of the question Jesus simply ignored altogether, thus detracting from the wisdom of his advice.

In the same chapter is yet another instance in which Jesus' argumentation leaves something to be desired. This arises in respect to the Sadducees' citation of the law of Moses that if a man dies without having fathered a child but has a brother, the brother is legally and morally obliged to have sexual intercourse with the widow so that children shall be born. The Sadducees relate the story of a family of seven brothers, each of which died in turn and each of which had sexual intercourse with the woman. The Sadducees conclude by asking,

> 23. In the resurrection [which we are told they do not believe in], therefore, when they shall rise, whose wife shall she be of them? for the seven had her to wife.

Jesus responds by accusing the Sadducees of not having a grasp of the relevant Scriptures. When the faithful rise from the dead, he reminds them, "they neither marry, nor are given in marriage; but are as the angels which are in heaven" (v. 25). This response may have carried the moment, but it simply will not bear the weight of even momentary analysis. The Sadducees were not asking which one of the seven brothers the woman should marry or be a sexual partner to in HEAVEN.

As for the reference to angels, an angel is, by definition, a being without a body. It may well be that all the inhabitants of Heaven are pure spirits with nothing physical about them. Unfortunately, elsewhere we are told that bodies *shall* be united with souls at the end of time, and this is the basis for some Christians' opposition to cremation.

Jesus also says something remarkably strange in Verse 27. Referring to the Almighty he says, "He is not God of the dead, but the God of the living . . ." Nowhere else in the Scriptures, or in churches and temples, are we told that God is not the God of those who have survived physical death, and yet that is precisely what Jesus is saying in this instance. If he is right in this instance, then a great deal of error is preached by the churches.

Fortunately, for simple common sense and for sustaining the belief of the faithful, Jesus preaches an admirable lesson indeed after he observes rich people contributing money to the treasury and then sees a poor widow give two copper coins.

43. And he called unto him his disciples, and saith unto them, "Verily I say unto you, That this poor widow hath cast more in, than all they which have cast into the treasury:

44. "For all they did cast in out of their abundance; but she of her want did cast in all that she had, even all her living."

A lovely lesson indeed.

Chapter 13. Like a good many of the alleged prophecies in the Old and New Testaments, Jesus' "prediction" that Jerusalem would be destroyed (v. 2) was probably written by Mark sometime around A.D. 70, the year Jerusalem *was* partially destroyed. The Romans had punished the inhabitants of Jerusalem severely for the previous three years, keeping it under tight siege; given Rome's mighty power at the time, it required no special gift to foresee the city's fate if Mark wrote *before* the actual event. *It is doubtless of more significance that John, Luke, and Matthew make no reference to such a prophecy.* A number of scholars simply assume that Mark wrote his "prediction" *after* the event it describes, a practice common among Old Testament authors.

The author of Mark then poses one of the gravest problems of Christian theology. Peter, James, John, and Andrew, sitting alone with Jesus, ask him how they shall know that various of his predictions shall be borne out. He then delivers his famous warning of a social situation characterized by a long list of calamities. Even the physical universe is to be shaken.

24. But in those days . . . the sun shall be darkened, and the moon shall not give her light.

25. And the stars of heaven shall fall, and the powers that are in heaven shall be shaken.

Unfortunately there is no way of knowing what Jesus meant in saying that the sun would be darkened. Perhaps he was indicating that there would be a great deal of fog or smoke or foreseeing industrial pollution that would obscure the sunlight. The moon has no light of its own, but perhaps Jesus (if he was the all-knowing God) was aware of common ignorance on the point and spoke in such a way as to be understood by his unsophisticated followers.

A more serious difficulty concerns the prediction that the stars in heaven would fall. Since there is neither up nor down in outer space, the word *fall* is meaningless. All the stars of the universe are, at any given moment, racing through space at incredible speeds; hence, we cannot be sure what message is intended to be conveyed by the statement.

Then we come to an exceedingly odd phrase which, if it is authentic, logically rules out the belief that Jesus was somehow identical with God, or was God in human form.

> 32. "But of that day or that hour no one knows, not even the angels in heaven, *nor the son,* but only the Father." (IA)

If it was indeed the case that Jesus personally did not know when the "last days" would occur, then there is absolutely no escape from acknowledging the fact that Jesus was not God in human form. No doubt most Christians will choose to retain their belief in the divinity of Jesus, which they may do, however, only by assuming that he never made the statement in Verse 32. But where does that concession leave the inerrancy of the New Testament?

Another and more commonly noted problem concerns the fact that if Jesus said what Mark attributes to him in Verse 30, then he was simply mistaken. "Verily, I say unto you, that this generation shall not pass, till all these things be done." The problem, of course, is that his generation *has* passed, along with *many* generations after it, and not a single one of the dire things that Jesus predicted has come to pass.

Chapter 14 tells the touching story of Jesus' solitary, anguished prayer in the place called Gethsemane.

> 35. And he went forward a little, and fell on the ground, and prayed that, if it were possible, the hour might pass from him.
> 36. And he said, "Abba, Father, all things are possible unto thee; take away this cup from me: nevertheless not what I will, but what thou wilt."

One's heart melts at contemplation of the sufferings of Jesus at such a moment. But these two verses are absolutely incompatible with the firm Christian dogma that Jesus was the Lord God, creator and ruler of the universe. In the scene it is inescapable that there are two separate personages, two separate minds, and that one, Jesus, is speaking to the other, God.

The statement attributed to Judas, that he would identify Jesus to his would-be captors by kissing him, is odd. We have previously been told story after story suggesting that Jesus was a famous person in that time and place. He had prayed with multitudes, spoken to multitudes, performed miracles for multitudes, constantly appeared in public places, and yet now, at this turn of events, it is as if he were some obscure figure who would not be immediately recognized.

Chapter 16. A thread of mystery runs through every portion of the

Bible. To this day, after centuries of work by the most dedicated and pain-staking scholars, most of whom have been sympathetic to Christian claims, some are still uncertain where the writer called Mark ended his Gospel. In the Vatican Codex, the book of Mark ends, plainly enough, at Chapter 16, Verse 8, and thus includes no reference to Jesus appearing to anyone after the RESURRECTION.

The incredible discovery called Codex Sinaiticus, found in the last century by the German scholar Konstantine von Tischendorf, is generally considered the oldest New Testament manuscript in existence. It, too, has Mark ending at 16:8.

Controversial Verses. Because of these manuscripts, some Bibles give only eight verses in Mark's last chapter. We do not know who wrote Verses 9–20 or when they were probably added. Verses 17 and 18 are especially problematical.

> 17. "And these signs shall follow them that believe: In my name shall they cast out devils; they shall speak with new tongues;
> 18. They shall take up serpents; and if they drink any deadly thing it shall not hurt them; they shall lay hands on the sick, and they shall recover."

It is necessary, of course, to separate the various components of this confi-dent prediction attributed to Jesus, which has been retained in some Bibles.

The popularity of books and films such as *The Exorcist* and *The Omen* may, to some extent, have revived an almost vanished popular faith in the existence of devils and the ability of at least the Catholic branch of the Christian clergy to "cast them out" of poor souls supposedly possessed by them. The larger question as to whether devils exist is an exceedingly strange one. No one has ever proved by scientific studies that they do. At the other extreme, the naturally superstitious mentality seems to derive a mixture of comfort and morbid fascination from believing in the embodiment of evil. One thing that can be said with certainty is that of the multitude of individuals said to have been possessed by demons over the centuries, a great many have been merely insane, epileptic, drugged, or victims of some other physical or psychological ailment.

The second component, "they shall speak with new tongues," has led to much speculation about a phenomenon known as *glossolalia*. The phrase quoted can mean one of four things: (1) Christian believers will learn other languages, which is not remarkable since anyone can learn another language; (2) they may suddenly speak in other languages without having previously made the slightest effort to learn them; (3) they shall speak in an unknown and undecipherable "tongue"; or (4) they shall find new *ways* of speaking, the word *tongues* being a metaphor. It is likely that the writer intended the last or else he made a prediction that cannot come true, since I know of no evidence that a person has suddenly awakened one morning and spoken a totally foreign language with great fluency. If there are such cases they ought to be investigated as scientifically as possible.

Much more remains to be learned, no doubt, about the strange phenomenon called "speaking in tongues." There seems little doubt that many alleged instances of glossolalia are only meaningless babbling, and it is also likely that those who claim to be able to interpret what are apparently random jumbles of spoken syllables are either dishonest or self-deluded. The possibility remains, however, that in some instances something quite mysterious—and certainly inexplicable by science at the moment—is taking place. If this is so, the ultimate explanation may be found in the same far reaches of psychology out of which emerge the mysteries associated with idiot savants, individuals who, though severely handicapped in brain function, nevertheless manifest startlingly superior abilities sometimes related to mathematics and in other instances to music and sculpture.

The third component of the quotation is puzzling: "They shall take up serpents." If he indeed said such a thing, Jesus probably meant that if those who believe in him took up *poisonous* serpents they would be in no danger of ill effects from the poison if bitten. This is a very dramatic promise indeed. Unfortunately there seems, in real life, to be no difference between the fate of Christians bitten by poisonous snakes and that of non-Christians similarly attacked.

In any event, it is surely significant that the overwhelming majority of Catholic and Protestant clergymen would not walk into a pit full of poisonous snakes for all the money in the world despite the sincerity of their faith. How they can possibly accommodate this reluctance on the one hand with the statement in the Gospel of Mark on the other I do not know.

The fourth component, concerning the power of healing, is in many respects as troublesome as those we have discussed: "they shall lay hands on the sick, and they shall recover."

There is perhaps not a great deal to say about this particular claim because of the impossibility of approaching it using standard methods of scientific control. As it happens, fortunately, people who are sick nearly always recover, until they acquire a terminal illness. The reader has no doubt been ill many times in his life and has subsequently recovered. If, at the onset of one of those illnesses a clergyman—or for that matter a bartender—had laid hands on him he might be inclined to assume that there was a cause-and-effect relationship between the two incidents, but we need not join him in that supposition.

We do know that up until modern times, when medicine began to make dramatic discoveries, which have saved millions of lives, the seriously ill of the world died in droves, despite the sincerity of their Christian convictions.

It is instructive to observe how Catholic priests and most Protestant ministers (with the exception of Christian Scientist healers) conduct themselves when a member of their flock is taken ill. They advise the person to avail himself of the best professional medical treatment he can afford and will sometimes recommend a neighborhood doctor or good local hospital. But there is precious little laying on of hands in such cases.

It may also be worth noting that anthropologists have observed non-Christian medicine men or *shamen* in traditional, isolated societies use the "laying on of hands" as part of their curing methods. Sometimes they are successful, sometimes not; it probably depends on three factors: the seriousness of the disease, the use of medicinal herbs whose healing properties modern medical science has not yet discovered, and the patient's faith in the would-be healer. But, as in the case of most Christians, the patient will recover from minor ills and sometimes from a serious one—no matter what is done.

To return to the basic question of the authenticity of Mark, the skeptical scholar and former Catholic priest Joseph McCabe, in his book *The Testament of Christian Civilization* (London: Watts, 1946), comments:

> We are by no means sure that the basic Gospel, that of Mark, now stands as he wrote it; on the contrary there is every reason to believe that it is full of the sophistications of editors and copyists. For example, *no competent scholar believes that its last twelve verses, beginning with Chapter 16:9, were written by Mark.* They are missing from most of the early manuscripts that have survived, whether Greek, Latin, Syrian, or Armenian. They were not cited by any of the early Fathers save Irenaeus, who did not quote them until the year 185 or thereabout; and they were apparently unknown to Luke and Matthew, who made heavy use of all the rest of Mark's Gospel.
>
> It was in Gaul that they seemed to have originated; Irenaeus himself was a bishop there. Not until the beginning of the 4th century were they accepted in the East, and even then they were still held suspect by the celebrated Eusebius of Caesarea (c. 260-340) who had access to the great library of Pamphilus and was the first critic to give the text of what is now the New Testament anything approaching scientific study.

But regardless of the authenticity of Mark, there is sometimes a sort of morbid recklessness which makes us rush to the opposite extreme from a long-held belief that has been seriously challenged. Dostoevsky made this error when he assumed that if there were no God, then anything would be morally permissible. Just so, some Christians assume that if Jesus is not God, then every aspect of the Christian religion is not grounded on truth and hence worthless. But it is by no means necessary to consider this to be the only alternative. There have been billions of devout believers in the *teachings* of Confucius, Buddha, and Mohammed who have revered these leaders even though none of them claimed to be divine or God. In Islam, such a claim would be blasphemy.

MATTHEW, GOSPEL ACCORDING TO ST. Although priests, ministers and Christian lay people all over the world, in referring to this Gospel, use phrases such as "Matthew says," "Matthew teaches," "What Matthew is saying," etc., the truth is that nobody knows who wrote this particular Gospel. The Gospel itself, like the other three, gives no clues as to its authorship. This is in sharp contrast to certain writings of PAUL, in which there is no room for doubt as to the author's identity.

The only reason that churchmen began to refer to this Gospel as Matthew's is that in approximately A.D. 130 a bishop of the city of Hieratolis, Papias by name, alleged that Matthew, a disciple of JESUS, had collected certain sayings of his master and written them in Hebrew. But as Howard Clark Kee observes, in his introduction to the Gospel of Matthew in the Abingdon Press'*Interpreter's One-Volume Commentary on the Bible* (1971), there are several difficulties with this assumption.

The best scholarship holds that, since Matthew appears to give no eyewitness accounts whatever, the author must have depended, in good part, on someone else's collection of the sayings of Jesus. Unfortunately, no such document now exists. This would have been the now-lost—or merely postulated—collection of sayings which, among scholars, is referred to as "Q" from the German word *Quelle*, which means *source*. (See "Q.")

The possibility also exists that there was once another full account of Jesus' public ministry, in addition to a series of sayings. Another complication is that, according to many scholars, the author of the Gospel of Matthew depended on the Gospel attributed to MARK as a source for his own separate account. Both of these Gospels, as it happens, were written not in Hebrew, but in Greek.

In view of these difficulties, Kee says, "It is plausible to assume that Papias is referring not to the Gospel Matthew as we know it, but to [the] now-lost collection of sayings of Jesus."

Another reason for questioning the long-held attribution was that Matthew the Apostle was older than Jesus, and by the year 90, when it would seem this particular Gospel was written, he would have been approximately 100 years old and therefore unlikely to have undertaken the writing of anything.

Another strange fact about Matthew is that it is the only one of the four Gospels to make any reference to two of the most important building-blocks of Christendom, the Lord's Prayer and the Sermon on the Mount. Given the obvious importance of these passages, it is an unexplained mystery as to why MARK, LUKE, and JOHN do not include them.

In addition, the famous saying which greatly comforts Catholics, that Peter is a rock on which Jesus built his church, is found in none of the other three Gospels.

There is, however, general agreement that, whatever sources the unknown author of Matthew may have used, oral tradition *was* one of them. The serious problem about oral reports grows out of the notorious weakness of human memory, which sometimes seems unable to relate anything whatever with total accuracy, although most people are usually competent enough to give the general gist of a message.

Concerning the notion of a now-lost collection of statements of Jesus, two observations are required. One is that we would have no way of knowing whether its individual attributions are, in fact, word-perfect. But an even more serious consideration is that, if such a vanished priceless document was indeed a source consulted by Matthew, that fact can scarcely be accommodated with the firm Christian belief that God has personally taken charge of every written word in the Bible.

Chapter 1. No one has ever understood why this Gospel opens with an extended genealogy. Fifteen generations are listed from ABRAHAM to DAVID, and 25 generations are numbered from David to JOSEPH, but this information is incompatible with the hypothesis that Joseph was not the natural father of Jesus. All Christian faiths insist that the true "father" of Jesus was the Holy Spirit. Why it was necessary for the Holy Spirit, the third person in the Trinity, to become the father of the second person in the Trinity is another of the impenetrable mysteries with which almost all religions abound.

Being a product of the Catholic tradition, I had always accepted the teaching that Mary, the mother of Jesus, was a life-long virgin. I had no doubts on the matter until I began the present study and read Verses 18-25. It is first stated that "when his mother Mary had been betrothed to Joseph, *before they came together,* she was found to be with child of the Holy Spirit" (v. 18) (IA). If one takes the phrase "before they came together" literally, one must assume that eventually Mary and Joseph did come together in a normal, sinless, healthy marital sexual union.

In Verse 19 we are told that "her husband Joseph, being a just man and unwilling to put her to shame, resolved to divorce her quietly," which suggests that Joseph did not at first believe Mary when she told him that although she was indeed pregnant she nevertheless had not had intercourse. The phrase in Verse 18 explaining that "she was found to be with child of the Holy Spirit" suggests that Mary was aware of the reason for her condition.

Chapter 2. We are told that when Jesus was born the WISE MEN came to Jerusalem saying:

> 2. "Where is he who has been born King of the Jews? For we have seen his star in the East, and have come to worship him."

When news of the presence of the three strangers reached Herod, he was troubled and shortly thereafter held a meeting of the chief priests and scribes. When Herod asked them where Jesus was to be born, they told him "in Bethlehem of Judea, for so it is written by the prophet":

> 6. "And you, O Bethlehem, in the land of Judah, are by no means least among the rulers of Judah; for from you shall come a ruler who will govern my people Israel."

Micah 5:2 is probably the source of the prophecy.

> 2. "But you, O Bethlehem Ephrathah,
>   who are little to be judged among the clans of Judah,
>   from you shall come forth for me
>   one who is to be ruler in Israel,
>   whose origin is from of old,
>   from ancient days."

Sometime after this meeting Herod summoned the Wise Men and questioned them as to their knowledge of the birth of Jesus.

A puzzling factor about the stories surrounding the birth of Jesus is that the details are rendered in a style different from that of reports about the adult Jesus. Concerning the remarkable events of his birth, it is strange that none of the Gospel authors report having talked to anyone who witnessed it. There is no record that Jesus ever shared any important information about his life with the APOSTLES.

Continuing the story of the Magi:

> 9. When they heard the king [Herod] they went their way; and lo, the star which they had seen in the East went before them, till it came to rest over the place where the child was.

Such men, in that day, were not kings, as Christians are frequently told; they were "wise men," specifically philosophers and astrologers. Given that they would have had a modest knowledge of the stars, it is by no means clear as to how they used such knowledge and the reported observation of a particular star to bring them to a specific point on the surface of the enormous planet earth. Since those were days when men imagined that planets and stars hung not terribly high above them, it is easy to see how such stories might have been believed. But we know now that stars are light-years away; it is therefore impossible to say that one of them could somehow hover over Bethlehem.

If we now check Luke to compare Magi stories, we are astonished by the fact that he seems to be unaware of the three Wise Men, if indeed there *were* three, for no number is given by Matthew. In any event, Luke reports that *simple shepherds* came and worshiped the baby, having been personally invited to the event by an angel.

Matthew describes the dwelling where the Holy Family was living after Jesus' birth as "the house." He says nothing about it being a stable. The implication is that it is merely the house in which Mary and Joseph happened to be living at the time. As Joseph is sleeping, perhaps a night or two later, an angel instructs him in a dream to flee to Egypt so as to avoid the murderous wrath of Herod.

Chapter 3. There now occurs a turn in the narrative so puzzling that after almost 2,000 years it has still not been explained. After we are introduced to the infant Jesus, we suddenly read: "In those days came JOHN THE BAPTIST, preaching in the wilderness of Judea," thus skipping some 30 years of Jesus' life. Why does the author of Matthew give no explanation for the omission? Why does he suddenly leave a blank where we would be grateful for any scrap of information about the individual who is considered by Christians as the most important person who ever lived?

There follows a description of the baptism of Jesus by John, concluding with the remarkable description of the voice from Heaven that says: "This is my beloved son, in whom I am well pleased" (v. 17). If, as billions of Christians have believed, Jesus was in some mysterious way God himself, then we can make no sense out of Verse 17. If it was truly God being baptized by John, why does a voice call the man in the River Jordan his son?

Chapter 4. Verse 3 tells us that the DEVIL came to tempt Jesus and said, "If thou be the Son of God, command that these stones be made bread." Jesus refuses to perform the requested miracle, giving as his reason: "Man shall not live by bread alone, but by every word that proceeds from the mouth of God" (v. 4).

Next we are told that the Devil takes Jesus and places him on the topmost point of the Temple in Jerusalem. Is it likely that the most despicable fiend imaginable would have the power to take God, or his beloved son, anywhere, much less to the top of a building? The story bears all the marks of human, not divine, authorship. The reported conversation is muddled and certainly not what is reasonable to expect from the leading spirits of good and evil. Jesus reminds the Devil: "Again it is written, thou shalt not tempt the Lord thy God" (v. 7).

This passage is interesting chiefly because in it Jesus clearly makes the claim that he was far more than a mere Son of God—that he was God himself. Since this is one of the very few places where Jesus makes that claim, it would not be amiss to suspect that it was inserted later to bolster a claim of Jesus' followers. But, despite that dazzling assertion, the Devil takes him away again, this time to "an exceeding high mountain" from which the two participants in our story can see "all the kingdoms of the world."

Now every schoolchild ought to know that the highest mountain on earth is Mt. Everest. But even from its topmost point, a victorious climber cannot see more than 100 miles in any direction, and it is incorrect to assert that from such a perch one could see "all the kingdoms of the world."

The story becomes even more preposterous when the Devil says he will give all the kingdoms of earth to Jesus, if he will simply fall down and worship him. Now, if Satan did know that the man to whom he was speaking was God in human form, then we must conclude that he is also the greatest dunce in history. There's nothing wrong with that unflattering opinion. Unfortunately for the ideal of overall scriptural consistency, we are told in numerous other instances that the Devil is exceedingly clever.

For Chapters 5-7, see SERMON ON THE MOUNT.

Chapter 10. We are introduced to the twelve apostles. In Verse 16 Jesus instructs the apostles to "be subtle as serpents." It is not clear what he meant by this. Very few evangelists have ever practiced subtlety in their sermons. They usually speak frankly, openly, and with considerable energy. What, then, has the quality of subtlety to do with the matter? God knows.

We encounter yet another mystery in Verse 23, where Jesus says, "I assure you that you will not have gone through the towns of Israel before the Son of man comes." By the Son of man he means, presumably, himself. But at that point he did not have to come since he was already there. If he was referring to what is commonly called the Second Coming, we know that remarkable event has not yet occurred. But his apostles did indeed go through the towns of Israel, almost 2,000 years ago. It is impossible to make sense of such passages when we relate them to evidential reality.

Chapter 11. As Jesus was speaking to a gathering of disciples, the subject of John the Baptist came up. That Jesus would praise him need not surprise us, but the degree of praise is quite remarkable. John, he says, is far "more than a prophet" (v. 9). In Verse 11 Jesus assures his hearers that "none has arisen among those born of women greater than" John the Baptist. Since Jesus himself was born of woman, we are presented with a problem here, but it is also odd that Jesus is reported to say that *no one* greater than John has ever lived. In other words, in Jesus' opinion on that day, John was greater than or equal to all the prophets and all the saints. Yet, curiously, he goes on to say that "he who is least in the kingdom of heaven is greater than [John]" (v. 11).

A highly instructive phrase is used in Verse 12. "And from the days of John the Baptist until now the kingdom of heaven suffers violence, and violent men take it by force." Generally, Christians believe that "the kingdom of heaven" has not yet been established. But here Jesus appears to be saying that it *has* been established and, furthermore, that it has been violently assailed.

Jesus clarifies nothing but only adds to our confusion when, in Verse 14, he says, "And *if you care to accept it,* he [John] is Elijah, who is to come." Nor are we enlightened by Verse 15: "He who has ears to hear, let him hear." The faithful have been listening to that verse for almost 2,000 years, and there's still considerable disagreement as to its meaning.

Another oddity occurs in Verses 20-24, when Jesus bitterly criticizes specific towns, Chorazin, Bethsaida, and Capernaum. They are not only criticized but threatened with a horrible, and not entirely clarified, fate on Judgment Day.

The reason for the Lord's anger is simply that his message was not properly attended to in those three communities and that their inhabitants had not repented of their sins. In the light of the Christian belief that Jesus was not merely a great saint or prophet but actually God, the possessor of all knowledge, is it really sensible for him to assert that all the residents of these particular towns are equally culpable for offenses committed merely by a portion of their inhabitants? There must have been, in those three small cities, babes in arms, little toddlers, the very aged and infirm, the deaf, the mentally handicapped, the merely uninformed, and others who could not possibly have attended to the message of Jesus. If any human judge handed down such a sentence he would be considered either insane or corrupt. Why then are such assertions and threats accepted by hundreds of millions of believers as the very epitome of divine wisdom?

Yet another perplexing statement attributed to Jesus is found in Verse 25. "I thank thee, Father, Lord of heaven and earth, that thou hast hidden these things from the wise and understanding and revealed them to babes."

It is a simple enough matter to discern here a certain sort of self-evident truth, which is that the mere possession of wisdom and knowledge does not always guarantee access to the truth. It sometimes happens that a relatively uninformed person, perhaps because of youth or naivete or goodness of heart, may possess a fraction of truth not grasped by well-educated adults. Unfortunately, while Jesus was alluding to this obvious-enough truth, he did not state it directly and clearly. He does not say that sometimes extremely intelligent and well-informed people are blinded by their own intellectual achievements, which can be the case. He is, rather, implying that the Lord God actually *prefers* the ignorant and therefore hides certain truths from the wise while simultaneously making them clearly evident to little children.

Chapter 12. Jesus, speaks first about himself as "lord of the sabbath" (v. 8) and then the author refers to him as the prophet predicted by ISAIAH, quoting: "He will not quarrel or cry out; nor will anyone hear his voice in the streets" (v. 19). It is absolutely clear, from other portions of the New Testament, that the voice of Jesus was constantly being heard in the streets. It is also beyond the possibility of denial that Jesus did indeed quarrel and cry out. Did he whisper to the moneychangers when he threw them out of the Temple?

Verse 36 makes a statement that provides ample reason for worry. "And I say to you, that every careless word that men shall speak, they shall render account for it in the day of judgment." Given the fact that all human beings speak a certain number of careless words every day of their lives, what are we to make of this assertion?

In Verse 38 we are told that some of the scribes and Pharisees asked Jesus for a sign—of what is not specified. There's nothing unreasonable in such a request, but the passage is nevertheless puzzling because we have been told throughout the Gospels that by this point in his life, Jesus had provided countless miracles. He had walked on water. He had calmed a storm. He had raised the dead. He had cast out demons, he had performed the miracle of the loaves and fishes. He had turned wine into water. He had cursed a tree and killed it. He had performed at least one miracle that seemed pointless and absurd, when he forced evil spirits into a herd of pigs, which then rushed headlong into the sea even though the poor animals were blameless. If indeed he had performed all the miracles described in Matthew, Mark, Luke, and John, what more did his questioners of the moment expect?

But the answer attributed to Jesus greatly increases the mystery, for, after having provided all kinds of signs, he now says, "An evil and adulterous generation craves for a sign; and yet no sign shall be given to it but the sign of Jonah the prophet" (v. 39). How can he possibly say that no sign will be given when he had already provided an impressive variety of signs and would, in fact, continue to do so?

Nor does the reference to Jonah add anything to the story except additional confusion. In Verse 40 Jesus says, "For just as Jonah was three days and three nights in the belly of the sea monster, so shall the Son of man be three days and three nights in the heart of the earth."

Jesus can be interpreted here as predicting his resurrection three days after his death, but part of the difficulty is that we are asked to believe that Jesus accepted the reality of the story of Jonah and the whale. For whatever the point is worth, millions of decent, God-fearing Christians in the present day, not to mention millions of Jews, do not believe that Jonah rode about in the belly of a whale.

Chapter 22. Jesus expounds a truly hateful message when he recounts the parable of the wedding guest who was not properly dressed. The message: such a one would be bound "hand and foot" and cast "into the outer darkness; there men will weep and gnash their teeth" (v. 13).

> 14. For many are called, but few are chosen.

Does this mean that God is capricious in whom he chooses to save? Some Christians have always believed that no amount of goodness can assure an individual of his place among "the Elect," as the Calvinists contend.

Chapter 23. William Neil, in his influential and well-thought-out *Harper's Bible Commentary,* makes an astonishing concession concerning the famous diatribe of Jesus against the Jewish religious leaders, which occupies most of this chapter.

Reminding ourselves that for long centuries Christians have insisted that every portion of the sacred record is the word of God, we find Neil saying:

> It is unlikely that our Lord would have been responsible for such a general tirade, which is obviously unfair to the Gamaliels, Nicodemuses, and Josephs, of whom there must have been many who would have agreed with this condemnation of some of their number.

This runs so counter to the official position of all Christian churches that the consciousness of the typical believer somehow automatically rejects the assertion. Neil has just stated that the unknown author of the Gospel has probably inserted a fictitious story, which may reflect his anticlerical views rather than those of Jesus.

Chapter 24. An error is attributed to Jesus in Verse 28 where, describing the last days of life on the planet, he is quoted as saying, "For wheresoever the carcass is, there shall be eagles gathered together." Eagles do not eat dead, rotting flesh; vultures and buzzards do. The only sensible question here is: Was the error made by Jesus, by the author of Matthew, or by an unknown translator? There is no way to resolve the question.

In the context of the explicit descriptions of the last days (vv. 7-44), it is interesting to note that there have probably been few years of Christian history during which someone has not become personally convinced that the end of the world was near. With the benefit of hindsight, it is of course easy to observe that all such predictions have been very wide of the mark. But the question remains: Why are they so common in all times and places where Christianity is preached? The answer is quite simple. The scenes that Jesus describes as characteristic of the last days are, in fact, *constantly occurring*.

> 6. "Ye shall hear of wars and rumors of wars. See that ye be not troubled, for all these things must come to pass. But the end is not yet.
> 7. For nation shall rise against nation, and kingdom against kingdom; and there shall be famines, and pestilences, and earthquakes in diverse places."

The part of Jesus' argument that is perfectly sensible is the moral component. He warns his followers to remain steadfast in virtue so that when the end comes they will be morally ready. But as for the practical details in Chapter 24, one can say only that the advice seems pointless. In Verse 16, for example, Jesus is quoted as recommending that those who happen to be living in Judea should flee into the mountains. Why? If the end of the world should ever come, what could it possibly matter whether one was on a mountain top or in a valley?

Chapter 25. The parable of the master who gave one of his servants five talents, another two, and another one is hardly edifying. The first two servants invest their money, make a profit, and are complimented. The third servant, who puts his money in the earth for safekeeping, is condemned. Jesus quotes the master as saying:

> 27. "Thou, oughtest, therefore, to have put my money to the ex- changers, and then at my coming I should have received mine own with usury."

For centuries the Christian church strongly condemned usury, yet here Jesus appears to recommend it. But whether theologians have taken a position on the practice of profiting from moneylending or not, Jesus' moral lesson is muddled or invalid: "but from him who has not, even what he has will be taken away" (v. 29).

Fortunately for moral education, the author returns to more solid ground when he quotes the Son of God as saying that, at the end:

> 34. Then the King will say to those at his right hand, "Come, ye blessed of my Father, inherit the kingdom prepared for you from the foundation of the world,
> 35. For I was hungry and you gave me meat. I was thirsty and you gave me drink. I was a stranger and you took me in,
> 36. I was naked and you clothed me. I was sick and you visited me. I was in prison and you came unto me."

This is wise and compassionate advice. The only pity is that very few Christians have ever been guided by it. There is even an irony in the fact that the Lord is quoted twice as recommending visits to prisons, inasmuch as today's conservative fundamentalists are active in the campaign for more and larger prisons, longer sentences, much harsher treatment of those incarcerated, and wide use of the death penalty. The lovely Verses 34, 35, and 36 are, of course, perfectly consistent with what conservatives consider the despicable heresy they call the social gospel. (See also COMMUNION; CRUCIFIXION; SLAUGHTER OF THE INNOCENTS.)

MESSIAH, THE. There has been so much concentration in church literature over the centuries on the mystical, prophetic element of messianism that there is a tendency to overlook the aspects of it which would be understandable and reasonable, even if there were no God.

To grasp this, we need to perceive only that in many times and places people have felt, usually quite rightly, that they lived in a dislocated, dangerous, and evil world. Down through the centuries we hear repeated denunciations of corruption, of the laxness of sexual morals, the rudeness and unruliness of the young, the concentration on selfish pleasure and economic gain to the exclusion of charity and spiritual considerations. Add to this the seemingly endless wars, conquests, oppression of the poor, plus the sufferings from natural disasters and diseases, and we can see that it is the most understandable thing in the world that men should long for a grand, heroic, virtuous figure who will lead them out of their misery to a more pleasant, more civilized tomorrow.

Men and women have usually felt such emotions in the context of their own interests. If soldiers, they longed for a military leader. If they were citizens, they longed for a political figure. If religiously oriented, they longed for a Messiah. There is still, in the 20th century, discussion about the hopes of one small tribe, the Jews, for a religious-political leader and whether the establishment of the state of Israel has contributed to that goal.

One can read in the daily papers about a rabbi in Brooklyn who refuses to go to Israel until the Messiah appears, but no one appears to know how to persuade the Messiah to come.

Christians, of course, believe that JESUS Christ was in fact the Messiah the Jews had long awaited—and was even more than a Messiah, since he was also God. Parenthetically, one must observe that if he was the Messiah, the Jews have not accepted the idea, since only a tiny fraction of them have acknowledged him to be their Messiah. It will help to understand the entire question more fully if we recognize its common-sense aspects.

The Jews and the early Jewish-Christians were by no means the only social groups yearning for special leadership. As Karl Bihlmeyer and Hermann Tuchle observe in their monumental *Church History* (Newman Press, 1966–1968):

> Pious pagans agonized with ardent yearning for enlightenment and help from above. The expectation that the world would be transformed and renewed (a "Golden Age"), indeed, even the expectation of an historical savior and redeemer, a great prophet and leader, is found among the Orientals and Greeks at an early date . . . . Even the Roman Emperor was given the honorary title of The Lord-God-Savior. The same idea is expressed . . . in the Stoic idea of a universally ruling *Logos*, the mediator between God and the world, who everywhere scatters the "seeds" of truth.

Are biblical references to the Messiah, scant as they are, reliable? It seems to me that in one sense they are. Although there are textual doubts about much of the Bible, it seems clear that messianic hope was long nurtured in Jewish hearts by the Scriptures simply because such hope is a perfectly reasonable response to periods of social unrest and oppression characterized by lack of effective leadership. We see this demonstrated even in relatively trivial social contexts.

In the 1930s and 1940s, when more white Americans were more *openly* racist than they are today, men spoke of "a great White Hope," a white pugilist competent to defeat the black champion Joe Louis, just as they had earlier looked for one to defeat the great Jack Johnson. And what Republican or Democrat in the U.S. has not longed for the emergence of a leader of heroic proportions, as contrasted with Nixon, Agnew, Reagan, Quayle, and other assorted lightweights or dishonest men so common in the present period?

Because such hopes are normal, we may therefore reasonably assume that the Jews did indeed long for a Messiah. This in itself, however, establishes nothing whatever about Jesus, other than that there was a vacuum into which any forceful, gifted, moral, and courageous leader could easily move.

Old Testament references to the Messiah are by no means as clear-cut as Christian apologists would like them to be. Bruce M. Metzger, George L. Collord Emeritus Professor of New Testament Language and Literature at Princeton Theological Seminary, has observed: "The term 'Messiah' is scarcely ever employed by an Old Testament author with the specialized meaning that only afterward came to be attached to it."

MOHAMMED. See Koran.

MOSES.
Few Bible scholars of the present day, however devout, believe that the stories of Moses' birth and early adventures in EXODUS are true. It is clear that Moses himself could not have written such an account because it was not set down until many centuries after his death. And, most importantly, Moses' birth story is remarkably similar to the account of the infancy of King Sargon of Akkad, who ruled Mesopotamia toward the end of the third millennium B.C. Concerning Sargon, it was written that as a baby he was put into a basket made of rushes and that it was sealed with pitch and set adrift on a river. An important person discovered the infant and, Sargon reports, "took me as his son and reared me."

Scholars are aware of similar stories in all of which a man who eventually assumes heroic stature is threatened in infancy, somehow escapes, and lives in relative obscurity during his early years until at last he achieves his rightful stature. It should not weaken the reader's personal faith in the Deity to be told that it is absurd to accept the story of Moses and the bullrushes as factual. What we must do is to get off our backs the people who insist that we are obliged to accept the story and that if we do not we are sinful, heretical, and socially dangerous.

Exodus 2. Beginning at Verse 11, we find one of several instances where, beyond the slightest question of ambiguity of interpretation, it is clearly stated not only that YAHWEH was *not* angered by an instance of murder but actually rewarded the murderer. I recall that in earlier years I was shocked and saddened when I read assertions by atheists, among others, that the Bible, far from teaching nothing but high ethical and moral behavior, actually *condoned* deceit, cruelty, slavery, murder, war atrocities, and other forms of evil behavior. But anyone who reads the Scriptures carefully and fully must inevitably concede that the critics' accusations are all too well supported.

Let the reader consider his response if he witnessed the following incident in his own community. Let us assume that a Native American and a Black man are engaged in heated argument and that the Indian finally assaults the Black. Suppose now that a third man, who happens to be Black, comes upon the scene and witnesses the struggle. Although he has the opportunity to try to separate the combatants or to warn the more aggressive of the two to desist, he instead kills the Native American on the spot. He is certainly a murderer.

The third man in the drama is Moses. It is nowhere suggested that he acted in a fit of uncontrollable fury. He therefore cannot plead temporary insanity. Nor can it be argued that the killing was accidental. Observe:

> 12. And he looked this way and that way, and when he saw that there was no man, he slew the Egyptian, and hid him in the sand.

In addition, there is nothing in the account to suggest that Moses felt the slightest guilt about his crime. In keeping with a common criminal attitude, he fears only that he will be caught, as a result of which he leaves Egypt.

Exodus 3. We are told the story of God's visit to Moses in the form of a voice that emanates from a bush which, though burning vigorously, is not consumed. Why it is necessary for God to impress Moses with such magician's trickery is nowhere explained. Shortly God gives Moses his orders.

> 10. "Come now therefore, and I will send thee unto Pharaoh, that thou mayest bring forth my people the children of Israel out of Egypt."

Oddly enough, the Almighty then seems to have had second thoughts:

> 19. "And I am sure that the King of Egypt will not let you go, no, not by a mighty hand.
> 20. "And I will stretch out my hand and smite Egypt with all my wonders which I will do in the midst thereof: And after that he will let you go."

303

Note that God is not quoted as saying that he will smite Pharaoh, or specific cruel Egyptian overseers, but rather that he will smite *Egypt itself,* which is to say that *millions of common Egyptians who have no connection whatever with the administration of their government will be punished.* When the Nazis committed atrocities of precisely this sort during World War II, they were regarded as depraved. It is not plausible or ethical that such behavior should be considered vicious in the one instance and blameless in the other.

Exodus 4. We are next told that Moses raised a reasonable objection. He points out that his people are unlikely to believe him when he says he comes to them by the direct order of God. God's solution to this is as puzzling as a great deal of other behavior attributed to the Almighty in the Old Testament. He performs a dramatic magic trick for Moses' edification, turning a walking stick into a snake. Moses jumps back in fear, whereupon the Lord converts the animal back into a wooden rod.

Since (1) Moses already honors God, and (2) there are no Israelite witnesses, the implication of the story is that the Lord is instructing Moses to go and perform such a trick for his people. Later, such tricks are performed for Pharaoh and an Eygptian audience. By now, the conscientious reader may have learned that, whatever virtues the Scriptures may possess, consistency and plausible reality are not always among them.

Despite these impressive demonstrations of divine power, Moses still meekly demurs, pointing out that he is not an effective public speaker. A wise human king or father would at this expression of modesty no doubt smile tolerantly, but the Lord's ways are not those of man. God's response is remarkably heated emotion. "And the anger of the Lord was kindled against Moses . . ." (v. 14).

In Verses 19-22 God instructs Moses to return to Egypt and perform his wonders for the Pharaoh personally, but now we encounter a puzzling instruction by Yahweh. Presumably, the only intelligent purpose for such a demonstration would be to convince the Pharaoh to let the Israelites leave Egypt, because the ruler, quite understandably, would be skeptical about religious claims concerning the power of the Israelite God and the urgency of releasing his CHOSEN PEOPLE. Says the Lord:

> 21. . . . I will harden his heart that he shall not let the people go.
> 22. And thou shalt say unto Pharaoh, "Thus saith the Lord, 'Israel is my son, even my firstborn:
> 23. 'And I say unto thee, Let my son go, that he may serve me: and if thou refuse to let him go, behold, *I will slay thy son, even thy firstborn.*' " (IA)

The Lord personally, through Moses, is threatening the Pharaoh with a crime which, if committed by any human, would merit a long prison sentence and, in the opinion of many conservatives, the death penalty. Incredibly, also, it is Yahweh who will "harden" Pharaoh's heart to begin with so that he can then be punished. The mind boggles—or ought to—at such a pathetically low level of moral teaching.

In Exodus 4 we read:

> 24. At a night encampment on the way, the Lord encountered [Moses] and sought to kill him.
> 25. So [his wife] Zipporah took a flint and cut off her son's foreskin and touched Moses' feet with it, saying, "You are truly a bridegroom of blood to me!"
> 26. And when he let him alone, she added, "a bridegroom of blood because of the circumcision."

This is a very bizarre story. We have no way of knowing whether this incident ever took place, but there are many reasons for strongly doubting that it did. Primary among these is that the report is not consistent with much that we know of human nature. If the account had been introduced into the literary record in any other way—imagine Zeus trying to kill Odysseus as he embarks for the Trojan War, and Penelope circumcising Telemachus on the dock—there is not a sensible individual on earth who would accept it as ever having happened.

To begin with, it is absurd to suggest that God—who is, by definition, everywhere at all times—could possibly "encounter" Moses. Secondly, if we persist in believing that God is supremely good, which is to say morally perfect, then we cannot argue convincingly that he would seek to kill one of his creatures in a face-to-face encounter.

With a sharp flint Zipporah cut off the tip of her son's penis. It must have been hideously painful. As we make our way through the details of the account, we may visualize the woman Zipporah standing with a small piece of human flesh in her hands. There is no suggestion that she was repulsed by her action, as the reader would be if he or she had performed or witnessed such an operation. She next touches the excised skin to Moses' feet. Why? And what are we to make of the statement, "You are truly a bridegroom of blood to me!"?

The next quotation appears to be intended as an explanation of the first. "A bridegroom of blood because of the circumcision." A circumcision is obviously bloody but what that has to do with a bridegroom is anybody's guess. In the centuries of speculation about this peculiar tale, no one has provided an enlightening explanation.

In Exodus 7 it is said that Moses and Aaron went to see the Pharaoh and performed the remarkable demonstration of turning a wooden stick into a snake. The Pharaoh, however, not to be outdone, calls his own sorcerers, who perform likewise.

Then Moses stages an even more remarkable demonstration at the bank of a nearby river. Moses and his brother stretch out their hands toward all the waters of Egypt—small lakes, rivers, streams, ponds, even small containers of water—and all water is at once turned to blood. Human blood? Animal blood? Why was it interpreted as blood? "And the fish in the Nile died; and the river stank, and the Egyptians could not drink of the water of the rivers; and there was blood throughout all the land of Egypt" (v. 21).

There is certainly no more impressive miracle in all recorded religious literature. A man would be a remarkable individual who would not bow down, upon witnessing such an event, to honor the unmistakable signs of the power of the Creator of the universe. Incredibly, however, nothing of the sort happens, for the magicians of Egypt at once performed the same trick! How could the Egyptian magicians turn the waters of Egypt into blood when Moses had already done so? The story grows ever more preposterous.

Exodus 9. Far from conducting himself with majestic dignity, the God of Moses is now made to seem little more than a demented, frustrated conniver.

> 1. And the Lord saith unto Moses, "Go unto Pharaoh and say unto him that thus saith the Lord, 'Let my people go that they may serve me.
> 2. 'And if thou refuse to let them go behold I will smite all thy borders with frogs.
> 3. 'And the river shall bring forth frogs abundantly, which shall go up and come into thine house, and into thy bedchamber, and upon thy bed. . . .' "

Aaron and Moses help the Lord work this horrendous wonder. Presumably bedlinens all over Egypt were at once crawling with frogs, which must have come as a most uninstructive spectacle to thousands of innocent people in distant parts of Egypt, who would have had no way of knowing why they were being so afflicted. Actually, the pair of traveling Hebrew wonder-workers sound as though they have escaped from a Grimm's fairy tale.

But then, as if there weren't frogs enough already, the Pharaoh's magicians produce their share of pests. We must consider also that God's and Pharaoh's magicians made millions of hopping creatures out of nothing. Let the reader respond to the point. Does he or she believe this truly happened in ancient Egypt? If one believes that Pharaoh's priests worked their wonders by the power of the Devil, then it follows that the Devil also can make something out of nothing, a proposition physicists say is impossible.

Let us pause briefly and consider the puzzling confidence of the Old Testament authors that the Pharaoh's magicians could so easily work such astounding feats. Homer W. Smith, in *Man and His Gods* (Boston: Little, Brown, 1955) refers to their claimed exploits.

> In the presence of the Pharaoh Khufu (Kheops) one magician decapitated a goose, a snake and a bull and then at his command each head moved back and rejoined its body. Another wonder-worker parted wide the waters of a deep lake that he might walk on dry ground to recover a lost jewel; another stopped the sun in its course, another rent the earth, another correctly prophesied the future; another read the contents of an unopened roll of papyrus. Nothing was impossible to these servants of the supernatural. And on occasion the more courageous sorcerer or priest threatened to pull down the very pillars that supported the heavens and to destroy the gods themselves if their demands were not obeyed immediately.

One may reason as follows: Miracles either occur or they do not. If they do not, then the many references to them testify to nothing more than the credulity and ignorance of ancient man. The story of Moses' plagues in Exodus is, therefore, made up; hence it is untrue.

If miracles do occur, then it is extremely unlikely that the power to perform them comes from God, since it is unreasonable that a rational deity would condone such nonsense in the first place or lend support and encouragement to hundreds of contradictory religious figures who claim the power to perform miracles for presumably opposing theological ends.

Bear in mind that when we are told that Pharaoh "hardened his heart," this means that he was reluctant to let the Hebrews leave his domain, which would seem a small price to pay to rid himself of plagues of frogs, bloody water, clouds of lice, and swarms of flies. The flies finally break Pharaoh's resistance, and he agrees to let Moses and his people leave Egypt. But no, wait; once again Pharaoh goes back on his word.

Moses turns once more to the alleged vicious nature and anger of God, who in this instance kills all the *cattle* of Egypt, except those belonging to the Israelites! This raises the ethical question as to why innocent beasts should suffer in a drama of which they understood nothing.

But lest he be thought unbalanced in punishing only Egyptian livestock, the Almighty now causes a terrible affliction of boils to break out upon the Egyptians themselves. This is followed by "a very grievous hail, such as have not been in Egypt since the foundation thereof" (v. 24).

Exodus 10-11. Incredibly, Pharaoh's heart—which by now, one would have thought, had already turned to stone—hardens again so that his obstinacy brings down yet another curse upon his country, a plague of locusts.

I do not see how any intelligent child could fail to conclude that there is a very great difference between the loving God one is taught to worship in Sunday School and catechism class and the violent and depraved deity described in Exodus. But a final injustice perpetrated on the innocent Egyptian people is to follow (in Chapter 11).

> 4. And Moses said, "Thus saith the Lord. 'About midnight will I go out in the midst of Egypt:
> 5. 'And *all the firstborn in the land of Egypt shall die,* from the firstborn of Pharaoh that sitteth upon his throne, even unto the firstborn of the maid servant that is behind the mill; and *all the firstborn of beasts.*' " (IA)

Exodus 12. In this chapter we are told of the supposed origin of the Passover. After a lamb is killed, its blood shall be smeared on the doorposts of Israelite homes.

> 13. "And the blood shall be to you for a token upon the houses where ye are: And when I see the blood, I will pass over you, and the plague shall not be upon you to destroy you, when I smite the land of Egypt."

One is asked to believe that a mighty God who knows all things would require some special help in discovering which innocent infants or young adults to spare as he made his murderous rampage through the land of Egypt.

In thinking of these violent actions that Yahweh is said to have taken against the Egyptians, instances from history, both ancient and modern, inescapably come to mind. One thinks of the mass slaughters by Hitler, Stalin, Mao, and Pol Pot. No one has suggested they had just cause to kill their innocent citizens or political opponents, but then *no crime had been committed* by innocent Egyptian children either.

29. And it came to pass that at midnight *the Lord smote all the firstborn in the land of Egypt,* from the firstborn of Pharaoh that sat on his throne unto the firstborn of the captive that was in the dungeon; and all the firstborn of cattle.

30. And Pharaoh rose up in the night, he, and all his servants, and all the Egyptians; And there was a great cry in Egypt; for *there was not a house where there was not one dead.* (IA)

It is an irony that Judaism, which is greatly respected for an emphasis on law and justice, began with a concept of a violent, angry god. Many children are taught Old Testament stories, as I was, but I somehow felt that the deity depicted in Exodus and elsewhere in the Old Testament was not the true God that I was supposed to pray to and worship. Yet at the same time I accepted as natural that the enemies of the Children of Israel were automatically the "enemies" of God.

It never occurred to me to ask: If there is only one God, then he must have made the Egyptians, the Canaanites, the Philistines also, and if so why is he so violently angry with them? I was taught that Christians should not hate others—and indeed was greatly disappointed to learn that some of us were deeply prejudiced against Jews—and that we should try to love everyone, including even our enemies. Why, then, did God not do so in Old Testament times?

As an adult, some of these violent stories cause me to wonder if the shameful attitude of ANTISEMITISM could be partly rooted in the interpretation by Christians that Hebrew Scripture and doctrine endorse the righteousness of the Jews' cause against all comers. It is especially curious that this blood-and-gore concept, which originated with such honored figures as Moses, ABRAHAM, and DAVID was retained when the earliest Old Testament Scriptures were finally written down or collated and edited around the time of the Babylonian Exile in the 6th century B.C. In Babylon the Hebrews probably came into contact with the tolerant practices of the Persians and highly ethical religion of Zoroastrianism, the official Persian religion.

Is it possible that today's highly charged Mideast problems originated back in biblical times with tenets said to have been established by Moses and his "employer," the vengeful Yahweh?

Since the early Hebrew documents have much to say about Egypt, it is a striking fact that Egyptian records, which are—fortunately for the purposes of scholarship—voluminous, apparently contain no reference to the Israelites. The one possible exception concerns a stela erected at Thebes at the instruction of the Egyptian king Merneptah, one of the many sons of Ramses. Had any of the incredibly dramatic miracles reportedly worked by Moses in the presence of the Egyptians actually taken place, it would be reasonable to suppose that they would be mentioned in Egyptian historical literature. The fact that nothing of the sort is found is suggestive evidence, though it cannot be conclusive, that no such dramatic acts ever took place.

Moses as Author of the Pentatauch. If one approaches the question as to whether Moses wrote the five books that synagogues and churches have long attributed to him, the first fact that emerges is that there is not the slightest suggestion in any of them that Moses was the author. He makes no such claim. Such evidence as is available, in fact, points in the *opposite* direction. The titles of the five books are certainly not part of the original text, nor are they called by those names in the Hebrew Scripture. Before the turn of the present century the theory that Moses wrote the Pentateuch had come into serious scholarly question. R. Heber Newton, in *Book of the Beginnings* (New York: G. P. Putnam's Sons, 1884), summed up the view common at that time by saying:

> We find that a brief record of a battle in Exodus (Chapter 17:8-13), a memorandum of camping stations in Numbers (Chapter 33:3-49), together with the ten words (Exodus, Chapter 34:28) and the book of Deuteronomy, in whole or in part, constitute *all* the narrative and legislation that is *claimed* to have been written by Moses. *The Pentateuch as a whole appears anonymous.* (IA)

It is important to understand that not only are there no longer any scholars who believe that Moses wrote these five books but, in fact, it is now the common academic view that they were not even written in the *time* of Moses, but many centuries later.

Whether Moses received the Commandments from God personally, as Exodus states, or whether he resorted to a legal fiction about a meeting with God on Mt. Sinai for the virtuous purpose of stimulating greater respect for the moral law among the Hebrews of his day, it would be quite reasonable to expect that, assuming Moses' literacy (which has not been established), he might have written, or dictated, certain documents about the matter and transmitted them to his tribe.

It is possible, therefore, that the actual authors of the great bulk of the first five books, the Pentateuch, had available to them (in some form concerning which we shall never be able to learn anything reliable) records left by Moses and/or his close associates. If, as scholars now believe, most of the first five books were compiled many centuries after Moses, it is unlikely that the written records available to them were ones that came from the *hand* of Moses, Aaron, or some scribe but rather were copies of copies of copies. As every scholar, teacher, or journalist is aware, errors inevitably creep in when copies are made.

Attempting an Analysis. Moses is a very problematic character, especially when we return to his association with the torment of presumably innocent Egyptians. The implication is that, since they were *not* God's Chosen People, they deserved whatever severe punishment God chose to mete out. But if this notion is accepted, then several obvious but troubling corollaries and questions follow.

1. Anyone who is *not* among God's Chosen—that is, any non-Jew who has ever lived in any part of the world, over 99 percent of the human race—may have terrible evils rained upon his or her head by a thoroughly dangerous God.

2. Why, then, if he so despised them, did God create all of those non-Chosen People? One Judaic tenet holds that God chose the Jews to enlighten Gentiles, to bring others to the knowledge of God given directly to Moses and other Old Testament prophets.

3. But if this is the case—if the Mosaic law was intended by God to be sufficient and all-encompassing—then why did he later send JESUS and proclaim a New Covenant? Jews would reply that he didn't; Christians insist that he did; while Muslims maintain that it took Mohammed and the KORAN to complete God's direct revelation to mankind.

Lest you think that I am spinning fanciful propositions or resurrecting old, discarded notions, a news story in the *New York Times* on August 13, 1989, focuses on this precise issue. Pope Paul II, on August 2 stated: "We consider the coming of the Holy Spirit at Pentecost as the fulfillment of the new and everlasting covenant between God and humanity," which was "sealed in the blood of Jesus." The *Times* article continues:

> He [the Pope] said that the Old Testament showed many instances of the Jewish people's "infidelity to God" and that the Prophets were sent "to call the people to conversion, to warn them of their hardness of heart and foretell a new covenant still to come.
>
> "The new covenant foretold by the Prophets was established through Christ's redemptive sacrifice and through the power of the Holy Spirit," he said.
>
> "This 'perfect gift from above' descends to fill the hearts of all people and to gather them into the church, constituting them the People of God of the new and everlasting covenant."

These remarks, quite understandably, were strongly protested by the Anti-Defamation League of B'nai B'rith, since they touch "on a fundamental

Jewish belief that God's covenant with the Jews, establishing them as the chosen people, has remained unbroken since the time of Moses."

It is easy to understand and sympathize with Jewish sensitivity about such a Roman Catholic theological position, since it clearly undercuts one basis of Judaic belief and can deteriorate into a base anti-Semitism. And yet that very belief in the Jews as chosen people, carried to extremes, is also reflected in the views of Jewish settlers on the West Bank, where Rabbi Yitzhak Ginsburg told a magistrate's court on June 3, 1989 (*Ha'aretz*), that "any trial based on the assumption that Jews and goyim are equal is a total travesty of justice," and that spilling "non-Jewish blood was not, in God's eyes, the same thing as spilling the blood of Jews." The newspapers in 1990 carried stories of Israeli attacks on Palestinians and of Jews who received very mild punishment for killing an Arab.

4. How can a God, who is supposed to embody all that is good, partake of what we are also taught in the Old Testament is evil? To accept as factually accurate the account of the Lord's behavior in Exodus is to give up any intelligible distinction between good and evil.

5. Even very uneducated primitive people, whose religion is termed *animistic*—that is, seeing spirits in all natural phenomena—attribute bad actions to bad spirits, not to a good God. A certain tribe, discovered in the almost impenetrable rain forest of central Panama when the Canal was being dug, seems more theologically sophisticated and logical than the authors of Scripture, in that the Panamanian natives propitiated only evil spirits, reasoning that a good god would not need to be opportuned to perform good acts and bring his children good fortune.

It almost seems that in their need to feel powerful—as any people naturally does—the ancient Hebrews' chief intention was to develop an image of an all-powerful God. That he showed his power by horribly punishing other tribes seemed reasonable to their primitive minds.

A serious question, however, then arises—and few are more urgent to address today—when two of the world's major religions accept with few, if any, reservations texts that are said to tell us all we need to know about God. But since, as we know, the Old Testament was composed long ago in less theologically enlightened times, why should we revere, or try to obtain more guidance from, Exodus than, say, the writings of Hans Kühn, Billy Graham, Albert Schweitzer, or Gandhi—or for that matter our own consciences?

That mankind is still capable of the murderous evils that have been committed in the 20th century may be due in part to the fact that Jews and Christians have totally incorporated, into their unconscious perhaps, extremely vengeful and "righteous" behavior as characteristic of the God they worship. If they have not, then why do not Jews and Christians reject publicly the more sadistically violent portions of the Bible? (See also DEUTERONOMY; COMMANDMENTS, TEN.)

N

NEW TESTAMENT. Difficulties facing those who would study the actual record of what JESUS did, thought, and taught are formidable, whether one is a true believer or a convinced nonbeliever. The first is that we do not, in the modern day, have the actual language of Jesus and his associates available to us. They probably spoke Aramaic, but the Gospels were written in Greek.

Secondly, the Gospels do not provide any information as to precisely how the words either truly spoken by Jesus or carelessly attributed to him were recorded and preserved. There was no method of shorthand transcription during that historical period, and, even if there had been, everyone who has ever been quoted, even by experienced professional journalists, is aware that totally accurate quotation at length is impossible.

A third difficulty, which we shall explore in some detail, concerns separate reports about a given incident, both of which cannot possibly be correct for the simple reason that they contradict each other.

A fourth problem concerns the factor of translation. Those who know little or nothing about it seem to assume that if one knows both relevant languages, the process involves nothing more difficult than replacing a word with its precise foreign equivalent. Unfortunately for clarity of communication, translation is a much more complex procedure, given that each language has separate rules, idioms, and formulations. In almost all of earth's languages, there are seldom precise equivalents in another language. This means that, at each separate thought or word, the individual translator has some freedom of choice. Consequently, if we give some quite simple document, such as the Lord's Prayer or the Preamble to the U.S. Constitution, to, say, a dozen people who speak Portuguese, we will not end up with twelve identical translations. No two, in fact, will be identical.

As an aid to understanding this difficulty, consider copies of the Bible in English, which is only one of about 3,000 languages spoken on our planet. English versions of the Scriptures vary widely, even with regard to the numerous quotations attributed to Jesus and/or God.

Another item from our litany of difficulties is that, even among those who are themselves in agreement as to particular groupings of words on a printed page, there is still that same annoying factor which causes all of us so much inconvenience as we daily communicate with others—the fact that separate individuals are quite likely to have their own personal *interpretations* of what appear to be even the simplest statements.

Consider, by way of example, one of the most quoted statements attributed to Jesus, "Blessed are the poor in spirit for theirs is the Kingdom of Heaven." It requires only a moment's reflection to perceive that the phrase *poor in spirit* may have several different meanings. Jesus might refer to those who are economically poor or those whose spirits are low, in the sense of depression, or he may speak of people whose spirits are impoverished, that is, shallow spiritually. Historian Charles Bradlaugh questions whether poverty of spirit is even a virtue at all. Vigor or manliness of spirit, he thinks—honesty of spirit—are virtues. But perhaps the phrase *the poor in spirit* simply refers to those who are humble. Although humility is certainly an appealing quality in people who are wealthy or hold great power, it can hardly be counted among the great virtues of someone who is poor and powerless. Have I now made it obvious how difficult agreement is?

It is important to attempt to determine to what extent New Testament accounts of events are historically accurate. The implications of this must first be grasped: if any significant portion of the Bible is *not* in accord with the established historical and scientific record, this is a very strong argument for the presumption that the biblical record cannot have been authorized or commissioned by the Almighty, since by definition an all-virtuous Deity cannot be the author of myths, fables, errors, contradictions, or falsehoods of any kind.

But, alas, the *partial* harmony of the New Testament with what is clear in the historical record by no means establishes that the Bible was either authored or inspired by God, nor even that it is otherwise factually reliable, whether there is a God or not. It would naturally be fortunate for the religious side of the argument if the entire Bible could be shown to be historically valid, since that would prevent the ground from being totally cut out from under the fundamentalist case. Nevertheless, instances of historical accuracy alone cannot totally validate that case.

There is constant repetition, in Christian apologetics, of a point that generally involves an unwarranted assumption. I refer to attempts by various scholars to suggest what a given writer of Scripture "intended" or "felt to be important." All such observations could be much improved, so far as reason is concerned, if they began with the word *perhaps* or some similar qualification. For in fact, we have not the slightest way of knowing what any scriptural author intended unless we get such information from the remainder of his work.

An example of such a questionable assumption is an observation by John Dart in *The Jesus of Heresy and History* (San Francisco: Harper and Row, 1988):

> By their selection, arrangement and omissions, the authors of Mark, Matthew and Luke *emphasized what each man felt to be important* in the life and death of Jesus. (IA)

One implication is that anything known from other sources but *not* mentioned in Mark, Matthew, or Luke is therefore unimportant because three illustrious authors considered it so. This might be acceptable in the abstract, but when one considers the many specifics not referred to by one or another of the authors, the weakness of the hypothesis becomes clear.

It has occurred, we are safe in assuming, to a good many Christians over the centuries that it might be possible to construct a purely New Testament version of the faith, an exercise considered desirable when the countless errors, discrepancies, contradictions, inconsistencies, and scandals of the OLD TESTAMENT become clear. But such a hope is doomed, for all available scriptural evidence shows that Jesus himself and his disciples accepted the bulk of the Old Testament as they found it. The early Church Fathers then constructed their own religious edifice squarely upon its foundation. It therefore inescapably follows that either the disturbing recognition that that foundation itself is invalid, or the conscious decision to reject its validity, forces a reconstruction of Christian belief so radical and far-reaching that nothing short of an entirely new version of Christianity would be the result.

One is perfectly free, of course, to undertake such a reconstruction; indeed, in the present age something like it seems to be occurring. But it is clear that the philosophical result would be nothing resembling Catholicism, Methodism, Episcopalianism, Lutheranism, Mormonism, or any other of the common variations of Christian theology.

As regards the common Christian belief that the four Gospels attributed to MATTHEW, MARK, LUKE, and JOHN were, in fact, written by the named individuals, Rudolf Augstein says in *Jesus, Son of Man* (New York: Urizen Books, 1977):

> None of the four evangelists is known, either by name or in any other way; all four of the Gospels have been handed down to us anonymously. It was the Phrygian bishop Papias who first named Mark, about the

middle of the second century; he saw Mark as a travelling companion and interpreter of Peter. Another version says that Mark was for a time one of Paul's companions. *The content of Mark's Gospel makes it evident that the author was neither the one nor the other,* and it is generally accepted today that Papias was trying to reinforce the credibility of this Gospel by appealing indirectly to an apostle. In early church circles—the evidence again comes from Papias—Matthew's Gospel was similarly given enhanced credibility by being *ascribed to the apostle Matthew, who, if he existed at all, is quite certainly not the author.* ("He modestly conceals in his gospel that this"—a tax-gatherer and Essene with Jesus—"was his standing, and that this was his house," to quote the commentary to the Luther Bible of 1964). (IA)

If the four versions of the life of Jesus in the Gospels were the only falsely attributed works in religious literature, the problem would be simplified. Unfortunately, there are libraries of such literature, practically all of which Christians and Jews insist are preposterous in the extreme. Even modern times show such instances, as for example, the founding documents of the Church of the Latter-Day Saints.

Early in the century Myron Phelps wrote about the Bahai religion, which has since attracted numerous adherents around the world, including a good many in the United States. Concerning the forerunner of Bahaism, Joseph McCabe says:

It arose out of the teachings of a Persian reformer, Ali Mohammed [called the Bab, or gate] . . . Like Christ, but in the year 1844 A.D. Ali Mohammed set out to reform the accepted creeds, to bring people back to the worship of a purely spiritual God. He and hundreds of his followers were put to death, in 1850, by a combination of Persian priests and government . . . but the significant point is this: two or three years after the death of [Ali Mohammed] his life was written, and it was a purely human account of a Christ-like man; but some decades later a new life appeared richly embroidered with miracles in the Gospel manner.

As regards reports of the experiences of Jesus, it is clear that the very fervency and sincerity of his early followers could, with the most innocent of intentions, give rise to the writing and subsequent elaboration of miraculous accounts, which were almost certain to contain factual errors.

The earliest known manuscript copy of the New Testament, the Codex Sinaiticus, probably dating from the last half of the fourth century, provides little assurance to the faithful insofar as the separation of inspired from uninspired documents is concerned, for in addition to most of the Old Testament and all of the New Testament books, it also contains the *Epistle of Barnabas* and part of the *Shepherd of Hermas.* The early church was quite certain that these last were inspired, but eventually the certainty dissipated and in time they were eliminated from the canon. No one has any ideas who wrote them or when they were written, although it is commonly assumed that they must have been composed before A.D. 150. Another manuscript, *The Teaching of the Twelve Apostles* or *The Didache,* seems to have an integral connection with the *Barnabas* and the *Hermas,* but it, too, is part of the general confusion of the early Christian period and is not accepted as divinely inspired or legitimate.

Human nature being what it is, we should not be surprised to observe that even well-intentioned skeptics tend to take the quotations attributed to Jesus at face value when they find them relatively easy either to refute or question, whereas when they are difficult to deal with, the accuracy and authenticity of the quotations are more likely to be called into question. It is fair, nevertheless, for a critic to cite a quotation in which he may have little confidence, so long as he is addressing others for whom it is perfectly authentic.

Recollection of Quotations. As an aid in understanding this process, the reader is referred to any ancient nonreligious literature in which an author quotes an illustrious figure at great length. Plato's dialogues are illustrative. Plato had enormous admiration and affection for his master Socrates and was therefore concerned to show him in the best possible light in his recollections of Socrates' teachings. Since dialogues, by definition, consist entirely of conversation, there are naturally many thousands of words attributed to Socrates by Plato in the *Protagoras,* the *Phaedo,* the *Symposium,* and his other writings. But Plato would have been astonished to hear that anyone ever imagined that the speeches of Socrates he presents were direct, word-for-word quotations. We may go so far as to assume that Plato was present when many of Socrates' instructional conversations took place, that he made copious notes, and that, being a genius, he had a prodigious memory. But, as any professional author knows, even these three assumptions fall far short of indicating that Plato was quoting Socrates' actual words.

If there were only one Gospel, it might be possible to defend the proposition that the sayings of Jesus were accurately quoted in it. But since there are at least four recognized as canonical, and others not so sanctioned, we are faced with the fact that there are many discrepancies among the various reports. It is therefore *logically inescapable that either all of the Gospels contain errors of quotation or that all but one do.* It is not possible to assert that all four are preserved from error of quotation by virtue of divine and miraculous intervention.

New Testament Ambiguity. The ambiguity, mystery, and confusion that face any serious searcher for the actual, historical Jesus cause a good deal of frustration. A clue to the general murkiness of the records drawn up in New Testament times is suggested by Ivan Havener in his *Q: The Sayings of Jesus:*

> But why was the sayings genre treated so circumspectly by the writers of the New Testament? An answer may lie in the very nature of the sayings genre itself, which is closely related to oral transmission of the material it contains. The proclaimers of such materials were prophets in their communities and these proclaimers of Jesus' sayings identified themselves so completely with him that they claimed to speak in his name, thereby *creating new sayings of Jesus that certainly did not go back to his historical person.* (IA)

(See "Q.")

It is, obviously, a matter of enormous importance to distinguish between the authenticated sayings of Jesus (if, in reality, any such thing is possible) and sayings not originated by Jesus but by certain of his followers. The latter were either (1) under the impression that they had been "inspired" by Jesus to create new "sayings," or (2) telling what are called "pious lies," which are deliberate distortions of the truth advanced for what is perceived as a good purpose. The first is probably the case. It is difficult, at almost 2,000 years remove from the scene, to understand exactly what Jesus' followers were experiencing that caused them to "enhance" his message as they did. What *is* important is to understand that *nobody*—pope or evangelist—can know for certain what Jesus said or did.

Protestants are perfectly correct in saying that individual Catholic officials, at certain times, in certain places, have discouraged the reading of the Bible. Early in the present century, for example, in a work titled "Le Feminisme Condamne par des Principes de Theologie et de Philosophie," a French Catholic priest wrote:

> In the Old Testament the Holy Spirit shows us so clearly the inferior status of women that the church has been more than justified in *forbidding the reading of the Bible in the vernacular.* If members of the opposite sex knew all that the spirit of truth has to say in a general way about their defects, they might well doubt the divine origin of our Holy Scriptures. (IA)

The Status of Tradition. Many Catholics who are aware of their church's insistence that tradition, as well as Scripture, is a source of truth believe that this doctrine dates from the time of Christ. They are mistaken; *up to the time of the Middle Ages all Christians assumed that the Bible was the only source of revelation.* As the church, however, began to feel increasingly obliged to condemn heresies, it was eventually perceived that there were certain Catholic doctrines and practices that could not, in fact, be directly supported by specific passages in the biblical record. The belief that the body of Mary, the mother of Jesus, had been physically assumed into Heaven is nowhere spelled out in the New Testament. It did not, in fact, become formal dogma until 1950. It was during the 14th century that Catholic theologians attempted to relieve the growing general embarrassment by suggesting that tradition as well as Scripture was a reliable source of truth.

The Protestant Reformers shortly opposed this view, as part of their attempt to simplify the faith or restore it to what they considered was its original purity. The Catholic Council of Trent (held between 1545 and 1563) responded to the Reformers' criticism by the peculiar argument that revelation was also drawn from the instruction received by the apostles from Jesus, even though such instruction had not subsequently been written into the documents comprising the New Testament. The average modern reader, now far removed in time, and perhaps bias, from the controversy, can perceive that there is something decidedly less than satisfactory about this last notion. If no one knows what the unwritten instructions were, they are clearly an undependable source for anything, much less something so important as "divine revelation."

It urgently needs to be explained to the faithful—although it is no longer necessary to repeat to theologians something with which they are so painfully familiar—that Catholic, Protestant and Jewish biblical scholars concede that the Bible includes many simple factual mistakes. But the churches are clearly uncomfortable with this concession; consequently they continue to make official pronouncements such as that of October 1965, in which the Second Vatican Council formally referred to the Gospels ". . . whose historicity the Church constantly affirms."

A factual error cannot be part of history. Let us deal with numbers, percentages. It is no longer asserted that any given book of the 27 comprising the New Testament is true history. What alternative position is there to fall back to? That a given book is 90 percent reliable? 70 percent? 50 percent?

Only statements that include such factors—even as estimates—will now be meaningful. But if the figures are anything less than 100 percent, what happens to the notion of divine inspiration?

NOAH AND THE ARK, a famous Old Testament story, found in Genesis 6–9.

Genesis 6. One of the biblical patriarchs, Noah was said to have lived for 950 years. He built an enormous boat. The reason he had to build it was that Almighty God, who theologians tell us knows all things, including the future, was suddenly surprised and depressed "that the wickedness of man was great in the earth." That is the first detail of the story that sounds plausible. Now attend closely to what happened.

> 6. And it repented the Lord that he had made man on the earth, and it grieved him at his heart.
> 7. And the Lord said, "I will destroy man whom I have created from the face of the earth; both man, and beast, and the creeping thing, and the fowls of the air; for it repenteth me that I have made them.

Even if we could believe anything so preposterous on its face as that God was *surprised* at the evilness of the human heart and cranky enough about his discovery to try to destroy the human race in the way a petulant child might knock down and cast aside a collection of toy soldiers, what would we think of any child, man, or God who decides to drown not only the offending human sinners but all the innocent beasts and birds as well?

The story is another insult to the Deity, and yet we are told, by poor thinkers who wrap themselves in the mantle of religion, that, preposterous as it sounds, it must be true. It is not such fairy tales that we need, good friends of the literalist persuasion. It is morality, decency, and respect for truth.

As for the poppycock about Noah taking pairs of "every living thing of all flesh," we are here faced, obviously, with a story written by a person so ignorant of biology that he assumed that only the few dozen living species with which he might have personally come into contact constituted the entire spectrum of animal life on planet earth. Schoolchildren know now that there are *millions* of forms of animal life when we include the insects.

There is a sense in which, as I recite these details of endless error or contradiction, I feel that it should really be unnecessary to continue further. Were every reader guided by even moderately rational principles, the case constructed here could be adequately established within a few pages. But so impervious is the mind of the committed believer even to the combination of common sense and factual evidence that one must continue with countless repetitions of what is really the same simple point. And even then, if one were to prepare endless volumes of such documented refutation, there would no doubt be believers who would still persist in their error. But the study must be continued, nevertheless, because literalist fundamentalists do, after all, constitute a percentage (happily, small) of the human population. Such a study as the present one therefore may serve as a sort of inoculation against the toxin of irrationality preached by the literalists.

A theme which is repeated in a number of instances in the Bible, and which certainly reflects not the slightest credit on either the abstract idea or the reality of God, is that of punishing animals for acts committed either by their owners or by human beings as a class. Again, we see that something which is absurd on its face, and would seem so even to a child, is nevertheless passionately believed in, for no other reason than that it is encountered in the Scriptures. An added element of absurdity concerns the fact that not all the animals of the earth are said to have merited destruction, but only those that lived on dry land or flew over it.

St. Francis of Assisi is universally respected because of his tender, loving concern for animals as well as humans. In this regard, then, Francis was clearly superior to whatever God is presented in the Old Testament story of Noah. But since it is not possible for a human being to be superior to that God who created him, it is evident that we are dealing with an absurdity and a false report.

Because of the profound importance of another point, let us pause here momentarily to reflect again on the fact that it is not necessary to cast doubt on the validity of the entire Bible to bring its accuracy as history or natural science into question. It would be sufficient, on purely logical grounds, to successfully call into question any single chapter or collection of verses within a chapter. If it could be established, let us say, that 20 percent of the Bible was stuff and nonsense, it would not follow, in the absence of additional argument, that there was definitely something questionable about the other 80 percent. But many of the world's Jews and Christians have always insisted that the Bible is God-inspired in each and every one of its parts. There is not even the remote theoretical possibility of error, they argue, and there is an appearance of reasonableness to such an argument if it is couched inside the larger assertion that God Almighty personally caused the Scriptures to be created since, by definition, God is incapable of error.

Whatever justice may lie in such an argument, considered abstractly, it is clear enough that unknown numbers of Christians and Jews have abandoned or modified their traditional faiths once it became evident to them that one portion or another of Scripture could not possibly be true.

It is still, of course, perfectly permissible to argue that, even if the Bible is generally unreliable so far as matters of science are concerned, and frequently in error as regards historical factors, much remains which may be construed as morally uplifting, psychologically insightful, or spiritually ennobling. But since the present work does not address such factors, and I am not concerned to challenge those portions of Scripture which are worthwhile, little more need be said about the matter here.

No more, that is, except that such beauty, insight, poetry, and sound moral advice as the Scriptures contain would now have to stand on their own inherent merits and could no longer be attributed to divine authority.

Chapter 6 of Genesis is interesting in that it includes the assertion that God decided that the rightful days of man "shall be a hundred and twenty years." Nevertheless, there is no evidence that after that point men lived to that age. Some of them, as in the present day, died at or shortly after birth and others at each year of age thereafter, perhaps to 90 or 100. Who were "the mighty men that were of old, the men of renown," no one knows nor, it is fair to assume, has anyone ever known. They cannot have been of much renown if not even their names were recalled by the biblical authors who remembered the names of such nonentities as Lamech.

The most bizarre aspect of the first several verses of Chapter 6 is the claim, in Verses 1-4, that after men began to multiply on the face of the earth and daughters were born to them, "the sons of God saw that the daughters of men were fair; and they took to wife such of them as they chose." Verse 4 also refers to "the sons of God" coming into the daughters of men, who bore children by them. The Bible itself gives no information as to who these sons of God were. Many scholars feel that such passages reflect nothing more than the belief, common among primitive peoples in most parts of the earth, that at some earlier point in their tribal history many gods had had sexual intercourse with human females and thereby created either a race of remarkably superior beings or at least certain individual superior specimens. But there can only be speculation about such matters, nothing resembling certain knowledge. In any event, no one today seems to believe such stories except a few of the uneducated.

Genesis 7. When I was a younger man, and still a loyal adherent of the Catholic faith, I used to resent criticisms from Protestants alleging that the Catholic church had deliberately discouraged the reading of the Bible by the masses. I subsequently learned that these allegations were perfectly correct. One of the reasons Catholic leaders were by no means enthusiastic about the faithful reading the Bible in vernacular languages was that scholars feared that the contradictions and discrepancies in the Scriptures might weaken the faith of many. There can be no question now but that this has frequently occurred. I do not see how any intelligent person can read, for example, Chapters 6 and 7 of Genesis, dealing with the two stories of Noah and the flood, and fail to have his faith in the inerrancy of the Bible badly shaken.

Again, it must be stressed that the number of creatures God wanted Noah to save in the ark would be staggeringly high, since the instruction is not just to take a few cattle and perhaps a small number of household pets but, in Verse 19 of Chapter 6, "Of every living thing of all flesh, two of every sort." Now, as it happens, there are today on this planet hundreds of thousands of animal species; since the story of Noah is alleged to have taken place just a few thousand years ago, we know that the same was true in those days. Indeed, we have clear fossil evidence of the existence of thousands of species millions of years earlier. How large a ship one would have to construct to house two of every sort of animal creature inhabiting the earth I personally do not know, but it would surely have to be larger than the most enormous modern ocean liner.

But wait, the ship-building problem must have been even more troublesome to Noah because the author of Chapter 7 tells a contradictory story:

2. "Of every clean beast thou shalt take to thee by sevens, the male and his female: and of beasts that are not clean by two, the male and his female.

3. "Of fowls also of the air by sevens, the male and the female; to keep seed alive upon the face of all the earth."

Now we have in the equation hundreds of thousands of species, many of which we must multiply by seven and others of which we must multiply by two. Perhaps an enormous *fleet* of ships would suffice for such a vast number of living creatures. No intelligent person can seriously suggest that one ship, made by hand with primitive tools and techniques by an amateur shipbuilder, would be equal to the task. Animals, of course, must eat, and anyone who has seen the enormous supplies of foodstuffs that must be trucked to even a small zoo or circus each day will understand the amount of food it would take to provide even one meal for hundreds of thousands of animals. Let us suppose each creature ate twice a day and did so for 40 days. This means 80 such meals would have to be served.

And this is not even to address the problem as to how a handful of human beings, living in one tiny geographic area, could possibly have rounded up vast armies of land creatures even so far as a hundred miles away, much less those that inhabited the whole globe at the time. It must be remembered that it would be impossible for even the most quick-thinking and physically agile human to capture even one of most of the creatures anyway. Some would have resisted being trapped simply by flying, running, or climbing out of Noah's way. Others would have reduced the members of Noah's family to lunchmeat within seconds, if closely approached.

Another problem which must have troubled Noah was that of the elimination from the ship of the mountains of waste matter, liquid and solid, that hundreds of thousands of animal creatures would have produced.

Since the fundamentalists tell us that Noah's voyage took place only a few thousand years ago, it inescapably follows that among the land creatures that were taken aboard the ark was a pair of skunks. Anyone knowing the habits of skunks is aware that they do not take kindly to social contact with other animals. Certainly anyone who has ever lived in a rural area will be familiar with the unpleasant odor they emanate. Had this happened during Noah's voyage, surely the overpowering smell would have been dramatic enough to occasion notice by the narrator of the story.

Skunks, of course, are New World animals so it is unclear how Noah would have found them—or any other species not living in the vicinity of the eastern Mediterranean.

Let us now consider what the size of Noah's ark must have been. Dimensions in *cubits* are given in Genesis 6:15. A cubit was always a less than scientific unit of measurement, inasmuch as it was based on the length of the forearm from the elbow to the tip of the middle finger. Scholars have generally figured that a cubit can vary from 18 to 22 inches.

Taking the figure of 20 inches for convenience, this would mean that Noah's craft was 500 feet long. Since most Americans have no reason to be able to estimate such lengths, I suggest that the reader bear in mind that a football field is 300 feet long. Imagine, then, a wooden craft so long that it could not be accommodated on the floor of the Los Angeles Coliseum or, for that matter, other large athletic facilities.

Another odd factor is that although the ark is supposed to have been of this enormous length, and perhaps even longer because of the imprecise length of a cubit, it was nevertheless, only 50 feet high.

In rabbinic scriptural analysis, incidentally, Genesis Rabba 30:7 states that Noah took 120 years to build the ark! A long time indeed to delay the Lord God's angry plan to substantially wipe out the human race, at the same time committing the first instance of the savage crime of genocide.

Why is the story of Noah believed? The explanation, I suggest, is not difficult. Indeed, I have found it in my own experience. I am a person of average intelligence, though perhaps more-than-average industry, and there was a sense in which I accepted such stories for at least half a century. How? *Simply by never once concentrating on the details of the stories in an analytical, which is to say intelligent, way.* This was achieved partly by the church's introducing the material to me when I was a small child.

A five-year-old will believe practically anything presented to him; the story of Noah and the flood is no more inherently preposterous to the immature mind than is the legend of Santa Claus or of Goldilocks and the Three Bears. But eventually, as adults, we cease to believe in Santa Claus, Goldilocks, and other imaginary characters and stories.

Why then do some people persist in believing equally impossible stories in the OLD TESTAMENT? For a simple reason. They have now been filed in a certain section of our internal mental computer classified as *religious*. We have been assured that the authority of God, indeed the very existence of God, is somehow bound up with such stories. This makes us unlikely to question them, for even to think of the possibility of doing such a thing is regarded as heresy, impiety, blasphemy. Consequently, that portion of our minds is somehow sealed off; the rational capabilities we bring to such tasks as the building of bridges, the designing of space vehicles, the performing of medical operations, the construction of space telescopes and other technological wonders is not directed toward the massive collection of odds and ends that comprise our individual belief-system.

Eventually the habit of faith, and perhaps a deep emotional need for a philosophical anchorage, becomes so powerful that mere reason is simply no match for it. We know from instances having nothing whatever to do with religion how simple it is for our poor reasoning powers to be overcome. Anger, fear, depression, lust, love, paranoia—any number of emotional states—can seize us as forcefully as a hurricane and toss us about like almost helpless dolls, plunging some of us into murders, hare-brained adventures, sexual escapades, and irrational behavior of all sorts. If the simple loss of a few hours of needed sleep, the missing of a meal, the ingestion of a few small glasses of alcohol can so strikingly diminish our modest powers of reason, why should we be surprised that the firm conviction that there is a God, and that he personally dictated certain ancient religious documents, may be in little serious danger when finally exposed to intelligent analysis?

Bad Archaeology. A depressing aspect of the debate over the authenticity of the Noah story, such as it is, concerns a book and motion picture of the 1970s, which raised the question as to whether a large wooden vessel which had been located in the Caucasus, near the Turkish-Soviet border, might be the actual craft built by Noah. The response to this is not in the least troublesome. I personally would not care if the ruins of 57 varieties of ancient, hand-hewn wooden ships were found in a like number of mountain ranges. Each one may be approximately dated by the carbon process. Let us assume each may be found to be just a few thousand years old. But even if there were many such vessels, they could not possibly have any connection with the story of Noah, because *it is clearly stated in Genesis* *that that event occurred not many centuries after the time of Adam,* which all Christian and Jewish scientists know must have been untold hundreds of thousands, perhaps millions, of years ago—if indeed such a story is to be intelligible at all.

Scholarship has shown that the general outlines of the story of Noah and the flood are encountered in Babylonian and other ancient literature. This suggests that there may well have been some actual instance, at a time and place now impossible to specify, when a farsighted individual, fearing a flood, built some sort of craft for himself, his family, and perhaps a few livestock and pets.

The Catholic authority, John McKenzie, S.J., in his *Dictionary of the Bible,* casually disposes of the Noah story by saying:

> . . . the shape and dimensions of the two stories are similar enough to indicate that the Ark of Noah is described *after* that of Utnapishtim, although the dimensions have been altered and the symbolism, if it is present, forgotten. *In neither case is such a fantastic vessel suitable even for a houseboat.* (IA)

In other words, there never was such a thing as Noah's ark; the entire Old Testament story is based on nothing remotely resembling divine inspiration but simply represents a reworking of an older pagan Mesopotamian story, which the Israelites thought might be used to draw a dramatic moral. (See FLOOD, THE.)

The reader is urged to consult the supplementary volume of the respected *Interpreter's Dictionary of the Bible* (Nashville: Abingdon Press, 1976), which states that attempts to test archaeologically the historicity of the flood narrative by examination of alluvial layers in the remains of Mesopotamian cities have "failed to indicate any single widespread deluge." The *Dictionary's* scholars explain that Genesis refers to no specific mountain in the phrase "the Ark came to rest upon the mountains of Ararat."

> Ararat is the Hebrew form of *Urartu,* an extensive country which covered parts of modern Turkey, Iran and the Soviet Union . . . later Christian tradition [called] . . . the southernmost of the great peaks . . . Agri Dag in N.E. Turkey, "Mt. Ararat." At its foot was built in the Middle Ages the Monastery of St. James, whose monks satisfied pilgrims by showing relics of Noah and his family.

Concerning reports of the modern discovery, at an altitude of some 14,000 feet, of a large wooden structure, the *Dictionary* states: "In 1970 the age of small fragments of wood was estimated, by the carbon-14 technique, to be not more than 1200 years." It seems likely that monks of the Monastery of St. James, sparing no effort to provide appropriate relics, may have built something to pass for the ark high up in the mountains. However that may be, nothing found on the latter-day "Mt. Ararat" has any relevance to the historicity of the biblical narrative.

Some of the least scientifically respectable searches in Asia Minor have involved well-intentioned but amateurish explorations to find the ark. The fact that an ark has never yet been located seems not to dismay the searchers, of whom professional archaeologists take an extremely dim view. The December 1984 issue of *Biblical Archaeologist* refers to yet another expedition to the remote promontory in northeastern Turkey. Comments Philip J. King, professor of biblical studies at Boston College:

> Radiocarbon analysis of wood fragments found there . . . yields a date no more ancient that the seventh to eighth centuries A.D. The most recent episode of searching for Noah's ark was reported by *The New York Times* whose headline read "Turks Hold American Over Claim to the Ark." The American, claiming to have found remains of the ark on Mount Ararat [sic], was carrying a bag of dirt and rocks from the mountain as proof of his discovery. After studying the confiscated material geologists at the Istanbul Archaeological Museum declared it had no historical value.

Genesis 8. Verse 13 says, "And it came to pass in the six hundred and first year . . ." For centuries this was taken to mean that, from the formation of the earth to the drying up of the flood that Noah lived through, exactly 601 years had passed. (The figure may, however, refer to the "age" of Noah, given as 600, in 7:11.)

But every well-informed person—whether Christian, atheist, or any other—is now perfectly aware that, whatever might have happened 601 years after the creation of the earth, there is certainly no record of it, since no humans existed. This again forces us to the conclusion that the story of Noah must be taken as the mixture of myth and legend that it obviously is. So long as we so interpret it, we may still believe in God, in the beauty and importance of the life of Jesus, and in any number of other comforting ideas. It is those who insist that such stories are literal history who cause the trouble that presently distracts us.

Genesis 9. Of all the commandments attributed to God in all the religious scriptures of the world, probably the most unnecessary is that which states: "be fruitful and multiply" (v. 7). Until modern times, when access to devices and substances that enable men and women to exert some control over the process, human conception took place in precisely the same way as do those of all other mammals. As soon as nature makes human males and females capable of sexual function, they begin to copulate, and this, in short order, for unknown ages, has led to pregnancy and childbirth. I doubt if there is a single recorded instance in which a human male and female, whether married or not, said to each other, "To tell you the truth, I have no particular interest in becoming a parent, nor, quite frankly, do I find you personally sexually desirable. Nevertheless I will now make the great sacrifice of having intercourse with you solely because I am mindful of the divine commandment to be fruitful and multiply."

After handing to Noah, presumably as representative of the whole human race, dominion over all animals, which therefore can be eaten as food, the bizarre qualification is added, "Only you shall not eat flesh with its life, that is, its blood" (v. 4). The passage has, of course, occasioned thousands of years of inconvenience for devout Jews, who interpret it as forbidding the eating of blood. First of all, the advice makes no sense and is unnecessary. Secondly, every Jew in the world who has ever eaten even the tiniest morsel of meat has, in the act, also eaten at least a bit of the blood that had coursed through the living creature's veins and capillaries.

Genesis at this point proceeds to attribute further foolishness to God.

> 5. Moreover, your blood, to the extent of your lives, shall I requite; from every beast shall I requite it, and from human beings, each from the other shall I requite human life.
> 6. Whoever sheds human blood, from mankind, his blood shall be shed for he [God] fashioned human beings in God's form.

The unknown author of this peculiar passage at least deserves credit for packing more absurdity into just a few words than one might commonly encounter. One element of that absurdity is that God appears to be saying that for every animal in the world that drinks the blood of another living creature, he personally shall exact a similar punishment. It happens to be a fact that millions of the earth's creatures sustain themselves by eating, usually alive, other living creatures. It would be insane to consider that there is moral evil in this, since animals are incapable of moral evil, and their eating habits are determined not by conjecture, philosophical speculation, or democratic compromise but are programmed into them by the very God that all Jews and Christians, in another breath, assure us created such creatures and determined their separate modes of physical existence.

It is a terrible waste of intellectual energy to try to "make sense" out of such scriptural assertions since they are, in essence, senseless. The only reasonable thing to do about them is assume that such foolishness could not possibly be authorized by Almighty God, given the fact that foolishness is typical of human but certainly not of divine behavior.

O

OLD TESTAMENT. What Christians call the Old Testament is, of course, the Jewish Bible. Given that specific books of the Old Testament are dealt with under separate headings, it will not be necessary here to provide an extended commentary.

I should like, first, to express my thanks to the authors and publishers of *The Voice of Wisdom,* subtitled "A Guide to the Wisdom Literature of the Bible for Youth and Adults," published by the Bureau of Jewish Education, Cleveland, Ohio, for permission to reproduce here a sketch-outline of the books of the Jewish Bible since, because it combines both written and pictorial elements, it impresses upon the reader the structure of the Old Testament in a more effective way than does the usual column listing.

The entire collection of books is obviously of enormous importance for reasons having to do not only with religion, but also philosophy, history, and literature, given that Western culture is permeated with biblical thought and references.

The primary philosophical problem posed by an unbiased and even casual study of the Old Testament concerns its sharply defined representation of the Almighty. Indeed, one of the most disturbing of all scriptural contradictions is that between the God referred to in the NEW TESTAMENT and that described in the Old.

Christians commonly assume that the Jews had their Scriptures in more or less their present form many hundreds of years before JESUS lived. This was not the case. While the books of the Jewish Bible were written down in pre-Christian times, they were not collected into any form recognized as official—which is to say they did not constitute a canon—until 90 A.D., at which time the Council of Yavneh made the necessary decisions. Nor should it be thought that such an official pronouncement came about as a result of a flash of divine inspiration or solely because of sage advice by a leading rabbi of the time, Johanen ben Zakkai. The decisions were

THE BOOKS OF THE BIBLE

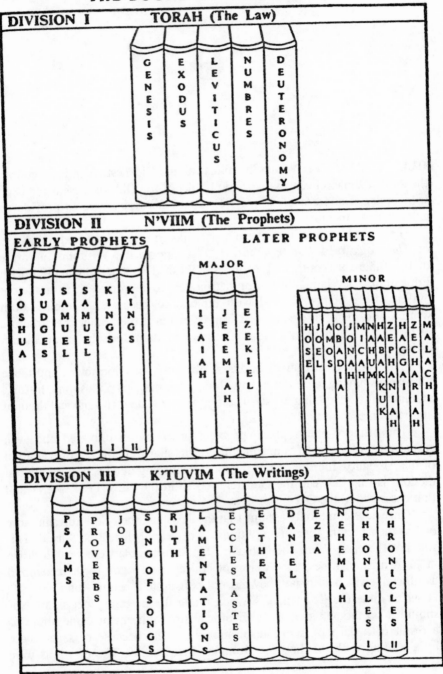

DIVISION I — TORAH (The Law)

GENESIS · EXODUS · LEVITICUS · NUMBRES · DEUTERONOMY

DIVISION II — N'VIIM (The Prophets)

EARLY PROPHETS

JOSHUA · JUDGES · SAMUEL I · SAMUEL II · KINGS I · KINGS II

LATER PROPHETS

MAJOR

ISAIAH · JEREMIAH · EZEKIEL

MINOR

HOSEA · JOEL · AMOS · OBADIA · JONAH · MICHA · NAHUM · HABAKKUK · ZEPHANIAH · HAGGAI · ZECHARIAH · MALACHI

DIVISION III — K'TUVIM (The Writings)

PSALMS · PROVERBS · JOB · SONG OF SONGS · RUTH · LAMENTATIONS · ECCLESIASTES · ESTHER · DANIEL · EZRA · NEHEMIAH · CHRONICLES I · CHRONICLES II made exactly the way they were by various Christian councils, which is to say by open debate, by committee, by haggling and bargaining, by concession and consensus. This happens to be an eminently reasonable way to go about such business, but it clearly rules out Divine Providence, unless the definition of God's will is so broad as to be essentially meaningless.

It is fascinating to observe who, in the present day, are the most vigorous defenders of the kind of Old Testament morality characterized by lies, murders, assassinations, and other moral abominations. It is certainly not most modern-day Jews, as might be expected, who could perhaps be forgiven for rallying around their spiritual ancestors. It is fundamentalist Christians, almost alone, who seek to rationalize and justify what, in reality, cannot possibly be justified, unless such words as *moral* and *just* are treated as cavalierly as the words which Lewis Carroll's Queen of Hearts spoke in *Alice in Wonderland*. The fundamentalists, of course, are caught in a trap from which there is no escape, except that of abandoning at least the more absurd of their arguments. If we start with the unquestioned assumption that there is a God and that he is, by definition, good, then it inescapably follows that the countless atrocities attributed to him in the Old Testament are not only lies, but insulting lies at that. Since this is something the fundamentalists cannot even consider, much less concede, they are, as I say, trapped in an intellectual prison. Their greatest anger, alas, is reserved for those who would do them the great service of freeing them from their prison.

ORIGINAL SIN. This term applies to the ancient belief that there is a *natural* tendency in humans to do evil, and that such a tragic flaw was deliberately implanted in man as a punishment for the disobedience of the first man, ADAM, who was not considered mythical when the dogma was created. Although few well-educated people now hold to such a belief in its simple, literal sense, the fact remains that all humans do, if only on rare occasions, commit acts commonly perceived as evil, immoral, or illegal. We therefore speculate endlessly about this tendency to make moral mistakes, to hurt others, or ourselves. The pure environmentalists in the old argument of heredity vs. environment—if indeed any ever existed—were mistaken, although there was considerable truth in the argument that negative experiences produce harmful effects on future behavior.

It is quite obvious that those who spent their early years under the care of loving, intelligent, essentially decent parents do better in life than those whose upbringing was characterized by verbal, physical, and sexual abuse, poverty, ignorance, and other destructive influences. But all of that, though of the most enormous importance, does not directly address the mystery as to why even those who have many advantages during their early conditioning are capable of wrongdoing.

One part of the explanation, I suspect, concerns the fact that we are born without the ability to speak, while at the same time, in infancy, we are creatures with essential, animal needs for water, food, sleep, physical contact, and protection from pain. Given the notorious forgetfulness of all adult humans, not excluding the most intelligent, the infant therefore must make his or her wants known. This is communicated by crying. A certain amount of anguished howling, therefore, is a necessary survival behavior. Adult humans are sensitive to such pitiful sounds and generally are moved by them to attend to an infant's desires and to alleviate its discomforts. But what all this means is that from their first days on earth new humans are conditioned to express emotions that in later contexts are viewed as negative and destructive. We are conditioned therefore to express sadness, fear, and anger, and to demand immediate gratification. Moreover, we learn that the communication of such emotional states produces rewards.

There is, alas, an enveloping sadness that surrounds such survival behavior, because not all parents respond affectionately to such signals from their offspring. Some respond by expressing annoyance, exasperation, even overt anger, which in turn may lead to physical or emotional abuse in varying degrees of severity.

This large pattern, then, must be part of the explanation as to why there is so much selfishness, anger, and destructiveness in the world. People unfamiliar with the particulars of the debate on original sin sometimes make the error of assuming that the concept must be valid because of what *appears* to be an innate tendency to do evil. The component factors of such an assertion must be separated and examined individually. We must understand what is intended by the word *evil* in this context. It is not meant to apply merely to dramatic and easily recognized crimes such as murder, physical assault, rape, arson, robbery, or thievery, since the majority of the inhabitants of the world will live out their lives without ever committing one or another of such serious crimes. If the commission of offenses of that order were the definition of evil, one would have to say that the evidence of most people's lives supports the view that there is a strong natural tendency to *avoid* evil.

But, short of extreme offenses, there is nevertheless a great deal of unhappiness and discord in the world, and it can be more responsibly argued that there is at least one component of human nature which sometimes does, in fact, produce negative or destructive results. This component, which may be rooted in nothing more diabolical or God-ordained than the human instinct for survival, is *selfishness*. The adult self, too, being either totally or largely part of our nature as animals, must be concerned that its bodily needs are satisfied, whether for food, water, sexual outlet, livable habitation, or protection from the elements. Because man tends to concentrate on the self (which is mostly a matter of unconscious tendencies and acts), when he finds himself in a competitive situation, he will slide imperceptibly from the demand for *enough* to the demand for *more*. We are each, after all, entitled to enough, and in highly competitive contexts even the satisfaction of this basic requirement can lead to the advantage of some and the disadvantage of others. But it is generally the tendency to demand *more than enough*—whether it be more food, more water, more sex, more money, more clothing, more territory—that provides the soil out of which grow acts commonly perceived as evil or sinful.

But though there is indeed a certain facet of human behavior that one can interpret as both *original* and *sinful*, this is totally irrelevant to the theological concept of original sin.

A most interesting commentary on this belief—*itself so fundamental that the entire validity of Christianity has been made to rest upon it*—has been provided by Jean de Fraine, S.J., in *The Bible and the Origin of Man* (Staten Island, N.Y.: Alba House, 1967). This is limited to a consideration of the basic belief that all members of the human species, present and past, have descended from a single ancestor called Adam. Father de Friane, a learned scholar, frankly reports that "theological monogenesis" *cannot* be established by Scripture. Lest the faithful be bowled over by this admission, Father de Friane "explains" that the Old Testament authors did not intend to develop or spawn any such notion.

I do not see how one can accept the latter assertion. If anything about the Old Testament seems inescapably clear, it is that not only the original authors but hundreds of millions of Christians and Jews of the last 2,000 years have insisted that Adam was literally the father of the human race, in as simple, personal, and direct a way as the reader may be the ancestor of his or her own children and grandchildren. Father de Friane concedes that, if one *denies* that Adam is the literal father of us all, then the idea that original sin has been transmitted to all his descendants can no longer be valid, at least in anything remotely resembling the traditional interpretation. But he suggests that this question can best be treated separately.

Again, all de Friane is concerned to demonstrate is that monogenesis *cannot* be proved from the Bible alone. He is indeed correct about this, but since the theory cannot be proved by any other means either, it is a good question as to where this leaves the entire structure of Christianity. Father de Friane is naturally of the opinion that, if something cannot be established from the Bible, it may nevertheless be legitimately taught by the authority of the church. For the moment, one can only say that this may well be the case, but that if it is so, the argument is convincing to few non-Catholic scholars, or, for that matter, to a relative minority of the human race. Being highly intelligent, Father de Friane emphasizes that *it is simply wrong to attempt to make the Bible compatible with science.* Everyone who knows science well is aware that this is the case, but so long as there are poorly informed defenders of Scripture who have not grasped the point, and who therefore continue to insist that the Bible can be harmonized with science, then studies such as the present volume must continue to be introduced.

While even the theological jury, over the centuries, has never been able to arrive at a unanimous verdict concerning the correct meaning of the term *original sin,* the early interpretations still dominate the discussion. For example, a new church-authorized book of instruction, *The Teaching of Christ: A Catholic Catechism for Adults,* states clearly enough that "each individual is born in a condition of sin, and can be freed from that condition only by the merits of Jesus Christ."

Although one can hardly fault the authors as regards clarity and directness of language, the fact remains that the two component factors of the assertion are subject to a variety of interpretations. Perhaps the first perplexity that confronts the unbiased student of the issue concerns the belief that all the humans who have ever lived since the time of Jesus—including, obviously, the billions who inhabit the earth today and the even larger number who will swarm across its surface in the future—are in the gravest possible danger unless they are (1) fortunate enough to hear the essential Christian message, and (2) accept it in their hearts.

At first glance this might appear an ominous and depressing pronouncement, but though it does point to a condition that is fatally serious, it also indicates a way out of the dreadful trap. The inescapable element of the difficulty, however, grows out of the inarguable fact that *only a small minority of our planet's inhabitants are Christians.* If we start by assuming that, however depressing, the basic assertion is as true as anything ever stated, then there is no way around the reality that the majority of the world's inhabitants, including even a number of our loved ones and dear friends, will not only fail to get to that sublime future state called HEAVEN, which would be a horrible enough fate, but will spend eternity in savagely painful flames every bit as real as those we presently encounter on earth. (See HELL.)

There is absolutely no way that Christian apologists can extricate themselves from this fearful conclusion by saying, "Well, what all of this demonstrates is the urgency of increasing our missionary efforts so that absolutely no one fails to have the opportunity for conversion to Christ." There is not even the remotest possibility that such a response can resolve the issue, given the clear fact that after almost 2,000 years of the most heroic missionary campaigns, including personal sacrifices by armies of good-hearted Christians, the great majority of the human race remains essentially uninterested in the Christian message.

Another point, though obvious, perhaps should be included here. It is that salvation, the avoidance of hell-fire, is by no means guaranteed by virtue of the fact that one is either born into the Christian faith or converted to it; otherwise we should have to conclude that such moral monsters as Adolf Hitler and Joseph Stalin, among many who might be cited, were entitled to admission into the divine realm, despite their hideous crimes.

De Friane is, of course, simply one of thousands of courageous scholars who have gradually, painstakingly come to perceive that the early chapters of GENESIS are the least reliable guide to truth when judged by common standards of science, history, or general scholarship itself. As regards certain particulars which in the past have been the subject of the most heated debate—concerning, for example, the AGE OF THE EARTH, the structure of the physical universe, the question as to whether MOSES wrote Genesis, etc.—it is possible now, after long periods of confrontation, to observe that Christian and Jewish groups still exist as such, despite the large areas of ground they have necessarily sacrificed in the interest of retaining the loyalties of intelligent people. After all, if God made the universe, it is hardly a matter of great *moral* importance if he made it a few thousand or few billion years ago. But we must return to one doctrinal question that cannot be so readily dismissed, for the same casual attitude cannot apply to the question of original sin.

If Genesis is as unreliable as regards the stories of forbidden fruit trees, talking snakes, and flaming swords as it is about a great many other details, then the very foundation of Christian belief is shown to have no validity. Jesus, after all, did not come to earth—within the context of common Christian assumptions—simply to suggest a better way of dealing with the problem of sin and the guilt that derives from it. He came, we are told, specifically because of what happened to an actual human being, Adam, an actual woman, Eve, and an actual loquacious serpent, at a specific place called the Garden of EDEN. It was in regard to this drama—and in regard to it *only*—that the concept and basic Christian dogma of original sin was introduced.

Here, then, we are at last face to face with the one biblical difficulty so great, so serious, that all others pale by comparison, so far as Christianity is concerned. If the majority of the human race is correct in its view that there is no such thing as original sin, then it inescapably follows that all Christian churches can be nothing more than human constructions, however admirable or productive on other grounds. It is possible to argue that those who established them were motivated entirely by virtuous considerations and that the purpose was not, as Thomas Paine suspected it was, "to terrify and enslave men and assist in the monopolization of power and profit." But this is as far as one can go in defending the churches, insofar as the record of Genesis is concerned.

To return again to the question of evil, for whatever the point is worth I happen to believe that all mankind does carry the potential and the capacity to do serious harm. The reader ought not to pass over the point lightly, whether to accept or reject it, for it has been the subject of philosophical debate for centuries. There are those, such as St. Augustine, John Calvin, and Martin Luther, who considered the question so clear-cut on the side of evil that the force of their belief drove them, logically enough, to the assumption that the great majority of mankind has always been dispatched to Hell and that this may, in fact, be a matter of divine predestination. This opinion is, in my view, shocking nonsense. Fortunately, the number who agree with it is not so large today as in past centuries.

But neither can I side with those good-hearted souls who assume that man is born totally innocent and becomes evil *only* as a result of a traumatic or otherwise destructive personal experience. If we draw back a bit from the question, we may perceive that each camp has apprehended a portion of the truth but mistaken it for the whole. It is clear that one can produce an army of Charles Mansons or other social monsters simply by subjecting innocent infants to horrible experiences. The question is: Can there be any *other* explanation for the fearful destructiveness that so often appears in human behavior, both individual and collective? The answer is: certainly. Nor is there anything the least bit mysterious about the other factor since it is merely a matter of man's evolutionary animal ancestry. The same blind, uncaring nature that produced man-eating sharks, saber-toothed tigers, cancer cells, and other voracious forms of life has also produced man.

It is relatively easy to grasp this fact as long so one performs the peculiar trick of exempting one's self from the general condemnation. But to do that is to miss the point by a very wide margin. There are no exceptions. As Carl Jung has put it:

> I am a man who has his share of human nature; therefore I am guilty
> with the rest and bear unaltered and indelibly within me the capacity

and the inclination to do [evil acts] again at any time. Even if, jurisdictionally speaking, we were not accessories to the crime, we are always, thanks to our human nature, potential criminals. In reality we merely lacked a suitable opportunty to be drawn into the infernal melee. None of us stands outside humanity's black collective shadow.

Jung wisely observes, "Only the fool can permanently neglect the conditions of his own nature." In fact, this negligence is one of the main reasons for a man becoming an instrument of evil.

This is by no means to argue that we are all equally guilty or that, as Calvin and Luther thought, most of us are headed straight for Hell. A good many people, despite the common potential for violence and cruelty, nevertheless manage to live generally peaceable, law-abiding, and productive lives. This is partly a matter of conscious virtue on their part, one may be willing to assume, but such fortunate individuals should never forget that their admirable record is also partly a matter of luck, of not having been driven to the point where their virtues would crumble and their evil natures be given free reign. It only takes a few seconds, after all, to convert a nonmurderer to a murderer. Almost all murderers have killed but once; we nevertheless refer to them as murderers.

Parenthetically, it is the general failure to perceive this psychological and moral reality that constitutes part of the danger of the world's predicament at the present moment of history. For if in the past the physical evil an individual could perpetrate was limited by the strength of his own hands or the effect of such simple instruments of destruction as he could hold, scientific ingenuity has now developed a lethal methodology far more sophisticated and extensive than anything the mind of the maddest tyrants of past history could have dreamed of.

Personal violence may be no more serious a problem, on one level, than it ever was. But organizational violence—mass cruelty perpetrated out of loyalty to an ethnic group or ideology—would appear to be worse in the present century than at any earlier time. The same psychological processes at work in the modern instances of loyalty to a nation, to Communism, to anti-Communism, to free enterprise, to democracy were in earlier ages usually activated by loyalty to a religious code, church, or tribe.

Part of the danger is that millions who would never dream of killing their neighbor or a member of their family nevertheless become willing instruments of murder once they are convinced—often by the state or religious leaders—that violent behavior is perfectly justified on the basis of political, religious, or other philosophical concerns or in response to real or imagined threats to their people, ideology, or country. Witness the homicides at Kent State in 1970 or the willingness of an American president to order an action that murdered perhaps thousands of defenseless civilians in Panama in 1989, during Christmas week. Their bodies were burned with flamethrowers and dumped into mass graves by young American servicemen. Can any Christian American justify such an assault in any terms but ones Hitler might have used? Did any clergyman or rabbi speak out?

To come full circle in the argument: Though there *is* something that resembles original sin, it is absurd to suggest that *the mere existence of this potential-for-evil in the human heart merits divine punishment,* or—to turn the coin over—that it requires the visit of a divine savior to take upon himself the guilt of all mankind resulting from our innate dangerousness. Had Jesus never come to earth, were the Messiah to be perceived only in the future and never in the past or present, debate on the point could perhaps be waged for all eternity. But there are hundreds of millions who believe that the Messiah has come. If he did, then it is unfortunately the case that his heroic sacrifice and death have *had no effect whatsoever on the very problem his coming might have been expected to address,* for history demonstrates, beyond question, that we Christians have been just as dangerous, singly and en masse, as non-Christians. No one having the slightest degree of familiarity with the savagely bloody, largely senseless religious and territorial wars, massacres, crusades, and pogroms of European history, in the American West, or in Central America in the 20th century could deny this.

The unknown authors of Genesis were as capable as any of us of recognizing the human capacity for evil; in speculating as to how such an unhappy reality had come to be they simply evolved a limited, personal story, a small drama taking place on a narrow stage, to account for it. To sum up: The phenomenon they were considering is all too real but their explanation was classic myth-formulation.

A reasonable case, however, could be made in support of the argument that Christ died for mankind's sins. It is certainly clear that most of us commit more than our share, and that too many of the total are atrocious and depraved is also painfully evident. If we assume that Jesus is in a special sense the Son of God, his personal suffering and death might be construed as intended to counterbalance the aggregate of all the evil done by the hundreds of millions of humans who ever lived or will live in ages to come. That, as I say, is a proposition which, while it will seem preposterous to some, may nevertheless at least be intelligently defended. But the proposition that the entire human race—consisting of enormous hordes of humanity—would be placed seriously in danger of a fiery eternity characterized by unspeakable torments *purely because a man disobeyed a deity by eating a piece of fruit offered him by his wife* is inherently incredible.

This is not to say that one can prove it so. If I assert, for example, that at 3:34 yesterday afternoon, in the basement of a certain house in Cleveland, Ohio, a quivering purple basketball hovered in the middle of the room for ten minutes, one may choose to believe or disbelieve such a report; it is not a simple matter to *prove* that such an event did not take place. But as for the story that the entire human race was damned because of one man's or woman's transgression, that is inherently unbelievable.

Orthodox Jews are unable to accommodate the evolutionary theory of the origin of human life, and they continue to search the horizons of the future for the Messiah. As for literalist Christians, they have even less opportunity for adjustment because it is the absolute essence of their faith that the only point of Jesus Christ's coming to earth was to undo the harm done by the sin of Adam. Obviously the traditional theory is tenable if, and only if, there was indeed a sole first inhabitant of the planet. If, therefore, it is possible to establish that it is absurd to speak of one individual progenitor of the human race, and that if God did introduce a rational soul at a certain point in the development of some slightly-lower-than-human-species on the planet earth, a species which, like all others, must have had many thousands of members, *then the entire structure of the theory of original sin collapses.*

As I have otherwise noted, it is possible to offer some sort of defense or argumentation in support of almost any case, however patently absurd, but there are instances where one must choose between alternatives simply because the two are mutually exclusive. This is such an instance.

After preparing a first draft of such observations on original sin as I was at the time competent to make, I then began to read widely on the subject. Concerning numerous points and questions, a variety of arguments had been advanced, over many centuries and continuing to the present, but in all of the literature I consulted there was one point I never encountered (though that does not prove that no one else had ever dealt with the question for the public record). It concerns the fact that, though Christians believe humankind was not always as depraved as it observably is at present, and, in fact, once lived in an ideal state, at all moments surrounded by an almost visible grace of God, even in that pure, happy, and blessed setting *man did sin.* If the basic Christian assertions about all this are valid, we quickly come to realize that it can hardly be surprising that man now sins so readily and in such vast daily numbers, given that Adam so casually succumbed to temptation, even in his original, innocent, God-washed state.

Concerning Eve's participation in the drama, although male scholars of Scripture have generally concurred with Adam in placing the blame for the FALL on her, the fact is that the command not to eat the fruit of the Tree of Knowledge was transmitted to Adam *before woman was created* (Gen. 2:17). Adam, therefore, may be said to have been guilty of a strikingly bold offense, whereas Eve's only sources for information were her husband and the talking snake that God permitted to advise her.

What is newsworthy at present on this issue is that there are separate categories of opinion. There is first the original assertion, which is an essential, dogma of the Christian faith. Second, there are the traditional philosophical defenses of the dogma. Third, there is a large amount of recent, rather astonishing theological revision of the traditional view, and fourth, there is what the average Christian believes, a set of opinions that does not take into account new Christian thinking on the subject.

P

PALESTINE. The Greek and Roman (*Palaestina*) name for a territory on the shores of the eastern Mediterranean, bounded roughly by the lower Litani River on the north, the Arabian desert on the east, and the Gaza Valley on the south. The Jews call this area Greater Israel; its sovereignty has been disputed in the last half of the 20th century by the state of Israel and the Palestinian people, who lived there for at least ten centuries prior to 1948. The name is thought to be derived from the Egyptian *Peleset* and the Hebrew *Pleshet,* which means land of the Philistines, one of the peoples who lived there when Israelite tribes first appeared in Canaan.

Palestine has been occupied since at least Middle Paleolithic times, possibly simultaneously by Neanderthal man and modern *Homo sapiens,* if archaeological finds in the 1980s have been dated correctly. Beginning in the 10th century B.C., many known peoples—including Canaanites, Phoenicians, Philistines, Hebrews (kingdoms of Israel and Judah), Galilean and Judean converts to Christianity, and Arab converts to Islam—have lived there. The area, or some part of it, was conquered at various times by the Assyrians, Egyptians, Babylonians, Persians, Greeks, Romans, Arabs, Crusaders, and Ottoman Turks. It was designated a British Mandate by the League of Nations from the end of World War I until 1948, when the first of several Israeli-Arab wars were fought there. (See also CANAAN.)

PAUL, ST. The best scholarship has long contended that the letters of Paul to his fellow Christians were the first portions of the New Testament written or that they are the earliest of materials written by Christians that have survived. The primary reason for this belief is that in all the Pauline epistles there is no reference, even indirectly, to the Gospels of MATTHEW, MARK, LUKE, or JOHN. While this is not proof for respective datings, it does seem highly probable that the Gospels either were not known to Paul or did not exist in his lifetime. He died about A.D. 64.

Another difficulty facing those who attempt to bring the actual events of New Testament times into the clearest possible focus is the fact that the majority of the letters written by St. Paul, to competing and sometimes separate branches of the new church, have been lost. This unfortunate fact poses at least one interesting question.

Many Christians believe that every word written by Paul was divinely inspired by God, a conclusion logically inescapable given that (1) St. Paul's writings are part of the Bible, and (2) Christians believe that the Bible is the word of God. But if, let us say, 60 percent of what Paul wrote has simply been lost, destroyed, or otherwise discarded, are we to conclude that God permitted divinely inspired works to be blown away by the winds of time? Or should we believe that only some of what Paul wrote was inspired and that the portion of it which was lost suffered the eventual fate it deserved?

Another intriguing question is: Is it possible that at least some portions of the lost Pauline papers were deliberately destroyed, or else withheld and then lost, by church leaders who took exception to one or another of Paul's observations? It is a pity that we shall never know.

But the difficulties facing historians in the 20th century are not the same as those that troubled the new Christians of the first. Despite obstacles, the church spread relatively quickly throughout the Mediterranean world. This happened for two reasons: (1) partly because of the merits of the new religion, as compared with the frequently absurd, superstitious, and preposterous pagan beliefs, the worshipping of idols, etc., and (2) partly, as a number of scholars have pointed out, because the Christian faith had the good fortune to be introduced, not side-by-side with the Mayan religion in the jungles of Guatemala or with a shamanistic religion in the wastes of Siberia, but at a crossroads of the highly settled world, an area where the Eastern and Western worlds encountered each other, where Greek philosophy had worked its short-term benefits, and where Roman political and military organization was already in the process of unifying that part of the world.

A Presbyterian minister and mathematician, the Rev. Andrew Q. Morton of Culross, Scotland, aware of academic disagreement concerning the question of whether St. Paul did in fact write all of the epistles attributed to him, in *Paul: The Man and the Myth* (1966), made a computer analysis of the original Greek of the letters, employing factors of sentence length, word pattern, and occurrence of common Greek words.

Taking care to check his hypothesis first by using the writings of Plato and Aristotle, Rev. Morton concluded that Paul in fact wrote Romans I and II, CORINTHIANS, Galatians, and Philemon. As for the remaining

seven epistles commonly attributed to Paul—Ephesians, Colossians, II Thessalonians, I and II TIMOTHY, Titus, and Hebrews—Morton satisfied himself
that they had at least five other authors, saying, "Even with a great margin
for error it is quite open-and-shut."

Although Morton's findings came as a shock to believers, he was not
the first to reach these conclusions, explaining that his computerized research
simply led him to share the views of F. C. Bauer and other scriptural critics
connected with Tübingen University in Germany in the 19th century. The
Tübingen reports were placed on the Index of books prohibited by the
Catholic church, a move understandable in light of the fact that, according
to Morton, if St. Paul did not write the seven epistles, Catholics would
have to revise their basic conception of his role in establishing the early
Christian church.

Walter M. Abbott, S.J., in criticizing the work of Morton, makes the
fascinating comment: "It was odd that a minister did not see that all the
books of the New Testament remained Scripture no matter who their human
authors were." The implication of Father Abbott's rejoinder is that it is
not a fundamentally important question who wrote one or another book
of the New Testament. I do not know how many other Catholic theologians
and Bible scholars agree.

The reason I raise this point is that if what has been learned about
the Old Testament—that there is great doubt concerning the authorship
of most of its books—is also the case with the New Testament, then this
fact itself, quite aside from any questions about the text itself, casts grave
doubt on the purity and integrity of the early Christian structure. Such
discoveries suggest, for example, that part of the early organization of the
Christian case was based on false premises.

Paul said, "The just shall live by faith." But many believers hold that
the just shall live by their justness and could not possibly "live"—which
is to say, achieve salvation—by their faith alone, unless it be argued that
the justice of God is inferior to, rather than superior to, that of man. Do
not we all know many individuals who are perfectly steadfast in their faith
but nevertheless live lives either partly or largely characterized by immorality?
If Paul is right, these people are just as assured of salvation as are the
highly virtuous, which is absurd.

PENTATEUCH, the first five books of the Old Testament. For many
centuries Jewish tradition has been firm in the belief that MOSES personally
wrote GENESIS, EXODUS, Leviticus, Numbers, and DEUTERONOMY. Early
Christian scholars naturally accepted the traditional belief. In fact, however,

there is no evidence that Moses authored or even compiled the books in question, but there *is* evidence, in particular passages, that he could *not* have done so. The most that responsible Jewish and Christian scholars assert presently is that Moses may possibly have been a contributor. The fact is that no one has the slightest idea—or is now likely to find out—who wrote these early books.

It is easy enough now for churchmen to say, "Well, when one thinks of it, it really doesn't matter very much who wrote these works. They are true, regardless of their authorship." But God forbid that any free-thinking soul should have made such a statement during the past 2,000 years. We shall never know how many were abused, imprisoned, and killed for expressing opinions no more heretical. But even the truth of the Pentateuch has been seriously questioned in recent years by historians and archaeologists.

A century ago Bishop Colenso, in *The Pentateuch Examined,* said:

> The books of the Pentateuch are never ascribed to Moses in the inscriptions of Hebrew manuscripts, or in printed copies of the Hebrew Bible. Nor are they styled the "Books of Moses" in the Septuagint or Vulgate, but only in our modern translations, after the example of many eminent Fathers of the church who—with the exception of Jerome and, perhaps, Origen—were, one and all of them, very little acquainted with the Hebrew language and still less with its criticisms.

The popular view that Moses wrote the Law would, oddly enough, have surprised the Jews who lived one or two thousand years before Jesus, since it was only around the beginning of the 3rd century B.C. (about a thousand years after Moses presumably lived) that there is *evidence* in Israelite literature that Moses was being touted as the author. That JESUS accepted the unanimous view of his time concerning Moses' authorship of the Pentateuch, far from settling any question about Moses, unfortunately raises what to Christians will be a much more troublesome question about Jesus. For if it is established that Moses could not possibly have authored the books of the Law, then the fact that Jesus is said to have *believed* he did so casts serious doubt on the dogma that Jesus was either the Son of God or was God himself. How could he have been either and not know that Moses did not author the Pentateuch?

Father Jean Levie (*The Bible: Word of God in Words of Men*) has explained:

> Modern critical discussion about the origin of the Pentateuch, initiated by the Oratorian Richard Simon in 1678 (Bossuet was in violent

opposition to his views) and continued by the Catholic doctor Jean Astruc in 1753, was developed on a scientific basis in the second half of the 19th Century . . . and found its principle exponent in J. Wellhausen (more especially after 1878).

But even though the first scholars to raise these specific doubts came from within the Christian faith, nevertheless, as Father Levie noted:

> Wellhausen's system appeared to Catholics and to orthodox Protestants as a complete denial of their religious view of the Old Testament. The ensuing controversy was long and animated.
>
> Nevertheless, at the conclusion of this extensive investigation certain details of the method gained acceptance, at least as the best working hypotheses in the present state of knowledge. The composite character of the Pentateuch is recognized by the majority of exegetes, and the four fundamental documents, or in any case three of them—J, D, P— seems sufficiently established to form a solid basis of interpretation.

("J," "D," and "P" refer to several strands of authorship. See YAHWIST, THE; DEUTERONOMIST, THE; PRIESTLY CODE, THE.)

In other words, Wellhausen and the other critics were right and the traditionalists were wrong. Continues Father Levie:

> *No one any longer regards Moses as the final author of the five books of the Pentateuch;* his influence and activity are sought rather at the origins of the legislation and the narrative. *What happened with the Pentateuch occurred also with the other books of the Old Testament.* (IA)

In graceful and frequently charming language Father Levie concedes that, in general, Catholic biblical scholarship of the last century was at first unequal to the task of either keeping abreast of the research of the leading Protestant scholars or of responding to even harder-hitting agnostic and atheistic criticism.

Levie's study refers to the sort of difficulties with which the present work is concerned. In his survey of scholarly disputation on the historical narratives of the Bible and the larger question of scriptural inerrancy he says:

> Were all the dates and figures, often difficult enough to reconcile with each other and with contemporary history, necessarily guaranteed by Scriptural inerrancy, or could they be regarded as ancient documents quoted by the inspired author . . . ? Taking into account the topography

of Palestine and Egypt, how could the accuracy be allowed of such figures as 600,000 men fit for military service, since this implied between two and a half and three million Israelites living within boundaries of the land of Goshen and making their way along the recorded route across the Sinai Peninsula?

For quite a long time, as Levie concedes, Christian and Jewish scholars attempted to explain these obviously erroneous figures as mistakes not of the inspired author but rather of well-intentioned but either ignorant or careless copyists. "But," observes Levie, "it soon became clear that this explanation was artificial and out-of-date and that a solution must be sought in the nature of ancient history itself."

And, of course, if God took care to inspire such important documents in the first place, he would hardly permit human carelessness or dishonesty to gradually erode his handiwork.

PRAYER. For me to appreciate is, in the same moment, for me to feel grateful. If I am appreciating a meal prepared for me, there is a sense of gratitude toward the preparer. In that sense, of course, it is not unusual that one reaction leads to the other. We respond by thanking the person who hands us a cold drink on a hot day, something to eat when we are hungry, or who does even less important favors or services. But I feel the same pairing of emotions about the gifts and splendors of nature, even though there is no way to determine whether they are available because of a creator's intent or are simply fortunate accidents.

At the moment I record these reflections, for example, my sense of gratitude has welled up because of a combination of physical circumstances: an ideal temperature in the low 80s, a clear sky, warm sun and, most pleasurable of all, a cooling breeze. Given that hosts of individuals on other parts of the planet are at this moment dying of thirst and hunger, it can hardly be intelligently argued that a God has purposely ignored their prayers and entreaties while going out of his way, at the same moment, to provide me with such pleasure. The sense of gratitude, nevertheless, is not only felt but recognized.

Perhaps this response grows out of nothing more mysterious than early social conditioning, since when we are young we take the attributes of nature for granted but feel appreciation for specific human beings who provide for our physical needs and comforts, as well as our emotional requirements. Thus, even in the absence of articulated instruction, we develop the habit of being grateful. That being so, it is probable that the children of atheists are just as grateful about many things as are the children of the most devout believers.

It has always been a difficult thing to determine the true value of prayer. Aristotle said it was "of no avail." Another philosopher suggested that saying prayers is equivalent to believing that the universe is governed by a Being who changes his mind if you ask him to. The religious mentality recoils at this analysis, but many of us who pray have brought the indictment down on our own heads by praying in the wrong manner. Some people, for example, are naïve enough to believe that all prayers are answered. Then when a particular plea elicits no response from HEAVEN they rush to the other extreme of unbelief.

Common sense indicates that much selfish prayer is doomed to reap no benefit. When two men, for example, pray for the same thing—when Notre Dame prays to beat Brigham Young on the football field while Brigham Young is praying for just the opposite result—it is obvious that Heaven could please only one group of supplicants. Very probably it is the one that is the better trained and coached. The same thing will be true of much prayer that is only entreaty: begging for a handout from Heaven. There are young girls praying for jobs as actresses who would be better off staying home, and students praying for help in passing tests for which they have not had the foresight to study. These and millions like them breach religious etiquette, often even asking God to satisfy their desires at the cost of depriving someone else.

Skeptics are fond of pointing out that there has never been a scientific test made of the efficacy of prayer in the same sense that experiments have been made to determine the power of medicines. A fair testing method might be to work with two groups of people, and ask one group to pray for certain things over a certain specified period and the other to refrain from prayer for these same things. Perhaps the group that did not pray would find just as many lost articles, get just as many desired jobs, win just as many football games, or have just as much rain fall on their farms. But this would only confirm what many of the most thoughtful people already suppose: that the most meaningful form of prayer is the prayer of thanksgiving, the prayer for grace, the prayer that we may be given strength to improve our spiritual selves.

If Jesus came to preach spiritual values and to deemphasize involvement with the tangible, why should we constantly pray for material things? God helps those who help themselves. If our wills are strong enough we usually can secure our material needs ourselves. We should pray rather for wisdom, for a love for peace, for an increase in charity. This is the sort of prayer that is answered in the very moment of its utterance; it is the sort of prayer that would be answered even if there were no God. Such prayer is unselfish because it makes us better able to love one another.

When I published these opinions in *Look* magazine some years ago, the response was both surprising and gratifying. Frankly, I had expected that I would be subjected to widespread criticism for expressing a viewpoint that I had assumed was of limited appeal. But of the several hundred letters received, very few took exception to my statement about prayer and many specifically endorsed it.

The most touching communication I received was from a man whom I shall identify only as a clergyman of one of the large Christian denominations. He told me that, because of a tragedy involving a loved one, he had for several months contemplated suicide. What brought him to this sad state was that he had always believed wholeheartedly in the power of prayer; yet now he was praying, for emotional reasons, for something that his reason told him simply could not be granted. To give a specific example, it has never been known that a child born, say, without feet grew them as a result of prayer. The clergyman explained that my article had resigned him to an understanding of what might be called the technical limits of the efficacy of prayer. Now he was praying for simple strength to bear the burden of his sorrow and for courage to face his problem.

Reading this letter and many of the others that arrived with it somewhat unnerved me. In writing an autobiographical article at *Look*'s request I had simply set down my ideas on a number of philosophical questions. The sudden realization that the publication of these ideas could affect the hearts and minds of others came as a shock to me. In television we commonly work no more significant effect than inducing a viewer to purchase a particular brand of canned beans or to laugh or cry at the contemplation of the antics or misfortunes of make-believe characters. This new kind of response to my efforts at communication touched me deeply.

The letters commenting on my views on prayer led me to make a study of the subject. But the reader must not assume that in a few paragraphs I am going to dispose satisfactorily of a question that will be debated so long as man exists on this earth. However, I have read a number of books and articles on prayer and understand the subject much better than I did before tragedy in my own life made clear to me the misapplication of prayer.

A provocative article on the subject was once written by C. S. Lewis. In the *Atlantic Monthly* Mr. Lewis made the point that it is a mistake for the churches to "sell" Christianity with slogans such as "prayer works." He does not believe that prayer is an infallible source of power by which Christians can "control or compel the course of nature." Neither do I, but judging from other articles and letters I have read, a great many Christians do. Lewis sharply repudiates the idea of the scientific testing of prayer. Concerning a proposal to test the efficacy of prayer by praying for patients in one hospital and not for those in another, the magazine *The Churchman,* commenting on Lewis' article, said, "but that would not be prayer, asking God to heal a group of perfect strangers." When I read this I sent the following letter to the editors:

Gentlemen:

In reference to the suggested scientific test of the efficacy of prayer—praying for one group of hospital patients while not praying for another test group—you state, "But that would not be prayer, asking God to heal a group of perfect strangers." May I respectfully disagree, pointing out that one is as much at liberty to pray for perfect strangers as one is to pray for one's own. Indeed both religious history and the contemporary scene offer numerous examples of prayer for "perfect strangers." Like yourself, Mr. Lewis tends to shy away from a test of this sort, claiming that the prayer could not be effective because the minds of those praying would be weakened and distracted by the knowledge that they were engaging in a scientific test (and what's wrong with that?) rather than just praying for prayer's sake. But I have written to Mr. Lewis to point out that this difficulty could be quite easily by-passed by the simple expedient of not informing the praying group of the nature of the experiment. They would simply be told to pray as hard as they could for the A-group of patients. Only the people conducting the test would know of its existence. If there is anything wrong with my reasoning in making this suggestion I should be indebted to either you or your readers for pointing the fact out.

In response, the editor of *The Churchman,* Guy Emery Shipler, wrote to me, "It seems to me that the idea of testing the efficacy of prayer . . . is to confuse the meaning of prayer. The efficacy of prayer does not need testing; it has already been attested to by our Lord Himself." The trouble with an argument of this sort is that while it may be appropriate for someone of my sympathies, it would hardly be convincing to one who is uncommitted and who hopes to arrive at a rational position on prayer or to reject it altogether.

Another viewpoint that I have frequently encountered is summed up in the statement that God does answer every prayer, but frequently the answer is *no.* While this is very clever, it is not a religiously satisfying argument.

Two significant events took place during the months in which I was continuing my study of prayer. One was the tragic fire at Our Lady of the Angels school in Chicago, in which scores of innocent children were burned to death; the other was the publication of a book by the Rev. Franklin Loehr called *The Power of Prayer on Plants.* Rev. Loehr's book related the fascinating history of an experiment he claims to have conducted in which prayed-for plants apparently grew more vigorously than a control group of unprayed-for plants.

Here, obviously, was one clergyman who saw nothing wrong with a scientific test of the efficacy of prayer and who, moreover, announced results calculated to gladden the hearts of all believers. I was greatly surprised therefore, shortly afterward, to note in *Time* magazine a letter from the Rev. Adrien Gauvreau, professor of theology at the Convent des Capucins, Ottawa, Canada. Speaking as both a Catholic and a clearly qualified authority on questions of this sort he wrote, "Prayer has never been intended to take the place of nature and interfere with poor innocent carrots and tomatoes. Mr. Loehr's idea of prayer belongs to superstitition and magic, not to Christian religion."

Another facet of the Loehr research that complicated the question was his reported discovery that just as plants could be aided in their growth by prayer so other plants could be harmed by violent *cursing.* But perhaps such destructive power may have come from some poorly understood psychic energy emanating from the minds of those doing the cursing rather than from a loving God.

During this period I received a few letters taking me to task for my remarks about prayer and mentioning Rev. Loehr's book as refutation of my statements. I answered them by saying, in part:

> The question of prayer . . . is a very subtle and difficult one and not at all as simple as we would like it to be. The recent tragic school fire in Chicago where almost a hundred children and several nuns died in flames while praying to God to be saved indicates that the issue is not precisely as it is usually represented to us as children. This one instance, as we know all too well, is not isolated or unusual but is repeated countless thousands of times each day all over our planet. (Earthquakes never detour around churches and if there are worshipers in them when disaster strikes they die the same as unbelievers. On the battlefield bullets seem no respecter of persons of religious affiliations. Every hospital is a scene of tragedy too depressing to contemplate for long. Against this there are, of course, the rare cures of a spontaneous nature which may well be, for all I know or care to suggest to the contrary, miracles, although there are many Christians who contend that such phenomena can be explained by the laws of God's nature. The Christian Scientists, in this connection, undoubtedly get sick less than the rest of us but not many people believe that their religion

is therefore necessarily true.) A number of people . . . have written to tell me of [Rev. Loehr's] research indicating that prayer has made plants grow taller than unprayed-for plants in an experimental laboratory. Assuming this to be truly the case it seems to me to indicate that some natural, but presently unknown, force might be involved, since it appears highly unlikely that God would go out of His way to add an inch to a petunia while leaving innocent children to burn in pitiful agony while they kneel in the very act of prayer. Naturally I cannot hope in the confines of this brief letter to exhaust the subject, but I hope I have indicated by these few remarks that the question is a very complicated one indeed.

Imagine, for a moment, that a man sets up a small table and advertising easel at a busy intersection in a large city. His signboard announces that he is raising funds to combat, let us say, the AIDS epidemic. Knowing that and nothing more, many passersby would no doubt be willing to make a financial contribution toward so worthy a cause. But now let us assume that those so charitably inclined draw closer and read some of the smaller print on the gentleman's public appeal, in which it is explained that his particular approach to the AIDS problem is to organize prayer groups in various parts of the country for the sole purpose of appealing to God to remove the AIDS curse, or at least to cure a good many of the millions of AIDS sufferers around the world. With that understanding, would the fundraiser accumulate so much as five dollars in a full eight-hour day?

To turn from fantasy to reality, all of the millions of dollars to fight AIDS, some contributed by government, are collected on the sound premise that, if a solution to that dread problem is ever devised, it will come about as a result of purely practical and scientific research.

It does not, at least on logical grounds, necessarily follow that there is no place whatever for prayer in human experience, nor has anyone ever suggested it is necessary to concentrate solely on prayer to the exclusion of more concrete approaches to life's difficult problems. The prayers of the afflicted, or those who care about them, are often simply a formalized expression of their most fervent emotional wishes. Who, seeing a loved one in pain, does not feel a natural tendency to lift up his head and somehow address the universe itself—whether that universe is listening or not— in a sort of blind, unplanned plea for help?

The question as to the proper role of *evidence* in the context of the ancient dialogue on the efficacy of prayer has always posed a difficulty for religious believers, regardless of the philosophy to which they adhere. On the one hand, believers gladly accumulate and publicly display such apparently relevant evidence as crutches, canes, glasses, hearing aids, and other objects no longer needed by those who have (1) been cured and (2) attribute their good fortune solely to the fact that they have been prayed for. That sort of evidence is quite comfortably accommodated within all religious belief-systems, absolutely no one of which, by the way, would dream of claiming a monopoly on such cures.

But when it comes to evidence of a purely objective nature, the situation becomes fraught with difficulty. If we lift our heads from the printed page and look about the world, we see that every human being dies. The situation would be at least somewhat simpler if no one ever died except "of old age," as the common expression has it. Unfortunately, fetuses die shortly after the moment of physical conception, more die in the womb, infants die at birth, and from the beginning to the end of life, millions of humans die at every age. In most of the tragic cases of the death of a child or young person or one in the prime of life, it is reasonable to assume that the most fervent prayers have been thought, whispered, spoken aloud, shouted, or sung to the heavens, and yet, despite the accumulated power of such hundreds of millions of daily prayers, neither an untimely death nor death itself would appear to be one whit delayed.

The situation is, of course, considerably confused by virtue of the fact that, quite regardless of whether prayer is a factor in a given medical equation or not, the great majority of people suffering physical ailments, major and minor, do recover from them. In that percentage of cases in which prayer has been resorted to, it would therefore be inevitable that a great many people would attribute their recovery to prayer. Medical science, of course, credits such happy outcomes to the personal intervention of doctors, the application of medicines, the availability of hospital services, and the wonderful power of the human immune system to attack and conquer invading organisms of disease. America's favorite humorist-philosopher, Mark Twain, used to say that it was wonderful to observe the calm confidence of a Christian— with four aces. By this he meant that even the most devout believer does well to be mindful of purely material factors and would, if wise, never dream of trusting his card-playing success or his own physical welfare entirely to the natural mercy of God or such power as prayer may have.

There was a professional criminal in Brooklyn in the 1950s named Harry Gross, among whose various rackets and scams was one that was quite ingenious. He caused it to be rumored around the neighborhood that he could secure exemption from the draft at the cost of $1,000 per customer. The offer was accompanied by a money-back guarantee. Great numbers of anxious mothers and young men paid Gross thousands of dollars. Some of these were later drafted; in these instances Gross promptly refunded the payment. A number of others were not required to serve.

The point is that Gross did nothing whatever, in any case. He was clever enough to perceive that a certain percentage of people would not be drafted; from each of these he made a very easy $1,000. The people who were not taken into the military naturally assumed that their good fortune had been produced by Gross's exertions. Something like the same procedure—it is possible—may be involved with respect to supplicatory prayer. We later do receive some of the things we pray for, just as in other cases our wishes are not satisfied.

While it may be comforting to assume that our good fortune occurs because God personally intervenes in the normal flow of human experience, as a direct result of our personal request to him, most theologians would be very careful before asserting that happy events come about as a result of divine intervention.

The belief that prayers are always, or at least frequently, answered favorably may stem from the fact that most of the things that happen to us during our lifetimes are either beneficial or neutral. The truly tragic or destructive instances are few, perhaps because it does not take very many of them to snuff out the life of so fragile a creature as man. To deal with the point statistically, using hazy estimates, if 65 percent of what happens to us is beneficial, then whenever we pray it will often be the case that some fortunate occurrence will take place after the prayer. Whether there is a cause-and-effect relationship between prayer A and event B is, alas, one of those difficult questions that mankind has wrestled with down through the ages. But such a statistic inclines some people to assume that there is some superhuman force at work in the universe that has our general goodwill at heart.

PRIESTLY CODE, THE, is one of the four strands of authorship scholars have discerned in the PENTATEUCH. It is the most extreme and was presumably the latest written. Much attention is given to the laws and rituals of the Levites, an order of priests. Comments Jabez Thomas Sunderland in *The Bible: Its Origin, Growth, and Character* (New York: J. P. Putnam's, 1893):

> This elaborate and long-drawn-out priestly document . . . is mechanical and dry in the extreme. There is no poetry in it, and no life. It is verbose, artificial, repetitious, tedious . . . the historical portion draws constantly upon the J [Yahwist] and E [Elohist] documents for data; but it so works over its narratives as to destroy all picturesqueness, all naturalness, all human interest.

(See also DEUTERONOMIST, THE; ELOHIST, THE; YAHWIST, THE.)

PRIMITIVE RELIGION. It may be instructive for us to consider some passages from the ancient religious documents of the Zaruba tribe of central Africa. The Zarubas are so ferocious that tales of their savagery appear even in the folk legends of their neighbors.

That the Zarubas have been guilty for centuries of dreadful slaughters is of course—while deplorable—nothing to mark them as unique among human tribes, for on every continent there is a more than ample record of battlefield and conquest atrocities. But the Zarubas do hold the dubious distinction of not only hating other tribes—an evil to which all are prone—but of glorying in such hatred. It is to be hoped that most men today, if moved to strong, sustained anger will not, except in the context of imminent military confrontation, attempt to justify their vindictive emotions; many will experience some guilt as a result of them.

There is scarcely any trace of such softening of heart in the religious literature of the Zarubas, however. They not only justify their anger, but they inculcate it through many centuries, from generation to generation, so that Zaruba children are trained from the cradle to despise those whose only offense is that they are born into non-Zaruba tribes. The Christian admonition to love the sinner, while hating the sin, to do good to those that curse us, to love the enemy, to turn the other cheek, would be an absurd heresy to the Zarubas, which is presumably why exceedingly few of them have ever been converted by Christian missionaries.

An unattractive mixture of paranoia and fawning subjection to their deity renders the Zaruba religious philosophy even less attractive to the modern mind, including the minds of young educated Africans of Zaruba ancestry.

The following excerpt from a Zaruba hymn of praise, which is typical, reveals this unedifying combination of emotions:

> Oh God, do not hold your blessings from me.
>
> For the mouth of the wicked and the lying speak against me.
>
> They speak words of hatred and fight against me without reason.
>
> I pray to God, but my enemies return evil and hatred for the good I do.
>
> Oh God, set an evil chief over my enemy and let Kimba [the devil] stand at his right hand.
>
> When my enemy be judged, condemn him. Let even his prayer be judged evil.
>
> Let his life be shortened and let another man take his village.
>
> Let his children have no father and his wife be a widow.

Let his children wander lost in the jungles, begging for their food.

Let thieves steal my enemy's property and let strangers spoil his work.

Oh, God, let nobody help this man. Do not even let anyone help his father and his children. Let his children in generations to come be cut off. Let their names be blotted out.

Let the sins of the fathers and the mothers harass the children down through generations.

But let the Lord God remember the sins that he may stamp out the memory of my enemies from the earth.

But as for me, Almighty Ruler, be good to me for I am poor and needy and my heart is wounded with a spear.

My knees are weak and I am thin.

This is hardly edifying prayer; it is cursing, invoking as it does the power of the Deity to bring suffering to those the Zaruba consider their enemy. It must be understood here that the word *enemy* is not interpreted in the personal, but rather in a corporate, military, or ethnic sense. It is as if the prayer were spoken by, say, a German and by *enemy* he means not only the soldiers but all inhabitants of France, male and female, children, and the aged. Clearly the emotions expressed are primitive, vengeful—what one might expect from at least some, though happily not all, primitive cultures.

The sentiments are particularly unattractive in the context of the fact that the Zaruba themselves are noted for their warlike behavior and for the ruthlessness with which they have, over many centuries, attacked and slaughtered their neighbors. A typical Zaruba prayer, for example, actually recommends, indeed blesses, the Zaruba tribe member who will capture the innocent infants of a neighboring tribe and dash their brains out against a stone. The exact quotation is:

Happy shall he be who takes and dashes the enemy's little ones against a stone.

As scholars of the Old Testament may have perceived, I have attempted to bypass, temporarily, certain prejudices, pro or con, in the minds of at least some readers of the present study by changing the name of the tribe of Judah to Zaruba, which I now explain is totally fictitious. Let the reader who a moment ago was rightly contemptuous of what he assumed was primitive African tribal behavior ponder the ethical and theological significance of his or her reactions.

My purpose in inventing this fictional tribe was to aid the reader in forming an opinion of typical Old Testament literature. The "Zaruba" prayer is actually a paraphrase of part of Psalm 109, with the last line taken from Psalm 137. I do not see how any unprejudiced reader can fail to be struck by its combination of fawning sycophancy on the one hand and psychotic hatred on the other.

I do not intend that the argument I set out by this simple illustration to have any relationship to another mindless sort of racism, antisemitism. Knowing hundreds of Jews as well as I do and holding them in the highest regard, I wonder if their remote ancestors were ever as bloodthirsty as is alleged in almost every portion of the Old Testament. It is not the Jews I suspect. It is rather the claim—made even by Christians—that such savage tales were personally inspired by God. In the modern day, thanks largely to the fact that technology makes it possible to induce the emotion of shame, some Jews and Christians believe and teach that a loving God seeks to discourage violent emotion and the shedding of blood to which it so commonly leads, although the right to self-defense is always reserved. Why must we hear ancient libels? Why are psalms like this in the Scriptures?

PROPHETS, OLD TESTAMENT. Whatever conclusions we may draw concerning the Bible's prophets, it is no longer possible to believe that they lay striking claims to much originality in respect to ideas. As regards monotheism and the search for a Messiah, these themes are encountered in history earlier than prophetic times. The Code of Hammurabi, which dates from about 1,800 years before Jesus and which embodies material considerably older than itself, has a high ethical tone and is generally considered to be unsurpassed until Roman times.

James Brown observes in "The New Old Testament: Ancient Israel in Its Near Eastern Setting" (*Commentary,* April 1956):

> Therefore we can . . . no longer think of the prophets as unique in their ethical concern; it seems more just to conclude with Gunnar Oestborn (in *Torah in the Old Testament*) that the special characteristic of Israelite religion is, more simply, the energy and consistency with which ethics is emphasized, as compared to what has—so far—been found elsewhere.

Such conclusions appear to be based on a consideration of the evidence, but Jewish and Christian scholars are, understandably enough, uneasy concerning the direction of such arguments, perceiving that they raise profoundly serious theological problems. Brown continues:

If Israel shared so much in common with her neighbors, what is the distinctive element in her religion which has made it of such unique significance to herself and others; in a word, what is the contribution of Judaism? Even prophecy, once thought to be original with Israel, is now known to have a pre-history. Ecstatic individuals and groups existed previously, and in other cultures. More than that, in some texts from Mari [a city] on the middle Euphrates which date from the end of the 18th Century B.C., we come upon a prototype of the Old Testament prophets, who appears, as they did, unasked and unbidden with an oracle, and making the same claim that "the God has sent me."

Brown does not follow the implications of his argument but retreats to an emphasis on the distinction between origin and significance.

Cult, kingship, priesthood and prophecy—these things did indeed exist for Israel, and even her very language is but one in a family, and a young one at that . . . but *we must never make the mistake of thinking that Israel and its neighbors meant the same thing by the institutions they had in common.* (IA)

One wonders why not. After we acknowledge that Old Testament prophets were not the first nor the only ones in the ancient Middle East, we may, however, note that they employed imagery that was often striking. Their purpose was chiefly to exhort their people to hold fast to the worship of one god, Yahweh, with whom they believed the people had a covenant and who they believed gave the people their laws, although these laws resemble the laws discovered by archaeologists in the 20th century throughout the Middle East, presumably "given" by other gods, such as Marduk, Baal, etc. (See also the books in the division of the Old Testament known in Hebrew as *Nevi'im* (Prophets): AMOS, EZEKIEL, HOSEA, ISAIAH, JEREMIAH, JOSHUA, KINGS.)

PROVERBS. Both Christian and Jewish tradition, as well as Chapter 1, Verse 1, ascribes the writing of Proverbs to Solomon. The tradition is in error. The book of Proverbs had several authors and was composed over an extended period of time. There is no longer any reason to suppose that Solomon was even one of the contributors.

It is not necessary to ascribe to the now-unknown authors the conscious intention to deceive by suggesting that Solomon's had been the hand that held the pen. Rather it was common in ancient times for professional scribes in the service of a king to honor a ruler by affixing his name to collections of writings they either created or compiled from earlier sources or traditions.

If a group of Catholic scholars were to produce a collection of Catholic wisdom at present, for example, and honor Pope John Paul II by attaching his name to the document, it would not necessarily follow that they wished others to assume that the pope himself had personally written or compiled the material. The error, with such books as those attributed to Solomon, was made by scholars of later generations who misinterpreted the original ascriptions.

It is difficult to be absolutely certain as to when the writing of Proverbs was either begun or finished. There is a loose scholarly agreement that the final stage of the process must have been completed sometime between 400 B.C. and A.D. 200, a period of some six centuries.

Jean Levie, S.J., in *The Bible: Word of God in Words of Men,* explains:

> The Egyptian Wisdom and moral literature has many similarities in thought and structure with the Wisdom literature of Israel and there is possibly some connection, direct or indirect, between the moral sentences of Amenenope and the Hebrew Book of Proverbs, 22:17 to 24:22.

PSALMS. With the psalms we are confronted not with clear knowledge but a mystery.

H. Keith Beebe, in his well-organized and informative *The Old Testament* (Belmont, Calif.: Dickenson, 1970), put the matter simply enough. "The precision achieved in dating most literary units of the Old Testament," he says, "is impossible with the Psalms, because the historical allusion in them is scanty." Some interpreters place the composition of the majority of psalms late in Israel's history; others put most of them during the divided monarchies of Israel and Judah. But no one knows for certain when they were composed or written down.

For those who might not have had the pleasure of reading Dr. Beebe's study, I should point out that he writes with enormous respect for the Bible, with, in his own words, "a full appreciation of the literary and historical significance, and the religious grandeur of these truly great books."

However, I do not feel that way about all of the psalms. Many are indeed beautifully written, and I acknowledge that they have been a source of inspiration, especially to Jews, although to Christians as well.

In what follows, I shall merely point out what I object to in *some* of the 150 psalms.

Psalm 52. The morality of part of this psalm is dubious. Verse 6 refers to the righteous men laughing at the downfall of the wicked. I think such laughter is sadistic and heartless. Wouldn't a better response to the downfall or sufferings of sinful people be sadness?

Psalm 53. The first verse includes the famous condemnation of atheism, "The fool hath said in his heart, there is no God." The following verses, however, are puzzling.

> 2. God looked down from heaven upon the children of men, to see if there were any that did understand, that did seek God.
> 3. Every one of them is gone back. They are altogether become filthy; there is none who doeth good, no, not one.

The odd thing about this condemnation is that no one has ever been able to assert that it applied to the human condition at any single point in time. Generally, both well-known and obscure religions are convinced that there is always at least a saving remnant, a small minority of the virtuous.

Psalm 58. This psalm expresses a remarkable philosophical approach to the mystery of human evil.

> 3. The wicked are estranged from the womb; they go astray as soon as they are born, speaking lies.

This is the "bad seed" theory of evil, that certain individuals are depraved and sinful from the moment of either conception or birth. But no psychologist, even those within the churches, holds to such a theory, nor is it now the official position of *any* religious group except perhaps among some fanatical cultists.

A few verses later another peculiar thought is expressed in unmistakable terms:

> 10. The righteous shall rejoice when he sees the vengeance. He shall wash his feet in the blood of the wicked.

No Jew or Christian now preaches any such vile notion. In yet one more instance, we find a specific portion of the Bible teaching a moral lesson abhorrent to all persons of the slightest ethical sensitivity.

Psalm 59. I was raised to believe that the psalms were a source of comfort, sweetness, and light, and the very fact that they are poetic somehow established their gentle reasonableness. This is, of course, not always the case. The unknown author of Psalm 59, for example, speaks as violently as any demagogue who ever lived.

10. My God in his steadfast love will meet me; my God will let me look in triumph on my enemies. . . .

12. For the sin of their mouths, and the words of their lips, let them be trapped in their pride. For the cursing and lies which they utter,

13. consume them in wrath, consume them till they are no more . . .

Psalm 68. The same sadism is encountered here, along with savage imagery.

21. But God will shatter the heads of his enemies, and the hairy crown of him who walks in his guilty ways.

22. The Lord said, "I will bring them [your enemies] back from Bashan, I will bring them back from the depths of the sea,

23. that you may bathe your feet in blood, that the tongues of your dogs may have their position from the foe."

Psalm 109. There is no way to tell, from simply reading this psalm, why it is addressed "To the Choirmaster." There is no reference to music in the text. The psalm is, however, a remarkable expression of an unedifying desire for vengeance. Referring to those who have responded to the speaker's love with hatred the psalmist says:

Appoint a wicked man against him; let an accuser bring him to trial. When he is tried, let him come forth guilty; let his prayer be counted a sin! May his days be few; may another seize his goods! May his children be fatherless, and his wife a widow! May his children wander about and beg; may they be driven out of the ruins they inhabit! May the creditor seize all that he has; may strangers plunder the fruit of his toil! Let there be none to extend kindness to him, nor any pity to his fatherless children! May his posterity be cut off; may his name be blotted out in the second generation! May the iniquity of his fathers be remembered before the Lord, and not let the sins of his mother be blotted out! (Verses 6-14)

There are several more verses in this vein. What spiritual or moral lesson is supposed to be inculcated by such expressions of spite is unclear.

Psalm 136 is a litany of affirmations and responses, which begins in a morally acceptable fashion.

1. O, give thanks unto the Lord; for He is good: For his mercy endureth forever.

2. Oh, give thanks unto the God of gods: For his mercy endureth forever.

This edifying tone is maintained until Verse 10, which begins, "To him that smote Egypt in their firstborn." The theme persists in the following verses:

17. To Him which smote great kings . . .
18. And slew famous kings . . .
19. Sihon, king of the Amorites . . .
20. And Og, the king of Bashan . . .

And the verses go on to glorify slaughter and murder.

Psalm 137 is not obscure or of questionable authenticity; it is in fact one of the more famous in Christian and Jewish religious literature. It could not have been written by David because the Babylonian Captivity occurred long after his reign. The shocking last line is generally omitted when this psalm is quoted.

1. By the rivers of Babylon, there we sat down, yea, we wept, when we remembered Zion.
2. We hung our harps upon the willows in the midst thereof.
3. For there they that carried us away captive required of us a song; and they that wasted us required of us mirth, saying, Sing us one of the songs of Zion.
4. How shall we sing the Lord's song in a strange land?
5. If I forget thee, O Jerusalem, let my right hand forget her cunning.
6. If I do not remember thee, let my tongue cleave to the roof of my mouth; if I prefer not Jerusalem above my chief joy.
7. Remember, O Lord, the children of Edom in the day of Jerusalem; who said, Raze it, raze it, even to the foundation thereof.
8. O daughter of Babylon, who art to be destroyed; happy shall he be, that rewardeth thee as thou hast served us.
9. *Happy shall he be, that taketh and dasheth thy little ones against the stones.* (IA)

Psalm 139 is said to have been written, every word, by King David. The personage addressed is God. Much of the psalm consists of beautiful poetic phrases, which the reader may consult in his or her Bible. But such high-minded beauty is discarded as we approach the following verses:

> 19. O that thou wouldst slay the wicked, O God,
>   and that men of blood would depart from me,
> 20. men who maliciously defy thee,
>   who lift themselves up against thee for evil!
> 21. Do I not hate them that hate thee, O Lord?
>   And do I not loathe them that rise up against thee?
> 22. I hate them with perfect hatred;
>   I count them my enemies.

It is impossible, if one assumes that David was divinely inspired to write these lines, to argue that there is anything wrong with hatred. It could still be held that the only sort of hatred the passage endorses is hatred of those who are anti-God. Alas for intellectual clarity, the meaning of the phrase *anti-God* is not easy to determine. To say that an individual is an atheist cannot possibly mean that he is anti-God, since it is an intellectual absurdity that one can be opposed to something that one does not believe exists.

Still, the reader must clearly perceive that such passages as the one just quoted cannot be reconciled with Christian moral theology, which preaches that though we are obliged to hate the sin, we must, in all circumstances, love the sinner. At the time Psalm 139 was written, and for centuries thereafter, did David's subjects and later Hebrews truly believe that it was not only permissible but morally obligatory to hate so fiercely?

If our minds were not clouded by long ages of respect for the so-called "Holy Scriptures," we could easily perceive the moral idiocy of what the quoted verses seek to justify.

Psalm 140. One of the most dependable sources of humor is incongruity, a factor that presents itself in the very first verse of this psalm. "Deliver me, O Lord, from the evil man. Preserve me from the violent man." We have just read the psalmist singing the praises of violence and hatred, and now we find a message of the opposite sort. The humor is consistent through much of the psalm, in which the psalmist calls down calamities upon the heads of those he dislikes: "Let burning coals fall upon them. Let them be cast into the fire, into deep pits, that they rise not up again" (v. 10).

Psalm 145. The psalms, like many other parts of the Scriptures, combine great beauty with elements of nonsense, error, unsound moral advice, and contradictions. In Verse 16, for example, we read, "Thou openest thine hand, and satisfiest the desires of every living thing."

It does not require even a moment's reflection to be aware that what this verse states is simply not the case. Many human desires are never satisfied. And among those that are satisfied, not all of them should be.

Verse 20 also cannot conform to the witness of evidence. "The Lord preserveth all them that love him, but all the wicked will he destroy." We can provide a lengthy list of the names of wicked people whose fortunes prosper, who are "rich and famous," powerful, honored and successful, and a list at least as long of the names of good, religious, law-abiding people who, despite their personal virtues, are struck by cancer, killed in automobile accidents, burned in fires, eaten by sharks, beaten down by poverty and suffering—who, in short, suffer any of the thousand and one ills that are all too typical of the human condition.

Q

"Q." While most Christians have gone to their graves without ever once hearing about a collection of hypothetical scriptural writings called "Q" by scholars (from the German *Quelle,* source), the fact is that there would probably be no New Testament at all, or at least not the one we are familiar with, were it not likely that such a source once existed. Scholars have produced a "document" of what they believe "Q" would have been by culling from two Gospels the sayings of JESUS—parables, beatitudes, etc.—that LUKE and MATTHEW have in common.

The average Christian no doubt assumes—largely because he has been taught—that the Gospel of Matthew was written by the apostle Matthew, that called Luke by a man of that name, and so forth. The truth is considerably more complex. There is now almost universal agreement among the best-informed scholars of Scriptures—including those who are sympathetic to claims of divine inspiration—that a vanished document of unknown authorship was the source from which the authors of the first and third Gospels drew part of the information included in their separate accounts of Jesus' life and teachings. There is also general agreement that if "Q" existed, it would have been one of the earliest Christian writings.

The hypothesis about "Q" leads to subsidiary questions, some of which are perplexing and troubling. Ivan Havener, O.S.B., of St. John's University in Collegeville, Minnesota, writes in *Q: The Sayings of Jesus* (Wilmington, Del.: Michael Glazier, 1987) that "Q" 's

> . . . view of Christianity challenges us to rethink the very beginnings of Christianity itself . . . a careful reading of the text of Q will disclose *numerous ideas that break or clash with our contemporary understanding of Christian Orthodoxy.* (IA)

The eminent German biblical scholar Martin Dibelius, who helped pioneer and apply the method of scriptural study known as form-criticism,

366

has this to say about "Q" ("The Synoptic Problem," in *The Origins of Christianity,* ed. R. Joseph Hoffman, Buffalo, N.Y.: Prometheus Books, 1985):

> This solution to the problem of Gospel sources is known as the "two-source theory," according to which Matthew and Luke used Mark and in addition a second source, "Q," now lost (p. 190).

Another scholar, G. A. Wells of Birkbeck College, London University, is a skeptic about whether Jesus ever existed. However, he notes:

> A very remarkable thing about Q (in so far as one can reconstruct it from *Matthew* and *Luke*) is that, although it sets Jesus' life in first-century Palestine by associating him with John the Baptist, it makes no mention of Pilate and gives not the slightest hint of the Passion, crucifixion, and resurrection. Nor does it represent Jesus as a great miracle-worker but rather as an obscure and rejected preacher. The Jesus of Q suffers in so far as he is rejected by men, but his suffering has no atoning power. . . . Q consists mainly of sayings in which Jesus predicts the coming of the kingdom and insists that only those who accept him and what he says will be saved when the Son of Man (a supernatural personage familiar in Jewish apocalyptic literature) comes to inaugurate it. He also provides a moral code ("love your enemies," "judge not") by which men are to live in preparation for the coming judgment (*The Historical Evidence for Jesus,* Buffalo, Prometheus Books, 1982, p. 213).

Wells thus discloses the "numerous ideas that break or clash with . . . Christian Orthodoxy," hinted at by Father Havener.

R

RESURRECTION. If the reader has studied the articles on MATTHEW, MARK, LUKE, and JOHN, he or she has seen that they are of little help in providing an accurate report of the birth of JESUS. The other most important event in the story of his life is the Resurrection. That he was crucified in itself establishes nothing special about him since many thousands have been crucified. (See CRUCIFIXION.) But if, after being crucified, he in fact rose from the dead, that is a remarkable matter indeed, and would have enormous religious significance. Unfortunately, no other historian of the time makes any reference to such a dramatic occurrence, so we are left with the Gospels as the only source of information. But the difficulty is compounded when we read closely and find that the Gospels give conflicting reports.

Comments Robert Coughlin in "Who Was the Man Jesus?" (*Life,* December 1964):

> The gospels are in full accord on two points: first, the central fact that the tomb of Jesus was empty; second, that faithful Mary Magdalene was initially responsible for this discovery. Otherwise, however, *there are hardly any details of the resurrection that match in any two of the gospels, let alone among all four.*
>
> Thus in Mark's story a young man "dressed in a white robe" greeted Mary Magdalene and her companions with the words "Do not be amazed; you seek Jesus of Nazareth, who was crucified. He has risen, he is not here. . . ."
>
> In Matthew, along with numerous other embellishments, there was an earthquake and an angel who "came and rolled back the stone," features absent from John, Luke and Mark.
>
> On the other hand, Luke is the only one to mention the ascension of Jesus to heaven from Bethany, on the side of a hill.
>
> As for Jesus' post-resurrection appearances, Mark is content to forecast that he will meet with the disciples in Galilee. According to

Matthew, the honor of being the first to see the risen Jesus belonged to Mary Magdalene and her companion that day, identified only as "the other Mary" . . .

The differences in the gospel accounts become even more baffling when they are compared with Paul's statement. Paul, after all, had discussed the Resurrection only a few years afterward with such authoritative witnesses as Peter. His first epistle to the Corinthians, in which he catalogues the appearances, moreover, was written in the very early 50s A.D.—*some 15 to 20 years before any of the gospels were.* ". . . he appeared to Cephas [i.e. Peter] then to The Twelve. Then he appeared to more than 500 brethren at one time, most of whom were still alive, though some have fallen asleep. Then he appeared to James, then to all the apostles. Last of all . . . he appeared also to me." (IA)

There is not the slightest question that the story of the Resurrection is the most important account in the New Testament. If Jesus did not rise from the dead, then a very great deal of what is believed by Christians is not valid. One among various possible conclusions, in that event, would be that Jesus—assuming he physically existed at all, which I do—was merely a very remarkable man, perhaps the most remarkable who ever lived, but only a man nevertheless, certainly not a uniquely chosen Son of God and equally not God himself in human form.

In recent years a number of books by Christian scholars have been published that deal specifically with the Resurrection. Among these are: *The Formation of the Resurrection Narratives* by Reginald H. Fuller (Macmillan), *The Resurrection of Jesus of Nazareth* by Willi Marxsen (Fortress Press), and *Resurrection and the New Testament* by C. F. Evans (A. R. Allenson). Reviewing these works, Father Richard J. Clifford, S.J., explains:

The New Testament evidence for the resurrection of Jesus, which is the natural starting point for any serious theological investigation, offers . . . its own peculiar problems. *The Gospel traditions are impossible to harmonize;* they are separate expressions of the Eastern faith, *redacted according to the special viewpoint of each evangelist.* Behind all these traditions, of course, is the conviction that Jesus of Nazareth lives, but his mode of living is differently conceived in the four Gospels. (IA)

Given the scholarly difficulties finally conceded in the face of what was initially skeptical criticism, it is both understandable and significant that Clifford would refer to "the considerable Biblical problems connected with the resurrection." He quotes Dr. Fuller of Union Theological Seminary to the effect—which will certainly startle, if not shock most Christian leaders—that *"the words spoken by the risen one are not to be taken as recordings of what was actually spoken by him, but as verbalizations of the community's understanding of the import of the resurrection."* (IA)

Resurrection of the Body. The Second Book of Maccabees speaks with clarity and directness of the resurrection of the body. The author believes that survival after death will not only result in the restoration of the body but reunion with members of one's family. Indeed, this concept that each of us will one day be reunited with our loved ones (those of them that did not merit, by their sins, eternal residence in a fiery Hell) is one of the more appealing features of such a belief. While it is perhaps meaningless to speak of what is *not* possible in a context where nothing seems to be predicated on the physical laws of the universe, nevertheless we are entitled to point to a certain logistical difficulty about belief in the reunion of family members. The reader may imagine, for example, that he will one day be reunited with his or her parents, spouse, and children. But each of these, in turn, would say the same, so that it is impossible to imagine how such a universal wish could be granted, except by perhaps an eternity-long process of visitation.

"Resurrection" Myths. While it may seem disrespectful to include the names of two popular young men of our time who carry no moral significance, Elvis Presley and James Dean, in the same sentence with that of Jesus Christ, it is nevertheless profitable to do so, because an examination of the public reaction to the untimely death of these figures of popular culture can help illuminate the mass psychology that might have operated in the days, weeks, and months following the crucifixion of Jesus.

In the case of Dean, news of his death came as a shock. He was "too young to die." His excellent portrayals of immature young men, in the few films he had made, had caused him to become a cult-figure, one with whom millions of American youth could identify. To them he seemed "one of us." His untimely death, therefore, led to a degree of public hysteria. As those who had reached adulthood at the time may recall, one response to the news of Dean's automobile accident was denial. There were rumors that he had been horribly disfigured and consequently hidden away. There were stories that someone else had stolen or borrowed his car and that it was this unknown figure, not Dean, who had been killed.

There was something in millions of young Americans that *needed* James Dean. That something was reluctant to let go of him and, to defend against the pain of loss, people began at once to construct myths and legends out of the raw material of rumor and hope. Those who had known Dean personally, if they were literate, began to publish reports about him. Those who had known him and were not able to write were endlessly interviewed by those who had not known the actor. Young people travelled from various parts of the world to visit his grave or the home of his aunt and uncle in Marion, Indiana.

The same phenomenon occurred in 1977, when Elvis Presley was found dead. People stood in line for hours to visit his coffin, wept publicly, scrambled to snatch souvenirs, bought out his albums in record stores the world over. Even journalists who should have known better wrote paeans of praise; professional critics applied their powers of analysis to the mostly innocuous music which Presley, by the force of his oddly attractive personality, had made popular.

Stories about his being alive have continued to appear. That such public reactions are not accorded all popular entertainers who die was demonstrated when Groucho Marx and Bing Crosby died about the same time Presley did. Yet there was no public hysteria over their deaths. Presley was "too young to die," as the saying goes; and he had appealed to the *emotions* of his admirers. That is what made the difference.

Religious figures such as Jesus, Mohammed, Mary Baker Eddy, Buddha, etc. also speak to the emotions, not the intellect, of their followers. The death of a young, much-admired, beloved leader such as Jesus—even to those who did not know him personally, or never saw him—would very likely have produced the same kinds of reactions Americans have seen in the two instances cited. Add to this the fact that religious figures are of more profound concern than popular culture figures, and it is not in the least difficult to understand the sort of soil from which confusing and contradictory stories about the Resurrection may have emerged.

REVIVAL, MODERN RELIGIOUS. There is no question but that the United States is experiencing a wave of religious fervor, which has been called a second Age of Faith. But it is unlike the earlier European Age of Faith, in which unanimity of opinion about theological matters was the norm and religion pervaded every aspect of human activity. The present revival is distinguished from that of the Middle Ages by a number of important factors.

First of all, only a small percentage of Americans are touched by the modern trend; the great majority continue in their accustomed ways. Secondly, there is anything but unanimity of belief. Despite the ecumenical tendency of recent years and some mergers of Protestant churches, such great differences still remain that any unification of all Christianity is not likely.

The new wave of faith, then, seems almost to be faith for its own sake, a desperate longing for certainty in a notoriously uncertain world. The problem of the multiplicity of forms of what was assumed to be the sole true faith is one that has troubled Christianity from its earliest days.

It must also be appreciated that the present phenomenon of religious conviction is by no means limited to Christian forms. Oriental religions are also experiencing a revival, and have reached the West. Indeed considerable numbers of young Christians and Jews have left their own faiths to kneel at various Buddhist or other Eastern shrines.

Nor are all the traditional Christian churches pleased by what is happening within the Christian fold. There are serious differences between such traditional Christians as Catholics, Methodists, Baptists, Presbyterians, Episcopalians, etc. on the one hand and affiliates of the "Jesus Freak" or communal groups on the other. About the latter we read of kidnappings, physical violence, lawsuits, and bizarre predictions.

One need refer then to no additional evidence to establish that the new revivalism is by no means a Christian reawakening of the sort that occurred on the American continent in the 19th century, but rather it is a partly blind and sometimes pathetic groping, toward which one must, however, be sympathetic and understanding.

The relevance of this to my thesis is that the Bible plays a central role in the new phenomenon, except in the case of Oriental religions, and—in keeping with the historical record of concentrated dependence on the Jewish-Christian Scriptures—the results are not such as to encourage unity but disunity, since almost every man considers himself the equal of the most sophisticated theologian or scholar when it comes to interpreting "the simple word of God."

The point demands frequent repetition: the Bible is in no sense the simple word of God. Either it is not the word of God at all or if it is there is nothing simple about it. It is rather a collection of books of incredible complexity, so impenetrable that, after some 2,000 years, some of its secrets remain inaccessible. To this day it is demonstrably the case that if, say, the Mormon religion is true and complete, then Christian Science, for example, is largely stuff and nonsense; that if the Baptist faith is truly of God, then the Catholic version is a monstrous affront to the Deity; that if Rome is right then Canterbury is sadly misguided; that if Jehovah's Witnesses constitute the true Christian fold then the Presbyterians ought to be ashamed of themselves, etc., ad infinitum.

None of this is intended to argue that no good can be produced by even the most misguided sect. Each can point to socially beneficial works: hospitals and universities, charitable efforts on behalf of the poor, the bringing of literacy to backward areas, the softening of the hearts of sinners, comfort brought to bereaved hearts, the preservation of families, etc. All of this is beautiful enough, and in sadly short supply, but probably only a Mormon or a Baptist, for example, will insist that such of it as occurs in his fold is a testimony to *the truth* of his philosophy. No one but a Christian Scientist is convinced of the truth of that particular faith simply by evidence of the virtuous lives led by many of its adherents.

What is appealing—it is important to grasp—is never the mere lighting of candles, repetition of certain prayers, superstitious insistence on ritual but rather the emphasis on ethics and morals. Shakespeare was right; it is good deeds in a naughty world that cast a warming light. It is the traditional virtues of truth, courage, honesty, and love that sustain and improve the world, and these may be shown by pagan, atheist, and believer alike.

Something else rarely perceived by those caught up in the religious revival is that the apparently secure rocks to which they are tying up their individual frail crafts are not unchanging bastions of certainty but are, like everything in nature, in an endless process of change. The primary reason this truth is obscured, of course, is that much change takes place so slowly as to be unnoticeable day by day. A Catholic, for example, will perceive no difference between his church this morning and that of a few years earlier. But one has only to consider the amazing changes in the Catholic church in the last quarter of a century to perceive the large, historical process at work. Questions once considered matters of life and death are no longer debated, papal pronouncements once thundered authoritatively are now forgotten and a source of embarrassment when remembered, sciences once decried as atheistic are now quietly taught at Catholic universities. And so it is with many religions. One may still derive deep comfort, even inspiration, from them. But whatever the source of such uplifting manifestations, it certainly is not a rock of never-changing solidity.

One need not look to supernatural causes in searching for an explanation of the present wave of religious revival. It would be at least consistent with reason to assume that some all-wise divinity was behind the phenomenon if, in reality, the social movement we see was all in one general direction. This would be the case if, for example, mankind was being swept up into the Christian faith exclusively, if practically everyone was being converted to Catholicism or charismatic Evangelicalism.

But when we observe reality, we see that the movement itself is chaotic and formless. Many people seem to be stampeding, for the most part blindly, into not one or a few, but hundreds of sects, both large and traditional and small and obscure. It can hardly be argued seriously that such a social tendency has God as its causative agent. Having ruled out one cause we must look for another.

The true explanation is that ours is a time of social dislocation, of political and scientific change so markedly accelerated that some of it is, and much of it appears to be, revolutionary. We criticize those of the 16th century who, though living in the Age of Exploration, took no particular notice of the remarkable discoveries of the adventurers. We ourselves are living in the dawn of the Space Age, which represents perhaps the most incredible scientific achievement in history, and yet most of us are not so much exhilarated as somehow vaguely disturbed by it.

Many Americans living today have lived through four major wars in this century, and we are both weary and wary, for war has certainly not been extinguished from our planet. The American taxpayer continues to fund many. In addition to localized and regional wars, there has been the all-too-real threat of international violence among the superpowers.

We live in the twilight of colonialism, in the context of an ongoing debate between capitalist and socialist powers, and in a time when many social institutions and governments are either collapsing or proving unequal to the tasks confronting them. In such a chaotic human panorama, it would be surprising indeed if many did not flock to one religion or another as a way of seeking certainty in an uncertain world.

There are some similarities between our period of unrest and that of 2,000 years ago, which led to the creation and development of Christianity. Then, too, there was a growing demand for a remedy for the ills of life more effective than what the prevailing philosophies and governments offered. Then, too, men were filled with a sense of spiritual unease. The ruling class was corrupt. Striking contrasts between great luxury and abject misery were notorious. The general insecurity of life made men feel that the world was in its last days and that it had been brought to its low estate by the sinfulness of man. By perceiving how such processes explain—indeed make inevitable— the religious revival of the present moment in history, we can more readily grasp the functioning of the same process at the time of Jesus.

RUTH. The reasons for the popularity of the book of Ruth are by no means evident to me. It is therefore puzzling to be told by the editors of the Dartmouth Bible (Boston: Houghton Mifflin) that:

> Few writings have been loved as much as this short book. Its spirit and style have brought it such superlatives as "the daintiest of love idyls" (Goethe), "the ideal pastoral romance," "the most delightful story ever penned."

The editors do not tell us the source of the last two compliments. (Perhaps since some of the other Old Testament books are so long and dreary, critics were responding primarily to the brevity of Ruth.) In any event, I believe that the superlatives are unjustified. It is understandable why mothers-in-law would find the story touching; one may also be pleased by the story's disregard of the belief—dear to many believers—that one should marry only within one's own religious sect.

Ruth is a peculiar book of the Bible. After reading its four short chapters twice, I confess that I can find no reason why it was included in the canon of the Scriptures. It is not a religious document, unless one considers any literature religious in which phrases such as "the Lord" are occasionally included. It is a moderately charming short story about an old widow named Naomi who, having lived some ten years in the land of Moab, decides after the death of her husband and two sons to return to her home in Judah. One of her daughters-in-law, Orpah, bids her an affectionate farewell. The other, a young woman named Ruth, decides to remain with Naomi.

Chapter 1, Verse 16 includes the oft-quoted speech of Ruth to Naomi: "Whither thou goest, I will go; and where thou lodgest, I will lodge. Thy people shall be my people and thy God my God."

What is of interest to me in the first chapter is the casual reference to polytheism. In Verse 15 Naomi mentions to Ruth that Orpah has "gone back to her people, and to her gods." This is not said with any horror or disapproval. When, therefore, Ruth mentions her willingness to worship Naomi's God rather than the one she is accustomed to worshiping, the conclusion is clear that the two gods are separate.

In any event the two women travel to Bethlehem, where there dwells a man named Boaz, a relative-in-law of Naomi. Ruth goes to a field belonging to Boaz and gathers a few ears of corn. When Boaz sees her he inquires about her identity and, upon meeting her, gives her permission to continue to glean grain. When Ruth more or less throws herself on his mercies, Boaz invites her to share his table.

In Chapter 3 Naomi suggests to Ruth that later that evening, Ruth should bathe, put on perfume and fresh clothes, wait until Boaz has finished eating and drinking, and then lie with him on the floor of the threshing room.

> 4. "And it shall be, when he lieth down, that thou shalt mark the place where he shall lie, and thou shall go in and uncover his feet, and lay thee down. And he will tell thee what thou shalt do."

The two spend the night together on the floor, although we are not to assume that they had sexual relations, since in Verse 14 it is asserted that

RUTH

Ruth "rose up before one could know another." Boaz, perhaps understandably, suggests that Ruth say nothing of the incident to others.

When Boaz learns that another male relative has no interest in acquiring Ruth as his property, he decides he will marry her himself.

> 13. So Boaz took Ruth, and she was his wife; and when he went
> in unto her the Lord gave her conception and she bare a son.

The son, according to the unknown author of Chapter 4, turns out some years later to be the great-grandfather of King DAVID.

All of this might be considered of moderate interest as family history, but there is not a bit of religious edification in it, although it is a popular Sunday School story.

S

SATAN. See **Devil, The.**

SABBATH. The Scriptures give various reasons for a heavy concentration on the importance of the Sabbath. The instructions about it are so important that they are included among the Ten COMMANDMENTS. There was not only the firm insistence that no work, of even the most necessary kind, could be done on the Sabbath Day but also the idea that if the law were broken bad fortune would certainly follow. Do unfortunate results follow from *working* on the Sabbath Day? The answer is simple: no, they do not.

It is still possible to argue that the Sabbath ought to be honored whether or not dishonoring it produces negative results, but if that answer is valid then those who advance it ought to set about reviving respect for the Sabbath.

Christians, by and large, feel that they fulfill their seventh-day obligations merely by attending church services and that otherwise they are as free to work on that day as they are on any other.

As a practical matter, of course, most people do take both Saturday and Sunday off, and doing so is an eminently reasonable practice. In ancient times almost all work was physically difficult and exhausting so there has, from the first, been a perfectly sensible reason for giving laborers a rest during part of each week.

But in discussing the Sabbath Day we are not talking about anything so reasonable. We are talking about the belief in a command, directly from God, that the Sabbath Day is somehow special and holy, in a way that all other days are not. As for the word itself, it is related to the Babylonian *Shabattum,* the day on which the moon was full. Many scholars argue that the Hebrews took their Sabbath customs from other, older civilizations.

I once heard a Black comedian tell a joke that, while it may be offensive to some people, and would, if delivered by a white performer, be considered racist, nevertheless made a point that applies to behavior on the Sabbath.

"Have you ever wondered," the comedian asked, "why it's so quiet in Los Angeles on Sunday morning? I'll tell you why that is. The Catholics are in church, the Protestants are playing golf, the Jews are all in Palm Springs, a lot of the Blacks are in jail, and the Mexicans can't get their cars started."

Offensive? Certainly, like a good deal of modern stand-up comedy. But the contents of the joke do relate, however grossly, to elements of social reality as well as to the question of the Sabbath. Many religious believers do attend church or synagogue services, but there is little evidence that for the rest of the day they treat it in any more holy a fashion than the other six days of the week, unless they are Orthodox Jews or one of a small number of fundamentalist Protestant sects.

SAMSON. The story of Samson begins in the 13th chapter of Judges. Samson, a Sunday School hero, was one of the worst monsters either in history or in the literature of myth. Of his crimes, sins, and general foolishness four chapters of the book of Judges give ample evidence. It is therefore of particular interest to note how he happened to be born. There is, alas, no shortage of moral monsters among the human population, and all of them are, so far as physical nature is concerned, conceived and born in the common manner. In the case of Samson, however—just as in the case of Jesus—God troubled himself to miraculous exertions.

> 2. And there was a certain man of Zorah, of the family of the Danites, whose name was Manoah; and his wife was barren.
> 3. And the angel of the Lord appeared unto the woman and said unto her, "Behold now, thou are barren; but thou shalt conceive and bear a son . . ."

Concerning the story of Samson's mother, Elizabeth Cady Stanton makes the observation:

> One would suppose that this woman, so favored of God, worthy to converse with angels on the most delicate of her domestic relations, might have had a name . . . instead of being mentioned merely as the wife of Manoah.

Considering that the Lord had troubled himself to make Samson such a remarkable physical specimen, it is necessary to observe to what uses such a natural endowment was put. Stanton observes further:

Even his physical prowess was not used by him for any great purpose. To kill a lion, to walk off with the gates of the city, to catch 300 foxes and to tie them together by their tails two-by-two, with firebrands to burn the cornfields and vineyards—all this seems more like the frolics of a boy than the military tactics of a great general or the statesmanship of a Judge in Israel.

One of the most astonishing discoveries one makes by a dispassionate study of the Old Testament concerns the sort of moral messages it inculcates. **Judges 14.**

> 2. And he [Samson] came up and told his father and mother and said, "I have seen a woman in Timnah of the daughters of the Philistines: now therefore get her for me to wife."

Samson's parents are understandably displeased that he wishes to marry a daughter of the enemy. It turns out, however, that although the parents do not perceive it Samson is actually doing the Lord's work, for he "sought an occasion against the Philistines; for at that time the Philistines had dominion over Israel" (v. 4).

Samson went to Timnah, where "a young lion roared against him." Samson grabbed it and tore it apart. We are, of course, called upon to admire his ability to tear a yearling lion apart with his bare hands, as he was apparently in the habit of doing to young goats and sheep.

Samson proceeds on his way and meets the woman, whom he again finds physically attractive.

> 8. And after a time he returned to take her, and he turned aside to see the carcass of the lion, and behold there was a swarm of bees and honey in the carcass of the lion.

It is possible to believe such an assertion only on the assumption that the event described is miraculous. And of course, when we say that a given event is the result of the miraculous intervention of divine power, we have deprived reason of a foothold since if one uses the word *all-powerful* to describe God it follows that no act is impossible for him. We can say with assurance that the rotting carcasses of animals are not used by bees— which are among the most efficient animals known to biological science— as dwellings. We also know that the insects that swarm around dead carcasses are flies and that this is part of nature's garbage-disposal system.

Samson invited 30 people to a feast and posed a riddle about the honey in the carcass, which they could not guess.

15. And it came to pass, on the fourth day, that they said unto Samson's wife, "Entice thy husband, that he may declare unto us the riddle, *lest we burn thee in thy father's house with fire:* have ye called us to take that we have? Is it not so?" (IA)

Let the reader ask himself what he would think of guests who, if asked to guess a riddle, went to a man's wife and said, "You'd better find out for us the answer and if you don't we will burn down your house." Equally atrocious threats are not unknown in our own time, but we associate them with members of the Charles Manson family, the Mafia, the Ku Klux Klan, and other depraved social entities.

Samson's wife wept for seven days about the matter "while their feast lasted," which must have put quite a damper on the party. Perhaps for that reason he eventually gave her the information, "and she told the riddle to the children of her people":

18. And the men of the city said unto him on the seventh day before the sun went down "What is sweeter than honey? And what is stronger than a lion?" And he said unto them, "If ye had not plowed with my heifer, ye had not found out my riddle."

It is quite understandable that Samson would be angered at the devious way in which his guests had contrived to solve his puzzle. Any intelligent person, in such an event, would respond by saying, "Since you have solved the riddle by deception, I am therefore under no obligation to give you the 30 sheets and 30 changes of garments I promised you. Get out of my house since I wish to have nothing to do with such deviousness." But one must get out of the habit of trying to rewrite the Old Testament according to our standards of reasonableness, psychology, morality, or literary art. Let's look at Samson's solution.

19. And *the spirit of the Lord* came upon him and he went down to Ashkelon *and slew thirty men of them,* and took their spoil, and gave change of garments unto them which expounded the riddle. (IA)

This is a puzzling verse. At first one supposes that the 30 killed were the 30 visitors, the dishonest souls who had cheated in playing the riddle game. But on a second reading we notice that Samson went to Ashkelon and "gave change of garments unto them which expounded the riddle." It therefore follows that Samson's crime is even more atrocious than we had first assumed. What he did was go to a nearby Philistine community and kill 30 strangers simply because of his anger at what some of their countrymen had done. We see from this "evidence" that Samson was not only a mass murderer but utterly irrational as well.

If this story were placed in a modern setting and dramatized on television, Samson would be a villain, and those presently criticizing the medium for excessive sex and violence would write angry letters to the Federal Communications Commission.

Judges 15. Samson is still in the grip of enormous fury. It is important that we now reflect on the subject of cruelty to animals. If the reader happens to see a man viciously beating a dog or a horse, is he not moved to a combination of pity and anger at the tragic spectacle? St. Francis of Assissi is venerated because of his tender, affectionate regard for animals. Let us contrast Francis with Samson.

> 4. And Samson went and caught three hundred foxes, and took firebrands and turned tail to tail, and put a fire-brand in the midst between two tails.

Imagine the suffering of the 300 innocent furry animals, who were not only trapped, no doubt painfully, but subsequently set afire.

Now man must often make painful moral choices in this world, and sometimes it is thought necessary to commit a small evil in order to produce a larger good. Let us see, therefore, what good might have justified such a sickeningly atrocious act.

> 5. And when he had set the brands on fire, he let them go into the standing corn of the Philistines, and burnt up both the shocks, and also the standing corn with the vineyards and olives.

Is there a Christian clergyman or Jewish rabbi anywhere who can say of such a vile passage that yes, somehow it does indeed represent an unquestioned instance of divine authorship and that it is edifying and morally instructive?

There is a sense, by God, in which it *is* instructive, but it is clearly not the sense intended by the Old Testament authors. Passages like this one refer to the vilest of crimes as if they were not only admirable but redounded to the greater glory of Israel and God Almighty. A more intelligent reader, granting that he has the benefit of several thousand years of moral progress, can recognize an atrocity when he hears of one, and therefore may learn a great deal about how *not* to conduct his affairs.

Verse 6, incidentally, resolves our earlier puzzlement as to whether the chief reason for Samson's fury was the riddle-game cheating or the fact that his wife was given to another man.

> 6. Then the Philistines said, "Who hath done this?" And they answered "Samson, the son-in-law of the Timnite, because he had taken his wife and given her to his companion." And the Philistines came up and burnt her and her father with fire.

The Philistines, apparently, were as vicious and uncivilized as the Israelites. Instead of looking for Samson and seeking revenge by intelligible means, they instead attacked an old man and a young woman, setting their bodies afire. Samson himself shortly sets upon them:

> 8. And he smote them hip and thigh with a great slaughter: and he went down and dwelt in the top of the rock Etam.

Thereafter the Philistines involve the men of Judah in their controversy with Samson. These men approach Samson, who strangely permits them to bind him and deliver him into the hands of the Philistines. The Lord personally gives Samson added strength, however, with the result that the cords binding his arms are broken. With his hands now free he does something even more remarkable, in the context of military history, than the smiting of hips and thighs.

> 15. And he found a new jawbone of an ass, and put forth his hand, and took it and slew a thousand men therewith.

That there is not a shred of historical truth in the story of Samson is strongly suggested by the similarity, in numerous details, between his story and that of the legendary Greek hero Hercules.

Judges 16. We have already seen that Samson is a liar, a mass murderer, and something of a madman. Let us learn more about him.

> 1. Then went Samson to Gaza and saw there an harlot and went in unto her.

Even as have some men of our own time, including at least two prominent evangelists, Samson enjoyed the sexual favors of whores. At midnight Samson awakened from his slumber in the prostitute's bed and, for reasons not evident, walked to the doors of the gates of the city, ripped them from their moorings, and carried them to the top of a nearby hill. Sometime later it occurred to him to seek out another woman.

We now come to the story small children and Cecil B. DeMille are familiar with.

> 4. And it came to pass afterward that he loved a woman in the valley of Sorek, whose name was Delilah.
> 5. And the lords of the Philistines came up unto her and said unto her, "Entice him, and see wherein his great strength lieth, and by what means we may prevail against him that we may bind him to afflict him: and we will give thee everyone of us eleven hundred pieces of silver."

Delilah nags Samson "so that his soul was vexed unto death."

> 17. Then he told her all his heart, and said unto her, "There hath not come a razor upon mine head; for I have been a Nazirite unto God from my mother's womb: if I be shaven then my strength will go from me, and I shall become weak and be like any other man."

Our interest in this is purely literary; as alleged reality it is nonsense.

> 19. And she made him sleep upon her knees; and she called for a man, and she caused him to shave off the seven locks of his head; and she began to afflict him, and his strength went from him.

Does the reader honestly believe that Samson would remain asleep while a mysterious stranger shaved his entire head?

Since there is now no person alive, however devoutly religious, who believes that there is any connection between the physical strength of a human being and the length of that person's hair, it therefore follows that in writing this tale the people of ancient times revealed one more form of their ignorance.

We are told that the Philistines now captured Samson, because his hair was cut off. They put out his eyes—an atrocity typical of the Old Testament—and brought him down to Gaza. Next comes a twist in the plot that is at least creative:

> 22. Howbeit the hair on his head began to grow again after he was shaven.

This detail creates suspense; one wonders if this new growth will renew Samson's strength.

The Philistines then organize an enormous feast and sacrifice to celebrate the capture of Samson. They send for Samson, who is brought, blind, from prison and stationed between two pillars. Note a description of the scene:

> 27. Now the house was full of men and women; and all the lords of the Philistines were there; and there were upon the roof about three thousand men and women, that beheld while Samson made sport.
> 28. And Samson called unto the Lord and said, "O, Lord God, remember me, I pray thee, and strengthen me, I pray thee, only this once, O God, that I may be at once avenged of the Philistines for my two eyes."

Note that Samson does not bring about the death of the men and women of Gaza solely by means of his own anger or by his natural physical strength, which would obviously be unequal to the task of budging two massive stone pillars. He specifically makes God a party to the atrocity he plans to commit.

> 29. And Samson took hold of the two middle pillars upon which the house stood, and on which it was borne up, of the one with his right hand, and of the other with his left.
> 30. And Samson said, "Let me die with the Philistines." And he bowed himself with all his might; and the house fell upon the lords, and upon all the people that were therein. So the dead which he slew at his death were more than they which he slew in his life.

In conclusion, it is stated that this mass murderer, liar, fornicator, torturer of animals, and pretender to miracles "judged Israel 20 years." The Israelites, it is clear, were by no means ashamed at having been led for two decades by such a moral monster. They are instructed to be proud of his achievements. Return to "biblical morality," anyone?

SARAH, wife (and half-sister?) of ABRAHAM and mother of ISAAC. (See these articles and also one on ABIMELECH, king of Gerer, with whom she may or may not have slept.) Sarah, first called Sarai, a variant spelling, is one of the most problematic figures in GENESIS.

Part of her story is suggestive of the miraculous impregnation of the Virgin Mary. Although the Old Testament is filled with specific passages such as "And he went in to Hagar, and she conceived" (16:4), the formula is different for Sarah. Three times the Lord makes a cryptic statement to Abraham:

> "I will give you a son by her." (17:16)
> "I will surely return to you in the spring, and Sarah your wife shall have a son." (18:10)
> "At the appointed time I will return to you, in the spring, and Sarah shall have a son." (18:14)

Parenthetically, since we ought to assume that if God exists he is present everywhere, it is not clear why we so often hear of him going, coming, or returning. We also read:

> "The Lord visited Sarah as he had said and the Lord did to Sarah as he had promised. And Sarah conceived and bore Abraham a son in his old age . . ." (21:1-2)

After Isaac is born, Abraham claims him as his son, but we must remember that JOSEPH functioned as JESUS' earthly father despite the reported miracle of the impregnation of Mary by the Holy Spirit.

But there may be another explanation. Sarah is called by Abraham his half-sister (20:12) and is offered as a wife to two men of royalty that we know of: the Egyptian pharaoh and King Abimelech, with the tribal chieftan Abraham telling both of them that she is only his sister. The textual critic of the Bible might be on safe ground in wondering if the author(s) of Genesis—writing down these ancient legends about the Hebrew progenitors long after they happened—might not have simply combined two traditions without resolving the contradiction: (1) that Abraham and Sarah were man and wife (11:31 and elsewhere) and (2) that they were both children of Terah (20:12).

Since the prohibition against incest is one of the oldest taboos in the world, this could explain the legend that Sarah was barren throughout her childbearing years. Perhaps Abraham took his half-sister sojourning with him, but may not have slept with her even though he might have been tempted to do so. Instead, he offered her to others, as a tribal leader of the time would naturally have done, to acquire wealth or important liaisons. If such is the case, then it was only the Lord who is made to appear confused, railing against the pharaoh and Abimelech for bedding her down—a clear implication if we try to follow the writer's confusing story of Sarah's sexual life.

But one is still troubled by the fact that Sarah is decidedly a senior citizen. Any rabbi, priest, or minister who is also a licensed psychiatrist is familiar with a particular and fortunately rare form of sexual perversion in which an adult male is sexually attracted not by a young, pretty, healthy female—as is normal—but by women of very advanced years.

Abraham was able to father ISHMAEL by Hagar and later all manner of other sons by a second wife, Keturah, after Sarah's death, and by slavewomen or concubines (25:1-6), but Sarah was only able to conceive Isaac with the Lord's special help. We are never told explicitly that Abraham impregnated Sarah.

Presumably, the writer wished to make certain that the later children of Israel, who by 586 B.C. (about the time Genesis may have received its final form) were in danger of being swallowed up in the Assyrian and Babylonian empires, would think of the legendary Abraham as their progenitor, even though the most powerful of the Abraham legends said both that Sarah was barren as Abraham's wife *and* that she was the mother of Isaac. Is it possible that Isaac was an illegitimate son of Abraham? Or was Isaac, as the father of JACOB (traditionally the father of the sons who formed the twelve tribes of Israel) considered to be a necessary link in the chain of necessary ancestors of the Hebrews?

All of this is the sort of muddle to be expected when written literature is based on hoary legends from an antiquity we can scarcely imagine. These legends were unsystematically incorporated into what became a sacred text by writers without modern standards of consistency and clarity. We should not hold the use to which these legends were put against the compilers of them, but we can set the tales of Abraham beside those of the legendary King Arthur, Siegfried, and the Irish kings. The early part of the Old Testament, at least, appears to consist of the legends and imaginative stories of one small group of tribes who traveled around the Fertile Crescent during the Bronze Age. The mischief arises when historical accuracy is claimed today to justify land titles in Israel and deportations of people with different origin-stories.

If we were to take Sarah seriously—that is, literally, as fundamentalists in both Orthodox Judaism and retrograde Christianity wish us to do— she sounds like a character in a television soap opera, with the usual seductions and mysterious, not altogether plausible, revelations about key characters.

In defense of Sarah, it is sometimes observed, correctly enough, that in giving her handmaiden Hagar to her husband to bear him children, she was simply following the custom of her time. Those who accept this explanation so readily would be unlikely to do so were the subject of debate to be the relativity of morals. Today, any woman who encouraged her husband to have sexual relations with her maid would be considered to be aiding and abetting adultery.

SERMON ON THE MOUNT. I have had a nagging question in the back of my mind for some years concerning Matthew 5, Verse 13, where JESUS tells the multitude:

> "You are the salt of the earth; but if salt has lost its taste, how shall its saltiness be restored? It is no longer good for anything except to be thrown out and trodden underfoot by men."

This observation perplexed me, for I was aware that provisions of salt many years old, kept in our home, nevertheless remained salty to the taste. Accordingly, one day I wrote to various salt companies with the question "Can salt lose its savor?" The answer was a clear-cut no. A letter from the Morton Salt Company said: ". . . salt does not lose its saltiness—literally salt does not become less salty upon storage or with age."

If Jesus believed that it was possible for salt to lose its savor, then the fact is inconsistent with the hypothesis that he was the most intelligent man who ever lived simply because he was in actuality God.

Matthew 5. Although the fundamentalist branch of Protestantism tends to deprecate "good works," Jesus says, in Verse 16:

> ". . . similarly let your light shine among people, so that they may observe your good works and give glory to your heavenly Father."

Verse 18 presents a puzzling problem. Jesus is quoted as saying:

> "For truly I say unto you, until heaven and earth pass away, not the smallest letter or stroke shall pass away from the Law, until all is accomplished."

The first element of the difficulty is that it is not possible to say with any assurance precisely what is meant by the phrase "until all is accomplished."

All what? Surely the meaning cannot be that every command of the OLD TESTAMENT shall, at some future time, actually be obeyed. It is clear enough that no such thing has ever occurred. But it is more important to understand that there is neither the practical nor even the abstract possibility of such a state of affairs, partly for the reason that certain portions of the Old Testament contradict other portions.

In the next verse Jesus speaks harshly of those who abolish "the least significant of these commands." But the Jews themselves have long ceased to observe certain of the recommendations of the PENTATEUCH, and there is an even greater number of Christians who are not obedient to them.

The reader is now urged to refer to the article on the COMMANDMENTS, which we are told came from face-to-face conversations between MOSES and God on Sinai. It will be recalled that a great many Commandments were given, far more than the traditional ten. It will also be recalled that the Catholic church, among others, teaches that the original commandments were intended for the Jews only. This astonishing teaching, is, of course, somewhat modified by the assertion that among the many Commandments are some worthy of respect because of their inherent moral reasonableness. This may well be the case but there cannot be the slightest question but that it logically excludes the statement of Jesus: "Whoever then relaxes one of the *least of these commandments* and teaches men so, shall be called least in the kingdom of heaven . . ." (v. 19). (IA)

There is a suggestion of intolerance here, in that the offense of which Jesus is critical does not seem to merit the pains of eternal torment, but he is strongly critical of such behavior nevertheless. A moment later, perhaps feeling that he has sounded too lenient a note, Jesus adds:

> 20. "For I tell you, unless your righteouness exceeds that of the scribes and pharisees, you will never enter the Kingdom of Heaven."

The commandent "Thou shalt not kill" is certainly direct. Those who believe it is permissible to kill in wartime and in self-defense prefer the rendering "Thou shalt not murder." But it is significant that Jesus used the Aramaic word for *kill*—not that for *murder*—in his next admonition.

> 21. "You have heard that it was said to the men of old, 'You shall not kill; and whoever kills shall be liable to judgment.'
> 22. "But I say to you that everyone who is angry with his brother shall be liable to judgment; whoever insults his brother shall be liable to the council, and whoever says 'You fool' shall be liable to the hell of fire."

It has generally been held that Jesus was on firm moral ground here, although there was nothing in the Old Testament law that even remotely discouraged anger and insults. What we find, in hundreds of instances in the Old Testament, are examples of great anger and verbal assault by Almighty God himself.

The admonition concerning the specific insult "You fool" has puzzled theologians for centuries. It is not that these gentlemen recommend the insult, but rather that they are puzzled as to why it should have been singled out for punishment in HELL.

The astonishing imbalance between the punishment and the crime would be apparent to anyone past the age of reason. How then do we explain that one who was either God or at least his most precious Son *made precisely a recommendation that from anyone else we would instantly consider cruel?* The fact is we cannot explain it.

We may be quite certain that of the millions of Catholics who this week will confess their sins not a one will confess to having called someone a fool, although tens of thousands of them may have done so.

Another portion of the Sermon on the Mount which has troubled many of the devout is the following:

29. "If your right eye causes you to sin, pluck it out and throw it away; it is better that you lose one of your members than that your whole body be thrown into hell.

30. "And if your right hand causes you to sin, cut it off and throw it away; it is better that you lose one of your members than that your whole body go into hell."

This dramatic illustration has frequently been held against Jesus, but on purely logical grounds it is not easy to see why. If we start with the assumption that (1) there is indeed such a thing as the actual, literal flames of Hell and that (2) untold millions of poor souls and bodies have been relegated to such a horrible place, then (3) I'm sure we would agree that every one of them would gladly change his state if the only price he had to pay was the sacrifice of one hand or one eye. The argument is not, of course, persuasive to those who think that belief in Hell is itself atrocious and/or ridiculous.

In Verses 33 to 37 Jesus refers to the Old Testament instructions not to swear falsely. But he goes much farther than that in saying "make no oath at all." He advises those who are asked to affirm that they are speaking the truth to simply say yes or no. Verse 37 says, "anything beyond these is of evil." There is simply no evading the clear message that the millions of law-abiding Christians who have been formally swearing to one thing or another for the past 2,000 years are committing this evil act at the direct instigation of the Devil. All over the world at this very moment large numbers of Christians are raising their hands—to God—or placing a hand on a copy of the Scriptures and doing precisely what Jesus absolutely forbids.

The list of problems with the sermon of Jesus is continued right through to Verse 48, which tells us, "Therefore you are to be perfect, as your heavenly

Father is perfect."

To speak as plainly as possible, this recommends what is literally impossible. No human being can be perfect. The mere idea of perfection properly applies only to God. We could convert the statement into something far more reasonable by rendering it as, "Therefore you must strive toward the perfection of your heavenly Father." Unfortunately, fundamentalists absolutely forbid any such revisions of difficult portions of Scripture, and in one sense they are perfectly right in doing so. It is no fair solution to the endless problems found in the Bible to "solve" them by simply rewriting for ourselves certain passages.

Matthew 6. If Jesus is accurately quoted in Verse 5, when he forbids his followers to pray like hypocrites, in public, to be seen by the people, he appears to rule out a kind of prayer common among fundamentalists. In Verse 6 he says:

> "But you, when you pray go into your inner room, and when you have shut your door, pray to your Father who is in secret, and your Father who sees in secret will repay you."

He also offers, in the following verse, advice that the Catholic church has totally ignored for almost 2,000 years.

> "And when you are praying, do not use meaningless repetition, as the Gentiles do, for they suppose that they will be heard for their many words."

In Verse 19 Jesus has advice that must dismay any capitalist Christian:

> "Do not lay up for yourself treasures upon earth, where moth and rust destroy and where thieves do break in or steal."

In Verse 21 he continues, "for where your treasure is, there will your heart be also."

Matthew 7. The first verse has probably been ignored by almost every Christian who has ever lived, "Do not judge lest you be judged." So far as pointing to the sins of others, Christians are a remarkably judgmental and censorious group. It can be argued that they should be, because there is a great deal of evil in the world, and it might well be the case that sin and evil should be criticized daily from the rooftops. But if this is so, then we are forced to conclude that Jesus was mistaken and that he offered foolish advice in this instance. Christians cannot have it both ways since it is obvious that the two views logically exclude one another.

One of the most staggering assertions in all Scripture is attributed to Jesus in Verses 13 and 14. After referring to the many who take the road to destruction he says, "For the gate is small, and the way is narrow that leads to life, and *few are those who find it.*" (IA) It is difficult to attach a precise number to the word *few,* but it obviously means a small minority. Let us be generous and say that *few* can be translated into 20 percent of Jesus' followers. It is then logically inescapable that Jesus is asserting that some 80 percent of God's sons and daughters are doomed to an eternity in the flames of Hell.

The famous warning against false prophets presents a difficulty in the analogy that Jesus draws, in Verses 15 through 20, when he asks if it is possible for a bad tree to produce good fruit. Unfortunately for the integrity of the analogy, the answer is—yes, it is perfectly possible. I have three small and stunted fruit trees. Some years they do not produce a good crop but in other years one of the trees produces large, beautiful, and extremely juicy lemons while another produces apricots of superb quality.

But, returning to the matter of false prophets, it is doubtful that even the worst prophet of all time, whoever he might have been, spoke nothing but lies and evil. Indeed, who would bother to listen to a false prophet if he lied all the time? It is obvious that all the prophets who have ever lived, all the theologians, popes, cardinals, bishops, ministers, rabbis, and lay lecturers have produced neither pure evil nor pure virtue and wisdom but that mixture of the two which is perfectly characteristic of human behavior.

In Verse 25, Jesus makes a highly questionable assertion when he says that if a house is built not on sand but on a rock it cannot collapse, even if attacked by floods and winds. Any child can see that houses built on firm foundations are more secure than those without such an advantage, but it's simply error to say that a house will certainly stand if it is built on firm foundations. Floods, hurricanes, earthquakes, tornadoes, typhoons, and other natural disasters are constantly destroying houses built on the firmest of foundations.

Hence, we see that even in one of the most highly acclaimed of all religious texts, the Sermon on the Mount, there is much that is wrong, shallow, or so obvious that any child might have said it. If Jesus did, indeed, preach marvelous, wise sermons, his illiterate disciples did not remember them accurately. Or perhaps he did not preach; perhaps these sermons were made up by not very well-educated (and unknown) men whose literary gifts or wisdom was not great. It is hard to understand, however, why Jesus should be considered the Son of or God himself on the basis of some of his quoted words.

SEX, WOMEN, AND RELIGION. While a good many things in Scripture, after hundreds of years of reputable scholarship, remain relatively confused and obscure, it is nevertheless the case that certain other ideas are absolutely clear and not subject to debate. One of these is a belief in the inferiority of women. In the apocryphal book of Ecclesiasticus (47:14) we read, "The badness of men is better then the goodness of women." The learned scholar Joseph McCabe reported, "Even in the older and more official books the mothers are condemned to do twice as long a penance for bearing a female as for a male child."

It is clear that Jews and Christians have by no means been alone in consigning women to an inferior status and in treating them accordingly, but this is no excuse for their doing so.

Good-hearted but relatively uninformed Christians might assume that, while there is no denying the shameful treatment accorded women in various Old Testament tales, the situation was vastly improved by the arrival of the beloved JESUS upon the scene. Would that it were so. While Jesus appears to have been a remarkably affectionate and compassionate individual, there is no evidence (1) that he ever addressed the problem of the disgraceful treatment of women during the thousands of years before his own birth, or (2) that he instituted procedures or beliefs to establish more just, humane treatment for womankind.

While PAUL by no means initiated the moral aversion to sex that has been such an essential element of Christian teaching for the past 2,000 years, he restated, with remarkable vigor and clarity, the case for contempt of women, including the hundreds of millions of them who have been married to Christian men over the centuries.

One aspect of the larger problem concerns the basic natural phenomenon of sexual attraction for the purpose of perpetuating all species. Nature has provided an intricate series of ways that normal, healthy males of all species would be strongly attracted by the mere sight of an attractive female. Given that this is something as perfectly natural as the human appetite for liquid and food, it was inevitable that the disgust with which many religious philosophers have viewed the feminine half of the human race would be no more readily accepted as moral advice than would the suggestion that, because of the sin of gluttony, one ought therefore to drink or eat absolutely nothing.

The writings of St. Jerome, St. Gregory of Nyssa, St. Ambrose, Origen, Clement, and other early fathers of the church simply carried on a tradition of aversion to sex as well as an aversion to women on the grounds that they provoked men to want sex.

As regards total abstention from sexual thought, word, or deed, we have no way of knowing if there is a single individual who has ever achieved it. That there are a few such people as virgins is clear enough, but it cannot be argued that because a woman has had no sexual contact with a male, she has eschewed all sexuality. In addition, there is no lack of evidence that millions of people who are unmarried—and even those who are—nevertheless perform the entirely natural act of self-stimulation to the point of orgasm.

It is quite probable that the majority of the human race has, at one time or another, wondered why God created this supreme pleasure, when many of his prophets and priests have told us that sex is degrading, vulgar, dirty, and essentially evil—unless it is engaged in for the specific purpose of creating a new life.

We also know, from the testimony of perfectly decent men who have left the Catholic priesthood that, although as priests they fully intended and hoped to lead a totally chaste life, they had in fact found it impossible to continue to do so.

Even the strictest theologians will concede that we are not morally responsible for whatever bizarre visions we see in our dreams, and we know that all sexually healthy men and women have erotic dreams of a sometimes remarkably pictorial sort. In young men such night visions commonly lead to a remarkable emission of a fluid that nature and/or God has designed for purpose of lubrication. In some people the dream-dramas are so intense as to lead to orgasm and, in the case of males, ejaculation of sperm.

Volumes have been written on male and female sexuality; it suffices to say here that abstention from sex is a remarkable moral ideal that is lived up to by a statistically insignificant percentage of well-intentioned Christians. Many of those who don't, used to—it is much less so at the end of the 20th century—be assailed by powerful storms of guilt and feelings of moral worthlessness. Indeed the more spiritually superior a young, healthy Christian is, the more intense will be the guilt occasioned by the inability to practice the ascetic ideal, whereas less conscientious individuals merely disregard preachments on such matters and arrange for the enjoyment of as much sexual pleasure as their social and financial circumstances might permit, with relatively little guilt.

It is important to explain that I am not exaggerating the historical Christian case against women and sexuality. Do most Catholics, for example, know that though Jesus said that love of money was the root of all evil St. Jerome thought that this was a perfect description of women, or that St. Ambrose, speaking to the women of his congregation, said, "God took a rib out of Adam's body, not a part of his soul" in making women and moreover that "she was not made of the image of God as man was"?

Once I came across a letter in the *Star-Ledger* of Patterson, N.J., that asserted that "those who regard sex itself as dirty and sinful" do so because "the Bible tells them so." This is a part-truth; the true situation is far more complex. I see no reason to doubt that for thousands of years before the various portions of the Scriptures were written there must have been many conflicting views about sex. It seems to me that there are two kinds of reasons why people are suspicious and fearful of what is clearly a natural phenomenon. To the extent that the Bible can be blamed for overtly puritanical attitudes, it is merely because it repeats ancient beliefs founded on these two reasons.

It is interesting that those who disapprove of sex often use the word *dirty* to describe it. I believe it is the very commonness of the word that provides a valuable clue to the mystery. The sense of dirtiness comes, I think, from nothing more mysterious than the fact that either God or nature contrived to place the organs of sex near or with those of elimination. Both human urine and fecal matter are waste products, generally malodorous and unappealing to all of the senses.

In former times, the mouth and orifices of elimination were quite unappealing. Vast and profitable industries exist in the present to provide soaps, toothpastes, mouthwashes, douches, bidets, and other artifacts connected with personal hygiene but that was not always so. In ages past, therefore, the simple fact of sexual appetites brought male and female into passionate copulatory contact that was probably diminished by the necessity of putting up with assorted odors.

The mistake was to assume that *dirty* equals *evil.*

As for the other understandable reason for the widespread fear, disgust, and distrust which many humans, even in the modern world, associate with sex, it has to do with the fact that the sexual appetite is notoriously anarchic, embarrassingly difficult—and at moments impossible—to control. Whether an individual willingly gives himself to the fullest possible and most often repeated sexual function or, out of moral or other considerations, tries to either diminish the sex drive itself or at least inhibit its acting out, almost all of us are sadly familiar with our inability to make relevant decisions purely on the basis of rational considerations. Not only is there a long list of sexual illnesses and depravities, almost all of which seem to have an obsessive-compulsive component to them, but even within the spectrum of healthy, normal sexual behavior this one human function, above all others, is unruly and restive under attempts by the will to control it. The sexual function is not the only one, of course, that is difficult to govern.

While presently celibate Catholic priests may assume that their difficulties would be over if they were simply permitted to marry, every married individual knows that the clergymen who might either be granted such relative freedom or simply take it without permission are but opening a door to a new way of life that has its own problems. A man may be married to "the most wonderful woman in the world," as the old saying has it, and yet in some situations find himself strongly tempted to establish sexual contact with another woman, either on a one-time basis or in the context of an ongoing relationship. And vice versa.

There are those who, addressing this particular aspect of sex, assume that it was a mistake to abandon the ancient practice, sanctioned in the Old Testament, of polygamy. Man is naturally polygamous, goes that particular argument, and there is not the slightest possibility of guilt about the matter if one lives in cultures and societies that condone the practice. It can hardly come as news to any reader past the age of ten that as regards sex there is simply no overall solution, no golden path whose traversing prevents sexual frustrations and problems.

Some of these problems, of course, are purely physical. One may contract AIDS, gonorrhea, syphilis, herpes, or other venereal infections. Other sorts of sexual problems are largely psychological and/or emotional. If we lived on a planet where there was some sort of activity that provided the pleasures now available only from sex except for the fact that new offspring were found wrapped in cabbage leaves or delivered by storks, the general array of sexual problems would be quite different. But we must deal with the reality that characterizes our world, and part of that reality is that the polygamous tendency in many men—and its equivalent in not a few women—runs counter to the orderly conduct of home life and the raising of children. Sexual promiscuity among the married, then, often leads to divorce, which in turn has destructive effects on the tender minds and hearts of the young. So that is the other reason why sexual problems will always trouble humanity. Those who wrote the Old Testament, then, were simply mindful of much, if not all of this, and cannot be blamed for having caused such difficulties in the first place.

SLAUGHTER OF THE INNOCENTS. Perhaps the strangest thing about the tale of the killing of innocent children by Herod is that although it is a strikingly dramatic story and certainly deals with an important subject, it appears only in the Gospel of MATTHEW (2:16). There is no reference to it in MARK, LUKE, or JOHN. Rationalist critics have suspected this casts strong doubt on its authenticity.

T. W. Doane, in *Bible Myths and Their Parallels in Other Religions* (1882), points out that "the myth of the dangerous child" has been part of the life story of various religious leaders such as Lord Krishna, Salivahana, and the Buddha. Doane comments:

> When a marvelous occurrence is said to have happened everywhere, we may feel sure that it has never happened anywhere. Popular fancies propagate themselves indefinitely, but historical events, especially the striking and dramatic ones, are rarely repeated.
>
> That this is a fictitious story is seen from the narratives of the birth of Jesus, which are recorded by the first and third Gospel writers, without any other evidence. In the one—that related by the Matthew narrator—we have a birth at Bethlehem—implying the ordinary residence of the parents there—and a hurried flight almost immediately after the birth from that place into Egypt, the slaughter of the infants, and a journey, after many months, from Egypt to Nazareth in Galilee. In the other story—that told by the Luke narrator—the parents, who have lived in Nazareth, came to Bethlehem only for business of the State, and the casual birth in the cave or stable is followed by a quiet sojourn, during which the child is circumcised, and by a leisurely journey to Jerusalem; . . . *There is no fear of Herod, who seems never to trouble himself about the child, or even to have any knowledge of him. There is no trouble or misery at Bethlehem, and certainly no mourning for children slain.* Far from flying hurriedly away by night, his parents celebrate openly, and at the usual time, the circumcision of the child; and when he is presented in the temple, there is not only no sign that enemies seek his life, but the devout saints give public thanks for the manifestation of the Savior. (IA)

The historian Josephus, who provides detailed information on many crimes and atrocities committed by Herod, makes no mention of the slaughter of all male children under two in the region of Bethlehem, a crime which— had it occurred—would certainly have occasioned widespread comment at the time.

SOLOMON. See KINGS, FIRST.

SUMERIANS. It is important, if one takes the Old Testament seriously, to know more about the Sumerians than the average person has the opportunity to learn. They were not, like the Hebrews, a small tribe of obscure people, but were the developers of a great civilization, perhaps the first. They may have come from the area of the Black and Caspian seas, from which they moved southwest to occupy lower Mesopotamia. Finding their new territory dotted with marshes, they set about the task of drainage, and then dug networks of ditches and canals to irrigate their fields, which otherwise would have baked in the sun.

At a later stage of Sumerian development, independent city-states emerged. One such city was Ur; others were Uruk, Larsa, Umma, and Lagash. For a thousand years the powerful Sumerian civilization flourished. The Sumerians developed a writing system on clay tablets and produced a literature, out of which came a number of remarkable epic poems, many of which concern a legendary figure called Gilgamesh. The poems give details of the creation of the world and of a great flood.

The significance of the information given in this brief outline of Sumer is that this civilization, with its highly developed religion and laws, existed *long before* that of the authors of the books of the Old Testament. Israelite culture, literature, and religion, in other words, did not influence the Sumerians; the influence ran in precisely the opposite direction at one period for the Semitic-speaking tribes, before they emerged as Israelites. It will also be helpful to the reader attempting to place the Old Testament in its proper context to be aware that the Sumerian city-states fell under the sway of a new tribe, the Akkadians, around 2300 B.C., under King Sargon I. Sargon and his successors united the Sumerian city-states, making Akkad the new empire's capital. It was the Sumerians, not MOSES, who gave the world its first code of laws. (See also AUTHORSHIP OF THE BIBLE; ENUMA ELISH AND GILGAMESH; FLOOD, THE; PROPHETS; OLD TESTAMENT.)

T

TIMOTHY, FIRST. For many centuries the Christian church has confidently asserted that the document identified as the first epistle to Timothy was written by PAUL. One can certainly see why Paul's authorship was assumed. If we were to find a message identified as the first letter of George Washington to Thomas Jefferson, we would be unlikely to suppose that it was actually written by James Madison or John Adams. But the church, nevertheless, now concedes that it was wrong and that Paul, in fact, did not write First Timothy. It does not follow, however, that there is no profit to be gained from reading the letter.

If the letter was not written by Paul, it is reasonable to ask if anyone named Timothy received it and, if he did, did he recognize Paul's name as a forgery? To the theologically immature, it seems shocking even to raise such questions. Unfortunately, it is the Bible itself which gives rise to them, not the hardness of heart of any scholars or critics.

Chapter 1. In Verse 4 the author says, "Neither give heed to fables and endless genealogies." Now that is eminently sound advice. One wishes that the writer had been specific about the fables that we need give no heed to. Are any of them to be found in the Bible? The advice about endless genealogies is also reasonable, largely because claims of perfect knowledge about long lists of ancestors have always been suspect. Even in the modern day, with greatly enriched opportunities for record-keeping, few people know anything definite about their ancestry more than five generations back. Is the writer referring to the two different genealogies of JESUS in the Gospels and the many lists in the Old Testament?

As a young Christian I was taught that, while it was all too painfully evident that the ranks of Christianity were hopelessly divided—and it was also obvious that an extremely small percentage of the fellow-Christians I knew seemed exemplary representatives of the faith they professed—it had nevertheless in the early days been otherwise. The record of history, alas, shows that this has never been the case. Even a casual reading of documents written by Paul, or by others using his name, show constant deviations from the faith, at least as Paul perceived it.

In this first chapter we read of problems:

> 6. Certain persons by swerving from these [love, pure heart, good conscience] have wandered away into vain discussion,
> 7. desiring to be teachers of the law, without understanding either what they are saying, or the things about which they make assertions.

The unknown author, starting with Verse 9, makes an interesting though debatable point: "The law is not made for a righteous man, but for the lawless and disobedient, for the ungodly and for sinners."

TOLERATION. The assumption that critics of a faith should be tolerated—which is to say, at the very least, not physically attacked, arrested, imprisoned, tortured or executed—is quite a modern idea and one by no means as yet universally accepted, as we see in the case of Salman Rushdie. It is but one small aspect of the larger modern experiment with freedom, which itself has never yet gained planetwide acceptance. Inasmuch as most people are quite insistent on their own freedom, they therefore make the irrational leap to the assumption that this somehow establishes that they are in favor of freedom itself. The difficult moment, of course, comes when such alleged defenders of freedom are brought into contact with those whose views they consider abhorrent or socially dangerous.

The authenticity of the Bible cannot possibly be said to stand or fall on the grounds of such considerations. It remains only to emphasize that those who are not in a position to address a large audience usually do not perceive the common process by which the social critic is punished.

Wherever it might be that the emotions generally considered uniquely Christian—those of compassion, cheek-turning, tolerance, unselfish love—are assumed to flow, they clearly have not been directed historically toward those who so much as question an article of faith. Christian attacks on freethinkers and other heretics have generally been quite severe. In the case of some blunt-speaking rationalists, this is perhaps understandable because these critics of dogma have spoken in strident tones themselves.

Once the validity of the True Faith is assumed, it cannot be tolerated that any public jury should be impressed by the charm, rationality, and decency of some of its critics. Therefore, not only their arguments but also they personally must be opposed and criticized, as bitterly as is thought necessary, lest their fair-mindedness be a reproach to the Faith.

This has, of course, been the case for centuries, but is even more so in the present age, since now the public expression of an opinion can reach a very wide audience through the press, radio, television, films, or tape-recordings. The difference today, however, is that in modern democracies expression is protected, and heretics and nonbelievers cannot be burned at the stake.

TRINITY, THE. Although practically all Catholics and a good many Protestants assert that the doctrine of the Trinity—three persons but somehow only one God—is of the most enormous and central importance, the puzzling fact remains that it never occurred to the author of JOHN to mention the subject in his Gospel.

Nor does it appear in any other Gospel. Unfortunately for the idea of clarity, when the concept of God the Father, his Son, and his Spirit is referred to, in the First Letter of John, the analogy drawn is of no help in explaining what even St. Augustine eventually conceded was un-explainable. In the Letter we find: "There are three witnesses, the Spirit, the water, and the blood" (5:8). How these relate to the Trinity is never explained.

There is simply no way of knowing what the author meant—by saying that water is somehow a witness of God. There are, of course, certain conclusions that might be drawn from an examination of a given amount of water. One could make a chemical analysis of it; one could determine whether it was "hard" or "soft"; one could determine whether there were microorganisms in it that would make it unsafe to drink. But if this is all that the author had in mind, then we are up against meaninglessness because if this sort of thing can be said of water, it can be said of every object in the universe.

As for blood, the difficulties are no less severe. To the extent that blood can bear witness, nothing was known of the matter until quite recently when it became possible to analyze the various types of blood and therefore do several things: (1) determine paternity; (2) use blood type as evidence in some kinds of criminal cases; (3) determine whether a newborn baby's blood is incompatible with its mother's and order a blood transfusion.

Whatever might have been the author's purpose in communicating with his early Christian brethren and sisters about the concept of three-persons-but-only-one-God, the method he chose can hardly have been intended as an attempt at explanation. But let us examine the text further. "There are three that bear witness in heaven, The Father, The Word and The Spirit, and these three are one." Again, this is an assertion and in no sense an explanation. If we assume that there is a God, and that, in some vague sense not entirely grasped, his natural habitat is a not-quite-possible-to-define place called HEAVEN, it is certainly reasonable to believe that God can do anything whatever in his Heaven, including bear witness.

Consider the term "to bear witness." It simply means to communicate something in a setting in which there is a call for evidence, that call being expressed either from the ground of total neutrality, or challenging doubt. One cannot bear witness in the abstract any more than one can speak in the abstract. If we speak, we speak about something. So the author's statement, then, boils down to nothing more remarkable than the assertion that God can communicate, can testify in Heaven.

W

WISE MEN, or **MAGI.** Not only is there nothing in the New Testament itself suggesting that the strange visitors to JESUS' birthplace were three in number but also there are no clues as to exactly how many came to Bethlehem. Early Eastern Orthodox tradition held that there were 12 visitors. An ancient painting in the cemetery of Sts. Peter and Marcellinus in Rome shows two and, according to Manly Palmer Hall, president of the Philosophical Research Society, an early vase shows the group as numbering eight.

A paragraph written by Richard Frohnen, religious editor of the *Los Angeles Times* (Dec. 25, 1960), referring to the views of Hall, stands as an all too typical instance of a certain kind of thinking, writing, and preaching on religious subject matter:

> By the time of Pope Leo I (A.D. 390–461) the idea that there were three Magi had gained popularity and they *gradually became symbols of the Trinity, of the three parts of the earth, and of the three divisions of the human race* descended from the sons of Noah, according to Hall. (IA)

The reader's attention is directed to the italicized portions—ideas that should not be blamed on Hall or Frohnen, since presumably they report a traditional view about the Magi. What the passage reveals is a form of substitute for thought that is asinine. Consider first the symbolic interpretation of the three Magi as *the Trinity.*

Why? On what evidence? There is no doubt that an endless series of speculative assertions can be made in response to these questions, but they will be no more convincing than an equally lengthy list of arguments supporting the hypothesis that the Andrews Sisters may be viewed, symbolically, as representative of the TRINITY.

Preposterous? Consider: (1) the Andrews Sisters, too, are three in number; (2) they reached great multitudes; (3) they brought joy to millions of hearts; (4) they were themselves religious believers; (5) they traversed the earth in airplanes, bringing glad tidings to many parts of the world. But why continue?

As for the three parts of the earth, is it necessary to point out that the earth is *not* divided into three parts? As for the three divisions of the human race, is it necessary to tell even a well-educated schoolchild that there are no such clearcut divisions?

WITCHCRAFT. It is depressing to realize how the degree of distance from the scene of a calamity decreases our sensitivity to it. One man killed in our presence, with his blood spattering our shoes, produces in us a more profound emotional reaction than does the news of ten such deaths only a mile away. Just so, distance in time also dulls us to the horror of past tragedies. When we read of the slaughter of untold thousands of poor women said to be witches, in allegedly civilized and Christian Europe, we treat this merely as a sad abstraction and rarely trouble ourselves to perceive such dramas as a series of specific horrifying tragedies.

Some authorities believe that 300,000 innocent women were killed *by both Catholic and Protestant churches* between 1484 and 1782. Some of this can be attributed to the Catholic Inquisition and some to the hysteria of extremist Puritans of New England.

In less than an hour, the Parliament of Toulouse, France, publicly burned 400 unfortunate women, having convicted them of crimes that existed only in the deluded minds of their sentencers. Five hundred women were burned at the stake in the city of Geneva in one month, and approximately a thousand were murdered in the Italian province of Como. A French judge, over the course of 16 years, could boast that he had sentenced some 800 women to the stake. This entire vast atrocity was said to be "justified" by the Bible. In reality, it is the Bible that is blackened by such crimes.

It is common knowledge that even in the present day there are women who regard themselves as witches. Some of these, no doubt, are simply deceitful manipulators, taking advantage of that gullibility which has always been one of the human race's less endearing characteristics, but others appear to be honestly under the impression that they are somehow set apart from the rest of us by possessing certain powers.

Still others call themselves witches in deference to what they term "the Old Religion," which they say preceded Christianity in Europe and was persecuted out of existence by the earliest priests and bishops. One of their reasons for harking back to this pre-Christian era is because they believe women played an important role as diviners, priestesses, etc.

The fact that no woman who calls herself a witch wants to say, to professional skeptical investigators, "Not only am I indeed a witch but I shall be happy to present myself at any time and place of your choosing for the purpose of demonstrating my remarkable abilities," seems to carry very little weight in our society. Its members not only have been given no training in critical, analytical thinking but also seem, by and large, unable to exercise such modest gifts for reason as they might otherwise have developed.

Some self-named witches write and publish "philosophical" and partly explanatory tracts, but I have found nothing in them that would make a reader say, "Aha, there are witches after all."

The traditional description of witches' black pointed hats, broomsticks, and muttered incantations is the stuff of children's story writers, and the evil repute assigned them came from their "enemies" in the churches. The fact that it took the churches so long to stamp out "witchcraft" (that is, a pre-Christian nature religion) and that the job was really done by rationalism and the 18th-century Enlightenment only shows how deeply rooted this "old religion" actually was.

Many Christians in our time are not only convinced that the hundreds of thousands (some authorities say millions) of women who were killed because they were thought to be witches were indeed such but also that there are true witches present in the United States and England.

Since the Bible clearly says that witches should be killed, it is not clear why there are no personal assaults, legal or illegal, on such individuals in our society at present. The Christian Reconstructionists are consistent on this point. They assert that the Bible is quite right in the matter and that witches indeed *must* be put to death. They add that such a campaign of slaughter will start as soon as the Reconstructionists' program has been successful enough to bring a majority of Americans around to their view.

A Christian Reconstructionist of my acquaintance has told me that a proper translation of the word *witch* is *poisoner*. Those who poison others, who murder them by that means are subject to whatever punishment the law prescribes. According to *Webster's Dictionary,* he is wrong. The root appears to come from Old High German *wih,* meaning "holy." Christian churches, when witch-burning took place, did not argue that the reason for killing men and women believed to be witches was that they killed others by poisoning them.

No one should forget that it was the dawning light of reason, of what is generally called the Enlightenment, the gradually emerging sun of Humanist thought (in which, thank God, some Christians were compassionate enough to participate) that put a stop to this hideous drama.

WYCLIFFE, JOHN (1320?–1384). Although the name Wycliffe means nothing to those nations speaking Russian, Chinese, or Portuguese, it does have importance in the English-speaking parts of the world, since Wycliffe was the first to translate the Scriptures into English, in about 1382. While it might be assumed that such a virtuous task would be warmly greeted, the reaction was the reverse. The fury of the criticism of Wycliffe was so great, in fact, that after his death his bones were dug up and burned and the ashes cast into a river. Latin and Greek were considered the only acceptable languages for Christians to read the Bible, which meant that very few could read it.

Wycliffe was a reformer, who denied the doctrine of transubstantiation and declared that the Bible, not the Catholic church, was the authority for Christian beliefs. Later, Protestant Reformation leaders considered Wycliffe an important forerunner.

Y

YAHWEH. Although I have consulted the writing of hundreds of authorities on the Scriptures, both believers and nonbelievers, I have been unable to locate any suggestion that the actual God of the universe (in a monotheistic religion) could possibly have a personal name. In a polytheistic context, when there are many gods, it obviously is necessary for each one to have a name. But if it is impossible for there to be more than one God, as Jews, Christians, and Muslims believe, it follows that it is patently absurd for that God to have a personal name.

In our general ignorance about such things, we might mistakenly assume that the word *Yahweh* is simply an ancient word that can be translated as *God*. But this is not the case. It was the designation of an individual, in no way different from the names Joseph, Moses, or John. The likely explanation of the fact that Hebrews gave God this name is that it was conceived in an era either when the ancient Hebrews believed in many gods or when they lived among people who had many gods with proper names.

YAHWIST, THE, also known as "J," or the Yahwistic source. According to a consensus developed in the 19th century among biblical scholars, the Yahwist was one of four strands that could be "isolated" in the PENTATEUCH.

William H. Stiebing, Jr., historian and author of *Out of the Desert?: Archaeology and the Exodus/Conquest Narratives* (Buffalo: Prometheus Books, 1989) points out:

> The Exodus story generally has been regarded as a composite account formed by blending together all of these sources. . . . Scholars usually assert that the earliest material about the Exodus is contained in the J tradition, generally thought to have been written down in the tenth century B.C., during the reign of Solomon or soon after his death.

However, after noting that Genesis and Numbers were thought to have "J" strands, Stiebing then explains newer scholarly thinking about Pentateuch authorship.

> But in recent years a number of scholars have argued persuasively that the Yahwistic material in the Pentateuch was *composed or collected during or after* the Babylonian Exile rather than in the tenth century B.C. If these scholars are correct, *historians could not assume the historical accuracy of any of the Pentateuchal traditions.* (IA)

In other words, nothing in the first five books of the Bible may be historical. Rather, the stories in GENESIS and EXODUS of the Hebrews' beginnings were a combination of much earlier Mesopotamian legends and the Hebrews' own fictional constructions.

Perhaps it would help the reader to place this startling information in perspective by setting the Pentateuch beside the Arthurian legends. No one can prove that Abraham, Joseph and his family, and Moses did not exist, just as no one can prove that a King Arthur did not rule a portion of historical England; but the accounts of both periods are so overlaid with myth and were written down so long after both are said to have occurred that it is unwise to believe that either the Arthurian romance or the Pentateuch contain any historical reality.

This is not to say that the Pentateuch is worthless. It gives the modern, unbiased reader a clear notion of how the 6th or 5th century Jews returning to Palestine after the Exile thought of themselves as they set about reconstructing their society from the shambles caused by Assyrian (722 B.C.) and Babylonian (586 B.C.) conquests of the divided kingdoms of Israel and Judah.

Z

ZECHARIAH, a Hebrew priest who lived at the time JESUS was born. The husband of Elizabeth, Mary's cousin, and the father of JOHN THE BAPTIST, he was another of those elderly men whose wives were barren, a type that abounds in the Bible.

Zechariah, too, had an angel, Gabriel, appear before him to announce his son's birth. The angel noted that the fetus would be filled with the Holy Spirit even in the womb, and implied that the child would grow up to be the equal of the great Elijah (Luke 1:15–17). This story appears only in LUKE, not in the other three Gospels.

It was shortly after this episode, according to Luke, that Gabriel appeared to Mary and told her that she too, although a virgin, would conceive and bear a son. The wording in Luke (1:35–37) implies that Mary and Elizabeth conceived in the same way. "For with God nothing will be impossible," says the angel. The implication in the Bible that women other than Mary had miraculous conceptions is overlooked by those who insist on the divine origin of Jesus. (See also SARAH.)

The purpose for the miracle that befell Zechariah's family is beautifully expressed by Zechariah himself after John was born.

> 71. "that we should be saved from our enemies,
> and from the hand of all who hate us;
> 72. to perform the mercy promised to our fathers,
> . . . .
> 74. to grant us that we, being delivered from the
> hand of our enemies,
> might serve him without fear,
> 75. in holiness and righteousness before him all the
> days of our life.
> 76. And you, child [John], will be called the prophet
> of the Most High;
> for you will go before the Lord to prepare his ways,

77. to give knowledge of salvation to his people
    in the forgiveness of their sins,
78. through the tender mercy of our God,
    when the day shall dawn upon us from on high
79. to give light to those who sit in darkness and in
        the shadow of death,
    to guide our feet into the way of peace."

Conclusion

No doubt some of my Christian friends, and a greater number of others whom I do not know, will wonder why I have written such a book. There are two factors alone which comprise the explanation.

The first is the Bible itself. During all the years of my fervent belief, I simply had no idea how many sorry and embarrassing passages there are in the scriptural record. I had encountered a few instances of critical literature, but it had largely bounced off the armored shell of my bias and loyalty to the Catholic church. I had unthinkingly accepted the argument that critics were atheistic and evil men who wished only to attack good, decent believers.

Now that I'm older, at least somewhat wiser, and certainly better informed, I am deeply ashamed of having held opinions so unconnected to reality. I've known very few atheists but, without exception, they have been men and women of principle, and admirable as citizens. Of the few truly despicable human beings I have encountered, I regret to report that almost every one of them was at least a nominal believer in one religion or another.

To deal with something more specific, consider the Mafia culture. It is thoroughly criminal, root and branch. It deals in murder, prostitution, torture, intimidation, violence, arson, drugs, illegal gambling, and so forth ad nauseam, as casually as other businessmen go about their separate trades. Mafioso claim to be Catholic, and I have rarely heard of their being refused Christian burial. This is an ugly fact, and one which most people are either too embarrassed or fearful to mention publicly, but it is a fact nevertheless.

White supremacists, White Citizen's Council types, John Birchers, Ku Klux Klaners, Posse Comitatus members, and paramilitary groups, with members armed to the teeth—every one of them considers the Bible and the cross as important as the flag. These people come from the ranks of fundamentalist Protestants. A few are law-abiding; many are not. Some are entirely sincere in their protestations that they revere God, respect the

Bible, and are good Christians and Americans. They do not, however, observe Constitutional guarantees to all their fellow Americans. The world regards their bigotry and propensity to violence with horror, which they explain to themselves by saying that the rest of the world is under the domination of Secular Humanists, Communists, Jews, Blacks, Catholics, liberal Protestants, intellectuals, the news media, and God knows what other distrusted branches of society. (Note that I am not charging the greater number of fundamentalists with being members of these perverted groups.)

Any model of the universe must incorporate all known and relevant facts to be intellectually plausible. That is why I have stressed act rather than theory in my modest dissertation. Equally important, I think it is unnecessary to concentrate on the sweet, uplifting, warm-hearted elements in Christian tradition and behavior and to ignore the rest of the record. Facts are facts, however uncomfortable it makes us to face some of them.

Some of the charming, dedicated Christians I have come to know, both laypeople and clergy, would, I believe, be more effective moral teachers if they radically revised their views about the Scriptures. Morals and ethics would continue to be of the most fundamental importance. We would still be aware that we are indeed our brothers' (and sisters') keepers, since the fact is morally obvious. We would still be concerned with maintaining the strength of the family and assuring children a decent upbringing, but we would be relieved of much of the dangerous nonsense that permeates the Scriptures.

Another reason I have undertaken this work grows out of intensive reading, particularly in recent years, in philosophy, biography, and history. Studying the details of the lives of such great thinkers and doers as Galileo, Darwin, Mendel, Copernicus, and Kepler, for example, I only gradually perceived a common factor. It was that the Bible, far from being confined to use as a source of spiritual inspiration down through the centuries, has frequently been employed as a dead hand of conservatism and reaction. It was a terrible, crushing, stifling force, against which free and creative minds had to contend, as if the concrete problems with which they wrestled were not already troublesome enough.

To those conditioned by a lifetime of bias in favor of the Bible, as I was, the response comes readily that it is not the Bible's fault that it has been so misused but is merely the fault of misguided men who have perverted the true intention of Scriptures. In time, however, I realized that such argumentation was specious and that it is not necessary to make a choice between Bible and individual churchmen in considering such a question. Both, in fact, have been at fault. For even the most well-intentioned churchmen had not the slightest freedom to contradict the Bible. On the contrary, they were under a solemn obligation to propagate its contents.

Some of those contents are clearly not only unscientific but antiscientific. They are also unhistorical. Modern, educated Christians and Jews cannot have it both ways. They cannot on the one hand develop their rightly esteemed universities, in which the physical sciences, archaeology, and history are taught, and at the same time talk about that perfection of Scripture which naturally follows from its being viewed as the Word of God. On this level, a choice must be made. If science and archaeology are correct about certain particulars, as is clearly the case, then as regards some of those same particulars, the Bible is in error.

I would be thunderstruck were every devout Christian or Jew reading the two preceding paragraphs to accept their wisdom instantly, since these ideas, simple as they are, took me several years to put together comfortably in my own mind.

Am I suggesting that the books of the Bible never should have been collected, copied, and published? Hardly. The various books of the Old and New Testaments are vitally important cultural and theological records. It is true that they are of greater religious interest to Jews and Christians than to the majority of the world's peoples, but that they are of legitimate value is not in question. The trouble came, not from the simple existence of the Bible, but from the formal, dogmatic insistence that its every word bore the imprimatur of God.

If the Bible were a simple one-page document, a document so dazzling in its simplicity and clarity that there could be no possibility of alternative interpretations, perhaps the notion that it was dictated or written by God would have endured throughout time. We know, however, that the Bible is very far indeed from such a record. It was, therefore, inevitable that once the analytical powers of the human mind came into studious contact with the Scriptures, there could no longer be any possibility of even general unanimity of interpretation and opinion.

The book the reader holds in his hands is, then, but one more instance in a centuries-old tradition of studying Scripture and applying to it the test of one's own God-given intelligence. With the forces of habit and tradition as powerful as they are, the Bible does not crack open the first instant the intelligence and/or moral senses find themselves unable to accommodate a particular scriptural passage.

But there does come a point when the analytical intelligence begins to perceive patterns, begins to notice that there is scarcely a page of the Bible on which an open mind does not perceive a contradiction, an unlikely story, an obvious error, an historical impossibility of one sort or another, so that the intelligence finally is no longer able to accommodate the absurd prejudice that the Bible is totally without error.

This leads, at least in the thoughtful individual, to the recognition that he or she wishes to separate scriptural truth or beauty on the one hand from error and dangerous anti-God nonsense on the other. That is the process by which intellectual rebellions and reformations occur.

There will be, perhaps, two inevitable reactions to this work, given the two categories into which its readers will fall. Those who are generally free-minded or antireligious will applaud the errors I have pointed out in the Scriptures. Others, psychologically and emotionally unable to countenance any criticism of the Bible, will angrily point out such errors as I have made in my research or commentary. Inevitably, there will be such. If, after all, the King James translation contains over 5,000 errors (and authorities insist that it does), how can I hope to have avoided mistakes, given the modesty of my credentials.

But if reaction consists chiefly of expressions of approval and disapproval I shall be disappointed. My primary intention has been to encourage readers to *read* the Scriptures and make up their own minds about them. They should also read scholarly studies, such as William H. Stiebing's *Out of the Desert?* (Buffalo, N.Y.: Prometheus Books, 1989), which demonstrates fairly conclusively that the Exodus and the conquest of Canaan by ten Israelite tribes never took place.

The majority of Protestants, Catholics, and Jews, though they may differ with specific aspects of my commentary, will probably agree that there ought to be more responsible Bible study in which unbiased scholarship and respect for evidence play a role. It is probably only fundamentalist Protestants and Catholics and Orthodox Jews, those who interpret every word of either one or both of the Testaments literally, who will be made uncomfortable by my bringing to public attention discoveries, insights, questions, doubts, and scholarly findings that have long been known to distinguished and pro-God students of Scripture.

The thing that most impresses me now, at the conclusion of my studies, is the amazing extent to which I was ignorant of scriptural questions for over half a century. Nor was my ignorance an instance of the type in which one at least acutely senses one's lack of knowledge. On the contrary, I assumed that I had a reasonably accurate picture of at least the New Testament. I had had courses in Bible history in Catholic grade schools, had been exposed to the subject briefly again at the high-school level, and throughout my childhood had heard hundreds of sermons, a good many of which dealt directly with the Gospels.

Moreover, in recent years, I took a course on the Bible as part of a class at a Presbyterian church in my neighborhood and augmented all this by occasional personal reading of the Scriptures over the years. Still I was, like millions of other Christians, not only lamentably uninformed but largely oblivious to the insufficiency of my information.

In my twenties, I somehow acquired the knowledge that there were "a few" difficult passages in the New Testament, a small number of apparent contradictions, but I assumed that Catholic Scripture specialists had such matters well in hand and that the mere fact that I was incapable of resolving such isolated problems need not pose the slightest threat to my faith.

All this would be laughable were it not so sad, and so typical. There are in the churches, thank God, responsible and decent men and women who are full-time scholars of Scripture. I have studied numerous volumes of their work in recent years and am impressed by the fact that it includes countless concessions that are apparently never brought to the attention of the great masses of the faithful.

Literalist compulsive fascination with the Bible, the belief that it is a court-of-last-authority in regard to all kinds of social and ethical questions, has been well-described by Alan Watts.

> This attitude is not faith. It is pure idolatry. The most deceptive idols are not images of wood and stone but are constructed of words and ideas—mental images of God. Faith is an openness and trusting attitude to truth and reality, whatever it may turn out to be. This is a risky and adventurous state of mind. Belief, in the religious sense, is the opposite of faith—because it is a fervent wishing or hope, a compulsive clinging to the idea that the universe is arranged and governed in such and such a way. Belief is holding to a rock; faith is learning how to swim—and this whole universe swims in boundless space. Thus, in much of the English-speaking world, the King James Bible is a rigid idol, all the more deceptive for being translated into the most melodious English and for being an anthology of ancient literature that contains sublime wisdom along with barbaric histories and the war songs of tribes on the rampage. All this is taken as the literal Word and counsel of God, as it is by fundamentalist Baptists, Jesus freaks, Jehovah's Witnesses, and comparable sects, which—by and large—know nothing of the history of the Bible, of how it was edited and put together. So we have with us the social menace of a huge population of intellectually and morally irresponsible people.

Some objections to atheistic or agnostic arguments are eminently respectable and deserve open-minded, intellectual consideration. Of certain others, however, the same cannot be said. One of the absurd arguments against the rationalist view is that its proponents would replace the worship of God with the worship of man.

The inability to locate today a single instance of an individual who worships humanity, either in the abstract or the concrete, seems to carry no weight with those who advance such arguments. It is theoretically possible, I suppose, that a naive, naturally high-minded and idealistic 12-year-old might imagine that somewhere, if not in his immediate neighborhood, there are adult humans of such moral perfection that their heroic stature would justify something close to adoration. But no one familiar with human nature could be guilty of such an inappropriate response.

One of the fascinating aspects of Bible study is that an uncritical acceptance of the scriptural record seems invariably to produce a peculiar suspension of those forms of moral judgment which are otherwise nearly universal.

To give an illustration, consider the wave of revulsion that floods the average person when he or she hears of the practice of human sacrifice by the Aztecs and other so-called primitive peoples. How savage and barbaric such practices seem. But when a Christian or Jew comes across human sacrifice in the Bible (see Jephthah's immolation of his daughter in Judges 11:30–40), is he or she repulsed? It is even possible to see the foreordained crucifixion of Jesus to "atone for our sins" as a throwback to human sacrificial practices. These are only two of the many instances of savagery that might be cited; others have been referred to throughout this volume.

Scholarly criticism of the Bible, which leads to either reservations or negative hypotheses, is not at all the same thing as "an attack on God." Nor is it an attack upon religion. Thousands have abandoned their original literalist confidence in the Scriptures only to reaffirm their faith in the Deity, and often to join another religious denomination. The supposed defender of the faith, therefore, who responds to intelligent, analytical criticism of Scripture passages by calling them attacks on religion or on God is behaving no more ethically, or sensibly, than the self-styled patriot who responds to responsible critics of a society's faults by accusing them of treason.

Although it would be ideal if all biblical scholars were guided merely by a search for truth and would let the evidence speak its own message, there is, I suspect, relatively little such research conducted. Rather the debate concerning the authenticity of the Bible resembles nothing so much as a legal trial. The rationalist critics are the prosecuting attorneys, having already concluded that the defendant's guilt is certain, while Christian and Jewish spokespersons are the attorneys for the defense. Alas, there is scarcely any public that could represent an impartial jury.

Most biblical scholars appear constrained to publish one sort of news that their intelligence has opened up to them: that the Bible is full of error, contradictions, and inconsistencies. Although such discoveries are startling and worthy of important public emphasis, the fact is that one must search scholarly journals carefully to unearth such nuggets of factual information and revised theory about the Bible. Can it be that most scholars are restrained by fear? Precisely what are they afraid of?

One answer is readily available: they are afraid of one another. They are also fearful that they will be personally attacked by their more traditionalist, conservative peers. To the extent that fear to tell the truth is unreasonable, it may dissipate upon being subjected to public scrutiny. One individual may be emboldened by even a modest display of courage in another. Another factor in the seemingly "watered down" reports of some scholars is their private acceptance of the Bible as sacred. They turn their capacity to reason to a defense of the text.

It is also obvious that some moderately learned individuals, even a number with degrees, conduct organized research into religious questions, but they are *absolutely without freedom* to be guided in their studies purely by their respect for evidence and truth. They are concerned merely to search out such evidence as can be made to appear consistent with the larger hypotheses to which they are already firmly committed. This is not unbiased scholarship but sophistry.

The basic theological problem for Protestantism—one for which it has never been possible to provide a satisfactory answer—concerns the principle according to which both the reformers and their subsequent followers were justified in casting off the authority of the dominant Christian church and replacing it with the assertion that *the individual believer has a clear right to interpret Scripture* as the combination of his intellect and conscience dictates. This, of course, relates to one of the essential questions about freedom itself. Ought we to submit to the dominance of well-intentioned institutions and leaders, or are we entitled to keep our own counsel? All true lovers of freedom have settled for a somewhat qualified version of the latter propostion.

As soon as the original Protestant reformers had so decided, they were necessarily letting certain influences and spirits loose, and it has never been possible to force them back into a rigid authoritarian structure, although Puritans and others have tried hard to do so and severely persecuted those who did not conform to the dogma of the moment, backed by political power.

The result, obviously enough, has been a great number of separate "heresies." To apply this lesson to the apparently endless debate on matters biblical, Catholic defenders of Scripture are in a somewhat less vulnerable position when they attack critical analysts of Scripture than are Protestants. The latters' insistence on their own freedom to believe that they know more about the Bible than does the church that originally produced the New Testament portion of it *has established the very principle which grants the same right to any scriptural critic to do the same.*

Do I want people to read the Bible less? No, I want them to read it more, because only by doing so will they finally get this puzzling work into clearer focus. What I would hope is that, regardless of whether a reader is at first biased pro or con as regards the Bible, he or she will employ his or her God-given intelligence in studying it. By doing so, the reader will perhaps then conclude, as did Thomas Jefferson, that certain portions of the Scriptures are beautiful and inspiring and others are shameful and degrading.

Eventually, driven by the thirst for inspiration and meaning, one may choose to concentrate on those portions of Scripture that even the most confirmed atheist can see are well-intentioned and wise. But the student of Scripture should also give careful study to the sordid, confused, meandering, and unedifying passages. In contemplating them, he or she will eventually be forced to face the question as to whether such passages could have been personally dictated, authorized, or inspired by a God who is the idealized embodiment of all virtue and knowledge.

I can easily envision a Utopian community in which the Bible is one of the books studied not only in religious but also in public schools— but not just the appealing portions of the Bible. Rather, *all* of it, in all its combined glory and shame would be read. That is the way to educate people on the issue, whether their other predilections lead them eventually to firm religious conviction, agnosticism, or atheism.

Perhaps the best scholarship—and, one hopes, ultimately the public— will arrive at a new position concerning those books now considered canonical: the same one adopted by the early church fathers, Origen and Jerome, toward the apocryphal books. Apparently largely on the basis of their discovery that *the Jews themselves had not considered such works divinely inspired,* they came in time to consider them of importance and interest but only on the grounds that they contained edifying passages that Christians might profitably read.

Millions in the present day have taken precisely this position as regards the Bible generally. It obviously contains hundreds of fascinating passages suitable for anyone to read. The problem is that all the controversy, the bloodshed, the savage cruelty that have characterized debate about the Scriptures over the centuries has arisen not from the books themselves but from the bizarre insistence that every one of them in the canon was divinely inspired. This is the source of the evil.

But since decisions as to which books belonged in the canon and which did not were made by fallible human beings after acrimonious debate among church fathers who thought in opposite ways (and those who lost the debate did so for political reasons), we can wonder if God was also around to tilt the debate toward the "winners" he wanted?

Among the many intriguing discoveries I have made while doing research is a publisher in Rockford, Illinois. A branch of the conservative movement, it has apparently emerged to satisfy a particular and rare sort of religious curiosity. Religion in its more pleasant and traditional aspects would appear to be of little interest to the thousands whose appetites are nourished by books such as those published by the Tam House. Such believers perceive a world which seems to have been created by Stephen King rather than God. The Devil is by no means relegated to a sort of dim limbo, as is the case with most Christians, but looms as a terrifyingly real, sharply focused figure. Social reality is perceived in terms of real, diabolical plots in which Communism, for example, is not simply a force for evil (which even the Russians are now conceding) but something created and directed by Satan himself.

Demonic possession, miracles, the efficacy of relics, the Antichrist, the Last Days—these are dominant themes among such Christians. To read their literature is to enter a strange, irrational world in which science is derided, reason has no natural home, the charitable social gospel is sulfurous heresy, and world events are viewed in a sort of green, house-of-horrors light.

As I write these words, I glance at a booklet titled *History of Anti-Christ* by the Rev. P. H. Ucheve, in which there is a perfectly serious reference to the theory of some of the holy fathers who "have concluded that [Enoch and Elias] dwell in terrestrial paradise" (p. 29). A footnote comments:

> This tradition may elicit skepticism from contemporary readers because we are given to understand today that the entire earth has been fully explored. However, the reader might consult *The Life of Anna Catherina Emmerick* by V. Rev. K. E. Schmoger, C.SS.R. (Maria Regina Guild, 1968), Vol. I, pp. 155-57, wherein the author discusses the prophecies of St. Hildegarde (1098-1179) and the visions of Bl. Lidwina of Schiedam (1380-1433) concerning paradise. The views of these two holy women support the opinion above. Notable in Schmoger's treatment is the statement of St. Hildegarde . . . : "When Adam and Eve were expelled from paradise, a wall of light was raised around it, and the Divine Power effaced from it all marks of their sin . . . *Paradise still exists, a region of joy, blooming in all its pristine loveliness, and imparting abundant fruitfulness to the sterile earth.*" (IA)

CONCLUSION

The rational mind staggers, not at such hypotheses, which are clearly absurd, but at the depressing reality that there are people to whom such speculation has far greater appeal than Christian literature dealing with what is known about our world.

I must reiterate a point that I have stressed publicly since 1960: Our culture's headlong flight into unreason will very likely continue, with frequently destructive social effects, until our educational curricula adds formal instruction in how to think or reason. There need be no fear that a society consisting entirely of reasonable individuals would solidify into some sort of unanimous consensus on all important questions. Social philosophers who respect the rules of evidence and logic nevertheless differ on a long list of questions important and trivial, but dialogue among them at least takes place on reasonable terms. Such discussion and study is civilized, rational, socially productive. Societies grow by such means. But feverish, paranoid theorizing, on the other hand, is a sign of social pathology.

In the end, then, it all comes down to Pascal's Gamble and the individual freedom to opt for faith. Pure science, pure reason are very largely on the side of the rationalists, agnostics, and atheists.

An important lesson of this study is that God in no sense depends on the Bible, the Koran, Joseph Smith's hypothetical golden plates, which no one has ever seen, or any other human document for authentication of his existence. They do not make his existence any more likely.

I consider it highly significant that so much of even the best, the most scholarly biblical commentary has an apologetic tone. The authors, decently conscious of the requirements of reason, seem to be pleading that the rational 20th-century student extend himself to understanding the literary forms, the ethnic and nationalistic biases, the *narrow religious concerns* of the original authors. To imagine that either a single sentence or a full-length work of alleged *divine* authorship should require such special pleading is something that in future centuries, I predict, will come to be regarded as a tragic joke. Man is sometimes a notoriously pathetic creature, of limited powers indeed. But God is not. It is therefore an insult to the Deity to be continually apologizing for the inadequacy, the narrowness, the vindictiveness, the absurdity, the illogicality, the stupidity of documents that he is supposed to have sanctioned.

Wherein lies the obvious appeal of those powers of human action and thought that we describe as religion? The question would be simple to answer if there were only one religion, for then we could concentrate on its particulars in seeking to come to a reasonable conclusion about it. We know, however, that there are thousands of religions, which are not all mutually exclusive, but, on the other hand, not all mutually compatible either. Even so, something about religious belief itself has a special appeal to the human heart and, indeed, to the mind as well.

What accounts for some of this appeal may be that we generally feel more socially comfortable in the company of others who are clearly attempting to do good and to avoid evil. Few of us would deliberately court the company of murderers, thieves, child-molesters, rapists, compulsive adulterers, embezzlers, or other criminals.

Another reason is that there is a certain hunger of the human heart for virtue and a certain inherent horror of evil. Some of this is inculcated in us as children, whether our parents are atheists or fervent believers. Most—if not all—parents encourage their children to behave in a reasonable manner and attempt to discourage the commission of destructive acts. So perhaps, then, the appeal of religion is partly a matter of wanting, as adults, the same kind of orderly good conduct for which we were rewarded as children.

Selected Bibliography

Allegro, John M. 1984. *The Dead Sea Scrolls and the Christian Myth.* Buffalo, N.Y.: Prometheus Books.

Arnheim, Michael. 1984. *Is Christianity True?* Buffalo, N.Y.: Prometheus Books.

Asimov, Isaac. 1968. *Asimov's Guide to the Bible: The Old Testament.* Garden City, N.Y.: Doubleday.

———. 1971. *The Land of Canaan.* Boston: Houghton, Mifflin.

Augstein, Rudolf. 1977. *Jesus, Son of Man.* Translated by Hugh Young. New York: Urizen Books.

Auzou, George. 1963. *The Formation of the Bible.* St. Louis: B. Herder.

Barnhart, Joe E. 1986. *The Southern Baptist Holy War.* Austin: Texas Monthly Press.

Baumer, Franklin L. 1960. *Religion and the Rise of Skepticism.* New York: Harcourt Brace.

Beardslee, William A. 1970. "Literary Criticism of the New Testament." In *Guides to Biblical Scholarship.* New Testament Series. Philadelphia: Fortress Press.

Bedau, Hugo Adam, ed. 1982. *The Death Penalty in America.* 3rd ed. New York: Oxford University Press.

Beebe, H. Keith. 1970. *The Old Testament.* Belmont, Calif.: Dickenson.

Bihlmeyer, Karl. 1966–68. *Church History.* 3 vols. Revised ed. by Hermann Tuchle. Westminster, Md.: Newman Press.

Bratton, Fred Gladstone. 1959. *A History of the Bible.* Boston: Beacon Press.

Bright, John. 1981. *A History of Israel.* 3rd ed. Louisville, Ky.: Westminster Press.

Brown, James. 1956. "The New Old Testament: Ancient Israel in Its Near Eastern Setting." In *Commentary,* April.

Bultmann, Rudolf. 1971. *The Gospel of John: A Commentary.* Louisville, Ky.: Westminster Press.

Burr, William Henry. 1987. *Self-Contradictions of the Bible.* Buffalo, N.Y.: Prometheus Books.

Burtchaell, James T. 1989. *The Giving and the Taking of Life: Essays Ethical.* South Bend, Ind.: University of Notre Dame Press.

Buttrick, George A., and Keith R. Crim, eds. 1976. *The Interpreter's Dictionary of the Bible.* 7 vols. Nashville, Tenn.: Abingdon Press.

Clemens, Thomas, and Michael Wyschogrod. 1987. *Understanding Scripture: Explorations of Jewish and Christian Traditions of Interpretation.* New York: Paulist Press.

Coe, Michael D. 1984. *Mexico.* London: Thames and Hudson.

Cohen, Edmund D. 1986. *The Mind of the Bible Believer.* Buffalo, N.Y.: Prometheus Books.

Collins, Raymond. 1988. *Letters That Paul Did Not Write.* Wilmington, Del.: Michael Glazier.

Comay, Joan, and Ronald Brownrigg. 1980. *Who's Who in the Bible: The Old Testament and the Apocrypha.* New York: Bonanza Books.

Coughlin, Robert. 1964. "Who Was the Man Jesus?" In *Life,* December.

Cross, Frank L., and Elizabeth A. Livingston, eds. 1974. *The Oxford Dictionary of the Christian Church.* New York: Oxford University Press.

Culpepper, R. Alan. 1983. *Anatomy of the Fourth Gospel: A Study in Literary Design.* Philadelphia: Fortress Press.

Dart, John. 1988. *The Jesus of Heresy and History: The Discovery and Meaning of the Nag Hammadi Gnostic Library.* Revised and expanded edition of *The Laughing Savior* (1976). San Francisco: Harper and Row.

De Vaux, R., and J. T. Milik. 1955–85. *Discoveries in the Judean Desert.* 7 vols. New York: Oxford University Press.

Dibelius, Martin. 1985. "The Synoptic Problem." In *The Origins of Christianity.* Edited by R. Joseph Hoffmann. Buffalo, N.Y.: Prometheus Books.

Dimont, Max I. 1964. *Jews, God and History.* New York: New American Library.

Doane, T. W. 1882. *Bible Myths and Their Parallels in Other Religions.* San Diego, Calif.: Truth Seeker Co.

Dunham, Barrows. 1964. *Heroes and Heretics: A Social History of Dissent.* New York: Alfred A. Knopf.

Encyclopedia Britannica, The New. 1974–86. "Biblical Literature," "Judaism." 15th ed. Chicago: Encyclopedia Britannica Company.

Engel, Frederic André. 1976. *An Ancient World Preserved: Relics and Records of Prehistory in the Andes.* New York: Crown.

Fraine, Jean de. 1967. *The Bible and the Origin of Man.* 2nd ed. Staten

Island, N.Y.: Alba House.

Friedell, Egon. 1953–54. *A Cultural History of the Modern Age.* New York: Alfred A. Knopf.

Funk, Robert W., Brandon Scott, and James R. Butts. 1988. *The Parables of Jesus.* Sonoma, Calif.: Polebridge Press.

Gaebelein, A. C. 1987. *What the Bible Says About Angels.* Grand Rapids, Mich.: Baker Books.

Hamblin, Dora Jane. 1973. *The First Cities.* Emergence of Man Series. New York: Time-Life Books.

Harrington, Daniel J. 1979. *Interpreting the New Testament.* Wilmington, Del.: Michael Glazier.

Hartshorne, Charles, and William L. Reese. 1976. *Philosophers Speak of God.* Chicago: University of Chicago Press.

Havener, Ivan. 1987. *Q: The Sayings of Jesus.* Wilmington, Del.: Michael Glazier.

Hawton, Hector. 1971. *Controversy: The Humanist/Christian Encounter.* London: Pemberton Books.

Helms, Randel. 1988. *Gospel Fictions.* Buffalo, N.Y.: Prometheus Books.

Henderson, John S. 1981. *The World of the Ancient Maya.* Ithaca, N.Y.: Cornell University Press.

Herklots, H. G. G. 1957. *How Our Bible Came to Us.* New York: Galaxy Books/Oxford University Press.

Herschel, Abraham J. 1962. *The Prophets.* New York: Harper and Row.

Hoffmann, R. Joseph, ed. 1985. *The Origins of Christianity: A Critical Introduction.* Buffalo, N.Y.: Prometheus Books.

Hoffmann, R. Joseph, and Gerald A. Larue, eds. 1988a. *Biblical vs. Secular Ethics.* Buffalo, N.Y.: Prometheus Books.

———. 1988b. *Jesus in History and Myth.* Buffalo, N.Y.: Prometheus Books.

Hoskyns, Edwyn, and Bart and Noel Davey. 1931. *The Riddle of the New Testament.* London: Faber and Faber.

Hunt, George. 1989. "American Catholic Intellectual Life." In *America,* May 6.

Hutchinson, Paul. 1955. "The Onward March of Progress." In *Life,* Dec. 26.

Isser, Stanley. 1990. "Two Traditions: The Law of Exodus 21:22–23 Revisited." In *Catholic Biblical Quarterly,* January.

Kaufmann, Yehezkel. 1960. *The Religion of Israel from Its Beginnings to the Babylonian Exile.* Chicago: University of Chicago Press.

———. 1970. *The Babylonian Captivity and Deutero-Isaiah.* New York: Union of American Hebrew Congregations.

Launderville, Dale. 1989. Review of John I. Durham, *Exodus* (Waco, Tex.:

Word Books, 1987). In *Catholic Biblical Quarterly,* April.

Laws, Sophie. 1988. *In the Light of the Lamb: Imagery, Parody and Theology in the Apocalypse of John.* Wilmington, Del.: Michael Glazier.

Laymon, Charles M., ed. 1971. *The Interpreter's One-Volume Commentary on the Bible.* Nashville, Tenn.: Abingdon Press.

Leaney, A. R.C. 1958. *Harper's New Testament Commentaries: The Gospel According to St. Luke.* New York: Harper.

Levie, Jean. 1962. *The Bible: Word of God in Words of Men.* New York: P. J. Kennedy.

Lloyd, Seton. 1984. *The Archaeology of Mesopotamia.* Rev. ed. London: Thames and Hudson.

Magnusson, Magnus. 1977. *B.C.: The Archaeology of the Bible Lands.* London: The Bodley Head.

Mangan, Celine. 1982. *1-2 Chronicles, Ezra, Nehemiah.* Wilmington, Del.: Michael Glazier.

Marty, Martin. 1989. "You're Going to Have to Be Institutionalized." In *The Critic,* Summer.

Matheson, Sylvia A. 1972. *Persia: An Archaeological Guide.* London: Faber and Faber.

McCabe, Herbert. 1986. *The Teaching of the Catholic Church.* Wilmington, Del.: Michael Glazier.

McCabe, Joseph. 1929. *The Story of Religious Controversy.* Boston: The Stratford Company.

———. 1946. *The Testament of Christian Civilization.* London: Watts.

McKenzie, John L. *The Dictionary of the Bible.* New York: Macmillan.

———. 1966. *The World of the Judges.* Englewood Cliffs, N.J.: Prentice-Hall.

Morton, Andrew Queen. 1966. *Paul, The Man and the Myth: A Study in the Authorship of Greek Prose.* London: Hodder and Staughton.

Neil, William. 1962. *Harper's Bible Commentary.* New York: Harper and Row.

Newton, R. Heber. 1884. *Book of the Beginnings.* New York: G. P. Putnam's Sons.

Nielsen, Kai. 1973; 1990. *Ethics Without God.* London: Pemberton Books, and Buffalo, N.Y.: Prometheus Books.

———. 1976. "Morality and the Will of God." In *Critiques of God.* Edited by Peter A. Angeles. Buffalo, N.Y.: Prometheus Books.

O'Malley, William J. 1989. "Scripture from Scratch." In *America,* Feb. 4.

Osborne, Charles, ed. 1975. *The Israelites.* Emergence of Man Series. New York: Time-Life Books.

Orwell, George (Eric Blair). 1931, 1968. "A Hanging." In *The Collected*

Essays, Journalism, and Letters. Vol. 1. New York: Harcourt, Brace.

Pfeiffer, Charles F. 1952. Introduction to the Revised Standard Version of the Bible. Philadelphia: A. J. Holman.

Prager, Dennis, and Joseph Telushkin. 1983. *Why the Jews?* New York: Touchstone Books/Simon and Schuster.

Richardson, Alan. 1959. *The Gospel According to St. John: Introduction and Commentary.* London: SCM Press.

Robertson, J. M. 1957. *A Short History of Free Thought.* New York: Russell.

Russell, Bertrand. 1967. *Why I Am Not a Christian and Other Essays on Religion and Related Subjects.* New York: Simon and Schuster.

Sandars, Nancy K. 1985. *The Sea Peoples: Warriors of the Ancient Mediterranean.* Rev. ed. London: Thames and Hudson.

Sanders, Jack. 1982. "The Salvation of the Jews in Luke–Acts." In *Seminar Papers: Society of Biblical Literature.* Atlanta: Scholars Press.

Shneour, Elie. 1986. "Occam's Razor." In *Skeptical Inquirer,* Summer.

Smith, George. 1876. *Chaldean Account of Genesis.* Out of print.

Smith Homer William. 1955. *Man and His Gods.* Boston: Little, Brown.

Smith, Morton. 1974. *The Secret Gospel.* New York: Harper and Row.

Smith, Morton, and R. Joseph Hoffmann, eds. 1989. *What the Bible Really Says.* Buffalo, N.Y.: Prometheus Books.

Stanton, Elizabeth Cady. 1895; 1972. *The Woman's Bible.* Reprint of 1st ed. Salem, N.H.: Ayer Company.

Stiebing, William H., Jr. 1989. *Out of the Desert?: Archaeology and the Exodus/Conquest Narratives.* Buffalo, N.Y.: Prometheus Books.

Stuhlmueller, Carroll. 1970. *Creative Redemption in Deutero-Isaiah.* Rome: Biblical Institute Press.

Sunderland, Jabez Thomas. 1893. *The Bible: Its Origin, Growth, and Character.* New York: G. P. Putnam's Sons.

Throckmorton, Burton H., ed. 1979. *Gospel Parallels: A Synopsis of the First Three Gospels.* Nashville/New York: Thomas Nelson.

Trible, Phyllis. 1984. *Texts of Terror: Literary-Feminist Readings of Biblical Narratives.* Philadelphia: Fortress Press.

Tyson, Joseph B. 1984. *The New Testament and Early Christianity.* New York: Macmillan.

Vawter, Bruce. 1956. *A Path Through Genesis.* New York: Sheed and Ward.

Voltaire, François-Marie Arouet de. 1962. *Philosophical Dictionary.* Vols. 1 and 2. New York: Basic Books.

Wells, G. A. 1975. *Did Jesus Exist?* Buffalo, N.Y.: Prometheus Books.

———. 1982. *The Historical Evidence for Jesus.* Buffalo, N.Y.: Prometheus Books.

Westermann, Claus. 1969. *Isaiah 40 to 66: A Commentary.* Louisville, Ky.:

Westminster Press.

White, Andrew Dickson. 1896; 1965. *A History of the Warfare of Science with Theology in Christendom.* Abridged ed. New York: Free Press.

Winchell, Paul. 1982. *God 2000: Religion Without the Bible.* Sylmar, Calif.: April Enterprises.

Zahn, Gordon. 1962. *German Catholics in Hitler's Germany.* New York: Sheed and Ward.